HOLY COMMUNION, VOL. 1

RESEARCH STUDY FROM GENESIS TO REVELATION

Rev. Prof. PETER PRYCE,
DSEF, BA, MA, B.Soc.Sc Pol Sci, IBA, PhD
Professor of French, USA

==============================

HOLY COMMUNION, VOL. 1

RESEARCH STUDY FROM GENESIS TO REVELATION

Rev. Prof. PETER PRYCE,
DSEF, BA, MA, B.Soc.Sc Pol Sci, IBA, PhD
Professor of French, USA

HOLY COMMUNION, VOL. 1

RESEARCH STUDY FROM GENESIS TO REVELATION

United States Library of Congress Catalog in Publication Data – Rev. Prof. Peter Pryce: *Holy Communion, Vol. 1 – Research Study from Genesis to Revelation.*

ISBN 978-1-77637-643-8 – Paper Edition

Printed and Published in the USA

ACKNOWLEDGEMENT

I acknowledge the Holy Spirit and dedicate this book to the Holy Spirit for giving me the wisdom to understand the Holy Scriptures to write this book in order to help others to also come to the understanding of The Word of God.

Isaiah 28:26 (KJV) For his God doth instruct him to discretion, *and* doth teach him.

Jeremiah 30:2 (KJV) Thus speaketh the LORD God of Israel, saying, Write thee all the words that I have spoken unto thee in a book.

John 14:26 (KJV) But the Comforter, *which is* the Holy Ghost, whom the Father will send in my name, he shall teach you all things, and bring all things to your remembrance, whatsoever I have said unto you.

Ephesians 5:11 (KJV) And have no fellowship with the unfruitful works of darkness, but rather reprove *them*.

Rev. Prof. PETER PRYCE,
DSEF, BA, MA, B.Scs. Pol Sci, IBA, PhD
A Scribe of the Law of the God of Heaven
Prophet of the Word of God
Professor of French, USA
Silver Spring, MD, USA
WWW.THEBIBLEUNIVERSITY.ORG
Accreditation Number: 07-QCTO/SDP120723172836
SAQA QUAL ID: Identification # 101997
WWW.BOOKSTORESITE.ORG
WWW.THEBIBLEUNIVERSITYCHURCH.ORG

DEDICATION

I dedicate this book to the Ministers of Jesus Christ who are obeying this commission:

Matthew 28:18 (KJV) And Jesus came and spake unto them, saying, All power is given unto me in heaven and in earth.

Matthew 28:19 (KJV) Go ye therefore, and teach all nations, baptizing them in the name of the Father, and of the Son, and of the Holy Ghost:

Matthew 28:20 (KJV) Teaching them to observe all things whatsoever I have commanded you: and, lo, I am with you alway, *even* unto the end of the world. Amen.

Acts 1:7 (KJV) And he said unto them, It is not for you to know the times or the seasons, which the Father hath put in his own power.

Acts 1:8 (KJV) But ye shall receive power, after that the Holy Ghost is come upon you: and ye shall be witnesses unto me both in Jerusalem, and in all Judaea, and in Samaria, and unto the uttermost part of the earth.

Rev. Prof. PETER PRYCE,
DSEF, BA, MA, B.Scs. Pol Sci, IBA, PhD

Aside from the more than 200 dreams and visions of my Calling that I have documented in writing, the following are the evidences from the Holy Scriptures of the Ministry to which I, Rev. Prof. Peter Pryce, was called of the LOD God Almighty, to function therein!

> **Ezra 7:10 (KJV)** For Ezra had prepared his heart to seek the law of the LORD, and to do *it*, and to teach in Israel statutes and judgments.
>
> **Ezra 7:11 (KJV)** Now this *is* the copy of the letter that the king Artaxerxes gave unto Ezra the priest, the scribe, *even* a scribe of the words of the commandments of the LORD, and of his statutes to Israel.
>
> **Ezra 7:12 (KJV)** Artaxerxes, king of kings, unto Ezra the priest, a scribe of the law of the God of heaven, perfect *peace*, and at such a time.
>
> **Ezra 7:14 (KJV)** Forasmuch as thou art sent of the king, and of his seven counsellers, to inquire concerning Judah and Jerusalem, according to the law of thy God which *is* in thine hand;
>
> **Ezra 7:15 (KJV)** And to carry the silver and gold, which the king and his counsellers have freely offered unto the God of Israel, whose habitation *is* in Jerusalem,
>
> **Ezra 7:16 (KJV)** And all the silver and gold that thou canst find in all the province of Babylon, with the freewill offering of the people, and of the priests, offering willingly for the house of their God which *is* in Jerusalem:
>
> **Ezra 7:17 (KJV)** That thou mayest buy speedily with this money bullocks, rams, lambs, with their meat offerings and their drink offerings, and offer them upon the altar of the house of your God which *is* in Jerusalem.
>
> **Ezra 7:18 (KJV)** And whatsoever shall seem good to thee, and to thy brethren, to do with the rest of the silver and the gold, that do after the will of your God.
>
> **Ezra 7:25 (KJV)** And thou, Ezra, after the wisdom of thy God, that *is* in thine hand, set magistrates and judges, which may judge all the people that *are* beyond the river, all such as know the laws of thy God; and teach ye them that know *them* not.

Here is the second evidence of my Calling!

> **Acts 8:26 (KJV)** And the angel of the Lord spake unto Philip, saying, Arise, and go toward the south unto the way that goeth down from Jerusalem unto Gaza, which is desert.

Acts 8:27 (KJV) And he arose and went: and, behold, a man of Ethiopia, an eunuch of great authority under Candace queen of the Ethiopians, who had the charge of all her treasure, and had come to Jerusalem for to worship,

Acts 8:28 (KJV) Was returning, and sitting in his chariot read Esaias the prophet.

Acts 8:29 (KJV) Then the Spirit said unto Philip, Go near, and join thyself to this chariot.

Acts 8:30 (KJV) And Philip ran thither to *him*, and heard him read the prophet Esaias, and said, Understandest thou what thou readest?

Acts 8:31 (KJV) And he said, How can I, except some man should guide me? And he desired Philip that he would come up and sit with him.

Acts 8:32 (KJV) The place of the scripture which he read was this, He was led as a sheep to the slaughter; and like a lamb dumb before his shearer, so opened he not his mouth:

Acts 8:33 (KJV) In his humiliation his judgment was taken away: and who shall declare his generation? for his life is taken from the earth.

Acts 8:34 (KJV) And the eunuch answered Philip, and said, I pray thee, of whom speaketh the prophet this? of himself, or of some other man?

Acts 8:35 (KJV) Then Philip opened his mouth, and began at the same scripture, and preached unto him Jesus.

Here is the third evidence of my Calling!

Luke 1:76 (KJV) And thou, child, shalt be called the prophet of the Highest: for thou shalt go before the face of the Lord to prepare his ways;

Luke 1:77 (KJV) To give knowledge of salvation unto his people by the remission of their sins,

Luke 1:78 (KJV) Through the tender mercy of our God; whereby the dayspring from on high hath visited us,

Luke 1:79 (KJV) To give light to them that sit in darkness and *in* the shadow of death, to guide our feet into the way of peace.

John 10:41 (KJV) And many resorted unto him, and said, John did no miracle: but all things that John spake of this man were true.

Here is the fourth evidence of my Calling!

Revelation 1:11 (KJV) Saying, I am Alpha and Omega, the first and the last: and, What thou seest, write in a book, and send *it* unto the seven churches which are in Asia; unto Ephesus, and unto Smyrna, and unto Pergamos, and unto Thyatira, and unto Sardis, and unto Philadelphia, and unto Laodicea.

ABOUT THE AUTHOR

Rev. Prof. Peter Pryce served for 10 years as a Public Servant French Teacher of the Maryland State Department of Education, USA, with competence in the IB Program, and is currently a Professor of Translation and Interpretation, a bilingual Scholar of Translation and Interpretation of the Holy Bible and the Qur'an, a French Language Scholar, a Theological Researcher and Scholar, a Christian Publisher, an Ordained Minister of the Gospel of Jesus Christ, an Anti-Racism Educator, a Bilingual Conference Interpreter, an Education Consultant, a Translator and Interpreter, and a Technical Writer. Rev. Prof. Peter Pryce holds a Ph.D. in Translation and Interpretation of French and English, with research interests in Translation Theory and Practice, and Sacred Text Analyses of the Bible and Qur'an.

I am a native-level English and French language expert. I hold the following School Administrator credentials for School Principal and Assistant Principal: Maryland Candidate ID # 03779397 ETS SCHOOL LEADERSHIP SERIES 02/02/2006 - ADMIN 1 & 2.

Rev. Prof. Peter Pryce taught Translation and Techniques of Expression in the Department of French, University of Education, Winneba, GHANA. He also taught Translation and Interpreting (French and English) in the Department of Modern Languages, University of Ghana, LEGON.

I am an Author of French and English textbooks for University Students. I have more than 65 textbook publications in the academic field of English and French Translation and Interpretation that are registered with the United States Library of Congress.

Rev. Prof. Peter Pryce often teaches on Radio and TV in the Bible and Qur'an Lecture Series drawing from his long experience as a Bible Commentary Writer, Corporate Language Instructor, Technical Writer with Nokia Corporation, French Embassy award-winning Poet, Conference Speaker, Book Editor, Presidential Speech Writer, and Author with intellectual properties registered with the United States Library of Congress Copyright Office in Washington, DC.

Four Presidents have encountered the writings of Rev. Prof. Peter Pryce namely: President Léopold Sédar Senghor of Senegal when Prof. Pryce was a student of French in the

University of Dakar, Head of State Ibrahim Badamosi Babangida of Nigeria when Prof. Pryce was a student of French in the University of Dakar, President Jerry John Rawlings of Ghana when Prof. Pryce was a Ph.D. Lecturer of French in the University of Education, Winneba and was selected to write the President's speech.

In July 2020, Rev. Prof. Peter Pryce received a formal Letter of Appreciation from the United States White House; from President Donald Trump, in appreciation, after the US President received some free textbooks from Rev. Prof. Peter Pryce.

Rev. Prof. Peter Pryce is currently devoting his time and energy to the writing and publishing of Christian Theological Research Textbooks for The Bible University and to the following services:

1. Anti-Racism Awareness Training and Education
2. Anti-Racism Research, Racism Policy and Social Justice Initiatives
3. Post-Racism Traumatic Syndrome Alleviation Counseling
4. Mental and Spiritual Health Counseling Therapy for Post-Racism Rehabilitate and Traumatic Stress Alleviation
5. Inter-Ministerial Pastoral Training and Pastoral Accountability
6. Theological Research and Christian Publishing
7. Bilingual Conference Interpretation and Translation
8. Technical Writing

Rev. Prof. PETER PRYCE,
DSEF, BA, MA, B.Soc.Sc Pol Sci, IBA, PhD
A Scribe of the Law of the God of Heaven
Prophet of the Word of God
Professor of French, USA
Silver Spring, MD, USA
WWW.THEBIBLEUNIVERSITY.ORG
Accreditation Number: 07-QCTO/SDP120723172836
SAQA QUAL ID: Identification # 101997
WWW.BOOKSTORESITE.ORG
WWW.THEBIBLEUNIVERSITYCHURCH.ORG

SUMMARY OF FORMAL EDUCATION

1. L'Université de Dakar, Diplôme Supérieur d'Études de Français (3ᵉ degré Supérieur), 1987
2. University of Calabar, B.A. (HONS.) French/German, 1988
3. University of Lagos, M.A. French (Emphasis on Translation), 1992
4. University of Helsinki, Finland, B.Scs. in Political Science, 1ˢᵗ Class, 1999
5. University of Applied Sciences, Finland, IBA Degree: Int. Business Acumen, 2000
6. Catholic University of America, USA, Graduate Teacher Certification Program, 2003
7. McDaniel University, USA, School Leadership and Administration I, 2005
8. School Leaders Licensure Assessment, SLLA Administration II, USA, 2006
9. University of Helsinki, Finland, PhD in Translation and Interpretation, English and French, 2007

SKILLS SUMMARY
1. French-English Translation and Interpretation
2. French Language Immersion Teacher
3. Conference Translator and Interpreter
4. Competence in IB and AP Program Implementation
5. Native-level English and French Language Expert
6. Editor of Publication Articles
7. Author of Textbooks with 37 publications registered with the US Library of Congress
8. Ordained Minister of the Gospel of Jesus Christ
9. Qur'an Scholar
10. Scholar of the Institute of Theologians, USA
11. Holder of School Administrator credentials for School Principal and Assistant Principal: Maryland Candidate ID # 03779397 ETS SCHOOL.

PUBLICATIONS BY REV. PROF., PETER PRYCE, PH. D.

Monographs and Books:

1. Pryce, Peter. (2003, 2018, 2019). *Foreignising Finnish – Necessary and Unnecessary English Imports into Translations* is peer-reviewed, accepted, and has a journal publication in 2003 by the University of Natal in South Africa. However, September 2018 is the first time that it was published as an e-book online and subsequently appeared as a hard cover book in March 2019. ISBN: 978-9988-8799-4-5

2. Pryce, Peter. (2006). *Measuring Attitudes in Translation: A Study of Nokia Business Reports*. Helsinki: Helsinki University Translation Studies Monographs 2, Vol. 2 Peter Pryce: Helsinki University Printing House. 324 pages. ISSN 1459-3246. ISBN 952-10-3414-9 (Paperback). ISBN 952-10-3415-7 (PDF)

3. Pryce, Peter. (2012, 2018, 2019). *Change as a Distinct Property of Language – Aspects of Language Variation, Acquisition, and Use* is peer-reviewed, accepted, and has a journal publication in 2012 by the University of Cape Coast, in Ghana. However, September 2018 is the first time that it was published as an e-book online and subsequently appeared as a hard cover book in March 2019. ISBN 978-9988-8799-0-7

4. Pryce, Peter. (2012, 2018, 2019). *Attitudes to Translation – Linguistique et didactique de langue et de littérature: problématiques contemporaines et perspectives* is peer-reviewed, accepted, and has a journal publication by the University of Lagos in Nigeria in 2012. However, September 2018 is the first time that it was published as an e-book online and subsequently appeared as a hard cover book in March 2019. ISBN 978–9988–2–7248–7

5. Pryce, Peter. (2013, 2018, 2019). *Techniques of Expression – The Conference Rapporteur* is peer-reviewed, accepted, and has a journal publication in 2013 by the University of Education, Winneba, in Ghana. However, September 2018 is the first time that it was published as an e-book online and subsequently appeared as a hard cover book in March 2019. ISBN 978-9988-8799-5-2

6. Pryce, Peter. (2013, 2018, 2019). *Norms of Academic Writing* is peer-reviewed, accepted, and was presented at the 3rd Annual International Colloquium of Language,

Literature and Communication: Contexts, Practice and Pedagogy, Faculty of Languages Education, the University of Education, Winneba, in Ghana, from Wednesday 13th November - Thursday 14th November 2013. However, September 2018 was its first publication, as an e-book online and subsequently appeared for the first time in print as a hard cover book in March 2019. ISBN 978-9988-8799-3-8

7. Pryce, Peter. (2018). *Topics in Translation Review – Testing the Perfect Harmony Theory of Translation and Interpreting*. Legon: Ghana Universities Press. 953 pages. ISBN 978-9988-2-2741-8.

8. Pryce, Peter. (2018). *Salvation – Anointed Teachings*. INGRAM. One Ingram Blvd., La Vergne, Tennessee, 37086: 615-793-5000. 756 pages. ISBN 978-9988-8799-1-4

9. Pryce, Peter. (2019). *Thematic Dictionary of Matthew – Intralingual Translation of Spiritual Themes*. INGRAM. One Ingram Blvd., La Vergne, Tennessee, 37086: 615-793-5000. 617 pages. ISBN 978-9988-8800-2-6

10. Pryce, Peter. (2019). *Language Migration* was first peer-reviewed, and accepted for journal publication by *Translation Watch Quarterly*, official journal of the Translation Standards Institute in Australia. However, September 2018 was its first publication, as an e-book online and subsequently appeared for the first time in print as a hard cover book in March 2019. ISBN 978-9988-8799-2-1

11. Pryce, Peter. (2019). *Français aux Anglophones – French for English Speakers*. INGRAM. One Ingram Blvd., La Vergne, Tennessee, 37086: 615-793-5000. 600 pages. ISBN: 978-9988-8801-4-9 (paper edition). ISBN: 978-9988-8803-1-6 (e-Book edition)

12. Pryce, Peter. (2020). *The Counseling Manual - Case Studies*. INGRAM. One Ingram Blvd., La Vergne, Tennessee, 37086: 615-793-5000. 416 pages. ISBN 978-9988-8800-4-0 – paper edition. ISBN 978-9988-8800-9-5 – eBook edition.

13. Pryce, Peter. (2020). *Threatened…by the Truth*. INGRAM. One Ingram Blvd., La Vergne, Tennessee, 37086: 615-793-5000. 654 pages. ISBN 978-9988-8801-8-7– paper edition. ISBN 978-9988-8800-1-9 – eBook edition.

14. Pryce, Peter. (2020). *Marriage is a Blood Covenant*. INGRAM. One Ingram Blvd., La Vergne, Tennessee, 37086: 615-793-5000. 348 pages. ISBN: 978-9988-8801-5-6 (Paper Edition). ISBN: 978-9988-8799-7-6 (e-Book Edition)

15. Pryce, Peter. (2020). *Strategies for Church Growth*. INGRAM. One Ingram Blvd., La Vergne, Tennessee, 37086: 615-793-5000. 456 pages. ISBN: 978-9988-8802-1-7 (Paper Edition). ISBN:978-9988-8802-2-4 (e-Book Edition)

16. Pryce, Peter. (2020). *But Suppose God is Black – What God says about Racism*. INGRAM. One Ingram Blvd., La Vergne, Tennessee, 37086: 615-793-5000. 284

pages. ISBN: 978-9988-8803-0-9 (paper edition). ISBN: 978-9988-8803-1-6 (e-Book edition)

17. Pryce, Peter. (2020). ***Anti-Racism Program for Christians – Methodology for Racist Detoxification***. INGRAM. One Ingram Blvd., La Vergne, Tennessee, 37086: 615-793-5000. 434 pages. ISBN: 978-9988-8799-9-0(paper edition). ISBN: 978-9988-8803-2-3(e-Book edition)

18. Pryce, Peter. (2020). ***Key to unlock Romans – 1449 Spiritual Revelations***. INGRAM. One Ingram Blvd., La Vergne, Tennessee, 37086: 615-793-5000. 582 pages. ISBN: 978-9988-8801-9-4 (paper edition). ISBN: 978-9988-8802-0-0(e-Book edition)

19. Pryce, Peter. (2020). ***Praise and Worship***. INGRAM. One Ingram Blvd., La Vergne, Tennessee, 37086: 615-793-5000. 276 pages. ISBN: 978-9988-8802-7-9 (paper edition). ISBN: 978-9988-8802-8-6(e-Book edition)

20. Pryce, Peter. (2020). ***Tithing – A Comprehensive Study from Genesis to Revelation***. INGRAM. One Ingram Blvd., La Vergne, Tennessee, 37086: 615-793-5000. 276 pages. ISBN: 978-9988-8800-0-2 (paper edition). ISBN: 978-9988-8802-9-3 (e-Book edition)

21. Pryce, Peter. (2020). ***Sermon Preparation – A Training Program for Pastors***. INGRAM. One Ingram Blvd., La Vergne, Tennessee, 37086: 615-793-5000. 276 pages. ISBN: 978-9988-8803-3-0 (paper edition). ISBN: 978-9988-8803-4-7 (e-Book edition)

22. Pryce, Peter. (January 2021). ***Theory of Bible Errors and Contradictions – Ministers' Essential Reference***. INGRAM. One Ingram Blvd., La Vergne, Tennessee, 37086: 615-793-5000. 1186 pages. ISBN: **978-9988-8803-5-4** (paper edition). ISBN: **978-9988-8803-6-1** (e-Book edition)

23. Pryce Peter. (July 2021). ***Key tothe Bible – Complete Bible Curriculum***. A 2600-page Christian Theological Research Textbook of Holy Spirit inspired Bible Teachings from Genesis to Revelation with search engine, as a Mobile App, for Android and IOS devices. Available on Google Play Store. Mobile App User Experience Functionality:

     i. Search engine for any word or topic in the Bible
     ii. Search results total count
     iii. Subject teachings with Book of the Bible references
     iv. Reading or audio functionality
     v. Font size increase or decrease
     vi. Text-to-voice audio function
     vii. https://play.google.com/store/apps/details?id=com.majesty. keytothebible

24. Pryce, Peter. (January 2022) *Méthode d'Enseignement de Traduction – Translation Textbook for Students*. INGRAM. One Ingram Blvd., La Vergne, Tennessee, 37086: 615-793-5000. 1098 pages. ISBN – 978-9988-8803-8-5 (Hard Cover Edition). ISBN – 978-9988-8803-9-2 (e-Book edition).

25. Pryce, Peter. (February 2022) *Spirituals of Money – Principles of Church Accounting*. INGRAM. One Ingram Blvd., La Vergne, Tennessee, 37086: 615-793-5000. 1166 pages. ISBN: 9781776376650 (Hard Cover Edition). ISBN: 9781776376681 (e-Book edition).

26. Pryce, Peter. (March 2022) *Complete Bible Curriculum Vol. 1 – Genesis – Exodus*. INGRAM. One Ingram Blvd., La Vergne, Tennessee, 37086: 615-793-5000. 695 pages. ISBN: 978-1-77637-622-3 (Hard Cover Edition). ISBN: 978-1-77637-623-0 (e-Book edition).

27. Pryce, Peter. (April 2022) *Complete Bible Curriculum Vol. 2 – Leviticus, Numbers, Deuteronomy*. INGRAM. One Ingram Blvd., La Vergne, Tennessee, 37086: 615-793-5000. 584 pages. ISBN: 978-1-77637-624-7 (Hard Cover Edition). ISBN: 978-1-77637-625-4 (e-Book edition).

28. Pryce, Peter. (May 2022) *Complete Bible Curriculum Vol. 3 – Joshua, Judges, Ruth, 1 and 2 Samuel*. INGRAM. One Ingram Blvd., La Vergne, Tennessee, 37086: 615-793-5000. 606 pages. **ISBN 978-1776376261** (Hard Cover Edition). **ISBN 9781776376278** (e-Book edition).

29. Pryce, Peter. (June 2022) *Topics in Qur'an and Bible Translation*. Legon: Ghana Universities Press, 2018. INGRAM. One Ingram Blvd., La Vergne, Tennessee, 37086: 615-793-5000. 707 pages. ISBN: (Hard Cover Edition). ISBN: (e-Book edition)

30. Pryce, Peter. (July 2022) *Complete Bible Curriculum Vol. 4 – 1 and 2 Kings, 1 and 2 Chronicles*. INGRAM. One Ingram Blvd., La Vergne, Tennessee, 37086: 615-793-5000. 604 pages. **ISBN 978-1776376261** (Hard Cover Edition). **ISBN 9781776376278** (e-Book edition).

31. Pryce, Peter. (August 2022) *Complete Bible Curriculum Vol. 5 – Ezra, Nehemiah, Esther, Job*. INGRAM. One Ingram Blvd., La Vergne, Tennessee, 37086: 615-793-5000. 382 pages. **ISBN 978-1-77637-630-8** (Hard Cover Edition). **ISBN 978-1-77637-631-5** (e-Book edition).

32. Pryce, Peter. (September 2022) *The Law of Writing Scriptures – A Comprehensive Research from Genesis to Revelation*. **ISBN 978-1-77637-632-2 – paper edition**. **ISBN 978-1-77637-633-9 – e-Book edition**. 779 pages. AMAZON PUBLISHING SOL, 5201 Great America Pkwy Unit 320 Santa Clara, CA 95054 United States, info@amazonpublishingsol.com, +(855) 408-6467.

33. Pryce, Peter. (October 2022) *Complete Bible Curriculum Vol. 6 – The Book of Psalms*. **ISBN 978-1-77637-634-6 – paper edition**. **ISBN 978-1-77637-635-3 – e-Book edition**. 523 pages. AMAZON PUBLISHING SOL, 5201 Great America Pkwy Unit 320 Santa Clara, CA 95054 United States, info@amazonpublishingsol.com, +(855) 408-6467.

34. Pryce, Peter. (November 2022) *Complete Bible Curriculum Vol. 7 – Hermeneutics and Exegesis of the Book of Proverbs*. **ISBN 978-1-77637-637-7 – paper edition**. **ISBN 978-1-77637-636-0 – e-Book edition**. 502 pages. AMAZON PUBLISHING SOL, 5201 Great America Pkwy Unit 320 Santa Clara, CA 95054 United States, info@amazonpublishingsol.com, +(855) 408-6467.

35. Pryce, Peter. (December 2022) *Complete Bible Curriculum Vol. 8 – Ecclesiastes, Song of Solomon*. **ISBN 978-1-77637-638-4 – paper edition**. **ISBN 978-1-77637-639-1 – e-Book edition**. 523 pages. AMAZON PUBLISHING SOL, 5201 Great America Pkwy Unit 320 Santa Clara, CA 95054 United States, info@amazonpublishingsol.com, +(855) 408-6467.

36. Pryce, Peter. (July 2023) *Complete Bible Curriculum Vol. 9 - THE BOOK OF ISAIAH*. **ISBN** – INGRAM. One Ingram Blvd., La Vergne, Tennessee, **– Hard Cover paper edition, 650 pages. ISBN 978-1-77637-650-6. eBook edition ISBN 978-1-77637-651-3.**

37. Pryce, Peter. (August 2023) *Her hair is given her for a Covering* –. **ISBN 979 8859067831 – Amazon Kindle Direct Publishing Paperback.** Sunday 27th August 2023. 233 pages.

38. Pryce, Peter. (September 2023) *Marriage Counseling Textbook for Ministers Vol. 1*. **Print ISBN 978-1-77637-640-7. E-book ISBN 978-1-77637-641-4. INGRAM Publishing. 518 pages.**

39. Pryce, Peter. (September 2023) **THE LAW OF HOLY COMMUNION, VOL. 1: WHAT LAWS GOVERN HOLY COMMUNION? – ISBN 979 8861352727 – Amazon Kindle Direct Publishing Paperback.** Thursday 14th September 2023. 123 pages.

40. Pryce, Peter. (October 2023) **THE LAW OF HOLY COMMUNION, VOL. 2: WHO HAS THE RIGHT TO SUPPLY HOLY COMMUNION BREAD? – ISBN 979-8868078910 – Amazon Kindle Direct Publishing Paperback.** Monday 2nd October 2023. 114 pages.

41. Pryce, Peter. (October 2023) **THE LAW OF HOLY COMMUNION, VOL. 3: THIS DO, IN REMEMBRANCE OF ME! – ISBN 979-8863155616 – Amazon Kindle Direct Publishing Paperback.** Monday 2nd October 2023. 266 pages.

42. Pryce, Peter. (October 2023) THE BIBLE UNIVERSITY PASTORAL CERTIFICATE TRAINING: MODULE 1 # 263601004-KM-01. — **ISBN 9798863610375. Amazon Kindle Direct Publishing Paperback.** Release date: October 6, 2023.107 pages.

43. Pryce, Peter. (October 2023) THE BIBLE UNIVERSITY PASTORAL CERTIFICATE TRAINING: MODULE 2 # 263601004-KM-01. — **ISBN 979-8863800417. Amazon Kindle Direct Publishing Paperback.** Release date: October 8, 2023.136 pages.

44. Pryce, Peter. (October 2023) THE BIBLE UNIVERSITY PASTORAL CERTIFICATE TRAINING: MODULE 3 # 263601004-KM-01. — **ISBN 979-8863905266. Amazon Kindle Direct Publishing Paperback.** Release date: October 9, 2023.121 pages.

45. Pryce, Peter. (October 2023) THE BIBLE UNIVERSITY PASTORAL CERTIFICATE TRAINING MODULE 4: THEORY AND PRACTICE OF BIBLE TRANSLATION AND INTERPRETATION. — **ISBN 9798863978338. Amazon Kindle Direct Publishing Paperback.** Release date: October 10, 2023. 104 pages.

46. Pryce, Peter. (October 2023) THE BIBLE UNIVERSITY PASTORAL CERTIFICATE TRAINING MODULE 5: TEMPLATE FOR BIBLE TRANSLATION, TEACHING, AND INTERPRETATION. — **ISBN 979-8864084694. Amazon Kindle Direct Publishing Paperback.** Release date: October 11, 2023. 114 pages.

47. Pryce, Peter. (October 2023) THE BIBLE UNIVERSITY PASTORAL CERTIFICATE TRAINING MODULE 6: METHODOLOGY FOR BIBLE INTERPRETATION. — **ISBN 979-8864196045. Amazon Kindle Direct Publishing Paperback.** Release date: October 12, 2023. 102 pages.

48. Pryce, Peter. (October 2023) THE BIBLE UNIVERSITY PASTORAL CERTIFICATE TRAINING MODULE 7: METHODOLOGY OF SPIRITUAL INTERPRETATION. — **ISBN 979-8864307342. Amazon Kindle Direct Publishing Paperback.** Release date: October 13, 2023. 131 pages.

49. Pryce, Peter. (October 2023) THE BIBLE UNIVERSITY PASTORAL CERTIFICATE TRAINING MODULE 8: DO I NEED HEBREW, GREEK, ARAMAIC, OR ARABIC TO UNDERSTAND GOD? — **ISBN 979-8864408537. Amazon Kindle Direct Publishing Paperback.** Release date: October 13, 2023. 119 pages.

50. Pryce, Peter. (October 2023) THE BIBLE UNIVERSITY PASTORAL CERTIFICATE TRAINING MODULE 9: METHODOLOGY FOR

CHRISTIAN APOLOGETICS. – ISBN 979-8864600184. **Amazon Kindle Direct Publishing Paperback.** Release date: October 17, 2023. 129 pages.

51. Pryce, Peter. (October 2023) THE BIBLE UNIVERSITY PASTORAL CERTIFICATE TRAINING MODULE 10: SONG MINISTRATION AS A METHODOLOGY FOR GOSPEL IMPARTATION. **ISBN-979-8864757185. Amazon Kindle Direct Publishing Paperback.** Release date: October 18, 2023. 129 pages.

52. Pryce, Peter. (October 2023) THE BIBLE UNIVERSITY PASTORAL CERTIFICATE TRAINING MODULE 11: TEACHING BIBLICAL HERMENEUTICS AND EXEGESIS. **ISBN 979-8865077749. Amazon Kindle Direct Publishing Paperback.** Release date: October 21, 2023. 132 pages.

53. Pryce, Peter. (October 2023) **SPIRITUAL SUPERIORITY OF THE BLACK MAN**, INGRAM. One Ingram Blvd., La Vergne, Tennessee, **– Hard Cover Color Paper Edition, ISBN 978-1-77637-652-0. 150 pages**. Release Date 13-OCT-2023.

54. Pryce, Peter. (September 14, 2023). **THE LAW OF HOLY COMMUNION, VOL. 1: WHAT LAWS GOVERN HOLY COMMUNION?** Amazon Kindle Direct Publishing Paperback. **ISBN-13: 979-8861352727**. 123 pages.

55. Pryce, Peter. (October 2, 2023). **THE LAW OF HOLY COMMUNION, VOL. 2: WHO HAS THE RIGHT TO SUPPLY HOLY COMMUNION BREAD?** Amazon Kindle Direct Publishing Paperback. **ISBN-13: 979-8863155616**. 114 pages

56. Pryce, Peter. (October 2, 2023). **THE LAW OF HOLY COMMUNION, VOL. 3: THIS DO, IN REMEMBRANCE OF ME! Amazon Kindle Direct Publishing Paperback. ISBN-13: 979-8863155616**. 266 pages.

57. Pryce, Peter. (November 18, 2023) **THE DOCTRINE OF CHRISTMAS AND BIRTHDAYS, VOL. 1. Amazon Kindle Direct Publishing Paperback. ISBN-13: 979-8868075650**. 153 pages.

58. Pryce, Peter. (November 18, 2023) **THE DOCTRINE OF CHRISTMAS AND BIRTHDAYS, VOL. 2. Amazon Kindle Direct Publishing Paperback. ISBN-13: 979-8868078910**. 124 pages

59. Pryce, Peter. (November 18, 2023). **THE DOCTRINE OF CHRISTMAS AND BIRTHDAYS, VOL. 3. ISBN-13: 979-8868080302**. 132 pages.

60. Pryce, Peter. (December 8, 2023). **FEMALE ORDINATION – VOL. 1. Amazon Kindle Direct Publishing Paperback. ISBN-13:** 979-8871181256. 114 pages.

61. Pryce, Peter. (December 8, 2023). **FEMALE ORDINATION – VOL. 2. Amazon Kindle Direct Publishing Paperback. ISBN-13:** 979-8871184752. 115 pages.

62. Pryce, Peter. (December 8, 2023). **FEMALE ORDINATION – VOL. 3. Amazon Kindle Direct Publishing Paperback. ISBN-13:** 979-8871186282. 134 pages.

63. Pryce, Peter. (December 13, 2023). **FEMALE ORDINATION – VOL. 4. Amazon Kindle Direct Publishing Paperback. ISBN** 979-8871747872. 203 Pages.

64. Pryce, Peter. (1st January 2024) *Complete Bible Curriculum Vol. 10 - THE BOOK OF JEREMIAH*. INGRAM. One Ingram Blvd., La Vergne, Tennessee, – **Hard Cover paper edition ISBN 978-1-77637-655-1. eBook edition ISBN 978-1-77637-656-8. 332 pages.**

65. Pryce, Peter. (1st February 2024) **Complete Bible Curriculum:** *How to Examine Pastors, Vol. 1 – What is the Church and why does it Matter?* One Ingram Blvd., La Vergne, Tennessee, – **Hard Cover paper edition ISBN 978-1-77637-654-4. eBook edition ISBN. 332 pages.**

66. Pryce, Peter. (1st March 2024) **Complete Bible Curriculum:** *How to Examine Pastors, Vol. 2 – Fundamental Concepts for Successful Christian Life: Covering: Matthew, Mark, Luke, John.* One Ingram Blvd., La Vergne, Tennessee, – **Hard Cover. ISBN 978-1-77637-657-5 – paper edition.** 300 pages.

67. Pryce, Peter. (1st April 2024) **Complete Bible Curriculum:** *How to Examine Pastors, Vol. 3 – Fundamental Concepts for Successful Christian Life: Covering: Acts, Romans.* One Ingram Blvd., La Vergne, Tennessee, – **Hard Cover. ISBN – paper edition.** 372 pages.

68. Pryce, Peter (1st May 2024) *Can the Minister of God also function as a Minister of Government?* One Ingram Blvd., La Vergne, Tennessee, – **Hard Cover. ISBN 9781776376421 – paper edition.** 470 pages.

69. Pryce, Peter. (1st June 2024) **Complete Bible Curriculum:** *How to Examine Pastors, Vol. 4 – Fundamental Concepts for Successful Christian Life: Covering: 1 and 2 Corinthians.* One Ingram Blvd., La Vergne, Tennessee, – **Hard Cover. ISBN – paper edition.** 422 pages.

70. Pryce, Peter. (1st July 2024) *Thirty Ways to Encounter the Voice of God – Research Study from Genesis to Revelatio*n. One Ingram Blvd., La Vergne, Tennessee, – **Hard Cover. ISBN – paper edition.** 472 pages.

71. Pryce, Peter. (1st August 2024) *Holy Communion, Vol. 1 – Research Study from Genesis to Revelation.* One Ingram Blvd., La Vergne, Tennessee, – **Hard Cover. ISBN – paper edition.** 352 pages.

72. Pryce, Peter. (1st September 2024) *Holy Communion, Vol. 2 – Research Study from Genesis to Revelation.* One Ingram Blvd., La Vergne, Tennessee, – **Hard Cover. ISBN – paper edition.** 352 pages.

73. Pryce, Peter. (1ˢᵗ October 2024) *Holy Communion, Vol. 3 – Research Study from Genesis to Revelation.* One Ingram Blvd., La Vergne, Tennessee, – **Hard Cover. ISBN – paper edition.** 352 pages.

74. Pryce, Peter. (1ˢᵗ November 2024) *Holy Communion, Vol. 4 – Research Study from Genesis to Revelation.* One Ingram Blvd., La Vergne, Tennessee, – **Hard Cover. ISBN – paper edition.** 352 pages.

75. Pryce, Peter. (1ˢᵗ December 2024) *Holy Communion, Vol. 5 – Research Study from Genesis to Revelation.* One Ingram Blvd., La Vergne, Tennessee, – **Hard Cover. ISBN – paper edition.** 281 pages.

76. Pryce, Peter. (1ˢᵗ January 2025) *Holy Communion, Vol. 6 – Research Study from Genesis to Revelation.* One Ingram Blvd., La Vergne, Tennessee, – **Hard Cover. ISBN – paper edition**. 240 pages

COMPLETED MANUSCRIPTS AND UP-COMING TEXTBOOKS

77. Pryce, Peter. (September 2023) *Water Baptism Vol. 1 - From Genesis to Revelation.*

78. Pryce, Peter. (November 2023) *Water Baptism Vol. 2 - From Genesis to Revelation.*

79. Pryce, Peter. (December 2023) *Water Baptism Vol. 3 - From Genesis to Revelation.*

80. Pryce, Peter. (January 2024) *Water Baptism Vol. 4 - From Genesis to Revelation.*

81. Pryce, Peter. (February 2024) *Water Baptism Vol. 5 - From Genesis to Revelation.*

82. Pryce, Peter. (2024) *Holy Communion - From Genesis to Revelation.*

REFEREED ARTICLES IN BLIND PEER-REVIEWED ACADEMIC JOURNALS

1. Pryce, Peter. (2003). Foreignising Finnish: Necessary/Unnecessary English Imports into Translations. *Current Writing: Text and Reception in Southern Africa 14/2* (October, 2003), 203-12.

2. Pryce, Peter. (2011). Gemeinschaft Concept of Community in Schools: Case Study of Prince George's County Public Schools. *International Journal of Basic Education*, vol. 2(1), 1-9.

3. Pryce, Peter. (2012). Attitudes to Translation. *Linguistique et didactique de langue et de littérature : Problématiques contemporaines et perspectives (Linguistics and Language / Literature Didactics : Contemporary Challenges and Prospects)*, 343-377.

4. Pryce, Peter. (2012). Change as a Distinct Property of Language. In Bariki, I., Kuupole, D. D. and Kambou, M. K. (Eds.), *Aspects of Language Variation and Use*. Cape Coast: University of Cape Coast Press, 1-14.

5. Pryce, Peter. (2013). Techniques of Expression. *International Journal of Educational Research and Development*, vol. 2 (1), 1-9. 235-246.

EVIDENCE OF ACCEPTANCE FOR PUBLICATION IN A REFEREED JOURNAL

6. Pryce, Peter. (2006). Nokia's Role as an Agent of Language Migration. *Translation Watch Quarterly*. Patterson Lakes, Victoria, Australia: Translation Standards Institute.

PUBLICATION OF CONFERENCE PROCEEDINGS

7. Pryce, Peter. (2002). Translation as a Medium for Transmitting New Ideas: Finland as a Case Study. In H. Kucerova & B. Knowlden (Eds.), XVI Vancouver World Congress of the International Federation of Translators: Translation: New Ideas for a New Century (151-155). Paris: Fédération internationale des traducteurs (FIT).

INTERNET PRESENCE

Professional Website: WWW.THEBIBLEUNIVERSITY.ORG
Author website: WWW.BOOKSTORESITE.ORG
Church Website: WWW.THEBIBLEUNIVERSITYCHURCH.ORG

SOCIAL MEDIA LINKS

Skype link: https://join.skype.com/invite/a7xNskRQG2Fj
https://www.facebook.com/BibleLecturesAndHumanServices
www.instagram.com/thebibleuniversity
www.twitter.com/TheBibleUniv
https://youtu.be/G2bMwBpt0jk
https://www.youtube.com/channel/UCa0RgmXpGm7bJhtY7j_-UHw
LinkedIn URL: https://www.linkedin.com/in/the-bible-university-by-rev-prof-peter-pryce-ph-d-38b021127/

Association of African Universities (AAU) TV Discussion Program with Rev. Prof. Peter Pryce:
Topic: How Religion Contributes to Peace and Security in Africa:
https://kzread.info/dash/aau-talks-how-religion-contributes-to-peace-and-security-in-africa/lHiu1NeJgrjKgaQ.html

https://thebibleuniversity.org/blog/

Author Website Bookstore: WWW.BOOKSTORESITE.ORG

United States Patent and Trademark Office (USPTO): TRADEMARK:
https://furm.com/trademarks/the-bible-university-by-rev-prof-peter-pryce-phd-97075519

Contact Info:
Phone: +1-301-793-7190
E-mail: Dr.Pryce@gmail.com

TRADEMARK INFORMATION

United States of America
United States Patent and Trademark Office

The Bible University by Rev. Prof. Peter Pryce, P.H.D.

Reg. No. 6,999,146

Registered Mar. 14, 2023

Int. Cl.: 41

Service Mark

Principal Register

Presentation Copy

THE BIBLE UNIVERSITY INC.
11779 Carriage House Drive
Silver Spring, MARYLAND 20904

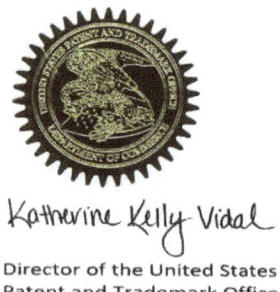

Katherine Kelly Vidal

Director of the United States
Patent and Trademark Office

TABLE OF CONTENTS

Table of Contents

FOREWORD

Dear Christians, Pastors, and Men of God:

I know that you believe in Holy Communion and you have been doing that offering and sacrifice even before I was born! But since there were False Teachers and False Christs right in the presence of the LORD Jesus Christ and immediately after HIS Death, Resurrection, and Ascension into Heaven, has it occured to you at all to ask yourself whether what you received as a Church Tradition from Church Elders called Holy Communion was maybe corrupted and falely presented to you as Truth when it was really NOT the Truth?

It is NOT a sin to question, examine, and test Doctrine, because God Almighty commands you so to do: **1 Thessalonians 5:21 (KJV)** Prove all things; hold fast that which is good. **1 John 4:1 (KJV)** Beloved, believe not every spirit, but try the spirits whether they are of God: because many false prophets are gone out into the world.

Secondly, supposing that you even agreed to have a second thought and to examine the Doctrine of Holy Communion, would the Word of God the Holy Bible be the best place for you to start searching for the Truth of that Doctrine? Certainly!

Thirdly, supposing that when you began to search the Scriptures, as the LORD Jesus Christ commanded, you found out that, truly, from Genesis to Revelation, there is nothing called "HOLY COMMUNION" in the entire Holy Bible? What would you say to that discovery?

Fourthly, what about if you also found out that from Genesis to Revelation, there is nothing physical, such as wafers, wine, and bread that has any spiritual power to connect you to Heaven, and that the LORD Jesus Christ Himself refers to your wafers, wine, and bread as toilet/dung items? How happy would you be, Brother, Sister, to find out, with solid incontrovertible Scriptures from the Bible that, in all these many years, you have actually been offering toilet/dung items to the LORD God Almighty as your "Holy Communion Sacrifice"?

Please, do not take my word for it, but read this Book to find out what very strange things the LORD God Almighty Himself and the LORD Jesus Christ have said about your "Holy Communion Sacrifice"!

God bless you!

Rev. Prof. PETER PRYCE,

DSEF, BA, MA, B.Soc.Sc Pol Sci, IBA, PhD

A Scribe of the Law of the God of Heaven

PREFACE

THE HEART IS ESTABLISHED WITH GRACE; NOT WITH MEATS!

Question 2380

1. The Holy Spirit revealed a Word about Holy Communion in **Hebrews 13:9-15 (KJV)**!

    i. **Hebrews 13:9 (KJV)** Be not carried about with divers and strange doctrines. For *it is* a good thing that the heart be established with grace; not with meats, which have not profited them that have been occupied therein.

    ii. **Hebrews 13:10 (KJV)** We have an altar, whereof they have no right to eat which serve the tabernacle.

    iii. **Hebrews 13:11 (KJV)** For the bodies of those beasts, whose blood is brought into the sanctuary by the high priest for sin, are burned without the camp.

    iv. **Hebrews 13:12 (KJV)** Wherefore Jesus also, that he might sanctify the people with his own blood, suffered without the gate.

    v. **Hebrews 13:13 (KJV)** Let us go forth therefore unto him without the camp, bearing his reproach.

    vi. **Hebrews 13:14 (KJV)** For here have we no continuing city, but we seek one to come.

    vii. **Hebrews 13:15 (KJV)** By him therefore let us offer the sacrifice of praise to God continually, that is, the fruit of *our* lips giving thanks to his name.

2. Now, the **FIRST SPIRITUAL LESSON** in **Hebrews 13:9-15 (KJV)** is this:

    i. "Meats have not profited them that have been occupied therein"! - **Hebrews 13:9 (KJV)**

3. Now, ask yourself this question:

    i. Are your Holy Communion wafers, bread, and wine classified as "meats/foods"?

    ii. The answer is: YES!

4. Well, then, there you have it!

5. The Holy Ghost is saying that your Holy Communion wafers, bread, and wine "have not profited them that have been occupied therein", meaning that they are very useless and vain!

6. Now, if you are a Pastor or a Bishop, and you were trained, and you are educated, and perhaps, you also declare yourself to be a Doctor or a Professor in Letters and in Theology, and yet you have been presenting vain sacrifices of Holy Communion wafers, bread, and wine unto God Almighty for about 50 years of your life, Sunday after Sunday, reading in the same Holy Scripture where the LORD God has been speaking to you and teaching you since the foundation of the world, and, yet, still, you have NOT attained unto the Wisdom of God, but you have rather remained too stupid to understand the Doctrines of Christ!

7. Or, in order to save yourself from shame, are you now going to deny that your Holy Communion wafers, bread, and wine are classified as "meats/foods"?

8. Since you DO NOT deny that Truth, then, the Holy Spirit is saying that "Meats/foods [meaning: your Holy Communion wafers, bread, and wine] have not profited them that have been occupied therein [meaning that they are vain and have zero spiritual significance nor acceptance in Heaven]"! - **Hebrews 13:9 (KJV)**

9. The **SECOND SPIRITUAL LESSON** in **Hebrews 13:9 (KJV)** is that:

   i. "For *it is* a good thing that the heart be established with grace; not with meats"!

   ii. Meaning that, your heart/mind/soul/spirit of Salvation that relates to the LORD God Almighty in Heaven, IS NOT established, founded, maintained, strengthened, secured, approved, sanctified, confirmed, grounded, anchored assured, and made holy by Holy Communion "meats/foods" of wafers, bread, and wine, BUT BY GRACE!

10. By the way, did you already know that "Grace" means "The Word of God" since "Grace" can be administered ONLY by "The Word of God"?

    i. **Romans 5:2 (KJV)** By whom also we have access by faith into this grace wherein we stand, and rejoice in hope of the glory of God.

    ii. **2 Corinthians 8:19 (KJV)** And not *that* only, but who was also chosen of the churches to travel with us with this grace, which is administered by us to the glory of the same Lord, and *declaration of* your ready mind:

    iii. **1 Peter 5:12 (KJV)** By Silvanus, a faithful brother unto you, as I suppose, I have written briefly, exhorting, and testifying that this is the true grace of God wherein ye stand.

    iv. **Acts 13:43 (KJV)** Now when the congregation was broken up, many of the Jews and religious proselytes followed Paul and Barnabas:

who, speaking to them, persuaded them to continue in the grace of God.

    v. **Acts 20:24 (KJV)** But none of these things move me, neither count I my life dear unto myself, so that I might finish my course with joy, and the ministry, which I have received of the Lord Jesus, to testify the gospel of the grace of God.

11. If it is "by grace are ye saved", and if "the word of his grace is able to build you up, and to give you an inheritance among all them which are sanctified", and if "the word of truth is the gospel of your salvation", and if it is "the engrafted word, which is able to save your souls", then, "Grace" means "The Salvation Word of God"!

    i. **Acts 20:32 (KJV)** And now, brethren, I commend you to God, and to the word of his grace, which is able to build you up, and to give you an inheritance among all them which are sanctified.

    ii. **Ephesians 2:8 (KJV)** For by grace are ye saved through faith; and that not of yourselves: *it is* the gift of God:

    iii. **Titus 2:11 (KJV)** For the grace of God that bringeth salvation hath appeared to all men,

    iv. **Acts 13:26 (KJV)** Men *and* brethren, children of the stock of Abraham, and whosoever among you feareth God, to you is the word of this salvation sent.

    v. **Ephesians 1:13 (KJV)** In whom ye also *trusted*, after that ye heard the word of truth, the gospel of your salvation: in whom also after that ye believed, ye were sealed with that holy Spirit of promise,

    vi. **James 1:21 (KJV)** Wherefore lay apart all filthiness and superfluity of naughtiness, and receive with meekness the engrafted word, which is able to save your souls.

12. So, then if "Grace" means "The Salvation Word of God" and the Holy Ghost is saying in **Hebrews 13:9 (KJV)** that:

    i. "For *it is* a good thing that the heart be established with grace; not with meats"!

    ii. Then, what the Holy Ghost is specifically saying is that:

    iii. "Holy Communion meats/foods, which are wafers, bread, and wine CANNOT establish the heart/the salvation of the saint and MUST be excluded to give way to the "Grace" meaning "The Salvation Word of God", which Salvation Word of God ALONE is able to establish the heart!

13. So, then, when you obey what the Holy Ghost is saying in **Hebrews 13:9 (KJV)**, then, you will and should be serving "The Grace/Salvation Word of God" at your

Holy Communion service and NOT the filth of man-made wafers, bread, and wine that you have been serving for the past 100 years!

14. The **THIRD SPIRITUAL LESSON** in **Hebrews 13:9 (KJV)** is that:

    i. The very Holy Communion wafers, bread, and wine that you have been serving in all your churches is the perfect evidence that you are "carried about with divers and strange doctrines"!

15. The Holy Ghost calls your Holy Communion wafers, bread, and wine "divers and strange doctrines", and truly, your Holy Communion services are doctrines of Devils!

    i. **1 Timothy 4:1 (KJV)** Now the Spirit speaketh expressly, that in the latter times some shall depart from the faith, giving heed to seducing spirits, and doctrines of devils;

    ii. **1 Timothy 4:2 (KJV)** Speaking lies in hypocrisy; having their conscience seared with a hot iron;

    iii. **1 Timothy 4:3 (KJV)** Forbidding to marry, *and commanding* to abstain from meats, which God hath created to be received with thanksgiving of them which believe and know the truth.

16. The **FOURTH SPIRITUAL LESSON** is in **Hebrews 13:10 (KJV**, and the lesson is a confirmation because in that same verse, we have the confirmation that the Holy Ghost is teaching about Holy Communion in **Hebrews 13:9-15 (KJV)**, because of the keywords: "altar, eat, serve the tabernacle"!

17. The **SIXTH SPIRITUAL LESSON** is in **Hebrews 13:10-14 (KJV**, where the Holy Spirit is revealing that, when it comes to the Flesh and Blood of the LORD Jesus Christ, IT IS FORBIDDEN TO EAT AT THE ALTAR!

    i. **Hebrews 13:10 (KJV)** We have an altar, whereof they have no right to eat which serve the tabernacle.

18. Now, ask yourself this: Do you eat and drink Holy Communion wafers, bread, and wine at the Altar in all your churches?

19. The answer is, YES, because that is exactly what you have been doing!

20. So, then, how does your Holy Communion eating compare with the command NOT TO EAT, which command is plainly written in **Hebrews 13:10 (KJV)**?

21. Do you now see how your Holy Communion Pastors and Bishops have been teaching doctrines of Devils, and you are yourselves Devils of Satan since you DO NOT obey the Word of God?

22. And, just in case you are still too stupid to understand what the Holy Spirit is teaching us on Holy Communion in **Hebrews 13:9-15 (KJV**, then, here is one more evidence for confirmation!

   i. **1 Corinthians 11:20 (KJV)** When ye come together therefore into one place, *this* is not to eat the Lord's supper.

23. Now, is the language in **1 Corinthians 11:20 (KJV)** plain enough for you?

24. Did you surely see the words: "NOT TO EAT THE LORD'S SUPPER"?

25. Did you also see in the same **1 Corinthians 11:20 (KJV)** that the Holy Ghost is saying that "When ye come together therefore into one place"?

26. What do you think that phrase means?

27. It means that:

   i. "When you meet as a congregation, as a church, then, that IS NOT the occasion to do a physical eating of the Lord's supper, the same thing that you foolishly do in your Holy Communion services"!

28. The **SEVENTH SPIRITUAL LESSON** is in **Hebrews 13:15 (KJV**, which is a natural ending for the entire lesson on Holy Communion!

   i. **Hebrews 13:15 (KJV)** By him therefore let us offer the sacrifice of praise to God continually, that is, the fruit of *our* lips giving thanks to his name.

29. Since, in **Hebrews 13:9-14 (KJV**, the Holy Ghost has condemned the physical eating of meats/foods, then, one would naturally ask what then is to be done instead, and **Hebrews 13:15 (KJV)** provides the answer!

30. In other words, **Hebrews 13:15 (KJV)** provides the answer to the question that: If we stop the physical eating of Holy Communion wafers, bread and wine, then, what shall we do in its place in order to obey the commandment of the LORD Jesus Christ, to wit: "this do in remembrance of me" in **Luke 22:19 (KJV)**?

   i. **Luke 22:14 (KJV)** And when the hour was come, he sat down, and the twelve apostles with him.

   ii. **Luke 22:15 (KJV)** And he said unto them, With desire I have desired to eat this passover with you before I suffer:

   iii. **Luke 22:16 (KJV)** For I say unto you, I will not any more eat thereof, until it be fulfilled in the kingdom of God.

   iv. **Luke 22:17 (KJV)** And he took the cup, and gave thanks, and said, Take this, and divide *it* among yourselves:

   v. **Luke 22:18 (KJV)** For I say unto you, I will not drink of the fruit of the vine, until the kingdom of God shall come.

   vi. **Luke 22:19 (KJV)** And he took bread, and gave thanks, and brake *it*, and gave unto them, saying, This is my body which is given for you: this do in remembrance of me.

   vii. **Luke 22:20 (KJV)** Likewise also the cup after supper, saying, This cup *is* the new testament in my blood, which is shed for you.

31. So, then, the answer is this:
    i. You stop the physical eating of Holy Communion wafers, bread and wine! - **Hebrews 13:10 (KJV), 1 Corinthians 11:20 (KJV)**
    ii. You "offer the sacrifice of praise to God continually" - **Hebrews 13:15 (KJV)**
    iii. You offer instead: "that is, the fruit of *our* lips giving thanks to his name" - **Hebrews 13:15 (KJV)**

32. "The fruit of *our* lips" means "The words of our lips", meaning that the true Holy Communion service should be serving words, specifically, the Words of the LORD Jesus Christ, because it is such words of thanksgiving and praise that give the true worship of Holy Communion unto God, NOT the filthy meats/foods of wafers, bread, and wine"!

33. In conclusion, here is the evidence that "The fruit of *our* lips" means "The words of our lips"!
    i. **Proverbs 18:20 (KJV)** A man's belly shall be satisfied with the fruit of his mouth; *and* with the increase of his lips shall he be filled.
    ii. **Isaiah 57:19 (KJV)** I create the fruit of the lips; Peace, peace to *him that is* far off, and to *him that is* near, saith the LORD; and I will heal him.
    iii. **Hebrews 13:15 (KJV)** By him therefore let us offer the sacrifice of praise to God continually, that is, the fruit of *our* lips giving thanks to his name.
    iv. **Matthew 7:15 (KJV)** Beware of false prophets, which come to you in sheep's clothing, but inwardly they are ravening wolves.
    v. **Matthew 7:16 (KJV)** Ye shall know them by their fruits. Do men gather grapes of thorns, or figs of thistles?
    vi. **Matthew 7:17 (KJV)** Even so every good tree bringeth forth good fruit; but a corrupt tree bringeth forth evil fruit.
    vii. **Matthew 7:18 (KJV)** A good tree cannot bring forth evil fruit, neither *can* a corrupt tree bring forth good fruit.
    viii. **Matthew 7:19 (KJV)** Every tree that bringeth not forth good fruit is hewn down, and cast into the fire.
    ix. **Matthew 7:20 (KJV)** Wherefore by their fruits ye shall know them.

The LORD Jesus Christ be with your spirit. The LORD Jesus Christ give you understanding.

Rev. Prof. PETER PRYCE,

DSEF, BA, MA, B.Soc.Sc Pol Sci, IBA, PhD
A Scribe of the Law of the God of Heaven
Prophet of the Word of God
Professor of French, Silver Spring, MD, USA
Scholar of the Institute of Theologians, USA
WWW.THEBIBLEUNIVERSITY.ORG
Accreditation Number: 07-QCTO/SDP120723172836
SAQA QUAL ID: Identification # 101997
WWW.BOOKSTORESITE.ORG
WWW.THEBIBLEUNIVERSITYCHURCH.ORG

Thursday 7th December 2023 @ 9:40 AM – 1:03 PM
While hearing and meditating on the Word of God.

CHAPTER 1

INTRODUCTION TO BIBLICAL HERMENEUTICS AND BIBLICAL EXEGESIS

ADINKRAHENE
"Chief of Adinkra symbols"
Asante philosophical symbol of Greatness, Charisma, Leadership

Hermeneutics is the study and establishment of the principles by which you interpret the Word of God. Thus, any rules, theoretical or practical, that you follow in order to bring out the meaning of a Bible text, is called "Biblical Hermeneutics".

The theoretical part is called "Hermeneutics" and then the actual application and implementation of the rules of Bible translation and interpretation, in order to bring out the hidden meaning, that is called "Biblical Exegesis"!

This introduction contains the entire theory that is at the foundation of how I teach the Word of God the way that I teach it, in other words: the why behind the what.

ABSTRACT

The aim of this research was to discover a scientific method of intralingual Bible interpreting where scientific means that (1) the faithfulness and accuracy of the translation are verifiable and (2) replicability of meaning at the message level of the interpreting process is assured once the method is mastered. The method used for the research was simple: (1) explain the Perfect Harmony Method for Bible Translation and Interpreting and the aim of interpreting, (2) read the entire English Bible: King James Version, (3) discover how meaning was rendered in the Bible using only the Bible (KJV), (4) in the light of the Scriptures, examine the rendered meaning for perfect harmony at the lexical level, at the message level, and at the context level such that the accuracy of the rendering or the accuracy of the intralingual interpretation is assured by its perfect harmony with the rest of the entire Bible. We found two illustrations of the Perfect Harmony Method of Bible Translation and Interpreting in Mark 12 and Mark 15. Thus, by using the Bible as its own interpreter, we achieve faithfulness to the source text and accuracy of expression apart from the assurance that the interpretation is not contradicted by any other verse in the entire Bible.

To the extent that there are University Professors and academics who are still ignorant of the three levels of translation to wit: Intralingual Translation (One language translation), Intralingual Translation (two or more language translation), and Intersemiotic Translation (non-verbal, non-linguistic translation), it is important to state plainly and categorically that this textbook is a work of interpretation and translation. It is a work of both interpretation and translation because we interpret to translate and we translate to interpret!

Keywords: Method, Intralingual Translation, Bible Interpreting, Perfect Harmony.

INTRODUCTION TO THE PERFECT HARMONY THEORY

Translation is the process of rendering meaning from an initiator to a receptor in order to achieve understanding of communication. In this paper, both translation and interpretation are used interchangeably given that during the cognitive process of translation, there is an interpretation segment that intervenes prior to writing the translation whereas, on the other hand, the act of note taking during interpreting is a clear intervention of a major translation activity of writing (cf. Seleskovitch, Danica, et Lederer, Marianne 2001).

We identify three types of translation known as *interlingual translation, intralingual translation* and *intersemiotic translation*. First, it is possible to render meaning from one language into another…that is called *interlingual translation*. Secondly, it is possible to render meaning within the same language such as when you take a Bible verse and explain it or when you explain a proverb in the same language to another…that practice is called *intralingual translation*.

Therefore Bible teaching, paraphrasing, summarizing, rephrasing, deverbalization, rapporteuring, commentary, journalistic reporting, recasting just to name those few, are all examples of *intralingual translation*. Thirdly, it is possible to render meaning by means of signs and objects such as road signs and drawings…that is called *intersemiotic translation* (Jakobson, 1971: 266).

The type of Bible interpreting exemplified in this book is intralingual translation and the English Bible: King James Version was used throughout. It is well understood that in translation, you render meaning by means of entities called words or signs or symbols. Therefore, words are vehicles that carry meanings. Just as meaning cannot be independent of the context, so Bible translation, whether interlingual or intralingual, must respect the *perfect harmony of the Scriptures*. The P*erfect Harmony Method of Bible Translation and Interpreting* simply means that Bible teaching or interpreting must not in any way contradict any part of the Bible from Genesis to Revelation.

THE LAW OF BIBLE TRANSLATION AND INTERPRETATION

1. Here in **Proverbs 21:16 (KJV)** is the Law of Bible Translation and Interpretation, otherwise known as Hermeneutics (Theory) and Exegesis (Interpretation)!

2. What is Understanding? What is the Way of Understanding?

    i. **Proverbs 21:16 (KJV)** The man that wandereth out of the way of understanding shall remain in the congregation of the dead.

3. "Understanding" is another name for the Word of God!

    i. **Deuteronomy 4:5 (KJV)** Behold, I have taught you statutes and judgments, even as the LORD my God commanded me, that ye should do so in the land whither ye go to possess it.

    ii. **Deuteronomy 4:6 (KJV)** Keep therefore and do *them*; for this *is* your wisdom and your understanding in the sight of the nations, which shall hear all these statutes, and say, Surely this great nation *is* a wise and understanding people.

    iii. **Job 28:12 (KJV)** But where shall wisdom be found? and where *is* the place of understanding?

    iv. **Job 28:20 (KJV)** Whence then cometh wisdom? and where *is* the place of understanding?

    v. **Psalm 119:104 (KJV)** Through thy precepts I get understanding: therefore I hate every false way.

    vi. **Psalm 119:130 (KJV)** The entrance of thy words giveth light; it giveth understanding unto the simple.

    vii. **Psalm 119:169 (KJV)** TAU. Let my cry come near before thee, O LORD: give me understanding according to thy word.

    viii. **Proverbs 2:6 (KJV)** For the LORD giveth wisdom: out of his mouth *cometh* knowledge and understanding.

    ix. **Proverbs 4:5 (KJV)** Get wisdom, get understanding: forget *it* not; neither decline from the words of my mouth.

    x. **Proverbs 4:7 (KJV)** Wisdom *is* the principal thing; *therefore* get wisdom: and with all thy getting get understanding.

    xi. **Proverbs 8:14 (KJV)** Counsel *is* mine, and sound wisdom: I *am* understanding; I have strength.

- xii. **Proverbs 9:10 (KJV)** The fear of the LORD *is* the beginning of wisdom: and the knowledge of the holy *is* understanding.
- xiii. **Proverbs 16:22 (KJV)** Understanding *is* a wellspring of life unto him that hath it: but the instruction of fools *is* folly.

4. Therefore, the real message in **Proverbs 21:16 (KJV)** is that: The moment you stray outside the Word of God, you have entered the territory of Death!

   - i. **Proverbs 21:16 (KJV)** The man that wandereth out of the way of understanding shall remain in the congregation of the dead.

5. Do you now understand why we say that in The Bible University, our ONLY textbook for the entire University is the Word of God, the Holy Bible the Gospel of the LORD Jesus Christ, from Genesis to Revelation?

6. So, then, as a true Man of God, you are forbidden to use any book aside the Word of God!

7. Are you a Pastor?

8. Do you have and do you consult other books that you keep in your Pulpit and in your Church Office, and you even use them to preach to the congregation?

9. Show me just one evidence where the LORD Jesus Christ used any other book aside the Word of God the Prophets!

   - i. **Luke 24:27 (KJV)** And beginning at Moses and all the prophets, he expounded unto them in all the scriptures the things concerning himself.
   - ii. **Luke 10:26 (KJV)** He said unto him, What is written in the law? how readest thou?
   - iii. **Matthew 4:4 (KJV)** But he answered and said, It is written, Man shall not live by bread alone, but by every word that proceedeth out of the mouth of God.
   - iv. **Matthew 4:7 (KJV)** Jesus said unto him, It is written again, Thou shalt not tempt the Lord thy God.
   - v. **Matthew 4:10 (KJV)** Then saith Jesus unto him, Get thee hence, Satan: for it is written, Thou shalt worship the Lord thy God, and him only shalt thou serve.

10. Do you also now understand why the same Law in **Proverbs 21:16 (KJV)** forbids you to use any other book when you want to translate and interpret the Word of God!

11. The entire theory of Bible Translation and Interpretation rests in this one verse:

    - i. **Proverbs 21:16 (KJV)** The man that wandereth out of the way of understanding shall remain in the congregation of the dead.

12. In other words, when you remove **Proverbs 21:16 (KJV)**, or when you despise and disregard **Proverbs 21:16 (KJV)**, then you have no Hermeneutics and Exegesis!

      i. **Isaiah 8:20 (KJV)** To the law and to the testimony: if they speak not according to this word, *it is* because *there is* no light in them.

      ii. **Proverbs 21:30 (KJV)** *There is* no wisdom nor understanding nor counsel against the LORD.

      iii. **Galatians 1:8 (KJV)** But though we, or an angel from heaven, preach any other gospel unto you than that which we have preached unto you, let him be accursed.

      iv. **Galatians 1:9 (KJV)** As we said before, so say I now again, If any *man* preach any other gospel unto you than that ye have received, let him be accursed.

13. Except when you are a fool and an ignorant person, that is when you will go outside of the Holy Bible to seek a theory, false theory, to use to teach, translate, examine, research, and interpret the Holy Bible, and then, in that case, your Hermeneutics and Exegesis will be from Satan!

14. Here in **Proverbs 21:30 (KJV)** is another Law of Bible Translation and Interpretation!

      i. **Proverbs 21:30 (KJV)** *There is* no wisdom nor understanding nor counsel against the LORD.

15. Proper Hermeneutics and Exegesis come from **Proverbs 21:30 (KJV)** and stipulates that you cannot translate and interpret the Word of God against the Word of God!

16. Instead, by that Theory of Bible Translation and Interpretation that you see in **Proverbs 21:30 (KJV)**, you must teach the Word of God to agree with the Word of God, you must translate the Word of God to agree with the Word of God, you must interpret the Word of God to agree with the Word of God!

      i. **Mark 9:39 (KJV)** But Jesus said, Forbid him not: for there is no man which shall do a miracle in my name, that can lightly speak evil of me.

      ii. **John 3:34 (KJV)** For he whom God hath sent speaketh the words of God: for God giveth not the Spirit by measure *unto him*.

      iii. **John 17:22 (KJV)** And the glory which thou gavest me I have given them; that they may be one, even as we are one:

      iv. **John 17:23 (KJV)** I in them, and thou in me, that they may be made perfect in one; and that the world may know that thou hast sent me, and hast loved them, as thou hast loved me.

17. That is the ONLY way, that is the only Theory, that is the only Hermeneutics available by which you can correctly teach, examine, research, expound, and interpret (Exegesis) the Word of God!

BIBLICAL EXEGESIS

Hermeneutics is the study and establishment of the principles by which you interpret the Word of God. Thus, any rules, theoretical or practical, that you follow in order to bring out the meaning of a Bible text, is called "Biblical Hermeneutics".

The theoretical part is called "Hermeneutics" and then the actual application and implementation of the rules of Bible translation and interpretation, in order to bring out the hidden meaning: that is called "Biblical Exegesis"! In the following paragraphs, we shall see an illustration of Biblical Exegesis.

Most importantly, and throughout the Holy Bible, the LORD God teaches the doctrine that the ONLY correct Bible Interpretation and Translation Theory is the one where the interpretation and translation are one, are in one accord, and are of one mind with the entire text of the Holy Scriptures from Genesis to Revelation!

> **Philippians 2:2 (KJV)** Fulfil ye my joy, that ye be likeminded, having the same love, *being* of one accord, of one mind.

SUMMARY OF THE THEORY OF BIBLICAL HERMENEUTICS

1. The Lord Jesus Christ used Psalm 110:1 (KJV) to teach Deductive Reasoning as a Methodology for Gospel Impartation!

    i. **Psalm 110:1 (KJV)** A Psalm of David. The LORD said unto my Lord, Sit thou at my right hand, until I make thine enemies thy footstool.

    ii. **Matthew 22:41 (KJV)** While the Pharisees were gathered together, Jesus asked them,

    iii. **Matthew 22:42 (KJV)** Saying, What think ye of Christ? whose son is he? They say unto him, *The Son* of David.

    iv. **Matthew 22:43 (KJV)** He saith unto them, How then doth David in spirit call him Lord, saying,

    v. **Matthew 22:44 (KJV)** The LORD said unto my Lord, Sit thou on my right hand, till I make thine enemies thy footstool?

    vi. **Matthew 22:45 (KJV)** If David then call him Lord, how is he his son?

    vii. **Matthew 22:46 (KJV)** And no man was able to answer him a word, neither durst any *man* from that day forth ask him any more *questions*.

2. First of all, the LORD Jesus Christ confirms in Matthew 22:41-46 (KJV) that David was saved in the Old Testament because David knew the LORD Jesus Christ in the Old Testament hence, he was writing about HIM!

3. Secondly, the LORD Jesus Christ is laying down "Deduction Reasoning" as an essential aspect of the Methodology for Gospel Impartation, saying that:

    i. If what you are teaching, affirming, explaining, translating, preaching, interpreting, evangelizing, and writing, does not make sense, then you are wrong in your Gospel Doctrine and in the Word of God!

    ii. If what you are teaching, affirming, explaining, translating, preaching, interpreting, evangelizing, and writing, violates any part of the entire Word of God from Genesis to Revelation, then you are wrong in your Gospel Doctrine and in the Word of God!

    iii. If what you are teaching, affirming, explaining, translating, preaching, interpreting, evangelizing, and writing, contradicts any part of the entire Word of God from Genesis to Revelation, then you are wrong in your Gospel Doctrine and in the Word of God!

iv. If what you are teaching, affirming, explaining, translating, preaching, interpreting, evangelizing, and writing, does not perfectly harmonize and agree with the entire remainder of the Word of God from Genesis to Revelation, then you are wrong in your Gospel Doctrine and in the Word of God!

v. In other words, you cannot teach the Word of God against the Word of God!

vi. In other words, you must teach the Word of God to agree with the Word of God!

4. Here are the evidences for the Perfect Harmony Theory for Bible Translation and Interpreting that the LORD Jesus Christ was teaching the erudite Pharisees, Sadducees, Synagogue Rulers, High Priests, Pastors, and Church Leaders!

5. In **Isaiah 8:20 (KJV)**, the LORD God Almighty declares that if you fail to teach the Word of God to agree with the Word of God, then it means that you are not even saved or born again!

i. **Isaiah 8:20 (KJV)** To the law and to the testimony: if they speak not according to this word, *it is* because *there is* no light in them.

6. In **Luke 10:25-28 (KJV)**, the LORD Jesus Christ is pointing out that, if you fail to seek, read, and study Salvation according to all that is written in the Law of God, then you will NOT be saved and you will NOT enter Heaven, effectively meaning that Salvation is actually a School Curriculum that you must read and study!

i. **Luke 10:25 (KJV)** And, behold, a certain lawyer stood up, and tempted him, saying, Master, what shall I do to inherit eternal life?

ii. **Luke 10:26 (KJV)** He said unto him, What is written in the law? how readest thou?

iii. **Luke 10:27 (KJV)** And he answering said, Thou shalt love the Lord thy God with all thy heart, and with all thy soul, and with all thy strength, and with all thy mind; and thy neighbour as thyself.

iv. **Luke 10:28 (KJV)** And he said unto him, Thou hast answered right: this do, and thou shalt live.

v. **2 Timothy 2:15 (KJV)** Study to shew thyself approved unto God, a workman that needeth not to be ashamed, rightly dividing the word of truth.

7. In **Acts 17:10-12 (KJV)**, the LORD God Almighty is revealing that Salvation is a Taught School Activity where the Salvation is attained when the Doctrine of Salvation is taught to Bible Students and where the Student of Salvation in turn reads and researches the Holy Bible to verify that what he/she has been taught conforms

to the rest of the Word of God, before he/she proceeds to believe what he/she has been taught, and then he/she will now attain unto Salvation!

     i. **Acts 17:10 (KJV)** And the brethren immediately sent away Paul and Silas by night unto Berea: who coming *thither* went into the synagogue of the Jews.

     ii. **Acts 17:11 (KJV)** These were more noble than those in Thessalonica, in that they received the word with all readiness of mind, and searched the scriptures daily, whether those things were so.

     iii. **Acts 17:12 (KJV)** Therefore many of them believed; also of honourable women which were Greeks, and of men, not a few.

8. In **Galatians 1:8-9 (KJV)**, the LORD God reveals that even if Angels from Heaven come and engage in teaching, affirming, explaining, translating, preaching, interpreting, evangelizing, and writing the Gospel of the LORD Jesus Christ, and then what the Angels teach do not perfectly harmonize and agree with the entire remainder of the Word of God from Genesis to Revelation, then those Angels are wrong in their Gospel Doctrine and in the Word of God, and for that matter, you the Man of God are even authorized to curse all such Angels!

     i. **Galatians 1:8 (KJV)** But though we, or an angel from heaven, preach any other gospel unto you than that which we have preached unto you, let him be accursed.

     ii. **Galatians 1:9 (KJV)** As we said before, so say I now again, If any *man* preach any other gospel unto you than that ye have received, let him be accursed.

9. In **1 Thessalonians 5:21 (KJV)** and in **1 John 4:1 (KJV)**, the LORD God Almighty reveals to us that if you fail to prove the Word of God by the Word of God, and if you fail to test, examine, and reason out the Word of God by the Word of God, then you are a false Christian and a false Prophet!

     i. **1 Thessalonians 5:21 (KJV)** Prove all things; hold fast that which is good.

     ii. **1 John 4:1 (KJV)** Beloved, believe not every spirit, but try the spirits whether they are of God: because many false prophets are gone out into the world.

10. All the above is the Perfect Harmony Theory for Bible Translation and Interpreting (Pryce, 2011) that I have been teaching in The Bible University and which the LORD Jesus Christ was first teaching the erudite Pharisees, Sadducees, Synagogue Rulers, High Priests, Pastors, and Church Leaders!

     i. **Matthew 22:41 (KJV)** While the Pharisees were gathered together, Jesus asked them,

    ii. **Matthew 22:42 (KJV)** Saying, What think ye of Christ? whose son is he? They say unto him, *The Son* of David.

    iii. **Matthew 22:43 (KJV)** He saith unto them, How then doth David in spirit call him Lord, saying,

    iv. **Matthew 22:44 (KJV)** The LORD said unto my Lord, Sit thou on my right hand, till I make thine enemies thy footstool?

    v. **Matthew 22:45 (KJV)** If David then call him Lord, how is he his son?

    vi. **Matthew 22:46 (KJV)** And no man was able to answer him a word, neither durst any *man* from that day forth ask him any more *questions*.

11. Specifically, the LORD Jesus Christ told them that there is contradiction (**Matthew 22:43 (KJV), Matthew 22:45 (KJV)**) in your reasoning and teaching of the Word of God, therefore, you are wrong!

12. Your ability as a Man of God to eliminate every contradiction in your teaching of the Word of God is your evidence that you have attained unto the Perfect Harmony of the Scriptures and unto the required Deductive Reasoning as the correct Methodology for Gospel Impartation!

THE BIBLE TRANSLATOR'S METHODOLOGY

THE BIBLE TRANSLATOR'S METHODOLOGY/THEORY (BIBLICAL HERMENEUTICS) TO EXPLAIN/TEACH/INTERPRET (BIBLICAL EXEGESIS) THE HOLY BIBLE

1. Here in **Isaiah 55:8-9 (KJV** is one of the major reasons why it is sheer folly and despicable beastly ignorance to try to explain the Word of God with human intellect and man-made methodologies!

    i. **Isaiah 55:8 (KJV)** For my thoughts *are* not your thoughts, neither *are* your ways my ways, saith the LORD.

    ii. **Isaiah 55:9 (KJV)** For *as* the heavens are higher than the earth, so are my ways higher than your ways, and my thoughts than your thoughts.

2. How can foolishness explain wisdom for it to be right?

    i. **1 Corinthians 2:14 (KJV)** But the natural man receiveth not the things of the Spirit of God: for they are foolishness unto him: neither can he know *them*, because they are spiritually discerned.

    ii. **Micah 7:3 (KJV)** That they may do evil with both hands earnestly, the prince asketh, and the judge *asketh* for a reward; and the great *man*, he uttereth his mischievous desire: so they wrap it up.

    iii. **1 Corinthians 1:20 (KJV)** Where *is* the wise? where *is* the scribe? where *is* the disputer of this world? hath not God made foolish the wisdom of this world?

    iv. **1 Corinthians 2:6 (KJV)** Howbeit we speak wisdom among them that are perfect: yet not the wisdom of this world, nor of the princes of this world, that come to nought:

    v. **1 Corinthians 3:19 (KJV)** For the wisdom of this world is foolishness with God. For it is written, He taketh the wise in their own craftiness.

3. How can corrupt thoughts produce an explanation or a methodology to assess and examine thoughts that are incorrupt and pure even as **Isaiah 55:8 (KJV)** reveals?

    i. **Proverbs 21:30 (KJV)** *There is* no wisdom nor understanding nor counsel against the LORD.

    ii. **Psalm 119:140 (KJV)** Thy word *is* very pure: therefore thy servant loveth it.

    iii. **Proverbs 30:5 (KJV)** Every word of God *is* pure: he *is* a shield unto them that put their trust in him.

4. How can continual liars (all men and all women) purport to examine, assess, evaluate, and offer a methodology/theory (Biblical Hermeneutics) to explain/teach (Biblical Exegesis) the words of He who never lied? Is that possible?

    i. **Genesis 6:5 (KJV)** And GOD saw that the wickedness of man *was* great in the earth, and *that* every imagination of the thoughts of his heart *was* only evil continually.

    ii. **Numbers 23:19 (KJV)** God *is* not a man, that he should lie; neither the son of man, that he should repent: hath he said, and shall he not do *it*? or hath he spoken, and shall he not make it good?

    iii. **1 Samuel 15:29 (KJV)** And also the Strength of Israel will not lie nor repent: for he *is* not a man, that he should repent.

    iv. **Proverbs 8:8 (KJV)** All the words of my mouth *are* in righteousness; *there is* nothing froward or perverse in them.

    v. **James 1:17 (KJV)** Every good gift and every perfect gift is from above, and cometh down from the Father of lights, with whom is no variableness, neither shadow of turning.

    vi. **1 Peter 2:21 (KJV)** For even hereunto were ye called: because Christ also suffered for us, leaving us an example, that ye should follow his steps:

    vii. **1 Peter 2:22 (KJV)** Who did no sin, neither was guile found in his mouth:

    viii. **John 14:6 (KJV)** Jesus saith unto him, I am the way, the truth, and the life: no man cometh unto the Father, but by me.

5. Ever since the world was created, was it ever possible for Darkness to dispel/explain Light? Was it ever possible for Darkness to examine, assess, evaluate, and offer a methodology/theory (Biblical Hermeneutics) to explain/teach (Biblical Exegesis) the words of He who is The Light?

    i. **John 8:12 (KJV)** Then spake Jesus again unto them, saying, I am the light of the world: he that followeth me shall not walk in darkness, but shall have the light of life.

    ii. **John 9:5 (KJV)** As long as I am in the world, I am the light of the world.

6. Shall He that brought Light (enlightenment) be examined by he that sat in darkness (the ignorant and the fools)?

     i.   **Genesis 1:1 (KJV)** In the beginning God created the heaven and the earth.

    ii.   **Genesis 1:2 (KJV)** And the earth was without form, and void; and darkness *was* upon the face of the deep. And the Spirit of God moved upon the face of the waters.

   iii.   **Genesis 1:3 (KJV)** And God said, Let there be light: and there was light.

   iv.   **Genesis 1:4 (KJV)** And God saw the light, that *it was* good: and God divided the light from the darkness.

7.   Shall one use the earthly to teach and to explain the Heavenly and not risk being called a fool?

     i.   **Luke 24:13 (KJV)** And, behold, two of them went that same day to a village called Emmaus, which was from Jerusalem *about* threescore furlongs.

    ii.   **Luke 24:14 (KJV)** And they talked together of all these things which had happened.

   iii.   **Luke 24:15 (KJV)** And it came to pass, that, while they communed *together* and reasoned, Jesus himself drew near, and went with them.

   iv.   **Luke 24:16 (KJV)** But their eyes were holden that they should not know him.

    v.   **Luke 24:17 (KJV)** And he said unto them, What manner of communications *are* these that ye have one to another, as ye walk, and are sad?

   vi.   **Luke 24:18 (KJV)** And the one of them, whose name was Cleopas, answering said unto him, Art thou only a stranger in Jerusalem, and hast not known the things which are come to pass there in these days?

  vii.   **Luke 24:19 (KJV)** And he said unto them, What things? And they said unto him, Concerning Jesus of Nazareth, which was a prophet mighty in deed and word before God and all the people:

 viii.   **Luke 24:20 (KJV)** And how the chief priests and our rulers delivered him to be condemned to death, and have crucified him.

   ix.   **Luke 24:21 (KJV)** But we trusted that it had been he which should have redeemed Israel: and beside all this, to day is the third day since these things were done.

    x.   **Luke 24:22 (KJV)** Yea, and certain women also of our company made us astonished, which were early at the sepulchre;

xi. **Luke 24:23 (KJV)** And when they found not his body, they came, saying, that they had also seen a vision of angels, which said that he was alive.

xii. **Luke 24:24 (KJV)** And certain of them which were with us went to the sepulchre, and found *it* even so as the women had said: but him they saw not.

xiii. **Luke 24:25 (KJV)** Then he said unto them, O fools, and slow of heart to believe all that the prophets have spoken:

xiv. **Luke 24:26 (KJV)** Ought not Christ to have suffered these things, and to enter into his glory?

xv. **Luke 24:27 (KJV)** And beginning at Moses and all the prophets, he expounded unto them in all the scriptures the things concerning himself.

8. Or, shall the profane and the physical be adequate to teach and to explain the holy and the spiritual without incurring the condemnation of fools?

i. **John 3:1 (KJV)** There was a man of the Pharisees, named Nicodemus, a ruler of the Jews:

ii. **John 3:2 (KJV)** The same came to Jesus by night, and said unto him, Rabbi, we know that thou art a teacher come from God: for no man can do these miracles that thou doest, except God be with him.

iii. **John 3:3 (KJV)** Jesus answered and said unto him, Verily, verily, I say unto thee, Except a man be born again, he cannot see the kingdom of God.

iv. **John 3:4 (KJV)** Nicodemus saith unto him, How can a man be born when he is old? can he enter the second time into his mother's womb, and be born?

v. **John 3:5 (KJV)** Jesus answered, Verily, verily, I say unto thee, Except a man be born of water and *of* the Spirit, he cannot enter into the kingdom of God.

vi. **John 3:6 (KJV)** That which is born of the flesh is flesh; and that which is born of the Spirit is spirit.

vii. **John 3:7 (KJV)** Marvel not that I said unto thee, Ye must be born again.

viii. **John 3:8 (KJV)** The wind bloweth where it listeth, and thou hearest the sound thereof, but canst not tell whence it cometh, and whither it goeth: so is every one that is born of the Spirit.

ix. **John 3:9 (KJV)** Nicodemus answered and said unto him, How can these things be?

     x. **John 3:10 (KJV)** Jesus answered and said unto him, Art thou a master of Israel, and knowest not these things?

     xi. **John 3:11 (KJV)** Verily, verily, I say unto thee, We speak that we do know, and testify that we have seen; and ye receive not our witness.

     xii. **John 3:12 (KJV)** If I have told you earthly things, and ye believe not, how shall ye believe, if I tell you *of* heavenly things?

9. When he that dwelt in the Darkness attempted to translate, interpret, explain, teach, examine, assess, evaluate, and offer a methodology/theory (Biblical Hermeneutics) to explain/teach (Biblical Exegesis) the words of He who dwells in The Bright Light, the result was a perpetual disaster of evil, wrath, condemnation, curses, and death!

     i. **1 Timothy 6:14 (KJV)** That thou keep *this* commandment without spot, unrebukeable, until the appearing of our Lord Jesus Christ:

     ii. **1 Timothy 6:15 (KJV)** Which in his times he shall shew, *who is* the blessed and only Potentate, the King of kings, and Lord of lords;

     iii. **1 Timothy 6:16 (KJV)** Who only hath immortality, dwelling in the light which no man can approach unto; whom no man hath seen, nor can see: to whom *be* honour and power everlasting. Amen.

     iv. **Romans 5:12 (KJV)** Wherefore, as by one man sin entered into the world, and death by sin; and so death passed upon all men, for that all have sinned:

     v. **1 Corinthians 15:22 (KJV)** For as in Adam all die, even so in Christ shall all be made alive.

10. Here is Professor Satan bringing his methodology/theory (Biblical Hermeneutics) to explain/teach (Biblical Exegesis) the words of He who dwells in The Bright Light!

     i. **Genesis 3:1 (KJV)** Now the serpent was more subtil than any beast of the field which the LORD God had made. And he said unto the woman, Yea, hath God said, Ye shall not eat of every tree of the garden?

11. Here is the ignorant and foolish Student of Professor Satan interacting with him in class when she had not prior read and assimilated her notes!

     i. **Genesis 3:2 (KJV)** And the woman said unto the serpent, We may eat of the fruit of the trees of the garden:

     ii. **Genesis 3:3 (KJV)** But of the fruit of the tree which *is* in the midst of the garden, God hath said, Ye shall not eat of it, neither shall ye touch it, lest ye die.

12. Here is Professor Satan who immediately recognized that his Student was a lazy Student who had refused to read and assimilate her notes before coming to class, and

so, he proceeded to impart unto her: false doctrines and an evil methodology/theory (Biblical Hermeneutics) on how best to understand the Word of God!

    i. **Genesis 3:4 (KJV)** And the serpent said unto the woman, Ye shall not surely die:

    ii. **Genesis 3:5 (KJV)** For God doth know that in the day ye eat thereof, then your eyes shall be opened, and ye shall be as gods, knowing good and evil.

13. Professor Satan's Student, Eve, has received the evil methodology/theory (Biblical Hermeneutics) on how best to understand the Word of God, and now, she is on her way to teach it and to implement it with her equally foolish and ignorant husband called Adam

    i. **Genesis 3:6 (KJV)** And when the woman saw that the tree *was* good for food, and that it *was* pleasant to the eyes, and a tree to be desired to make *one* wise, she took of the fruit thereof, and did eat, and gave also unto her husband with her; and he did eat.

14. Then, suddenly, they both died!

    i. **Genesis 3:7 (KJV)** And the eyes of them both were opened, and they knew that they *were* naked; and they sewed fig leaves together, and made themselves aprons.

    ii. **Genesis 2:16 (KJV)** And the LORD God commanded the man, saying, Of every tree of the garden thou mayest freely eat:

    iii. **Genesis 2:17 (KJV)** But of the tree of the knowledge of good and evil, thou shalt not eat of it: for in the day that thou eatest thereof thou shalt surely die.

    iv. **Hosea 13:1 (KJV)** When Ephraim spake trembling, he exalted himself in Israel; but when he offended in Baal, he died.

    v. **Romans 5:12 (KJV)** Wherefore, as by one man sin entered into the world, and death by sin; and so death passed upon all men, for that all have sinned:

15. What then shall we do, how shall we approach the Word of God, and with what methodology/theory (Biblical Hermeneutics) shall we approach and understand the Word of God?

16. Since every man and woman is corrupt and the Word of God is incorrupt, the only choice left is to use the methodology/theory (Biblical Hermeneutics) that the LORD God Himself has provided, and to learn from the ONLY Professor who is qualified to teach and to reveal the Word of God who is: The Holy Spirit!

17. Here is God's methodology to understand, to explain, and to teach the Word of God!

    i. **Proverbs 21:30 (KJV)** *There is* no wisdom nor understanding nor counsel against the LORD.

    ii. **Isaiah 8:20 (KJV)** To the law and to the testimony: if they speak not according to this word, *it is* because *there is* no light in them.

    iii. **1 Corinthians 2:6 (KJV)** Howbeit we speak wisdom among them that are perfect: yet not the wisdom of this world, nor of the princes of this world, that come to nought:

    iv. **1 Corinthians 2:7 (KJV)** But we speak the wisdom of God in a mystery, *even* the hidden *wisdom*, which God ordained before the world unto our glory:

    v. **1 Corinthians 2:8 (KJV)** Which none of the princes of this world knew: for had they known *it*, they would not have crucified the Lord of glory.

    vi. **1 Corinthians 2:9 (KJV)** But as it is written, Eye hath not seen, nor ear heard, neither have entered into the heart of man, the things which God hath prepared for them that love him.

    vii. **1 Corinthians 2:10 (KJV)** But God hath revealed *them* unto us by his Spirit: for the Spirit searcheth all things, yea, the deep things of God.

    viii. **1 Corinthians 2:11 (KJV)** For what man knoweth the things of a man, save the spirit of man which is in him? even so the things of God knoweth no man, but the Spirit of God.

    ix. **1 Corinthians 2:12 (KJV)** Now we have received, not the spirit of the world, but the spirit which is of God; that we might know the things that are freely given to us of God.

    x. **1 Corinthians 2:13 (KJV)** Which things also we speak, not in the words which man's wisdom teacheth, but which the Holy Ghost teacheth; comparing spiritual things with spiritual.

18. The words: "comparing spiritual things with spiritual" means that you must compare each understanding of the Word of God that you get with all the remainder of the Scriptures from Genesis to Revelation, before you can claim to have understood anything!

19. The reason for the arduous, diligent, and painstaking comparison from Genesis to Revelation is that: There should be no confusion, violation, or contradiction between your understand and the rest of the Word of God, no, not even one contradiction, else, you do not have Truth but a false doctrine, if you fail to do the comparison!

20. Here is the LORD Yeshua the Christ teaching the same correct God's methodology that I have just shown you, and He is condemning their Bible Teaching, because it has a contradiction, and therefore, it is a lie and not acceptable!

i. **Matthew 22:41 (KJV)** While the Pharisees were gathered together, Jesus asked them,

ii. **Matthew 22:42 (KJV)** Saying, What think ye of Christ? whose son is he? They say unto him, *The Son* of David.

iii. **Matthew 22:43 (KJV)** He saith unto them, How then doth David in spirit call him Lord, saying,

iv. **Matthew 22:44 (KJV)** The LORD said unto my Lord, Sit thou on my right hand, till I make thine enemies thy footstool?

v. **Matthew 22:45 (KJV)** If David then call him Lord, how is he his son?

vi. **Matthew 22:46 (KJV)** And no man was able to answer him a word, neither durst any *man* from that day forth ask him any more *questions.*

21. Consequently, since a fool cannot teach a wise person wisdom, in other words, since humans cannot teach Holy Spirit the Word of God, then, the only correct methodology left for translating, interpreting, and teaching the Word of God is to teach the Word of God to agree with the Word of God! Any other methodology is false and a lie!

   i. **1 Corinthians 2:6 (KJV)** Howbeit we speak wisdom among them that are perfect: yet not the wisdom of this world, nor of the princes of this world, that come to nought:

   ii. **1 Corinthians 2:7 (KJV)** But we speak the wisdom of God in a mystery, *even* the hidden *wisdom,* which God ordained before the world unto our glory:

   iii. **1 Corinthians 2:10 (KJV)** But God hath revealed *them* unto us by his Spirit: for the Spirit searcheth all things, yea, the deep things of God.

   iv. **1 Corinthians 2:11 (KJV)** For what man knoweth the things of a man, save the spirit of man which is in him? even so the things of God knoweth no man, but the Spirit of God.

   v. **1 Corinthians 2:12 (KJV)** Now we have received, not the spirit of the world, but the spirit which is of God; that we might know the things that are freely given to us of God.

   vi. **1 Corinthians 2:13 (KJV)** Which things also we speak, not in the words which man's wisdom teacheth, but which the Holy Ghost teacheth; comparing spiritual things with spiritual.

22. The LORD Jesus Christ be with your spirit. The LORD Jesus Christ give you understanding.

Rev. Prof. PETER PRYCE,
DSEF, BA, MA, B.Soc.Sc Pol Sci, IBA, PhD
A Scribe of the Law of the God of Heaven
Prophet of the Word of God
Professor of French, Silver Spring, MD, USA
Scholar of the Institute of Theologians, USA
WWW.THEBIBLEUNIVERSITY.ORG
Accreditation Number: 07-QCTO/SDP120723172836
SAQA QUAL ID: Identification # 101997
WWW.BOOKSTORESITE.ORG
WWW.THEBIBLEUNIVERSITYCHURCH.ORG

Saturday 27th May 2023 @ 12:40 PM – 2:30 PM

GOD'S THEORY FOR BIBLE TRANSLATION AND INTERPRETATION

Question 2366

Answer:

1. God Almighty reveals a Theory for Bible Translation and Interpretation in **Jeremiah 10:14 (KJV)**!

2. Because every man is brutish, a fool, and ignorant of the knowledge of God, this is the reason why it is impossible, yea, beyond the capacity of man, to devise a methodology for Bible Translation and Interpretation!

3. That leaves us with only one choice!

4. When you exclude all humans, then, you are left with ONLY God Almighty!

5. Hence, only God has the correct methodology for Bible Translation and Interpretation!

6. It is NOT possible for the Superior God to give HIS Superior Word to an inferior man to figure out and to develop a methodology on how to Translate and Interpret that superior Word of God!

7. That is why you cannot find any correct methodology for Bible Translation and Interpretation outside of the Holy Bible!

8. The correct way, methodology, technique, approach, and theory to understand, translate, teach, explain, and interpret the Word of God, is in the Word of God and by the Word of God ONLY!

    i. **Jeremiah 10:14 (KJV)** Every man is brutish in *his* knowledge: every founder is confounded by the graven image: for his molten image *is* falsehood, and *there is* no breath in them.

    ii. **Job 32:8 (KJV)** But *there is* a spirit in man: and the inspiration of the Almighty giveth them understanding.

    iii. **John 14:26 (KJV)** But the Comforter, *which is* the Holy Ghost, whom the Father will send in my name, he shall teach you all things, and bring all things to your remembrance, whatsoever I have said unto you.

    iv. **John 15:26 (KJV)** But when the Comforter is come, whom I will send unto you from the Father, *even* the Spirit of truth, which proceedeth from the Father, he shall testify of me:

     v. **John 16:13 (KJV)** Howbeit when he, the Spirit of truth, is come, he will guide you into all truth: for he shall not speak of himself; but whatsoever he shall hear, *that* shall he speak: and he will shew you things to come.

     vi. **Acts 2:4 (KJV)** And they were all filled with the Holy Ghost, and began to speak with other tongues, as the Spirit gave them utterance.

     vii. **2 Timothy 3:16 (KJV)** All scripture *is* given by inspiration of God, and *is* profitable for doctrine, for reproof, for correction, for instruction in righteousness:

     viii. **2 Timothy 3:17 (KJV)** That the Man of God may be perfect, throughly furnished unto all good works.

9. Here is the theory in **Jeremiah 10:14 (KJV)**!

10. This declaration by God Almighty: "Every man is brutish in *his* knowledge" disqualifies every man from putting forth a theory to examine the Word of God since that theory will constitute "his knowledge"!

11. The LORD God Almighty is saying in **Jeremiah 10:14 (KJV** that, if you want to see the evidence of a man's foolishness, his brute capacity, his ignorance, his treachery, his stupid thoughts, his evil proclivity, then, examine his words/his knowledge!

     i. **Matthew 12:34 (KJV)** O generation of vipers, how can ye, being evil, speak good things? for out of the abundance of the heart the mouth speaketh.

     ii. **Luke 6:45 (KJV)** A good man out of the good treasure of his heart bringeth forth that which is good; and an evil man out of the evil treasure of his heart bringeth forth that which is evil: for of the abundance of the heart his mouth speaketh.

12. As you can see in **Jeremiah 10:14 (KJV**, there is no exception to the falsehood that is in man, because "Every man is brutish in *his* knowledge"!

     i. **Genesis 6:5 (KJV)** And GOD saw that the wickedness of man *was* great in the earth, and *that* every imagination of the thoughts of his heart *was* only evil continually.

     ii. **Jeremiah 17:9 (KJV)** The heart *is* deceitful above all *things*, and desperately wicked: who can know it?

13. Every theory or methodology devised by men for Bible Translation and Interpretation that does not come 100% from the Word of God, is a work of error!

     i. **Jeremiah 10:15 (KJV)** They *are* vanity, *and* the work of errors: in the time of their visitation they shall perish.

14. Furthermore, there are other injunctions in the Word of God that sets the Approach to Bible Translation! Here is one of them:

     i. **Proverbs 19:27 (KJV)** Cease, my son, to hear the instruction *that causeth* to err from the words of knowledge.

15. Now, here is the meaning of **Proverbs 19:27 (KJV)**!

16. The ONLY "words of knowledge" that we know is the Word of God the Holy Scriptures from Genesis to Revelation!

17. Now, God says in **Proverbs 19:27 (KJV)** that ANYTHING, ANY WORD, ANY INSTRUCTION, ANY THEORY, ANY METHODOLOGY, ANY APPROACH, ANY TEACHING, ANY PREACHING, ANY EXPLANATION, ANYTHING AND EVERYTHING that departs from, deviates from, separates from, decouples from, and diverges from "the words of knowledge", which is the Word of God the Holy Scriptures from Genesis to Revelation: "CEASE, MY SON, TO HEAR IT"!

18. That injunction means that:

     i. "The moment you as a Translator, Interpreter, Preacher, Pastor, Apostle, Bishop, or anyone, the moment you step outside the boundaries (Genesis to Revelation) of the Word of God, for any assistance, to bring that outside thing into the Word of God, you are in error"!

19. Here is a confirmation of the same injunction above, showing that anything and everything and everyone that is outside the realm of the Word of God: IS FOOLISHNESS AND IS A FOOL!

     i. **Proverbs 14:7 (KJV)** Go from the presence of a foolish man, when thou perceivest not *in him* the lips of knowledge.

20. Here is another confirmation of the same injunction above, this time from the LORD Jesus Christ, showing that "Garbage in, Garbage out", or, "when you leave aside the Word of God to go and take foolishness to examine the Word of God, you will surely get foolishness as your result"! Jesus also means that "If you are in the Word of God and you take heed to exclude everything that is outside the perimeter of the Word of God, then more revelation in the Word of God will be given to you"!

     i. **Mark 4:24 (KJV)** And he said unto them, Take heed what ye hear: with what measure ye mete, it shall be measured to you: and unto you that hear shall more be given.

21. Here is another confirmation of the same injunction above, this time from Apostle Paul, showing that the ONLY way you can successfully execute any Theory of Bible Translation is by excluding/separating that theory away from unbelievers, away from unrighteousness, away from darkness, away from Belial, away from infidels, and away from idols, since anything and everything that are outside the realm of the Word of God are certainly what I have just listed! Succinctly, therefore, your Theory for Bible Translation and Interpretation CANNOT come from outside the Word of God

because anything and everything that are outside the Word of God are "unbelievers, unrighteousness, darkness, Belial, infidels, and idols"!

      i. **2 Corinthians 6:14 (KJV)** Be ye not unequally yoked together with unbelievers: for what fellowship hath righteousness with unrighteousness? and what communion hath light with darkness?

      ii. **2 Corinthians 6:15 (KJV)** And what concord hath Christ with Belial? or what part hath he that believeth with an infidel?

      iii. **2 Corinthians 6:16 (KJV)** And what agreement hath the temple of God with idols? for ye are the temple of the living God; as God hath said, I will dwell in them, and walk in *them*; and I will be their God, and they shall be my people.

      iv. **2 Corinthians 6:17 (KJV)** Wherefore come out from among them, and be ye separate, saith the Lord, and touch not the unclean *thing*; and I will receive you,

      v. **2 Corinthians 6:18 (KJV)** And will be a Father unto you, and ye shall be my sons and daughters, saith the Lord Almighty.

22. Here is another confirmation of the same injunction above, this time from King Solomon, showing that:

      i. "the moment your Bible Translation, Interpretation, Teaching, Explanation, Theory, Hermeneutics, Exegesis, Methodology, or Counsel goes against the LORD/Word of God, then, that is the same moment that you entered into error and falsehood"!

      ii. **Proverbs 21:30 (KJV)** *There is* no wisdom nor understanding nor counsel against the LORD.

23. Consequently, since anything that proceeds from the realm and imagination of all humans is "only evil continually, deceit above all things, and desperately wicked", therefore, the ONLY parameter within which you can find the true and correct theory for translating and interpreting the Word of God is the Word of God itself!

24. Having now understood the requirements of the theory, the next step now is to locate within the limits of the Holy Bible, from Genesis to Revelation, models of the translation and interpretation theory that the LORD God Almighty and the LORD Jesus Christ themselves have already successfully used and applied for our instruction!

The LORD Jesus Christ be with your spirit. The LORD Jesus Christ give you understanding.

Rev. Prof. Peter Pryce, Ph.D.

A Scribe of the Law of the God of Heaven
Prophet of the Word of God
Friday 3rd November 2023 @ 10:37 AM – 11:03 AM
While hearing and meditating on the Word of God in my bedroom
WWW.THEBIBLEUNIVERSITY.ORG
WWW.BOOKSTORESITE.ORG
WWW.THEBIBLEUNIVERSITYCHURCH.ORG

GOD'S METHODOLOGY FOR BIBLE TRANSLATION AND INTERPRETATION

Question 2388

1. In order to solve and answer spiritual controversies, the LORD God Almighty already gave us a 5-Step Approach and Methodology to handle Spiritual Controversies and Bible Questions!
    a. **STEP 1**: Identify the controversy, the Bible Question, or the misunderstanding!
    b. **Deuteronomy 17:8 (KJV)** If there arise a matter too hard for thee in judgment, between blood and blood, between plea and plea, and between stroke and stroke, *being* matters of controversy within thy gates: then shalt thou arise, and get thee up into the place which the LORD thy God shall choose;
    c. **STEP 2**: Go to the Priest, who is the God-appointed Judge of the Word of God, the Scribe of the Law of the God of Heaven, the Man of God, and bring the specific Bible Question to him, so that he can shew thee the sentence of judgment!
    d. **Deuteronomy 17:9 (KJV)** And thou shalt come unto the priests the Levites, and unto the judge that shall be in those days, and inquire; and they shall shew thee the sentence of judgment:
2. **STEP 3**: The contract for coming to the Man of God to shew thee the sentence of judgment of God is that, thou shalt observe to do according to all that they, the Men of God, inform thee!
    a. **Deuteronomy 17:10 (KJV)** And thou shalt do according to the sentence, which they of that place which the LORD shall choose shall shew thee; and thou shalt observe to do according to all that they inform thee:
    b. **STEP 4**: The Man of God shall teach and explain the controversy or Bible Question ONLY from within the Law of God and according to the sentence of the Law of God!
3. Once the Man of God has finished his work to teach you, to explain to you, and to show you the good understanding of the Bible Question or controversy, thou shalt not decline from the sentence which they shall shew thee, *to* the right hand, nor *to*

the left! The moment you hear the Word of God from the mouth of a true Man of God, you are bound by that Word whether you like it or not!

a. **Deuteronomy 17:11 (KJV)** According to the sentence of the law which they shall teach thee, and according to the judgment which they shall tell thee, thou shalt do: thou shalt not decline from the sentence which they shall shew thee, *to* the right hand, nor *to* the left.

b. **STEP 5**: Now, here is the curse of death that comes with going to the Man of God to teach you the Word of God, especially if that man is a true Man of God living in Truth and Righteousness daily!

4. After you have heard the Word of God from the true Man of God, and you reject it, despise it, decline it, argue against it, cast it aside, despise the Man of God, lie to him, not take his advice, leave his teaching aside to carry on with your life…well, in that case, the LORD God Almighty says that only death is good for you then, because it is such a great evil for the Word of God to come to you and you refuse to obey it!

a. **Deuteronomy 17:12 (KJV)** And the man that will do presumptuously, and will not hearken unto the priest that standeth to minister there before the LORD thy God, or unto the judge, even that man shall die: and thou shalt put away the evil from Israel.

b. **Deuteronomy 17:13 (KJV)** And all the people shall hear, and fear, and do no more presumptuously.

5. We shall, therefore, use this **5-Step Approach and Methodology to handle Spiritual Controversies and Bible Questions** that I have just presented to you; to answer this question on Female Ordination in the Churches!

The LORD Jesus Christ be with your spirit. The LORD Jesus Christ give you understanding.

Rev. Prof. PETER PRYCE,
DSEF, BA, MA, B.Soc.Sc Pol Sci, IBA, PhD
A Scribe of the Law of the God of Heaven
Prophet of the Word of God
Professor of French, Silver Spring, MD, USA
Scholar of the Institute of Theologians, USA
WWW.THEBIBLEUNIVERSITY.ORG
Accreditation Number: 07-QCTO/SDP120723172836
SAQA QUAL ID: Identification # 101997
WWW.BOOKSTORESITE.ORG
WWW.THEBIBLEUNIVERSITYCHURCH.ORG

Tuesday 19th December 2023 @ 2:40 PM – 4:01 PM
While writing another Book.

THEORETICAL APPROACH TO BIBLE INTERPRETATION AND TRANSLATION

Question 2458

If you want to accomplish a successful Bible Interpretation and Translation, then follow this theoretical approach:

1. A correct translation of the Holy Bible begins with a correct understanding of the text (Hermeneutics) of the Holy Bible!

2. A correct understanding of the Holy Bible precedes a correct interpretation (Exegesis) of the text of the Holy Bible!

3. A correct interpretation of the Holy Bible requires achieving perfect harmony/coherence and zero conflict of thought and doctrine between your understanding of the Bible text in question and the entire remainder of the Holy Bible!

4. A correct translation of the Holy Bible is the final step and a rendering in writing of the above intellectual process!

5. The Holy Scriptures is The Book that prescribes its own Approach and Methodology of Interpretation and it is contained in the Book of 1 Corinthians chapter 1!

6. There is a restricted audience that is identified for the interpretation and translation of the Holy Scriptures!
   i. **1 Corinthians 1:1 (KJV)** Paul, called *to be* an apostle of Jesus Christ through the will of God, and Sosthenes *our* brother,
   ii. **1 Corinthians 1:2 (KJV)** Unto the church of God which is at Corinth, to them that are sanctified in Christ Jesus, called *to be* saints, with all that in every place call upon the name of Jesus Christ our Lord, both theirs and ours:

7. In other words, the Holy Scriptures is NOT for everyone, but ONLY for:
   i. Those who are called to its tenets and doctrines.
   ii. Those who are identified as the Church of Christ and profess themselves so to be.
   iii. Them that are sanctified/cleansed/washed in Christ Jesus.
   iv. To be sanctified/cleansed/washed means to be washed from all thoughts that are contrary to the mind of Christ and to take on in its place, or to be imbued, impregnated, inspired, filled with, permeated, infused, poured into, soaked, or endued with: the mind of Christ!

  v. **Luke 24:49 (KJV)** And, behold, I send the promise of my Father upon you: but tarry ye in the city of Jerusalem, until ye be endued with power from on high.

  vi. **Acts 1:5 (KJV)** For John truly baptized with water; but ye shall be baptized with the Holy Ghost not many days hence.

  vii. **Acts 1:8 (KJV)** But ye shall receive power, after that the Holy Ghost is come upon you: and ye shall be witnesses unto me both in Jerusalem, and in all Judaea, and in Samaria, and unto the uttermost part of the earth.

  viii. Them that in every place call upon the name of Jesus Christ as the LORD and Source of that knowledge that is derived from the Holy Scriptures!

8. Now, therefore, if you are NOT identified in the above portrait or profile of people who should access the text of the Holy Scriptures, then what are you doing with it?

  i. **Psalm 50:16 (KJV)** But unto the wicked God saith, What hast thou to do to declare my statutes, or *that* thou shouldest take my covenant in thy mouth?

  ii. **Psalm 50:17 (KJV)** Seeing thou hatest instruction, and castest my words behind thee.

9. The next cardinal step in the theoretical approach to Bible Interpretation and Translation is called: the reciprocal confirmation of the knowledge of Christ!

  i. **1 Corinthians 1:5 (KJV)** That in every thing ye are enriched by him, in all utterance, and *in* all knowledge;

  ii. **1 Corinthians 1:6 (KJV)** Even as the testimony of Christ was confirmed in you:

  iii. **1 Corinthians 1:7 (KJV)** So that ye come behind in no gift; waiting for the coming of our Lord Jesus Christ:

  iv. **1 Corinthians 1:8 (KJV)** Who shall also confirm you unto the end, *that ye may be* blameless in the day of our Lord Jesus Christ.

10. In other words, in **1 Corinthians 1:5-8 (KJV)**, we learn that the knowledge and understanding of the text of the Word of God that you have, must be reciprocated and confirmed in both what you understand, interpret, say, and write on the one hand, and then on the other hand, in what is written in the Holy Scriptures itself!

  i. **Luke 20:9 (KJV)** Then began he to speak to the people this parable; A certain man planted a vineyard, and let it forth to husbandmen, and went into a far country for a long time.

    ii. **Luke 20:10 (KJV)** And at the season he sent a servant to the husbandmen, that they should give him of the fruit of the vineyard: but the husbandmen beat him, and sent *him* away empty.

    iii. **Luke 20:11 (KJV)** And again he sent another servant: and they beat him also, and entreated *him* shamefully, and sent *him* away empty.

    iv. **Luke 20:12 (KJV)** And again he sent a third: and they wounded him also, and cast *him* out.

    v. **Luke 20:13 (KJV)** Then said the lord of the vineyard, What shall I do? I will send my beloved son: it may be they will reverence *him* when they see him.

    vi. **Luke 20:14 (KJV)** But when the husbandmen saw him, they reasoned among themselves, saying, This is the heir: come, let us kill him, that the inheritance may be ours.

    vii. **Luke 20:15 (KJV)** So they cast him out of the vineyard, and killed *him*. What therefore shall the lord of the vineyard do unto them?

    viii. **Luke 20:16 (KJV)** He shall come and destroy these husbandmen, and shall give the vineyard to others. And when they heard *it*, they said, God forbid.

    ix. **Luke 20:17 (KJV)** And he beheld them, and said, What is this then that is written, The stone which the builders rejected, the same is become the head of the corner?

    x. **Luke 20:18 (KJV)** Whosoever shall fall upon that stone shall be broken; but on whomsoever it shall fall, it will grind him to powder.

11. Quite simply, the singleness of thought must be evident in your Bible Interpretation as well as in the text of the Holy Bible itself, to the extent that discord, contrariness, and divergence of thought are outlawed!

12. In **Luke 20:9-15 (KJV)**, we see the LORD Jesus Christ engaged in a Bible Interpretation and Translation!

13. In **Luke 20:16 (KJV)**, the LORD Jesus Christ renders an interpretation that is in perfect harmony, in one accord, is consistent with the contents in **Luke 20:9-15 (KJV)**!

14. At the end of **Luke 20:16 (KJV)**, the other Bible Interpreters come to a different, divergent, inconsistent, contrary interpretation, rejecting the interpretation of the LORD Jesus Christ with their words: "God forbid"!

15. In **Luke 20:17 (KJV)**, the LORD Jesus Christ shows them the evidence of their error in Bible Interpretation by pointing out the actual text that refutes and contradicts their interpretation, thereby establishing that Perfect Harmony is the required standard in Bible Interpretation and Translation!

16. Finally, in **Luke 20:18 (KJV)**, the LORD Jesus Christ uses metaphoric language to illustrate that, either way, both from the perspective of the bad Bible Interpreter and the bad Bible interpretation itself, there will be brokenness and a shattering of harmony and coherence!

17. The next cardinal step in the theoretical approach to Bible Interpretation and Translation is called: Faithfulness in Interpretation and Translation!

    i. **1 Corinthians 1:9 (KJV)** God *is* faithful, by whom ye were called unto the fellowship of his Son Jesus Christ our Lord.

18. This is where you seek to replicate the faith attribute of the owner of the text, which translation requirement is also mentioned elsewhere in the Holy Bible!

    i. **2 Chronicles 19:9 (KJV)** And he charged them, saying, Thus shall ye do in the fear of the LORD, faithfully, and with a perfect heart.

    ii. **Jeremiah 23:28 (KJV)** The prophet that hath a dream, let him tell a dream; and he that hath my word, let him speak my word faithfully. What *is* the chaff to the wheat? saith the LORD.

19. It is a reiteration of the requirement for zero conflict of thought and doctrine between your understanding of the Bible text in question and the entire remainder of the Holy Bible!

20. The next cardinal step in the theoretical approach to Bible Interpretation and Translation is captured in:

    i. **1 Corinthians 1:10 (KJV)** Now I beseech you, brethren, by the name of our Lord Jesus Christ, that ye all speak the same thing, and *that* there be no divisions among you; but *that* ye be perfectly joined together in the same mind and in the same judgment.

21. Now, the correct interpretation of the command in **1 Corinthians 1:10 (KJV)** is this:

    i. Speak the same thing as the original Bible text is saying!

    ii. Ensure that there be no divisions at all between your translation and the Bible text!

    iii. An examination of your translation and the original Bible text must reveal your translation to be perfectly joined together in the same mind and in the same judgment as the original Bible text!

22. The reason to (1) speak and write the same thing, (2) that there be no divisions at all, and (3) that your translation be perfect in mind and in judgment, is that, as I wrote above, the Holy Scriptures is the only Book that prescribes its own Approach and Methodology of Interpretation and Translation whereby, there is nothing that you can understand, interpret, or write which is contrary to what is already contained in the Holy Bible itself that will stand! The Holy Bible itself, as a text, outlaws contrary opinion and interpretation!

        i. **Proverbs 21:30 (KJV)** *There is* no wisdom nor understanding nor counsel against the LORD.

23. Failure to heed to the command in **1 Corinthians 1:10 (KJV)** and in **Proverbs 21:30 (KJV)** draws the following condemnation!

        i. **Isaiah 8:20 (KJV)** To the law and to the testimony: if they speak not according to this word, *it is* because *there is* no light in them.

24. It is very important to understand that the Holy Bible does NOT lend itself to contentious interpretations neither in the persons of the many theorists of translation and interpretation nor in the doctrines, subjects, themes, and topics that they present!

25. The Holy Bible lends itself to only one interpretation and translation that come from within itself to create a perfect harmony, as I have shown above:

        i. **1 Corinthians 1:11 (KJV)** For it hath been declared unto me of you, my brethren, by them *which are of the house* of Chloe, that there are contentions among you.

        ii. **1 Corinthians 1:12 (KJV)** Now this I say, that every one of you saith, I am of Paul; and I of Apollos; and I of Cephas; and I of Christ.

        iii. **1 Corinthians 1:13 (KJV)** Is Christ divided? was Paul crucified for you? or were ye baptized in the name of Paul?

        iv. **1 Corinthians 1:14 (KJV)** I thank God that I baptized none of you, but Crispus and Gaius;

        v. **1 Corinthians 1:15 (KJV)** Lest any should say that I had baptized in mine own name.

        vi. **1 Corinthians 1:16 (KJV)** And I baptized also the household of Stephanas: besides, I know not whether I baptized any other.

26. Hence, it does not matter at all whether the Bible Scholar is called Paul, or Apollos; or Cephas, or Christ, and it also does not matter at all whether the doctrine, subject, theme, or topic is Crucifixion or Baptism or whatever!

27. What matters in Bible Interpretation and Translation is the exclusion of man's wisdom in the exposition of the Doctrine of Christ!

        i. **1 Corinthians 1:17 (KJV)** For Christ sent me not to baptize, but to preach the gospel: not with wisdom of words, lest the cross of Christ should be made of none effect.

        ii. **1 Corinthians 1:18 (KJV)** For the preaching of the cross is to them that perish foolishness; but unto us which are saved it is the power of God.

iii. **1 Corinthians 1:19 (KJV)** For it is written, I will destroy the wisdom of the wise, and will bring to nothing the understanding of the prudent.

iv. **1 Corinthians 1:20 (KJV)** Where *is* the wise? where *is* the scribe? where *is* the disputer of this world? hath not God made foolish the wisdom of this world?

28. Not only is the exclusion of man's wisdom in Bible Interpretation and Translation one of the cardinal requirements, but also the exclusion of man's theories, man's methodologies, man's approaches, and man's techniques in Bible Interpretation and Translation, because the Holy Bible has concluded all human wisdom as vile, corrupted, and as foolishness!

i. **Isaiah 55:8 (KJV)** For my thoughts *are* not your thoughts, neither *are* your ways my ways, saith the LORD.

ii. **Isaiah 55:9 (KJV)** For *as* the heavens are higher than the earth, so are my ways higher than your ways, and my thoughts than your thoughts.

iii. **Micah 7:1 (KJV)** Woe is me! for I am as when they have gathered the summer fruits, as the grapegleanings of the vintage: *there is* no cluster to eat: my soul desired the firstripe fruit.

iv. **Micah 7:2 (KJV)** The good *man* is perished out of the earth: and *there is* none upright among men: they all lie in wait for blood; they hunt every man his brother with a net.

v. **Micah 7:3 (KJV)** That they may do evil with both hands earnestly, the prince asketh, and the judge *asketh* for a reward; and the great *man*, he uttereth his mischievous desire: so they wrap it up.

vi. **Micah 7:4 (KJV)** The best of them *is* as a brier: the most upright *is sharper* than a thorn hedge: the day of thy watchmen *and* thy visitation cometh; now shall be their perplexity.

vii. **1 Corinthians 2:14 (KJV)** But the natural man receiveth not the things of the Spirit of God: for they are foolishness unto him: neither can he know *them*, because they are spiritually discerned.

29. In other words, how can foolishness interpret and translate wisdom? Therefore, you must rely on the Holy Bible to interpret and translate itself! You CANNOT teach the Bible against the Bible! You MUST ALWAYS teach the Bible to agree with the Bible!

30. Your reliance on the Holy Bible to interpret and translate itself should bring you to believe the text/word and the self-interpretation and the self-translation that it says it is able to accomplish!

i. **1 Corinthians 1:21 (KJV)** For after that in the wisdom of God the world by wisdom knew not God, it pleased God by the foolishness of preaching to save them that believe.

31. This act of believing in the text/word of the Holy Scriptures to self-interpret and to self-translate does NOT rise to the level of unverifiable faith/belief or impregnable esoterism, but is the same act of using your pre-research data to believe in your scientific theory and research findings before you start the actual experiment!

i. **1 Corinthians 1:22 (KJV)** For the Jews require a sign, and the Greeks seek after wisdom:

32. In fact, as you can see in **1 Corinthians 1:22 (KJV)**, this theoretical approach to Bible Interpretation excludes not only signs, miracles, and wonders as justification for believing in the efficacy of the theory, but also, this same theoretical approach excludes all human wisdom!

33. And so, yes, just as a scientific experiment would seem foolish in the beginning but later turn out to be viable, so also will a Bible Translation that uses this Bible-prescribed theoretical approach to Bible Interpretation seem foolish in the beginning, but as record has it, it has never been proved inadequate or wrong whereas all the theories of Bible Translation and Interpretation that men devised have all fallen short of complete reliability!

i. **1 Corinthians 1:23 (KJV)** But we preach Christ crucified, unto the Jews a stumblingblock, and unto the Greeks foolishness;

34. What is certain is that all those who fall outside the above portrait or profile of people who should access the text of the Holy Scriptures, they will surely, like did the Jews in **1 Corinthians 1:23 (KJV)**, find this theoretical approach to Bible Interpretation a stumblingblock, and like did the Greeks, they will find it to be foolishness!

35. On the other hand, all those who are called or those who have received inspiration to understand the Word of God, shall attain unto much wisdom in the Gospel of Christ, NOT outside of it, because everything that is outside of the Gospel of Christ is foolishness!

i. **1 Corinthians 1:24 (KJV)** But unto them which are called, both Jews and Greeks, Christ the power of God, and the wisdom of God.

ii. **1 Corinthians 1:25 (KJV)** Because the foolishness of God is wiser than men; and the weakness of God is stronger than men.

36. They shall attain unto much wisdom in the Gospel of Christ and they shall also attain unto the Power of Christ that is in the text/word of the Holy Scriptures, which Power of Christ in the Text/Word of God is identifiable in its ability to transform

the mind of the inquirer to the renewal of itself unto the reproduction of itself (Text/Word of God) by the thirties, by the sixties, and by the hundreds!

   i. **Matthew 13:3 (KJV)** And he spake many things unto them in parables, saying, Behold, a sower went forth to sow;

   ii. **Matthew 13:4 (KJV)** And when he sowed, some *seeds* fell by the way side, and the fowls came and devoured them up:

   iii. **Matthew 13:5 (KJV)** Some fell upon stony places, where they had not much earth: and forthwith they sprung up, because they had no deepness of earth:

   iv. **Matthew 13:6 (KJV)** And when the sun was up, they were scorched; and because they had no root, they withered away.

   v. **Matthew 13:7 (KJV)** And some fell among thorns; and the thorns sprung up, and choked them:

   vi. **Matthew 13:8 (KJV)** But other fell into good ground, and brought forth fruit, some an hundredfold, some sixtyfold, some thirtyfold.

   vii. **Matthew 13:9 (KJV)** Who hath ears to hear, let him hear.

37. In other words, a good Student of the Theoretical Approach to Bible Interpretation and Translation that I am showing you here, should, in the end, be able to replicate in his own words, the same Thoughts and Doctrines of Christ as contained in the Holy Bible, by the thirties, by the sixties, and by the hundreds:

   i. **Philippians 2:5 (KJV)** Let this mind be in you, which was also in Christ Jesus:

38. Again, the LORD God Almighty reiterates that the Theoretical Approach to Bible Interpretation and Translation requires the exclusion of all human wisdom in order to attain unto the wisdom which is in the Word of God!

   i. **1 Corinthians 1:26 (KJV)** For ye see your calling, brethren, how that not many wise men after the flesh, not many mighty, not many noble, *are called*:

39. Wherefore, even though the interpretation and translation of the Bible by the Bible may seem incongruous and foolish on the face of it, yet still must thou persist in its own foolishness, even though it is NOT foolishness but it seems and sounds foolish because of the very foolishness and corruption that are in all humans, therefore, do some see a mirror image of their own foolishness and corruption in the Holy Bible!

   i. **1 Corinthians 1:27 (KJV)** But God hath chosen the foolish things of the world to confound the wise; and God hath chosen the weak things of the world to confound the things which are mighty;

ii. **1 Corinthians 1:28 (KJV)** And base things of the world, and things which are despised, hath God chosen, *yea*, and things which are not, to bring to nought things that are:

iii. **1 Corinthians 1:29 (KJV)** That no flesh should glory in his presence.

40. But thou must persist in the Bible's own foolishness because the Holy Bible being a mirror of the human face and character that it is, the foolishness and the contradictions that you see in the Holy Bible are a reflection of your own foolishness and contradictions, and they do hide a multitude of wise counsel ONLY when you exclude yourself, as **1 Corinthians 1:28-29 (KJV)** reveals, and allow the Word of God to speak, to translate itself, and to interpret itself!

   i. **Numbers 27:21 (KJV)** And he shall stand before Eleazar the priest, who shall ask *counsel* for him after the judgment of Urim before the LORD: at his word shall they go out, and at his word they shall come in, *both* he, and all the children of Israel with him, even all the congregation.

   ii. **Deuteronomy 32:28 (KJV)** For they *are* a nation void of counsel, neither *is there any* understanding in them.

   iii. **Judges 20:18 (KJV)** And the children of Israel arose, and went up to the house of God, and asked counsel of God, and said, Which of us shall go up first to the battle against the children of Benjamin? And the LORD said, Judah *shall go up* first.

   iv. **Psalm 33:11 (KJV)** The counsel of the LORD standeth for ever, the thoughts of his heart to all generations.

   v. **Proverbs 27:19 (KJV)** As in water face *answereth* to face, so the heart of man to man.

   vi. **Isaiah 58:13 (KJV)** If thou turn away thy foot from the sabbath, *from* doing thy pleasure on my holy day; and call the sabbath a delight, the holy of the LORD, honourable; and shalt honour him, not doing thine own ways, nor finding thine own pleasure, nor speaking *thine own* words:

   vii. **Ezekiel 3:4 (KJV)** And he said unto me, Son of man, go, get thee unto the house of Israel, and speak with my words unto them.

   viii. **Hebrews 4:12 (KJV)** For the word of God *is* quick, and powerful, and sharper than any twoedged sword, piercing even to the dividing asunder of soul and spirit, and of the joints and marrow, and *is* a discerner of the thoughts and intents of the heart.

41. In the end, the LORD God is showing you that the efficacy of your exercise of the Theoretical Approach to Bible Interpretation and Translation will be made evident in

your true and faithful reflection of the meaning of the Word of God devoid of any form of contrariness when compared against the Word of God!

    i. **1 Corinthians 1:30 (KJV)** But of him are ye in Christ Jesus, who of God is made unto us wisdom, and righteousness, and sanctification, and redemption:

    ii. **1 Corinthians 1:31 (KJV)** That, according as it is written, He that glorieth, let him glory in the Lord.

42. In other words, by means of comparison, your interpretation and translation of the Word of God must be one with the Word of God!

The LORD Jesus Christ be with your spirit. The LORD Jesus Christ give you understanding.

Rev. Prof. PETER PRYCE,
DSEF, BA, MA, B.Soc.Sc Pol Sci, IBA, PhD
A Scribe of the Law of the God of Heaven
Prophet of the Word of God
Professor of French, Silver Spring, MD, USA
Scholar of the Institute of Theologians, USA
WWW.THEBIBLEUNIVERSITY.ORG
Accreditation Number: 07-QCTO/SDP120723172836
SAQA QUAL ID: Identification # 101997
WWW.BOOKSTORESITE.ORG
WWW.THEBIBLEUNIVERSITYCHURCH.ORG

Thursday 4th January 2024 @ 7:10 AM – 4:44 PM
While hearing and meditating on the Word of God.

APPROACHES TO BIBLE INTERPRETATION AND BIBLE TRANSLATION – 1

Question 2461

1. The Testimony of God, or, the Holy Scriptures, or, the Holy Bible, has only one theme, namely, Jesus Christ and Him crucified!
    i. **1 Corinthians 2:1 (KJV)** And I, brethren, when I came to you, came not with excellency of speech or of wisdom, declaring unto you the testimony of God.
    ii. **1 Corinthians 2:2 (KJV)** For I determined not to know any thing among you, save Jesus Christ, and him crucified.
2. It means that all the Books and writings in the entire Holy Bible are about the LORD Jesus Christ!
    i. **John 5:46 (KJV)** For had ye believed Moses, ye would have believed me: for he wrote of me.
    ii. **John 14:6 (KJV)** Jesus saith unto him, I am the way, the truth, and the life: no man cometh unto the Father, but by me.
    iii. **Acts 10:43 (KJV)** To him give all the prophets witness, that through his name whosoever believeth in him shall receive remission of sins.
3. Therefore, a successful Bible Interpretation or Translation is the one that also has as its theme: Jesus Christ and Him crucified.
4. It also means that a Bible Interpretation or Translation that deviates from the LORD Jesus Christ and the Doctrines of the LORD Jesus Christ, is incorrect and false, just the same way as you cannot argue against the Constitution of a Country and be successful, because normally, the correct and accepted norm is that Judges and Lawyers speak and write from the strength, from the point of view, from the spirit, and from the prescriptions of the Law whereby, a Judge or a Lawyer is NOT a Judge or a Lawyer anymore when he speaks and writes against and contrary to the Constitution of the Land, and the same is with the Holy Bible the Word of God and the Law Book of God!
5. The speech, the preaching, or the writings of a true Man of God must be presented in a way to enhance and demonstrate the Spirit and Power of God!
    i. **1 Corinthians 2:4 (KJV)** And my speech and my preaching *was* not with enticing words of man's wisdom, but in demonstration of the Spirit and of power:

        ii. **1 Corinthians 2:5 (KJV)** That your faith should not stand in the wisdom of men, but in the power of God.

6. What do the Spirit and Power of God do?

7. Here is the answer:

        i. The Power of God produces Salvation in every person who believes the report and witness of the LORD Jesus Christ!

8. How does this production of Salvation happen? By what means?

9. By means of speaking, preaching, writing, and teaching the Gospel of Christ to people, to the effectual renewing of their mind toward God Almighty!

        i. **Romans 1:15 (KJV)** So, as much as in me is, I am ready to preach the gospel to you that are at Rome also.

        ii. **Romans 1:16 (KJV)** For I am not ashamed of the gospel of Christ: for it is the power of God unto salvation to every one that believeth; to the Jew first, and also to the Greek.

        iii. **Romans 1:17 (KJV)** For therein is the righteousness of God revealed from faith to faith: as it is written, The just shall live by faith.

10. The revelation in **Romans 1:15-17 (KJV)** is that, when a Man of God claims to have power from God in Ministry, then, you should be able to measure or identify the source of that power through the following two steps:

        i. **ONE** – Are the words of the Man of God 100% derived from the Gospel of Christ, from the Word of God, form the Holy Scriptures?

        ii. **TWO** – When that Man of God speaks, preaches, teaches, or writes his words, do people hear or read it and become convinced of its contents and believe the contents of the speech or writing such that they turn away from the thoughts that they previously held to now embrace the new thoughts of Christ that are contained in the speech or writings of the Man of God?

11. The moment that the above two steps are successfully accomplished through the speech or writings of a Man of God, then, that is the same moment that he has demonstrated the Power of God unto Salvation, because, Salvation is first measured in the mind before it appears in the deeds of the flesh!

        i. **Colossians 1:21 (KJV)** And you, that were sometime alienated and enemies in *your* mind by wicked works, yet now hath he reconciled

        ii. **Romans 12:2 (KJV)** And be not conformed to this world: but be ye transformed by the renewing of your mind, that ye may prove what *is* that good, and acceptable, and perfect, will of God.

      iii. **Titus 3:5 (KJV)** Not by works of righteousness which we have done, but according to his mercy he saved us, by the washing of regeneration, and renewing of the Holy Ghost;

12. Since **Romans 1:16 (KJV)** tells us that the Gospel of Christ is the Power of God unto Salvation, your belief/faith should be anchored in this Power of God, meaning, in the Gospel of Christ!

      i. **Romans 1:16 (KJV)** For I am not ashamed of the gospel of Christ: for it is the power of God unto salvation to every one that believeth; to the Jew first, and also to the Greek.

      ii. **1 Corinthians 2:5 (KJV)** That your faith should not stand in the wisdom of men, but in the power of God.

13. This same Gospel of Christ, though it might sound foolish to some, yet it is the ultimate wisdom that can be accessed ONLY through the revelation and inspiration from the Holy Spirit of God!

      i. **1 Corinthians 2:6 (KJV)** Howbeit we speak wisdom among them that are perfect: yet not the wisdom of this world, nor of the princes of this world, that come to nought:

14. What are revelation and inspiration?

15. Revelation and inspiration are simply different shades of thought that come to your mind as a result of reading the text of the Gospel of Christ!

16. It is the same as what Academics, Judges, and Lawyers call "the spirit of the text", meaning that there is an unseen thought, imagery, picture, understanding, poetry that accompanies a text while still remaining invisible and untouchable!

17. When this unseen thought, imagery, picture, understanding, poetry accompanies an ordinary text, it is called "the spirit of the text"!

18. When this same unseen thought, imagery, picture, understanding, poetry accompanies the text of the Holy Scriptures, it is called "the Holy Spirit"!

      i. **Job 32:8 (KJV)** But *there is* a spirit in man: and the inspiration of the Almighty giveth them understanding.

      ii. **2 Timothy 3:16 (KJV)** All scripture *is* given by inspiration of God, and *is* profitable for doctrine, for reproof, for correction, for instruction in righteousness:

19. Therefore, according to **1 Corinthians 2:6 (KJV)**, when a man operates according to, or under "the spirit of the text", meaning that his life is predicated on all sorts of texts that are outside the realm of the Gospel of Christ such as all academic and intellectual and scientific texts and pursuits of study, then, such a man has wisdom but his wisdom is worldly wisdom and is vain wisdom!

       i. **1 Corinthians 2:6 (KJV)** Howbeit we speak wisdom among them that are perfect: yet not the wisdom of this world, nor of the princes of this world, that come to nought:

20. Such a worldly wisdom vain man is NOT yet one with the Holy Bible and its only one theme of Jesus Christ and Him crucified as **1 Corinthians 2:2 (KJV)** reveals!

       i. **1 Corinthians 2:1 (KJV)** And I, brethren, when I came to you, came not with excellency of speech or of wisdom, declaring unto you the testimony of God.

       ii. **1 Corinthians 2:2 (KJV)** For I determined not to know any thing among you, save Jesus Christ, and him crucified.

21. On the other hand, when the man is completely one with the Holy Bible and its singular theme of Jesus Christ and Him crucified as **1 Corinthians 2:2 (KJV)** reveals, then, his spirit and the Spirit of the Word of God have become one Spirit!

       i. **Philippians 1:27 (KJV)** Only let your conversation be as it becometh the gospel of Christ: that whether I come and see you, or else be absent, I may hear of your affairs, that ye stand fast in one spirit, with one mind striving together for the faith of the gospel;

       ii. **1 Corinthians 6:17 (KJV)** But he that is joined unto the Lord is one spirit.

22. On the other hand, according to the same **1 Corinthians 2:6 (KJV)**, when a man operates according to, or under "the Holy Spirit", meaning that his life is mainly predicated on the text of the Holy Scriptures and he believes in and lives by its contents, then, such a man has perfect wisdom, has the ultimate wisdom, and has wisdom that becomes his Key of entry into another realm of spirit existence called Heaven!

23. Now, this wisdom that has the ability to transform my thinking here on Earth as well as guarantee my entry into the next Realm of Heaven, how accessible is this wisdom?

       i. **1 Corinthians 2:7 (KJV)** But we speak the wisdom of God in a mystery, *even* the hidden *wisdom*, which God ordained before the world unto our glory:

24. The wisdom of God is either accessible or hidden "to every man according to his several ability"!

       i. **Matthew 25:15 (KJV)** And unto one he gave five talents, to another two, and to another one; to every man according to his several ability; and straightway took his journey.

       ii. **Romans 14:5 (KJV)** One man esteemeth one day above another: another esteemeth every day *alike*. Let every man be fully persuaded in his own mind.

25. The wisdom of God does NOT become more accessible because of one's social standing, money, rank, education, or intellectual ability!

      i. **1 Corinthians 2:8 (KJV)** Which none of the princes of this world knew: for had they known *it*, they would not have crucified the Lord of glory.

      ii. **1 Corinthians 2:10 (KJV)** But God hath revealed *them* unto us by his Spirit: for the Spirit searcheth all things, yea, the deep things of God.

26. Concerning **1 Corinthians 2:10 (KJV)**, the meaning is that, just as the understanding of literature or legal text is hard to some yet easy to others who are endowed with certain inexplicable abilities, so also is the understanding of the Word of God easy to those who are filled with the Word of God the Gospel of Christ!

      i. **Deuteronomy 17:14 (KJV)** When thou art come unto the land which the LORD thy God giveth thee, and shalt possess it, and shalt dwell therein, and shalt say, I will set a king over me, like as all the nations that *are* about me;

      ii. **Deuteronomy 17:15 (KJV)** Thou shalt in any wise set *him* king over thee, whom the LORD thy God shall choose: *one* from among thy brethren shalt thou set king over thee: thou mayest not set a stranger over thee, which *is* not thy brother.

      iii. **Deuteronomy 17:18 (KJV)** And it shall be, when he sitteth upon the throne of his kingdom, that he shall write him a copy of this law in a book out of *that which is* before the priests the Levites:

      iv. **Deuteronomy 17:19 (KJV)** And it shall be with him, and he shall read therein all the days of his life: that he may learn to fear the LORD his God, to keep all the words of this law and these statutes, to do them:

      v. **Deuteronomy 17:20 (KJV)** That his heart be not lifted up above his brethren, and that he turn not aside from the commandment, *to* the right hand, or *to* the left: to the end that he may prolong *his* days in his kingdom, he, and his children, in the midst of Israel.

      vi. **Joshua 1:8 (KJV)** This book of the law shall not depart out of thy mouth; but thou shalt meditate therein day and night, that thou mayest observe to do according to all that is written therein: for then thou shalt make thy way prosperous, and then thou shalt have good success.

      vii. **Proverbs 14:6 (KJV)** A scorner seeketh wisdom, and *findeth it* not: but knowledge *is* easy unto him that understandeth.

viii. **Colossians 1:9 (KJV)** For this cause we also, since the day we heard *it*, do not cease to pray for you, and to desire that ye might be filled with the knowledge of his will in all wisdom and spiritual understanding;

27. Just as it requires interrogating a man in order to know the unseen intent and the thoughts of his deed, so also does it require interrogating the Word of God in the Word of God so that the unseen Spirit in the Text of the Word can yield inspiration and understanding of the Word unto you!

    i. **1 Corinthians 2:11 (KJV)** For what man knoweth the things of a man, save the spirit of man which is in him? even so the things of God knoweth no man, but the Spirit of God.

    ii. **Job 32:8 (KJV)** But *there is* a spirit in man: and the inspiration of the Almighty giveth them understanding.

    iii. **2 Timothy 3:16 (KJV)** All scripture *is* given by inspiration of God, and *is* profitable for doctrine, for reproof, for correction, for instruction in righteousness:

28. That is why it is impossible to access the Word of God from outside the Word of God, just as it is impossible to access the true meanings of the Constitution of a country from outside a prior legal training in its jurisprudence!

29. Therefore, the Spirit of God mentioned in **1 Corinthians 2:11 (KJV)**: that is the catalyst and the means to access and understand the Word of God the Holy Scriptures, and it is the equivalent of the legal training that you need in order to correctly access and understand the contents of a legal text!

    i. **1 Corinthians 2:12 (KJV)** Now we have received, not the spirit of the world, but the spirit which is of God; that we might know the things that are freely given to us of God.

30. Now, the means or the methodology through which to access and understand the Word of God the Holy Scriptures, by the teaching or inspiration of the Holy Spirit, is called: Comparing Spiritual Things with Spiritual!

    i. **1 Corinthians 2:13 (KJV)** Which things also we speak, not in the words which man's wisdom teacheth, but which the Holy Ghost teacheth; comparing spiritual things with spiritual.

31. Just as "the spirit of the text", as they say, is not seen but works in the mind as you read, to the effectual understanding of a literature text or a legal text, so also the Spirit of God is not seen but works in the mind to the effectual understanding of the Word of God as you read it, and when the understanding thereof is hidden, then, it is hidden, NOT because of some esoteric unverifiable non-faith clairvoyance or the

lack thereof, because of the inherent incapacity and mental inadequacy of the person himself who lacks the intellectual capacity to grasp deep and difficult concepts!

    i. **1 Corinthians 2:14 (KJV)** But the natural man receiveth not the things of the Spirit of God: for they are foolishness unto him: neither can he know *them*, because they are spiritually discerned.

    ii. **2 Corinthians 4:3 (KJV)** But if our gospel be hid, it is hid to them that are lost:

32. What does it mean: Comparing Spiritual Things with Spiritual?

33. Based on **1 Corinthians 2:11-13 (KJV)**, we understand that "comparing spiritual things with spiritual" is the methodology to access and to understand the deep thoughts, the concepts, and the doctrines that are hidden in the Word of God!

34. In order to correctly understand the phrase "comparing spiritual things with spiritual", we first need to understand what "spiritual" is!

35. What does "spiritual" mean?

36. Here is the answer!

    i. **John 1:1 (KJV)** In the beginning was the Word, and the Word was with God, and the Word was God.

    ii. **John 1:2 (KJV)** The same was in the beginning with God.

    iii. **John 1:14 (KJV)** And the Word was made flesh, and dwelt among us, (and we beheld his glory, the glory as of the only begotten of the Father,) full of grace and truth.

    iv. **Romans 7:14 (KJV)** For we know that the law is spiritual: but I am carnal, sold under sin.

    v. **1 Corinthians 6:17 (KJV)** But he that is joined unto the Lord is one spirit.

    vi. **2 Corinthians 3:17 (KJV)** Now the Lord is that Spirit: and where the Spirit of the Lord *is*, there *is* liberty.

37. As you can see from the above body of evidence, we do not need to travel outside the Holy Scriptures the Word of God into some unknown esoteric great beyond, in order to pluck off the meaning of the word "spiritual"!

38. As you can see, you need a prior rich understanding of figures of speech in order to correctly understand the personification, the metaphor, the irony, the hyperbole, the paradox, the poetry, the geography, and every sort of human intellectual sphere that is contained in the Holy Scriptures the Word of God!

39. Hence, the Word of God the Holy Scriptures, is God!

40. Then, the same Word of God the Holy Scriptures is a Man with flesh called Yeshua Christ!

41. Then, the same Word of God the Holy Scriptures, is "spiritual"!

42. Then, the same Word of God the Holy Scriptures turns a person into a spirit once that person fully believes the same Word of God the Holy Scriptures!

43. Then, the same Word of God the Holy Scriptures is the Holy Spirit who gives you that inspiration and understanding to understand the same Word of God the Holy Scriptures!

    i. **Haggai 2:5 (KJV)** *According to* the word that I covenanted with you when ye came out of Egypt, so my spirit remaineth among you: fear ye not.

44. Now that we have understood the word "spiritual", we shall return to the question that says: What does it mean: Comparing Spiritual Things with Spiritual?

45. From our prior understanding of "the spiritual", it becomes easy to define the phrase: "Comparing Spiritual Things with Spiritual", and it means: "comparing the Word of God the Holy Scriptures with the Word of God the Holy Scriptures"!

    i. **1 Corinthians 2:13 (KJV)** Which things also we speak, not in the words which man's wisdom teacheth, but which the Holy Ghost teacheth; comparing spiritual things with spiritual.

46. Therefore, as a good Bible Interpreter and Translator, your success in rendering a good and correct Bible Interpretation and Translation lies in your ability to successfully compare your understanding and interpretation of the text of the Holy Bible to each and every verse in the entire Holy Bible, with the express aim of eliminating all contradiction to attain zero contradiction, zero variableness, and with the express aim of achieving "Perfect Harmony" between your translation and the entire remainder of the Holy Bible!

47. Can a Bible Interpreter or Translator set aside these approaches and still attain a good Bible Translation? NO!

    i. **1 Corinthians 2:14 (KJV)** But the natural man receiveth not the things of the Spirit of God: for they are foolishness unto him: neither can he know *them*, because they are spiritually discerned.

48. Your ability to come to the correct understanding of the Word of God the Holy Scriptures derives 100% from your 100% immersion into the Word of God the Holy Scriptures!

    i. **1 Corinthians 2:15 (KJV)** But he that is spiritual judgeth all things, yet he himself is judged of no man.

    ii. **1 Corinthians 2:16 (KJV)** For who hath known the mind of the Lord, that he may instruct him? But we have the mind of Christ.

The LORD Jesus Christ be with your spirit. The LORD Jesus Christ give you understanding.

Rev. Prof. PETER PRYCE,
DSEF, BA, MA, B.Soc.Sc Pol Sci, IBA, PhD
A Scribe of the Law of the God of Heaven
Prophet of the Word of God
Professor of French, Silver Spring, MD, USA
Scholar of the Institute of Theologians, USA
WWW.THEBIBLEUNIVERSITY.ORG
Accreditation Number: 07-QCTO/SDP120723172836
SAQA QUAL ID: Identification # 101997
WWW.BOOKSTORESITE.ORG
WWW.THEBIBLEUNIVERSITYCHURCH.ORG

Saturday 6th January 2024 @ 7:02 AM – 3:33 PM
While hearing and meditating on the Word of God.

APPROACHES TO BIBLE INTERPRETATION AND BIBLE TRANSLATION – 2

Question 2462

1. In Approaches to Bible Interpretation and Bible Translation – 1, I identified two men or two Translators:

2. The Worldly Wisdom Vain Man who is NOT yet one with the Holy Bible and its only one theme of Jesus Christ and Him crucified as required in **1 Corinthians 2:2 (KJV)**!

   i. **1 Corinthians 2:1 (KJV)** And I, brethren, when I came to you, came not with excellency of speech or of wisdom, declaring unto you the testimony of God.

   ii. **1 Corinthians 2:2 (KJV)** For I determined not to know any thing among you, save Jesus Christ, and him crucified.

3. Then, you have The Spiritual Man who has become completely one with the Holy Bible and its singular theme of Jesus Christ and Him crucified as **1 Corinthians 2:2 (KJV)** reveals, and, because of that oneness, his spirit and the Spirit of the Word of God have become one Spirit!

   i. **Philippians 1:27 (KJV)** Only let your conversation be as it becometh the gospel of Christ: that whether I come and see you, or else be absent, I may hear of your affairs, that ye stand fast in one spirit, with one mind striving together for the faith of the gospel;

   ii. **1 Corinthians 6:17 (KJV)** But he that is joined unto the Lord is one spirit.

4. Now, in this chapter, we are going to find out how to identify The Worldly Wisdom Vain Man whose other names are The Carnal Man and The Babe in Christ!

   i. **1 Corinthians 3:1 (KJV)** And I, brethren, could not speak unto you as unto spiritual, but as unto carnal, *even* as unto babes in Christ.

5. The Worldly Wisdom Vain Man, The Carnal Man, or, The Babe in Christ can be identified by reason of the milk that he drinks!

   i. **1 Corinthians 3:2 (KJV)** I have fed you with milk, and not with meat: for hitherto ye were not able *to bear it*, neither yet now are ye able.

6. To be a Babe in Christ who drinks milk is to be unable or to lack the mental and intellectual and spiritual capacity to grasp deep difficult spiritual concepts in the Holy Bible the Word of God!

    i. **John 16:12 (KJV)** I have yet many things to say unto you, but ye cannot bear them now.

    ii. **John 16:13 (KJV)** Howbeit when he, the Spirit of truth, is come, he will guide you into all truth: for he shall not speak of himself; but whatsoever he shall hear, *that* shall he speak: and he will shew you things to come.

    iii. **John 16:14 (KJV)** He shall glorify me: for he shall receive of mine, and shall shew *it* unto you.

    iv. **2 Peter 3:14 (KJV)** Wherefore, beloved, seeing that ye look for such things, be diligent that ye may be found of him in peace, without spot, and blameless.

    v. **2 Peter 3:15 (KJV)** And account *that* the longsuffering of our Lord *is* salvation; even as our beloved brother Paul also according to the wisdom given unto him hath written unto you;

    vi. **2 Peter 3:16 (KJV)** As also in all *his* epistles, speaking in them of these things; in which are some things hard to be understood, which they that are unlearned and unstable wrest, as *they do* also the other scriptures, unto their own destruction.

7. Another way to identify The Worldly Wisdom Vain Man, The Carnal Man, or, The Babe in Christ is his penchant, because of his weakness in Christ Doctrine, and because he is destitute of the Truth of the Gospel of Christ, to go outside of the Holy Bible into the world to use theories, lessons, examples, thoughts, ideas, jokes, references, books, personalities, personal testimonies, and non-Biblical stories, to preach and to teach a sermon! That is wrong and promptly reveals the speaker as The Carnal Man!

    i. **Proverbs 26:18 (KJV)** As a mad *man* who casteth firebrands, arrows, and death,

    ii. **Proverbs 26:19 (KJV)** So *is* the man *that* deceiveth his neighbour, and saith, Am not I in sport?

    iii. **Ephesians 5:4 (KJV)** Neither filthiness, nor foolish talking, nor jesting, which are not convenient: but rather giving of thanks.

    iv. **1 Timothy 1:1 (KJV)** Paul, an apostle of Jesus Christ by the commandment of God our Saviour, and Lord Jesus Christ, *which is* our hope;

    v.   **1 Timothy 1:2 (KJV)** Unto Timothy, *my* own son in the faith: Grace, mercy, *and* peace, from God our Father and Jesus Christ our Lord.

   vi.   **1 Timothy 1:3 (KJV)** As I besought thee to abide still at Ephesus, when I went into Macedonia, that thou mightest charge some that they teach no other doctrine,

  vii.   **1 Timothy 1:4 (KJV)** Neither give heed to fables and endless genealogies, which minister questions, rather than godly edifying which is in faith: *so do.*

 viii.   **1 Timothy 4:6 (KJV)** If thou put the brethren in remembrance of these things, thou shalt be a good minister of Jesus Christ, nourished up in the words of faith and of good doctrine, whereunto thou hast attained.

   ix.   **1 Timothy 4:7 (KJV)** But refuse profane and old wives' fables, and exercise thyself *rather* unto godliness.

    x.   **2 Timothy 4:1 (KJV)** I charge *thee* therefore before God, and the Lord Jesus Christ, who shall judge the quick and the dead at his appearing and his kingdom;

   xi.   **2 Timothy 4:2 (KJV)** Preach the word; be instant in season, out of season; reprove, rebuke, exhort with all longsuffering and doctrine.

  xii.   **2 Timothy 4:3 (KJV)** For the time will come when they will not endure sound doctrine; but after their own lusts shall they heap to themselves teachers, having itching ears;

 xiii.   **2 Timothy 4:4 (KJV)** And they shall turn away *their* ears from the truth, and shall be turned unto fables.

 xiv.   **Titus 1:14 (KJV)** Not giving heed to Jewish fables, and commandments of men, that turn from the truth.

  xv.   **Titus 1:15 (KJV)** Unto the pure all things *are* pure: but unto them that are defiled and unbelieving *is* nothing pure; but even their mind and conscience is defiled.

 xvi.   **Titus 1:16 (KJV)** They profess that they know God; but in works they deny *him*, being abominable, and disobedient, and unto every good work reprobate.

 xvii.   **2 Peter 1:16 (KJV)** For we have not followed cunningly devised fables, when we made known unto you the power and coming of our Lord Jesus Christ, but were eyewitnesses of his majesty.

8. Another way to identify The Worldly Wisdom Vain Man, The Carnal Man, or, The Babe in Christ is the division, the deviation, the contradiction, the discord, the

contrariness, the divergence, or the disharmony that his Bible Interpretation and Bible Translation reveal when compared to and examined in the entire Holy Bible!

    i. **1 Corinthians 3:3 (KJV)** For ye are yet carnal: for whereas *there is* among you envying, and strife, and divisions, are ye not carnal, and walk as men?

9. In other words, his Bible Interpretation and Bible Translation do NOT reflect oneness or one accord with the entire Holy Bible hence that Bible Interpretation or Bible Translation has to be rejected! Here is the LORD Jesus Christ rejecting a Bible Interpretation that goes against another verse in the Holy Bible in another part of the Bible!

    i. **Luke 20:9 (KJV)** Then began he to speak to the people this parable; A certain man planted a vineyard, and let it forth to husbandmen, and went into a far country for a long time.

    ii. **Luke 20:10 (KJV)** And at the season he sent a servant to the husbandmen, that they should give him of the fruit of the vineyard: but the husbandmen beat him, and sent *him* away empty.

    iii. **Luke 20:11 (KJV)** And again he sent another servant: and they beat him also, and entreated *him* shamefully, and sent *him* away empty.

    iv. **Luke 20:12 (KJV)** And again he sent a third: and they wounded him also, and cast *him* out.

    v. **Luke 20:13 (KJV)** Then said the lord of the vineyard, What shall I do? I will send my beloved son: it may be they will reverence *him* when they see him.

    vi. **Luke 20:14 (KJV)** But when the husbandmen saw him, they reasoned among themselves, saying, This is the heir: come, let us kill him, that the inheritance may be ours.

    vii. **Luke 20:15 (KJV)** So they cast him out of the vineyard, and killed *him*. What therefore shall the lord of the vineyard do unto them?

    viii. **Luke 20:16 (KJV)** He shall come and destroy these husbandmen, and shall give the vineyard to others. And when they heard *it*, they said, God forbid.

    ix. **Luke 20:17 (KJV)** And he beheld them, and said, What is this then that is written, The stone which the builders rejected, the same is become the head of the corner?

10. Here, again, is the LORD Jesus Christ rejecting a Bible Interpretation that goes against another verse in the Holy Bible in another part of the Bible!

    i. **Matthew 22:41 (KJV)** While the Pharisees were gathered together, Jesus asked them,

    ii. **Matthew 22:42 (KJV)** Saying, What think ye of Christ? whose son is he? They say unto him, *The Son* of David.

    iii. **Matthew 22:43 (KJV)** He saith unto them, How then doth David in spirit call him Lord, saying,

    iv. **Matthew 22:44 (KJV)** The LORD said unto my Lord, Sit thou on my right hand, till I make thine enemies thy footstool?

    v. **Matthew 22:45 (KJV)** If David then call him Lord, how is he his son?

    vi. **Matthew 22:46 (KJV)** And no man was able to answer him a word, neither durst any *man* from that day forth ask him any more *questions*.

11. Another way to identify The Worldly Wisdom Vain Man, The Carnal Man, or, The Babe in Christ is that he uses men's theories to do his Bible Interpretation, Translation, and Sermon Preparation instead of using God's Theory for Bible Interpretation and Translation, as I have already identified in my writings!

    i. **1 Corinthians 3:4 (KJV)** For while one saith, I am of Paul; and another, I *am* of Apollos; are ye not carnal?

    ii. **1 Corinthians 3:5 (KJV)** Who then is Paul, and who *is* Apollos, but ministers by whom ye believed, even as the Lord gave to every man?

    iii. **1 Corinthians 3:6 (KJV)** I have planted, Apollos watered; but God gave the increase.

    iv. **1 Corinthians 3:7 (KJV)** So then neither is he that planteth any thing, neither he that watereth; but God that giveth the increase.

12. For the very reason that there is no wisdom of man that is qualified to examine the wisdom of God since all of man's wisdom is classified as foolishness, therefore being foolishness, it cannot be used to examine wisdom!

    i. **1 Corinthians 1:20 (KJV)** Where *is* the wise? where *is* the scribe? where *is* the disputer of this world? hath not God made foolish the wisdom of this world?

    ii. **1 Corinthians 2:6 (KJV)** Howbeit we speak wisdom among them that are perfect: yet not the wisdom of this world, nor of the princes of this world, that come to nought:

    iii. **1 Corinthians 3:19 (KJV)** For the wisdom of this world is foolishness with God. For it is written, He taketh the wise in their own craftiness.

13. So, then, Bible Interpretation and Bible Translation have to be Bible-centered and God-centered in order to correctly accomplish the task of transmitting the correct information, message, and meaning, for it is impossible for the Created to examine the Creator!

    i. **1 Corinthians 3:9 (KJV)** For we are labourers together with God: ye are God's husbandry, *ye are* God's building.

    ii. **1 Corinthians 3:10 (KJV)** According to the grace of God which is given unto me, as a wise masterbuilder, I have laid the foundation, and another buildeth thereon. But let every man take heed how he buildeth thereupon.

14. Now, even though the theory is one for all Bible Interpreters and Translators as **1 Corinthians 3:11 (KJV)** reveals, the final work will be different for all Bible Interpreters and Translators by reason of each other's training, several ability, and mental capacity!

    i. **1 Corinthians 3:8 (KJV)** Now he that planteth and he that watereth are one: and every man shall receive his own reward according to his own labour.

    ii. **1 Corinthians 3:11 (KJV)** For other foundation can no man lay than that is laid, which is Jesus Christ.

    iii. **Matthew 25:15 (KJV)** And unto one he gave five talents, to another two, and to another one; to every man according to his several ability; and straightway took his journey.

15. Another way to identify The Worldly Wisdom Vain Man, The Carnal Man, or, The Babe in Christ is through the testing of his Bible Interpretation, Bible Translation, and Sermon Preparation in the Holy Scriptures to see whether there is 100% harmony!

    i. **1 Corinthians 3:12 (KJV)** Now if any man build upon this foundation gold, silver, precious stones, wood, hay, stubble;

    ii. **1 Corinthians 3:13 (KJV)** Every man's work shall be made manifest: for the day shall declare it, because it shall be revealed by fire; and the fire shall try every man's work of what sort it is.

    iii. **1 Corinthians 3:14 (KJV)** If any man's work abide which he hath built thereupon, he shall receive a reward.

    iv. **1 Corinthians 3:15 (KJV)** If any man's work shall be burned, he shall suffer loss: but he himself shall be saved; yet so as by fire.

16. The testing of Bible Interpretation, Bible Translation, and Sermon Preparation in the Holy Scriptures is what is rendered in metaphorical language in **1 Corinthians 3:12-15 (KJV)** as: "it shall be revealed by fire; and the fire shall try every man's work of what sort it is", because of the very reason that the Word of God the Holy Scriptures itself is Fire, again, a metaphor!

    i. **Deuteronomy 4:24 (KJV)** For the LORD thy God *is* a consuming fire, *even* a jealous God.

    ii. **Deuteronomy 9:3 (KJV)** Understand therefore this day, that the LORD thy God *is* he which goeth over before thee; *as* a consuming fire he shall destroy them, and he shall bring them down before thy face: so shalt thou drive them out, and destroy them quickly, as the LORD hath said unto thee.

    iii. **John 1:1 (KJV)** In the beginning was the Word, and the Word was with God, and the Word was God.

    iv. **Hebrews 12:29 (KJV)** For our God *is* a consuming fire.

17. A Bible Interpreter and a Bible Translator who has become one with the Spirit of the Text of the Word of God, as I have already explained heretofore, is also called: The Temple of God!

    i. **1 Corinthians 3:16 (KJV)** Know ye not that ye are the temple of God, and *that* the Spirit of God dwelleth in you?

18. To become a Temple of God and fall back from the requirements of remaining a Temple of God through the total adherence to the Word of God the Holy Scriptures, is to make a shipwreck of your life!

    i. **1 Corinthians 3:17 (KJV)** If any man defile the temple of God, him shall God destroy; for the temple of God is holy, which *temple* ye are.

    ii. **1 Timothy 1:18 (KJV)** This charge I commit unto thee, son Timothy, according to the prophecies which went before on thee, that thou by them mightest war a good warfare;

    iii. **1 Timothy 1:19 (KJV)** Holding faith, and a good conscience; which some having put away concerning faith have made shipwreck:

    iv. **1 Timothy 1:20 (KJV)** Of whom is Hymenaeus and Alexander; whom I have delivered unto Satan, that they may learn not to blaspheme.

19. Again, as I mentioned before, you cannot hold the wisdom, concepts, and theories of this world and access the knowledge in the Word of God at the same time, no, you have to drop the one in order to take up the other, and since the Word of God the Holy Bible comes entirely in metaphors, in proverbs, in parables and in dark sayings, very often, the first impression from people on the Word of God is that it is foolishness and it does not make sense, and yes, it was deliberately made so, seemingly senseless, in order to weed out the misfits and the undesirables away from the Word of God!

    i. **1 Corinthians 3:18 (KJV)** Let no man deceive himself. If any man among you seemeth to be wise in this world, let him become a fool, that he may be wise.

    ii. **1 Corinthians 3:19 (KJV)** For the wisdom of this world is foolishness with God. For it is written, He taketh the wise in their own craftiness.

    iii. **1 Corinthians 3:20 (KJV)** And again, The Lord knoweth the thoughts of the wise, that they are vain.

20. Hence, you have to drop your worldly wisdom to become a fool in the Word of God in order to appreciate the foolishness of the Word of God!

    i. **Ecclesiastes 7:25 (KJV)** I applied mine heart to know, and to search, and to seek out wisdom, and the reason *of things*, and to know the wickedness of folly, even of foolishness *and* madness:

    ii. **1 Corinthians 1:18 (KJV)** For the preaching of the cross is to them that perish foolishness; but unto us which are saved it is the power of God.

    iii. **1 Corinthians 1:21 (KJV)** For after that in the wisdom of God the world by wisdom knew not God, it pleased God by the foolishness of preaching to save them that believe.

    iv. **2 Corinthians 4:3 (KJV)** But if our gospel be hid, it is hid to them that are lost:

    v. **Psalm 78:2 (KJV)** I will open my mouth in a parable: I will utter dark sayings of old:

    vi. **Proverbs 1:6 (KJV)** To understand a proverb, and the interpretation; the words of the wise, and their dark sayings.

    vii. **Matthew 13:34 (KJV)** All these things spake Jesus unto the multitude in parables; and without a parable spake he not unto them:

    viii. **Mark 4:34 (KJV)** But without a parable spake he not unto them: and when they were alone, he expounded all things to his disciples.

21. As guided by the verses in the Holy Scriptures which often uses repetition for emphasis, we conclude this chapter with a repetition of what I wrote earlier regarding **1 Corinthians 3:4-7 (KJV)** saying: Another way to identify The Worldly Wisdom Vain Man, The Carnal Man, or, The Babe in Christ is that he uses men's theories to do his Bible Interpretation, Translation, and Sermon Preparation instead of using God's Theory for Bible Interpretation and Translation, and here, in this conclusion, the correct approach is: DO NOT USE MEN'S THEORIES TO DO BIBLE INTERPRETATION, BIBLE TRANSLATION, AND SERMON PREPARATION!

    i. **1 Corinthians 3:21 (KJV)** Therefore let no man glory in men. For all things are yours;

ii. **1 Corinthians 3:22 (KJV)** Whether Paul, or Apollos, or Cephas, or the world, or life, or death, or things present, or things to come; all are yours;

iii. **1 Corinthians 3:23 (KJV)** And ye are Christ's; and Christ *is* God's.

The LORD Jesus Christ be with your spirit. The LORD Jesus Christ give you understanding.

Rev. Prof. PETER PRYCE,
DSEF, BA, MA, B.Soc.Sc Pol Sci, IBA, PhD
A Scribe of the Law of the God of Heaven
Prophet of the Word of God
Professor of French, Silver Spring, MD, USA
Scholar of the Institute of Theologians, USA
WWW.THEBIBLEUNIVERSITY.ORG
Accreditation Number: 07-QCTO/SDP120723172836
SAQA QUAL ID: Identification # 101997
WWW.BOOKSTORESITE.ORG
WWW.THEBIBLEUNIVERSITYCHURCH.ORG

Sunday 7th January 2024 @ 6:11 AM – 8:21 AM
While hearing and meditating on the Word of God.

SEVEN STEPS ON HOW TO CORRECTLY TEACH THE WORD OF GOD

Question 2483

1. It is inconceivable that the LORD God should give us such an imeasurably powerful instrument of Salvation, which is the Gospel of Christ, and not also give us any methodology to administer it!

    i. **Romans 1:16 (KJV)** For I am not ashamed of the gospel of Christ: for it is the power of God unto salvation to every one that believeth; to the Jew first, and also to the Greek.

    ii. **2 Corinthians 4:7 (KJV)** But we have this treasure in earthen vessels, that the excellency of the power may be of God, and not of us.

2. Therefore, thinking along the lines of the error of a lack of a Bible Interpretation Methodology in the Holy Scriptures, many humans have come up with several theories for Bible Translation and Interpretation without reasoning whether it makes any sense that God would call all human wisdom *foolishness* and then, the same God would return and hand over the translation and interpretation of what God calls *wisdom* to the same humans whom God has already condemned as foolish!

    i. **1 Corinthians 1:21 (KJV)** For after that in the wisdom of God the world by wisdom knew not God, it pleased God by the foolishness of preaching to save them that believe.

    ii. **1 Corinthians 3:19 (KJV)** For the wisdom of this world is foolishness with God. For it is written, He taketh the wise in their own craftiness.

3. How can foolish human beings exercise the power of correct understanding and interpretation of that which is NOT foolish but pure wisdom?

    i. **Deuteronomy 4:5 (KJV)** Behold, I have taught you statutes and judgments, even as the LORD my God commanded me, that ye should do so in the land whither ye go to possess it.

    ii. **Deuteronomy 4:6 (KJV)** Keep therefore and do *them*; for this *is* your wisdom and your understanding in the sight of the nations, which shall hear all these statutes, and say, Surely this great nation *is* a wise and understanding people.

iii. **Psalm 119:140 (KJV)** Thy word *is* very pure: therefore thy servant loveth it.

iv. **Proverbs 30:5 (KJV)** Every word of God *is* pure: he *is* a shield unto them that put their trust in him.

v. **Jeremiah 4:22 (KJV)** For my people *is* foolish, they have not known me; they *are* sottish children, and they have none understanding: they *are* wise to do evil, but to do good they have no knowledge.

vi. **Haggai 2:14 (KJV)** Then answered Haggai, and said, So *is* this people, and so *is* this nation before me, saith the LORD; and so *is* every work of their hands; and that which they offer there *is* unclean.

4. If sinful men, and NOT God, shall decide on the correct meaning of the instrument (Word of God) that takes men to Heaven, then where is the need for the LORD God to write the Word of God Himself and not rather leave it to men to do so?

i. **Exodus 34:28 (KJV)** And he was there with the LORD forty days and forty nights; he did neither eat bread, nor drink water. And he wrote upon the tables the words of the covenant, the ten commandments.

ii. **Exodus 31:18 (KJV)** And he gave unto Moses, when he had made an end of communing with him upon mount Sinai, two tables of testimony, tables of stone, written with the finger of God.

iii. **Deuteronomy 9:10 (KJV)** And the LORD delivered unto me two tables of stone written with the finger of God; and on them *was written* according to all the words, which the LORD spake with you in the mount out of the midst of the fire in the day of the assembly.

iv. **Exodus 34:1 (KJV)** And the LORD said unto Moses, Hew thee two tables of stone like unto the first: and I will write upon *these* tables the words that were in the first tables, which thou brakest.

v. **Deuteronomy 10:2 (KJV)** And I will write on the tables the words that were in the first tables which thou brakest, and thou shalt put them in the ark.

vi. **Jeremiah 31:33 (KJV)** But this *shall be* the covenant that I will make with the house of Israel; After those days, saith the LORD, I will put my law in their inward parts, and write it in their hearts; and will be their God, and they shall be my people.

vii. **Hebrews 8:10 (KJV)** For this *is* the covenant that I will make with the house of Israel after those days, saith the Lord; I will put my laws into their mind, and write them in their hearts: and I will be to them a God, and they shall be to me a people:

    viii. **Hebrews 10:16 (KJV)** This *is* the covenant that I will make with them after those days, saith the Lord, I will put my laws into their hearts, and in their minds will I write them;

    ix. **Revelation 3:12 (KJV)** Him that overcometh will I make a pillar in the temple of my God, and he shall go no more out: and I will write upon him the name of my God, and the name of the city of my God, *which is* new Jerusalem, which cometh down out of heaven from my God: and *I will write upon him* my new name.

5. That is why every Theory for Bible Translation and Interpretation, and every Methodology for Bible Translation and Interpretation, and every Approach to Bible Translation and Interpretation, that was devised by humans, is condemned as foolishness even before it sees the light of day, because man is the sum product of all his error thoughts, of all his error words, and of all his error deeds, which triple levels of error are also transferred into every Theory for Bible Translation and Interpretation that he devises!

    i. **Matthew 12:37 (KJV)** For by thy words thou shalt be justified, and by thy words thou shalt be condemned.

    ii. **John 3:18 (KJV)** He that believeth on him is not condemned: but he that believeth not is condemned already, because he hath not believed in the name of the only begotten Son of God.

    iii. **Hebrews 11:7 (KJV)** By faith Noah, being warned of God of things not seen as yet, moved with fear, prepared an ark to the saving of his house; by the which he condemned the world, and became heir of the righteousness which is by faith.

    iv. **Romans 11:32 (KJV)** For God hath concluded them all in unbelief, that he might have mercy upon all.

    v. **Galatians 3:22 (KJV)** But the scripture hath concluded all under sin, that the promise by faith of Jesus Christ might be given to them that believe.

    vi. **Romans 7:18 (KJV)** For I know that in me (that is, in my flesh,) dwelleth no good thing: for to will is present with me; but *how* to perform that which is good I find not.

    vii. **2 Corinthians 2:17 (KJV)** For we are not as many, which corrupt the word of God: but as of sincerity, but as of God, in the sight of God speak we in Christ.

6. **STEP #1**:

7. In order to correctly teach or preach the Word of God, the first step is to learn how to "speak in Christ" as **2 Corinthians 2:17 (KJV)** reveals!

8. What does it mean to "speak in Christ"?

9. It simply means to speak ONLY what the Gospel of Christ speaks, permits, directs, and allows!

   i. **Numbers 22:20 (KJV)** And God came unto Balaam at night, and said unto him, If the men come to call thee, rise up, *and* go with them; but yet the word which I shall say unto thee, that shalt thou do.

   ii. **Ezekiel 3:4 (KJV)** And he said unto me, Son of man, go, get thee unto the house of Israel, and speak with my words unto them.

   iii. **John 3:34 (KJV)** For he whom God hath sent speaketh the words of God: for God giveth not the Spirit by measure *unto him.*

   iv. **Numbers 22:35 (KJV)** And the angel of the LORD said unto Balaam, Go with the men: but only the word that I shall speak unto thee, that thou shalt speak. So Balaam went with the princes of Balak.

   v. **Numbers 22:36 (KJV)** And when Balak heard that Balaam was come, he went out to meet him unto a city of Moab, which *is* in the border of Arnon, which *is* in the utmost coast.

   vi. **Numbers 22:37 (KJV)** And Balak said unto Balaam, Did I not earnestly send unto thee to call thee? wherefore camest thou not unto me? am I not able indeed to promote thee to honour?

   vii. **Numbers 22:38 (KJV)** And Balaam said unto Balak, Lo, I am come unto thee: have I now any power at all to say any thing? the word that God putteth in my mouth, that shall I speak.

   viii. **Revelation 19:10 (KJV)** And I fell at his feet to worship him. And he said unto me, See *thou do it* not: I am thy fellowservant, and of thy brethren that have the testimony of Jesus: worship God: for the testimony of Jesus is the spirit of prophecy.

10. In other words, if the power to speak is given to you by God according to **John 12:49 (KJV)**, and if the words that you are speaking are NOT yours but were given to you by God according to **John 17:8 (KJV)**, then you have zero entitlement to profess any meanings to those same words that do NOT belong to you in the first place!

    i. **Jeremiah 23:30 (KJV)** Therefore, behold, I *am* against the prophets, saith the LORD, that steal my words every one from his neighbour.

    ii. **John 14:10 (KJV)** Believest thou not that I am in the Father, and the Father in me? the words that I speak unto you I speak not of myself: but the Father that dwelleth in me, he doeth the works.

      iii. **John 12:49 (KJV)** For I have not spoken of myself; but the Father which sent me, he gave me a commandment, what I should say, and what I should speak.

      iv. **John 17:8 (KJV)** For I have given unto them the words which thou gavest me; and they have received *them*, and have known surely that I came out from thee, and they have believed that thou didst send me.

11. The real Owner of the words, being God Almighty, retains the right to define what HIS Words mean hence, all human Theories for Bible Translation and Interpretation are nonsense, void, and excluded!

12. STEP #2:

13. The second step to correctly teach or preach the Word of God is to measure the efficacy of the teaching, NOT in terms of pastoral commendation and approval one of the other, but in terms of actual men and women who have received the teachings of Christ from you, and, being led of the Holy Spirit, are actually walking in Truth and Righteousness daily!

      i. **2 Corinthians 3:1 (KJV)** Do we begin again to commend ourselves? or need we, as some *others*, epistles of commendation to you, or *letters* of commendation from you?

      ii. **2 Corinthians 3:2 (KJV)** Ye are our epistle written in our hearts, known and read of all men:

      iii. **2 Corinthians 3:3 (KJV)** *Forasmuch as ye are* manifestly declared to be the epistle of Christ ministered by us, written not with ink, but with the Spirit of the living God; not in tables of stone, but in fleshy tables of the heart.

      iv. **2 Corinthians 10:12 (KJV)** For we dare not make ourselves of the number, or compare ourselves with some that commend themselves: but they measuring themselves by themselves, and comparing themselves among themselves, are not wise.

14. STEP #3:

15. The third step to correctly teach or preach the Word of God is to acknowledge our own insufficiency and yield our insufficiency to the sufficiency of God who owns the words that we are preaching and teaching!

      i. **2 Corinthians 3:4 (KJV)** And such trust have we through Christ to God-ward:

      ii. **2 Corinthians 3:5 (KJV)** Not that we are sufficient of ourselves to think any thing as of ourselves; but our sufficiency *is* of God;

16. STEP #4:

17. The fourth step to correctly teach or preach the Word of God is to identify and to recognize the two-prong meanings in the Word of God, which are "the letter of the text" (the physical meaning) and "the spirit of the text" (the spiritual meaning), and, then, in your preaching or teaching, to emphasize and focus on "the spirit of the text", because God is Spirit and never physical!

    i. **2 Corinthians 3:6 (KJV)** Who also hath made us able ministers of the new testament; not of the letter, but of the spirit: for the letter killeth, but the spirit giveth life.

    ii. **John 4:23 (KJV)** But the hour cometh, and now is, when the true worshippers shall worship the Father in spirit and in truth: for the Father seeketh such to worship him.

    iii. **John 4:24 (KJV)** God *is* a Spirit: and they that worship him must worship *him* in spirit and in truth.

    iv. **Acts 7:48 (KJV)** Howbeit the most High dwelleth not in temples made with hands; as saith the prophet,

    v. **Acts 17:24 (KJV)** God that made the world and all things therein, seeing that he is Lord of heaven and earth, dwelleth not in temples made with hands;

    vi. **Acts 17:25 (KJV)** Neither is worshipped with men's hands, as though he needed any thing, seeing he giveth to all life, and breath, and all things;

18. **STEP #5**:

19. The fifth step to correctly teach or preach the Word of God is to recognize the consequence of dwelling on the physical in God-worship, which consequence is death! That form of preaching and teaching the Word of God that considers the physical meaning of the Word of God as essential is called "the ministration of death"! In other words, all the Old Testament physical forms of God-worship were NOT unto life but into death!

    i. **2 Corinthians 3:7 (KJV)** But if the ministration of death, written *and* engraven in stones, was glorious, so that the children of Israel could not stedfastly behold the face of Moses for the glory of his countenance; which *glory* was to be done away:

    ii. **Romans 3:20 (KJV)** Therefore by the deeds of the law there shall no flesh be justified in his sight: for by the law *is* the knowledge of sin.

    iii. **Romans 8:13 (KJV)** For if ye live after the flesh, ye shall die: but if ye through the Spirit do mortify the deeds of the body, ye shall live.

    iv. **Romans 3:20 (KJV)** Therefore by the deeds of the law there shall no flesh be justified in his sight: for by the law *is* the knowledge of sin.

v. **Galatians 2:16 (KJV)** Knowing that a man is not justified by the works of the law, but by the faith of Jesus Christ, even we have believed in Jesus Christ, that we might be justified by the faith of Christ, and not by the works of the law: for by the works of the law shall no flesh be justified.

20. Hence, for example, it is called "the ministration of death", or, it is understood that you the Pastor or Bishop, you are administering death to the congregation when you read **Luke 22:19-20 (KJV)** and then you proceed to think and to preach that the LORD Jesus Christ wants you to eat and drink physical bread, wafers, and wine!

   i. **Luke 22:19 (KJV)** And he took bread, and gave thanks, and brake *it*, and gave unto them, saying, This is my body which is given for you: this do in remembrance of me.

   ii. **Luke 22:20 (KJV)** Likewise also the cup after supper, saying, This cup *is* the new testament in my blood, which is shed for you.

21. The moment that you choose to stay with the physical meaning of **Luke 22:19-20 (KJV)**, that is the same moment that you fell into the condemnation of **2 Corinthians 3:6 (KJV)**, and also, are in violation of the same!

22. The same doctrine of "the ministration of death" is applicable in all instances of the Word of God where you choose to present/minister the physical instead of the spiriual side of the same, why? Because the physical is already done away with! When was that? The physical was abolished in **John 4:23-24 (KJV)**!

   i. **2 Corinthians 3:8 (KJV)** How shall not the ministration of the spirit be rather glorious?

   ii. **2 Corinthians 3:9 (KJV)** For if the ministration of condemnation *be* glory, much more doth the ministration of righteousness exceed in glory.

   iii. **2 Corinthians 3:10 (KJV)** For even that which was made glorious had no glory in this respect, by reason of the glory that excelleth.

   iv. **2 Corinthians 3:11 (KJV)** For if that which is done away *was* glorious, much more that which remaineth *is* glorious.

   v. **John 4:23 (KJV)** But the hour cometh, and now is, when the true worshippers shall worship the Father in spirit and in truth: for the Father seeketh such to worship him.

   vi. **John 4:24 (KJV)** God *is* a Spirit: and they that worship him must worship *him* in spirit and in truth.

23. **STEP #6**:

24. The sixth step to correctly teach or preach the Word of God is to be fully convinced that the greatness of dropping the physical aspects of God-worship and placing all

hope in the "ministration of the Spirit", or, in the act of "speaking in Christ", lies in the fact that you assume zero responsibility for all things spiritual, because it is then the Holy Spirit who is in control and responsible for the words of the LORD God Almighty, and not you!

    i. **2 Corinthians 3:12 (KJV)** Seeing then that we have such hope, we use great plainness of speech:

    ii. **2 Corinthians 3:13 (KJV)** And not as Moses, *which* put a vail over his face, that the children of Israel could not stedfastly look to the end of that which is abolished:

25. STEP #7:

26. The seventh step to correctly teach or preach the Word of God is to learn that all the physical blindness that the LORD Jesus Christ healed were nothing in themselves since all of the healed people were going to die again anyway!

27. The reason being that the most precious healing of their blindness was NOT in their ability to physically see the world and the things in the world, but, rather, that the blindness of their minds hindering their ability to correctly understand the Word of God was taken away by Jesus Christ, and this is the same spiritual healing of the blind that you the Pastor and the Bishop should be practising and ministring in your preaching and teaching of the Word of God!

    i. **2 Corinthians 3:14 (KJV)** But their minds were blinded: for until this day remaineth the same vail untaken away in the reading of the old testament; which *vail* is done away in Christ.

28. Therefore, I testify to you by the Holy Ghost, that blindness is in the mind and in the head, and this is the real blindness that you are commanded to heal, given the fact that the eyes of man are in his head and NOT on his face!

    i. **Ecclesiastes 2:14 (KJV)** The wise man's eyes *are* in his head; but the fool walketh in darkness: and I myself perceived also that one event happeneth to them all.

    ii. **Matthew 10:8 (KJV)** Heal the sick, cleanse the lepers, raise the dead, cast out devils: freely ye have received, freely give.

    iii. **Isaiah 42:6 (KJV)** I the LORD have called thee in righteousness, and will hold thine hand, and will keep thee, and give thee for a covenant of the people, for a light of the Gentiles;

    iv. **Isaiah 42:7 (KJV)** To open the blind eyes, to bring out the prisoners from the prison, *and* them that sit in darkness out of the prison house.

    v. **Acts 26:17 (KJV)** Delivering thee from the people, and *from* the Gentiles, unto whom now I send thee,

vi. **Acts 26:18 (KJV)** To open their eyes, *and* to turn *them* from darkness to light, and *from* the power of Satan unto God, that they may receive forgiveness of sins, and inheritance among them which are sanctified by faith that is in me.

vii. **Isaiah 61:1 (KJV)** The Spirit of the Lord GOD *is* upon me; because the LORD hath anointed me to preach good tidings unto the meek; he hath sent me to bind up the brokenhearted, to proclaim liberty to the captives, and the opening of the prison to *them that are* bound;

viii. **Luke 4:18 (KJV)** The Spirit of the Lord *is* upon me, because he hath anointed me to preach the gospel to the poor; he hath sent me to heal the brokenhearted, to preach deliverance to the captives, and recovering of sight to the blind, to set at liberty them that are bruised,

29. How very stupid are you as a Man of God teaching the physical meaning of the Word of God, when you claim that it was the LORD Jesus Christ who called you into Ministry, and yet you are blind in the spiritual meaning of the Word of God, not knowing what the Word of God means, NOT having the Holy Spirit who is The Teacher of Truth, and therefore, you go about teaching the Word of God in error and in corruption, alas, to the utter destruction of your own soul in Hell

    i. **2 Corinthians 3:15 (KJV)** But even unto this day, when Moses is read, the vail is upon their heart.

    ii. **2 Corinthians 3:16 (KJV)** Nevertheless when it shall turn to the Lord, the vail shall be taken away.

    iii. **2 Corinthians 2:17 (KJV)** For we are not as many, which corrupt the word of God: but as of sincerity, but as of God, in the sight of God speak we in Christ.

    iv. **Acts 13:10 (KJV)** And said, O full of all subtilty and all mischief, *thou* child of the devil, *thou* enemy of all righteousness, wilt thou not cease to pervert the right ways of the Lord?

    v. **Galatians 1:7 (KJV)** Which is not another; but there be some that trouble you, and would pervert the gospel of Christ.

30. In conclusion, the Man of God who focuses on the spiritual side of the Word of God is demonstrating liberty in Chirst! Liberty from what? Liberty or breaking away from the physical and affinity with the Spirit of the Lord!

    i. **2 Corinthians 3:17 (KJV)** Now the Lord is that Spirit: and where the Spirit of the Lord *is*, there *is* liberty.

    ii. **2 Corinthians 3:18 (KJV)** But we all, with open face beholding as in a glass the glory of the Lord, are changed into the same image from glory to glory, *even* as by the Spirit of the Lord.

The LORD Jesus Christ be with your spirit. The LORD Jesus Christ give you understanding.

Rev. Prof. PETER PRYCE,
DSEF, BA, MA, B.Soc.Sc Pol Sci, IBA, PhD
A Scribe of the Law of the God of Heaven
Prophet of the Word of God
Professor of French, Silver Spring, MD, USA
Scholar of the Institute of Theologians, USA
WWW.THEBIBLEUNIVERSITY.ORG
Accreditation Number: 07-QCTO/SDP120723172836
SAQA QUAL ID: Identification # 101997
WWW.BOOKSTORESITE.ORG
WWW.THEBIBLEUNIVERSITYCHURCH.ORG

Saturday 20th January 2024 @ 11:01 AM – 3:37 PM
While hearing and meditating on the Word of God at home.

THE CORRECT THEORY FOR BIBLE TRANSLATION AND INTERPRETATION!

Question 2557

1. Here is the LORD Jesus Christ receiving HIS Anointing to go and begin HIS Ministry of Salvation!

    i. **Matthew 3:13 (KJV)** Then cometh Jesus from Galilee to Jordan unto John, to be baptized of him.

    ii. **Matthew 3:14 (KJV)** But John forbad him, saying, I have need to be baptized of thee, and comest thou to me?

    iii. **Matthew 3:15 (KJV)** And Jesus answering said unto him, Suffer *it to be so* now: for thus it becometh us to fulfil all righteousness. Then he suffered him.

    iv. **Matthew 3:16 (KJV)** And Jesus, when he was baptized, went up straightway out of the water: and, lo, the heavens were opened unto him, and he saw the Spirit of God descending like a dove, and lighting upon him:

    v. **Matthew 3:17 (KJV)** And lo a voice from heaven, saying, This is my beloved Son, in whom I am well pleased.

2. Here is the very first assignment of the LORD Jesus Christ in HIS Ministry, where we see the LORD Jesus Christ teaching to Satan the correct Doctrine and The Correct Theory for Bible Translation and Interpretation!

    i. **Matthew 4:1 (KJV)** Then was Jesus led up of the Spirit into the wilderness to be tempted of the devil.

    ii. **Matthew 4:2 (KJV)** And when he had fasted forty days and forty nights, he was afterward an hungred.

    iii. **Matthew 4:3 (KJV)** And when the tempter came to him, he said, If thou be the Son of God, command that these stones be made bread.

3. **The Correct Theory for Bible Translation and Interpretation: Step #1**:

    i. **Matthew 4:4 (KJV)** But he answered and said, It is written, Man shall not live by bread alone, but by every word that proceedeth out of the mouth of God.

4. Eliminate all forms and traces of esoteric unverifiable translations and interpretation that are NOT inside the written Word of God, which form of unverifiable interpretations Satan was presenting in **Matthew 4:3 (KJV)**!

5. Stay focus ONLY on the written Word of God just as the LORD Jesus Christ taught Satan in **Matthew 4:4 (KJV)**!

6. Your understanding of the written Word of God must be reasonable and the reasoning must come ONLY from the text of the written Word of God and NOT from outside the written Word of God!

7. **The Correct Theory for Bible Translation and Interpretation: Step #2**:

    i. **Matthew 4:4 (KJV)** But he answered and said, It is written, Man shall not live by bread alone, but by every word that proceedeth out of the mouth of God.

8. Two important features of The Correct Theory for Bible Translation and Interpretation derive from **Matthew 4:4 (KJV)**!

9. When the LORD Jesus Christ says that "It is written, Man shall not live by bread alone, but by every word that proceedeth out of the mouth of God", HE is saying that, together with **Matthew 4:7 (KJV)**, where "Jesus said unto him, It is written again", particularly, this word "again", that is indicative of one very important aspect in The Correct Theory for Bible Translation and Interpretation!

10. Those two references in **Matthew 4:4 (KJV)** and **Matthew 4:7 (KJV)** mean that you cannot, and it is also forbidden, to make a theory or to do an interpretation or translation based only on one verse in the Holy Bible, or, some few verses, or, based on an incomplete corpus of the entire number of relevant verses of the Bible that relate to the topic, subject, or theme that you are translating or interpreting!

11. In other words, you do NOT have correct translation or interpretation, neither do you have any Truth when you proceed to translate and interpret some section of the Holy Bible when you have not yet seen and read ALL the other relevant verses that also pertain to your text, to your theme, to your key word, to your topic, to your subject, and to your main idea!

12. **The Correct Theory for Bible Translation and Interpretation: Step #3**:

13. This expression: "by every word that proceedeth out of the mouth of God" means that your Bible Translation and Interpretation is NOT complete until you have checked it against "every word" in the entire Holy Bible from Genesis to Revelation and you have assured yourself that there is not a single contradiction of thought between what you have translated and the entire remainder of the Holy Bible!

    i. **Isaiah 8:20 (KJV)** To the law and to the testimony: if they speak not according to this word, *it is* because *there is* no light in them.

    ii. **Proverbs 21:30 (KJV)** *There is* no wisdom nor understanding nor counsel against the LORD.

14. **The Correct Theory for Bible Translation and Interpretation: Step #4**:

    i. **Matthew 4:5 (KJV)** Then the devil taketh him up into the holy city, and setteth him on a pinnacle of the temple,

    ii. **Matthew 4:6 (KJV)** And saith unto him, If thou be the Son of God, cast thyself down: for it is written, He shall give his angels charge concerning thee: and in *their* hands they shall bear thee up, lest at any time thou dash thy foot against a stone.

    iii. **Matthew 4:7 (KJV)** Jesus said unto him, It is written again, Thou shalt not tempt the Lord thy God.

15. **Matthew 4:5-7 (KJV)** reveals that you must achieve consistency and perfect harmony at all times throughout the entire translation and interpretation of the Word of God!

16. The words: "Thou shalt not tempt the Lord thy God" means that you cannot pit one section of the Word of God against another section of the same Word of God!

17. In other words, you cannot cause one part of the Holy Bible to violate another part of the same Holy Bible!

18. In other words, you cannot make the Word of God to speak against the Word of God!

19. In other words, you must translate and interpret the Word of God to agree perfectly with the Word of God!

20. Furthermore, the answer of the LORD Jesus Christ saying that "Thou shalt not tempt the Lord thy God" means that it is forbidden to inject or infuse your own personal intentions and thoughts and reasoning into the translation and interpretation process of the Word of God!

    i. **2 Peter 1:19 (KJV)** We have also a more sure word of prophecy; whereunto ye do well that ye take heed, as unto a light that shineth in a dark place, until the day dawn, and the day star arise in your hearts:

    ii. **2 Peter 1:20 (KJV)** Knowing this first, that no prophecy of the scripture is of any private interpretation.

    iii. **2 Peter 1:21 (KJV)** For the prophecy came not in old time by the will of man: but holy men of God spake *as they were* moved by the Holy Ghost.

21. Additionally, you cannot use the Word of God to support and justify a private evil intent or, in order to prove a private personal intent!

22. If it is your personal desire to cast yourself down from a hilltop to prove your own personal point, when the LORD God Almighty did NOT expressly command you so to do, then, by all means, please do so without roping in God Almighty to prove anything or to confirm anything since it was NOT God who first asked you to perform that gymnastics!

23. In other words, you must translate and interpret in the Word of God for its own intent, you must use the Word of God for the same intent for which God meant it, which intent must come from the Holy Bible itself and NOT from you the man!

24. **The Correct Theory for Bible Translation and Interpretation: Step #5**:

   i. **Matthew 4:5 (KJV)** Then the devil taketh him up into the holy city, and setteth him on a pinnacle of the temple,

   ii. **Matthew 4:6 (KJV)** And saith unto him, If thou be the Son of God, cast thyself down: for it is written, He shall give his angels charge concerning thee: and in *their* hands they shall bear thee up, lest at any time thou dash thy foot against a stone.

   iii. **Matthew 4:7 (KJV)** Jesus said unto him, It is written again, Thou shalt not tempt the Lord thy God.

25. There is a second feature of The Correct Theory for Bible Translation and Interpretation! that derives from **Matthew 4:5-7 (KJV)**!

26. In those verses, we see that while Satan used the *Literal Translation Method*, or, *Bible Translation and Interpretation According to the Letter of the Scripture* to render his Bible Translation and Interpretation, the LORD Jesus Christ rejected that method as false and instead used the *Obligatory Modulation Method of Translation* to render His Bible Translation and Interpretation of those same verses!

27. By the LORD Jesus Christ using this *Obligatory Modulation* technique, we see that His correct translation did NOT translate words into the target *intralingual* meaning, but HE translated the thought, the idea, and the intention within the text!

28. Hence, in The Correct Theory for Bible Translation and Interpretation, we translate the thought, the idea, and the intention within the text and NOT the words!

29. In Bible Translation, we translate and interpret thought, NOT words.

30. Here is the original thought/Wod of God:

   i. **Psalm 82:6 (KJV)** I have said, Ye *are* gods; and all of you *are* children of the most High.

31. Then, here is the translation/interpretation, with a large omission, from the LORD Jesus Christ: "I said, Ye are gods"!

   i. **John 10:34 (KJV)** Jesus answered them, Is it not written in your law, I said, Ye are gods?

32. So, for the original text, we have: "I have said, Ye *are* gods; and all of you *are* children of the most High." **Psalm 82:6 (KJV) [16 words]**

33. Then, for the translation/interpretation, we have: "I said, Ye are gods" **John 10:34 (KJV) [5 words]**

34. Then, for the Translation Omission, we have: "have, and all of you *are* children of the most High" **[11 words]**

35. Now, why was the Translation Omission non-impactful, or, why did the Translation Omission NOT affect the desired understanding of the communication?

36. Because in Bible Translation, you do NOT translate words, but thoughts, and the thought in that Source Text is adequately rendered in the Target Translation contained in these fewer words: "I said, Ye are gods"!

37. **The Correct Theory for Bible Translation and Interpretation: Step #6**:

    i. **Matthew 4:8 (KJV)** Again, the devil taketh him up into an exceeding high mountain, and sheweth him all the kingdoms of the world, and the glory of them;

    ii. **Matthew 4:9 (KJV)** And saith unto him, All these things will I give thee, if thou wilt fall down and worship me.

    iii. **Matthew 4:10 (KJV)** Then saith Jesus unto him, Get thee hence, Satan: for it is written, Thou shalt worship the Lord thy God, and him only shalt thou serve.

    iv. **Matthew 4:11 (KJV)** Then the devil leaveth him, and, behold, angels came and ministered unto him.

38. In **Matthew 4:8-11 (KJV)**, the LORD Jesus Christ is showing us that you must never consider the reward of Bible Translation and Interpretation as the reason to translate, preach, teach, explain, and interpret the Word of God in a certain way to please your audience and paymasters, but let the Word of God speak all the time!

    i. **Deuteronomy 1:17 (KJV)** Ye shall not respect persons in judgment; *but* ye shall hear the small as well as the great; ye shall not be afraid of the face of man; for the judgment *is* God's: and the cause that is too hard for you, bring *it* unto me, and I will hear it.

    ii. **Deuteronomy 16:19 (KJV)** Thou shalt not wrest judgment; thou shalt not respect persons, neither take a gift: for a gift doth blind the eyes of the wise, and pervert the words of the righteous.

    iii. **2 Chronicles 19:7 (KJV)** Wherefore now let the fear of the LORD be upon you; take heed and do *it*: for *there is* no iniquity with the LORD our God, nor respect of persons, nor taking of gifts.

    iv. **Ephesians 6:9 (KJV)** And, ye masters, do the same things unto them, forbearing threatening: knowing that your Master also is in heaven; neither is there respect of persons with him.

    v. **Colossians 3:25 (KJV)** But he that doeth wrong shall receive for the wrong which he hath done: and there is no respect of persons.

    vi. **James 2:1 (KJV)** My brethren, have not the faith of our Lord Jesus Christ, *the Lord* of glory, with respect of persons.

vii. **James 2:9 (KJV)** But if ye have respect to persons, ye commit sin, and are convinced of the law as transgressors.

viii. **1 Peter 1:17 (KJV)** And if ye call on the Father, who without respect of persons judgeth according to every man's work, pass the time of your sojourning *here* in fear:

ix. **Acts 10:34 (KJV)** Then Peter opened *his* mouth, and said, Of a truth I perceive that God is no respecter of persons:

39. The rejection of Satan by the LORD Jesus Christ is the communication to you that all the wealth and riches of the world CANNOT buy the Truth of the Word of God neither should all monies in the world be able to entice you to make the Holy Bible say what is NOT in the Bible!

40. For example, when so-called murderous Zionist Christian evangelicals in America and in Apartheid Israel say and preach that these same genocide-practising, nazi, lying, population exterminating white people in 1948 Israel are Jews and Hebrews, when they are NOT and have never shared a single DNA with any true semitic indigene from that Land, when they do that, then, they are forcing the Holy Bible to say that they are Semites, Jews, and Hebrews when they are NOT, but are actually, truly, and by DNA evidence, from the European caves of the Russian Khazars and Nazi Germany, and have never been Jews, Semites, or Hebrews, but they are rather blood-drinking Colonial Settler Land-Stealing Devils from Europe! The LORD Jesus Christ knows them very well and rejected them many centuries ago in **Revelation 2:9 (KJV)** and that is why all the Jews in 1948 Israel hate Jesus Christ and will arrest you by their Apartheid Police when you try to preach Jesus Christ over there!

i. **Exodus 3:6 (KJV)** Moreover he said, I *am* the God of thy father, the God of Abraham, the God of Isaac, and the God of Jacob. And Moses hid his face; for he was afraid to look upon God.

ii. **Exodus 3:15 (KJV)** And God said moreover unto Moses, Thus shalt thou say unto the children of Israel, The LORD God of your fathers, the God of Abraham, the God of Isaac, and the God of Jacob, hath sent me unto you: this *is* my name for ever, and this *is* my memorial unto all generations.

iii. **Revelation 2:9 (KJV)** I know thy works, and tribulation, and poverty, (but thou art rich) and *I know* the blasphemy of them which say they are Jews, and are not, but *are* the synagogue of Satan.

iv. **Revelation 3:9 (KJV)** Behold, I will make them of the synagogue of Satan, which say they are Jews, and are not, but do lie; behold, I will make them to come and worship before thy feet, and to know that I have loved thee.

41. This assertion of the LORD Jesus Christ: "Thou shalt worship the Lord thy God, and him only shalt thou serve", means that there is ONLY one focus in Bible Translation and Interpretation, and that focus is God Almighty Himself/the LORD Jesus Christ, NOT the audience of the translation!

    i. **Proverbs 24:23 (KJV)** These *things* also *belong* to the wise. *It is* not good to have respect of persons in judgment.
    ii. **Proverbs 28:21 (KJV)** To have respect of persons *is* not good: for for a piece of bread *that* man will transgress.
    iii. **Romans 2:11 (KJV)** For there is no respect of persons with God.
    iv. **Galatians 1:10 (KJV)** For do I now persuade men, or God? or do I seek to please men? for if I yet pleased men, I should not be the servant of Christ.
    v. **John 5:46 (KJV)** For had ye believed Moses, ye would have believed me: for he wrote of me.

42. Hence, one cardinal pillar in Bible Translation and Interpretation is that you do NOT translate to please the audience of your translation, but you translation to please ONLY the Author of the Text of the Holy Bible, which Author is the LORD God Almighty!

    i. **1 Peter 1:10 (KJV)** Of which salvation the prophets have inquired and searched diligently, who prophesied of the grace *that should come* unto you:
    ii. **1 Peter 1:11 (KJV)** Searching what, or what manner of time the Spirit of Christ which was in them did signify, when it testified beforehand the sufferings of Christ, and the glory that should follow.
    iii. **2 Peter 1:19 (KJV)** We have also a more sure word of prophecy; whereunto ye do well that ye take heed, as unto a light that shineth in a dark place, until the day dawn, and the day star arise in your hearts:
    iv. **2 Peter 1:20 (KJV)** Knowing this first, that no prophecy of the scripture is of any private interpretation.
    v. **2 Peter 1:21 (KJV)** For the prophecy came not in old time by the will of man: but holy men of God spake *as they were* moved by the Holy Ghost.

43. As you can see in **2 Peter 1:19 (KJV)**, the prophecy (meaning the Bible Translation and Interpretation) is "more sure, certain, correct, accurate, without blemish" ONLY when it reflects and conforms 100% to what the Holy Ghost is saying from Genesis to Revelation, but NOT when it conforms to cultural or audience influences and expectations! Those characteristics of target culture influences belong to all secular and business translation, but NOT to Bible Translation. The theoretical requirement

of Faithfulness in Translation derives from the Word of God and NOT from carnal secular ideas of the world!

    i. **Acts 10:42 (KJV)** And he commanded us to preach unto the people, and to testify that it is he which was ordained of God *to be* the Judge of quick and dead.

    ii. **Acts 10:43 (KJV)** To him give all the prophets witness, that through his name whosoever believeth in him shall receive remission of sins.

    iii. **Jeremiah 23:28 (KJV)** The prophet that hath a dream, let him tell a dream; and he that hath my word, let him speak my word faithfully. What *is* the chaff to the wheat? saith the LORD.

44. When Satan proposed a Bible Translation and Interpretation Theory, saying that: "All these things will I give thee, if thou wilt fall down and worship me", that statement meant that:

    i. If you will allow the Word of God to say what I want it to say, or, if you will allow me to impose my will on the Word of God and lie to the people, then, I will reward you with great wealth and riches!

    ii. **Matthew 28:1 (KJV)** In the end of the sabbath, as it began to dawn toward the first *day* of the week, came Mary Magdalene and the other Mary to see the sepulchre.

    iii. **Matthew 28:2 (KJV)** And, behold, there was a great earthquake: for the angel of the Lord descended from heaven, and came and rolled back the stone from the door, and sat upon it.

    iv. **Matthew 28:3 (KJV)** His countenance was like lightning, and his raiment white as snow:

    v. **Matthew 28:4 (KJV)** And for fear of him the keepers did shake, and became as dead *men*.

    vi. **Matthew 28:5 (KJV)** And the angel answered and said unto the women, Fear not ye: for I know that ye seek Jesus, which was crucified.

    vii. **Matthew 28:6 (KJV)** He is not here: for he is risen, as he said. Come, see the place where the Lord lay.

    viii. **Matthew 28:7 (KJV)** And go quickly, and tell his disciples that he is risen from the dead; and, behold, he goeth before you into Galilee; there shall ye see him: lo, I have told you.

    ix. **Matthew 28:8 (KJV)** And they departed quickly from the sepulchre with fear and great joy; and did run to bring his disciples word.

x. **Matthew 28:9 (KJV)** And as they went to tell his disciples, behold, Jesus met them, saying, All hail. And they came and held him by the feet, and worshipped him.

xi. **Matthew 28:10 (KJV)** Then said Jesus unto them, Be not afraid: go tell my brethren that they go into Galilee, and there shall they see me.

xii. **Matthew 28:11 (KJV)** Now when they were going, behold, some of the watch came into the city, and shewed unto the chief priests all the things that were done.

xiii. **Matthew 28:12 (KJV)** And when they were assembled with the elders, and had taken counsel, they gave large money unto the soldiers,

xiv. **Matthew 28:13 (KJV)** Saying, Say ye, His disciples came by night, and stole him *away* while we slept.

xv. **Matthew 28:14 (KJV)** And if this come to the governor's ears, we will persuade him, and secure you.

xvi. **Matthew 28:15 (KJV)** So they took the money, and did as they were taught: and this saying is commonly reported among the Jews until this day.

45. One unique feature of Bible Translation and Interpretation is that, whereas cultural, business, commercial, client, and audience considerations, norms, and expectations dictate and overbear on the translation and interpretation process, outcomes and output, there is ONLY one text in the entire world that does NOT conform to those corrupt ethics, and that text is the Word of God!

    i. **Matthew 4:8 (KJV)** Again, the devil taketh him up into an exceeding high mountain, and sheweth him all the kingdoms of the world, and the glory of them;

    ii. **Matthew 4:9 (KJV)** And saith unto him, All these things will I give thee, if thou wilt fall down and worship me.

    iii. **Matthew 4:10 (KJV)** Then saith Jesus unto him, Get thee hence, Satan: for it is written, Thou shalt worship the Lord thy God, and him only shalt thou serve.

    iv. **Matthew 4:11 (KJV)** Then the devil leaveth him, and, behold, angels came and ministered unto him.

    v. **John 15:5 (KJV)** I am the vine, ye *are* the branches: He that abideth in me, and I in him, the same bringeth forth much fruit: for without me ye can do nothing.

46. The second unique feature of Bible Translation and Interpretation is that, whereas in secular literary translation and interpretation, the Translator/Interpreter can insert

himself/herself in the translation process where he/she thinks there is some textual inadequacy or a lacune or a cultural inconsistency, and for that reason introduce his own words, explain, make additions, amplifications, adjustments, and subtractions, the same Translator/Interpreter is strictly forbidden to do the same in a correct Bible Translation Process!

    i. **Deuteronomy 4:2 (KJV)** Ye shall not add unto the word which I command you, neither shall ye diminish *ought* from it, that ye may keep the commandments of the LORD your God which I command you.

    ii. **Deuteronomy 12:32 (KJV)** What thing soever I command you, observe to do it: thou shalt not add thereto, nor diminish from it.

    iii. **Jeremiah 26:2 (KJV)** Thus saith the LORD; Stand in the court of the LORD'S house, and speak unto all the cities of Judah, which come to worship in the LORD'S house, all the words that I command thee to speak unto them; diminish not a word:

    iv. **Revelation 22:18 (KJV)** For I testify unto every man that heareth the words of the prophecy of this book, If any man shall add unto these things, God shall add unto him the plagues that are written in this book:

    v. **Revelation 22:19 (KJV)** And if any man shall take away from the words of the book of this prophecy, God shall take away his part out of the book of life, and out of the holy city, and *from* the things which are written in this book.

47. Here is another illustration of the Law of Bible Translation and Interpretation that prohibits the Translator/Interpreter from inserting himself/herself into the translation process by the means of addition, expansion, amplification, or textual gain!

48. Moses inserted himself in the doctrine of divorce by means of a totally new addition to the original spiritual thought and message, and the LORD Jesus Christ reversed Moses' translation/interpretation of the law of divorce as unbiblical and unscriptural!

49. Here was the wrong translation/interpretation of the law of divorce that Moses gave:

    i. **Deuteronomy 24:1 (KJV)** When a man hath taken a wife, and married her, and it come to pass that she find no favour in his eyes, because he hath found some uncleanness in her: then let him write her a bill of divorcement, and give *it* in her hand, and send her out of his house.

    ii. **Deuteronomy 24:2 (KJV)** And when she is departed out of his house, she may go and be another man's *wife*.

iii. **Deuteronomy 24:3 (KJV)** And *if* the latter husband hate her, and write her a bill of divorcement, and giveth *it* in her hand, and sendeth her out of his house; or if the latter husband die, which took her *to be* his wife;

iv. **Deuteronomy 24:4 (KJV)** Her former husband, which sent her away, may not take her again to be his wife, after that she is defiled; for that *is* abomination before the LORD: and thou shalt not cause the land to sin, which the LORD thy God giveth thee *for* an inheritance.

50. Then, here is the correction from the LORD Jesus Christ to replace the wrong translation/ interpretation of Moses!

i. **Matthew 19:1 (KJV)** And it came to pass, *that* when Jesus had finished these sayings, he departed from Galilee, and came into the coasts of Judaea beyond Jordan;

ii. **Matthew 19:2 (KJV)** And great multitudes followed him; and he healed them there.

iii. **Matthew 19:3 (KJV)** The Pharisees also came unto him, tempting him, and saying unto him, Is it lawful for a man to put away his wife for every cause?

iv. **Matthew 19:4 (KJV)** And he answered and said unto them, Have ye not read, that he which made *them* at the beginning made them male and female,

v. **Matthew 19:5 (KJV)** And said, For this cause shall a man leave father and mother, and shall cleave to his wife: and they twain shall be one flesh?

vi. **Matthew 19:6 (KJV)** Wherefore they are no more twain, but one flesh. What therefore God hath joined together, let not man put asunder.

vii. **Matthew 19:7 (KJV)** They say unto him, Why did Moses then command to give a writing of divorcement, and to put her away?

viii. **Matthew 19:8 (KJV)** He saith unto them, Moses because of the hardness of your hearts suffered you to put away your wives: but from the beginning it was not so.

ix. **Matthew 19:9 (KJV)** And I say unto you, Whosoever shall put away his wife, except *it be* for fornication, and shall marry another, committeth adultery: and whoso marrieth her which is put away doth commit adultery.

x. **Matthew 19:10 (KJV)** His disciples say unto him, If the case of the man be so with *his* wife, it is not good to marry.

xi. **Matthew 19:12 (KJV)** For there are some eunuchs, which were so born from *their* mother's womb: and there are some eunuchs, which were made eunuchs of men: and there be eunuchs, which have made themselves eunuchs for the kingdom of heaven's sake. He that is able to receive *it*, let him receive *it*.

51. When you become a Bible Translator/Interpreter, you have to completely remove yourself, you have to completely remove your own words and your own thoughts and your own opinions away from the translation/interpretation and let ONLY the LORD God to speak, NOT you!

i. **Ezekiel 3:1 (KJV)** Moreover he said unto me, Son of man, eat that thou findest; eat this roll, and go speak unto the house of Israel.

ii. **Ezekiel 3:2 (KJV)** So I opened my mouth, and he caused me to eat that roll.

iii. **Ezekiel 3:3 (KJV)** And he said unto me, Son of man, cause thy belly to eat, and fill thy bowels with this roll that I give thee. Then did I eat *it*; and it was in my mouth as honey for sweetness.

iv. **Ezekiel 3:4 (KJV)** And he said unto me, Son of man, go, get thee unto the house of Israel, and speak with my words unto them.

v. **John 3:34 (KJV)** For he whom God hath sent speaketh the words of God: for God giveth not the Spirit by measure *unto him*.

vi. **Isaiah 58:13 (KJV)** If thou turn away thy foot from the sabbath, *from* doing thy pleasure on my holy day; and call the sabbath a delight, the holy of the LORD, honourable; and shalt honour him, not doing thine own ways, nor finding thine own pleasure, nor speaking *thine own* words:

vii. **Isaiah 58:14 (KJV)** Then shalt thou delight thyself in the LORD; and I will cause thee to ride upon the high places of the earth, and feed thee with the heritage of Jacob thy father: for the mouth of the LORD hath spoken *it*.

52. Therefore, The Correct Theory for Bible Translation and Interpretation that the LORD Jesus Christ gave to us in **Matthew 4:10 (KJV)** is that:

i. In Bible Translation and Interpretation, there is ONLY one Source and ONLY one Target to please, which is: the Word of God itself!

The LORD Jesus Christ be with your spirit. The LORD Jesus Christ give you understanding.

Rev. Prof. PETER PRYCE,
DSEF, BA, MA, B.Soc.Sc Pol Sci, IBA, PhD
A Scribe of the Law of the God of Heaven
Prophet of the Word of God
Professor of French, Silver Spring, MD, USA
Scholar of the Institute of Theologians, USA
WWW.THEBIBLEUNIVERSITY.ORG
Accreditation Number: 07-QCTO/SDP120723172836
SAQA QUAL ID: Identification # 101997
WWW.BOOKSTORESITE.ORG
WWW.THEBIBLEUNIVERSITYCHURCH.ORG

Sunday 28th April 2024 @ 7:07 AM – 5:07 PM

While hearing and meditating on the Word of God in the bathroom.

BIBLE INTERPRETATION AND TRANSLATION THEORY STATEMENT

Question 2582

1. **How to be Sober and Watch: Lesson #9**:

    i. **1 Peter 4:11 (KJV)** If any man speak, *let him speak* as the oracles of God; if any man minister, *let him do it* as of the ability which God giveth: that God in all things may be glorified through Jesus Christ, to whom be praise and dominion for ever and ever. Amen.

2. Furthermore, if you want to be sober, if you want to strengthen your Christian life, and if you want to have a good prayer life as a true child of God, then, learn to speak as the oracles of God!

3. What does it mean to speak as the oracles of God? Or, what are oracles?

4. Oracles are simply the Word of God hence, the entire Word of God from Genesis to Revelation, while they are called Books of the Bible, or the Holy Bible, or the Holy Scriptures, or the Scripture of Truth, they are also called: The Oracles of God!

    i. **Acts 7:38 (KJV)** This is he, that was in the church in the wilderness with the angel which spake to him in the mount Sina, and *with* our fathers: who received the lively oracles to give unto us:

    ii. **Romans 3:2 (KJV)** Much every way: chiefly, because that unto them were committed the oracles of God.

    iii. **Hebrews 5:12 (KJV)** For when for the time ye ought to be teachers, ye have need that one teach you again which *be* the first principles of the oracles of God; and are become such as have need of milk, and not of strong meat.

5. Therefore, these words: "If any man speak, *let him speak* as the oracles of God" are actually a summary statement of the true and correct Bible Interpretation and Translation Theory or Methodology!

6. That Bible Interpretation and Translation Theory Statement means that:

    i. You the Bible Interpreter/Translator, you are totally 100% excluded from the Bible interpretation and translation process!

    ii. You cannot and must never insert your own thoughts, opinions, ideas, or suggestions!

    iii. You must always allow the Word of God (the Oracles of God) to speak from itself, to speak for itself, and to speak by itself, because the Holy Living God is well able to speak for Himself and explain His own Word without you the dead sinner!

iv. You have no power, authority, or assumption to speak or write anything against the Word of God!

v. When you interpret and translate the Word of God, you must reproduce faithfully, without adding or diminishing anything, the thoughts of God in the Word of God "as of the ability which God has given you", meaning that if you have the education, training, and mind of someone who did not go further than a secondary school education, then, you will interpret, translate, and teach the Word of God with the mind of a secondary school graduate, but the man who has acquired the education, training, and mind of a Doctor of Laws and its equivalent Disciplines, he shall also interpret, translate, and teach faithfully the Word of God "as of the ability which God has given you"!

vi. Just as **1 Peter 4:11 (KJV)** reveals, if you do not speak, interpret, translate, and teach the Word of God as the oracles of God, then you are disqualified!

vii. Your entire Bible Interpretation and Translation, using this Theory in **1 Peter 4:11 (KJV)**, must have and satisfy this one objective: "that God in all things may be glorified through Jesus Christ,"!

viii. That Bible Interpretation and Translation objective means that, in Bible Interpretation and Translation, it is NOT the audience or the Target Audience that you must seek to please or receive their approval and acceptance, no, in Bible Interpretation and Translation, the Target Audience does NOT matter at all, because it is the Author of the Holy Bible, the LORD God Almighty, whom you must seek to please for ever and ever, and NOT the Target Audience!

ix. **1 Peter 4:11 (KJV)** If any man speak, *let him speak* as the oracles of God; if any man minister, *let him do it* as of the ability which God giveth: that God in all things may be glorified through Jesus Christ, to whom be praise and dominion for ever and ever. Amen.

The LORD Jesus Christ be with your spirit. The LORD Jesus Christ give you understanding.

Rev. Prof. PETER PRYCE,
DSEF, BA, MA, B.Soc.Sc Pol Sci, IBA, PhD

A Scribe of the Law of the God of Heaven
Prophet of the Word of God
Professor of French, Silver Spring, MD, USA
Scholar of the Institute of Theologians, USA
WWW.THEBIBLEUNIVERSITY.ORG
Accreditation Number: 07-QCTO/SDP120723172836
SAQA QUAL ID: Identification # 101997
WWW.BOOKSTORESITE.ORG
WWW.THEBIBLEUNIVERSITYCHURCH.ORG

Wednesday 22nd May 2024 @ 5:13 AM – 9:47 PM
While hearing and meditating in the Word of God at home.

CONCLUSION

In this research, we set out to discover a scientific method for intralingual Bible translation/interpretation whose scientific edge derives from the ability to verify the rendered interpretation across the entire Bible from Genesis to Revelation and replicate the understanding contained in the interpretation without any contradiction whatsoever from any part of the Bible.

We noted in the introduction that translation and interpreting overlap and are therefore one and same thing depending on what emphasis one applies to both terms.

We also explained three types of translation known as *interlingual translation*, *intralingual translation* and *intersemiotic translation* and subsequently noted that the type of Bible interpreting exemplified in this paper is intralingual translation.

We then explained the *Perfect Harmony Theory for Bible Translation and Interpreting* and provided Biblical justifications for its use. In the section titled "Ten Roadmaps to Understanding Perfect Harmony", we supplied the chronological development of thoughts that help to anchor the importance and efficacy of this Bible interpreting method while reiterating that to master the *Perfect Harmony Method for Bible Translation and Interpreting* is to successfully blend the communicative objective of translation and interpreting with thorough Bible scholarship enriched by research and study of the Word from Genesis to Revelation.

In order to see how this Bible interpreting method works, we illustrated it with the Book of Daniel and with Mark Chapter 12. We then we tested the illustration with an interpretation assessment or verification exercise, which equally provided ten lessons on how to replicate it.

With pertinent references and explanatory commentaries following Mark Chapter 12, and in order not to have it seem as a one-off attempt to explain the *Perfect Harmony Method for Bible Translation and Interpreting*, we presented a second exposé of the method with a view to increasing its threshold of credibility by examining Mark chapter 15 with its own interpretation assessment and verification exercise. In fact, we conducted four interpretation assessment or verification exercises just to prove that, indeed, the theory works!

We believe that by removing self and allowing the Bible to interpret itself, we achieve faithfulness to the source text and we ensure accuracy of Bible interpreting apart from the assurance that the interpretation is not contradicted by any other verse in the entire Bible:

Jeremiah 23:28 (KJV) The prophet that hath a dream, let him tell a dream; and he that hath my word, let him speak my word faithfully. What *is* the chaff to the wheat? Saith the LORD.

One way forward would be an extended project where the *Perfect Harmony Theory for Bible Translation and Interpreting* is used to anchor a complete Commentary of the Bible. In that case, the objective would be to answer the perennial question: what does the verse mean?

REFERENCES

1. Bible, The. (1611). King James Version (Authorized Version) (Public domain).
2. Jakobson, Roman (1971[1959]). "On Linguistic Aspects of Translation." In R. Jakobson, Roman O. (1959). *Selected Writings, II.* The Hague, Mouton, pp. 260-266.
3. Jakobson, Roman O. (1959). On Linguistic Aspects of Translation. In L. Venuti (ed), (2004), *The Translation Studies Reader.* London, New York and Canada: Routledge, pp. 113-118.
4. Pryce, Peter. (2011). Méthode de Traduction intralinguale de thèmes bibliques, paper presented to 8th Inter-University Conference on the Co-Existence of Languages in West Africa, Department of French Education, University of Education, Winneba, Ghana, Monday June 13, 2011 – Saturday June 18, 2011.
5. Pryce, Peter. (2018). *Thematic Dictionary of Matthew.* Ingram, USA.
6. Seleskovitch, Danica. (1977). « Take care of the sense and the sounds will take care of themselves or Why interpreting is not tantamount to Translating Languages. » *The Incorporated Linguist*, 16, pp. 27-33.
7. Seleskovitch, Danica. & Lederer, Marianne. (1993). *Traduire pour interpréter.* Publication de la Sorbonne, Didier Erudition, Coll. « Traductologie 1 ».
8. Seleskovitch, Danica, et Marianne Lederer. (2001). *Interpréter pour traduire, Quatrième édition.* Paris, Didier Erudition.
9. Vinay, Jean-Paul, and Jean Darbelnet. (1958). *Stylistique Comparée du Français et de l'anglais : Méthode de Traduction*, Paris : Didier, 69-70, 103, 107-108, 110, 124.
10. Vinay, Jean-Paul, and Jean Darbelnet. (1995 [1958]). *Comparative Stylistics of French and English: a Methodology for Translation.* (Ed. And translators) Juan C. Sager and M.-J. Hamel, Amsterdam: John Benjamin.

The LORD Jesus Christ be with your spirit. The LORD Jesus Christ give you understanding.

Rev. Prof. PETER PRYCE,
DSEF, BA, MA, B.Soc.Sc Pol Sci, IBA, PhD
A Scribe of the Law of the God of Heaven
Prophet of the Word of God
Professor of French, Silver Spring, MD, USA

Scholar of the Institute of Theologians, USA
WWW.THEBIBLEUNIVERSITY.ORG
Accreditation Number: 07-QCTO/SDP120723172836
SAQA QUAL ID: Identification # 101997
WWW.BOOKSTORESITE.ORG
WWW.THEBIBLEUNIVERSITYCHURCH.ORG

Wednesday 8th July 2020 @ 6:37 AM
While hearing, and meditating on the Word of God

CHAPTER 2

WHERE IS THE EVIDENCE THAT JESUS DRANK WINE AND GAVE WINE FOR HOLY COMMUNION?

AKOBEN

"War horn"

Asante philosophical symbol of Vigilance, Wariness

Question 2324

Answer:

PROVERBS 20

1. If the LORD God Almighty condemns wine as a mocker, as a deceiver, and as an inducer of lack of wisdom, or and an inducer of foolishness, then how could the same LORD God Almighty counsel you to drink wine at your Holy Communion sacrifices? Let us consider the following verses to confirm our doctrine:

    i. **Proverbs 20:1 (KJV)** Wine *is* a mocker, strong drink *is* raging: and whosoever is deceived thereby is not wise..

2. Is not this very doctrine of Holy Communion in all your churches the evidence of your own spiritual nakedness and depravity?

    i. **Leviticus 10:9 (KJV)** Do not drink wine nor strong drink, thou, nor thy sons with thee, when ye go into the tabernacle of the congregation, lest ye die: *it shall be* a statute for ever throughout your generations:

    ii. **Numbers 6:3 (KJV)** He shall separate *himself* from wine and strong drink, and shall drink no vinegar of wine, or vinegar of strong drink, neither shall he drink any liquor of grapes, nor eat moist grapes, or dried.!

    iii. **Judges 13:7 (KJV)** But he said unto me, Behold, thou shalt conceive, and bear a son; and now drink no wine nor strong drink, neither eat any unclean *thing*: for the child shall be a Nazarite to God from the womb to the day of his death.

    iv. **Jeremiah 35:6 (KJV)** But they said, We will drink no wine: for Jonadab the son of Rechab our father commanded us, saying, Ye shall drink no wine, *neither* ye, nor your sons for ever:

3. Shall the LORD God accept that which mocks God (wine) and is a deceiver as part of the LORD's sacrifice? Thou fool! Do you not know, that anything that is labeled "a Deceiver" is of Satan?

    i. **2 John 7 (KJV)** For many deceivers are entered into the world, who confess not that Jesus Christ is come in the flesh. This is a deceiver and an antichrist.

4. If wine is a deceiver, and if **Proverbs 20:1 (KJV)** is the Truth of God, then wine is surely of Satan, and you are presenting the instrument of Satan to the LORD God Almighty in your so-called Holy Communion?

    i. **Malachi 1:14 (KJV)** But cursed *be* the deceiver, which hath in his flock a male, and voweth, and sacrificeth unto the Lord a corrupt thing: for I *am* a great King, saith the LORD of hosts, and my name *is* dreadful among the heathen.

    ii. **2 John 7 (KJV)** For many deceivers are entered into the world, who confess not that Jesus Christ is come in the flesh. This is a deceiver and an antichrist.

5. Is the LORD God Almighty the author of confusion to teach you in **Proverbs 20:1 (KJV)** that wine is a mocker and a deceiver, and then the same LORD God will later teach you to drink wine and offer it in your Holy Communion?

    i. **Numbers 23:19 (KJV)** God *is* not a man, that he should lie; neither the son of man, that he should repent: hath he said, and shall he not do *it*? or hath he spoken, and shall he not make it good?

    ii. **1 Corinthians 14:33 (KJV)** For God is not *the author* of confusion, but of peace, as in all churches of the saints.

6. Now, since all you Holy Communion Pastors, Apostles, Bishops, Arch Bishops, and General Overseers claim that it was the LORD Jesus Christ who taught you to drink wine and to offer wine unto God Almighty, please show me just one verse in the

entire Holy Bible from Genesis to Revelation where the LORD Jesus Christ drank wine or used wine as part of God-worship!

 i. **Matthew 26:27 (KJV)** And he took the cup, and gave thanks, and gave *it* to them, saying, Drink ye all of it;

 ii. **Mark 14:23 (KJV)** And he took the cup, and when he had given thanks, he gave *it* to them: and they all drank of it.

 iii. **Luke 22:17 (KJV)** And he took the cup, and gave thanks, and said, Take this, and divide *it* among yourselves:

 iv. **1 Corinthians 11:25 (KJV)** After the same manner also *he took* the cup, when he had supped, saying, This cup is the new testament in my blood: this do ye, as oft as ye drink *it*, in remembrance of me.

7. If the Prophet of the LORD Jesus Christ, who was John the Baptist, obeyed the Word of God in **Leviticus 10:9 (KJV)** and therefore drank no wine, then how did his Master the LORD Jesus Christ violate the Word of God in **Leviticus 10:9 (KJV)** to start drinking wine?

 i. **Leviticus 10:9 (KJV)** Do not drink wine nor strong drink, thou, nor thy sons with thee, when ye go into the tabernacle of the congregation, lest ye die: *it shall be* a statute for ever throughout your generations:

 ii. **Luke 1:15 (KJV)** For he shall be great in the sight of the Lord, and shall drink neither wine nor strong drink; and he shall be filled with the Holy Ghost, even from his mother's womb.

 iii. **Luke 1:76 (KJV)** And thou, child, shalt be called the prophet of the Highest: for thou shalt go before the face of the Lord to prepare his ways;

 iv. **Luke 7:33 (KJV)** For John the Baptist came neither eating bread nor drinking wine; and ye say, He hath a devil.

8. This is the evidence that the LORD Jesus Christ drank no wine!

 i. **Numbers 6:3 (KJV)** He shall separate *himself* from wine and strong drink, and shall drink no vinegar of wine, or vinegar of strong drink, neither shall he drink any liquor of grapes, nor eat moist grapes, or dried.

 ii. **Mark 15:23 (KJV)** And they gave him to drink wine mingled with myrrh: but he received *it* not.

9. So, how did the Man who drank no wine teach you to drink wine and even taught you to offer wine unto the LORD God Almighty in your Holy Communion sacrifices?

10. If the LORD Jesus Christ drank wine and also taught His Disciples to drink wine and to offer wine in the Pulpit, then why is there not even a single record of it in the entire Holy Bible? Why is there no record of offering wine in the Pulpit in the entire Ministries of Jesus Christ and all the Apostles?

    i. **Isaiah 5:22 (KJV)** Woe unto *them that are* mighty to drink wine, and men of strength to mingle strong drink:

    ii. **Titus 1:7 (KJV)** For a bishop must be blameless, as the steward of God; not selfwilled, not soon angry, not given to wine, no striker, not given to filthy lucre;

    iii. **1 Timothy 3:3 (KJV)** Not given to wine, no striker, not greedy of filthy lucre; but patient, not a brawler, not covetous;

11. Shall wine be good for the spiritual sacrifice of Holy Communion and still be a curse, both at the same time unto the LORD God Almighty?

    i. **Isaiah 5:22 (KJV)** Woe unto *them that are* mighty to drink wine, and men of strength to mingle strong drink:

12. Shall the same wine that is preferred by sinners also serve as God's choice for Holy Communion in your eyes? What has the LORD God Almighty to do with the sons of belial?

    i. **Isaiah 22:13 (KJV)** And behold joy and gladness, slaying oxen, and killing sheep, eating flesh, and drinking wine: let us eat and drink; for to morrow we shall die.

    ii. **2 Corinthians 6:14 (KJV)** Be ye not unequally yoked together with unbelievers: for what fellowship hath righteousness with unrighteousness? and what communion hath light with darkness?

    iii. **2 Corinthians 6:15 (KJV)** And what concord hath Christ with Belial? or what part hath he that believeth with an infidel?

    iv. **2 Corinthians 6:16 (KJV)** And what agreement hath the temple of God with idols? for ye are the temple of the living God; as God hath said, I will dwell in them, and walk in *them*; and I will be their God, and they shall be my people.

    v. **2 Corinthians 6:17 (KJV)** Wherefore come out from among them, and be ye separate, saith the Lord, and touch not the unclean *thing*; and I will receive you,

    vi. **2 Corinthians 6:18 (KJV)** And will be a Father unto you, and ye shall be my sons and daughters, saith the Lord Almighty.

13. Shall the LORD God Almighty allow the thing (wine) that causes Men of God to err in doctrine to be used in sacrifice unto the same God?

14. If errant Men of God have also erred in doctrine through wine, shall the LORD God Almighty then allow the use of wine in order to further destroy the good Doctrine of God? Is the LORD God then in the business of destroying His own Word? God forbid!

    i. **Isaiah 28:7 (KJV)** But they also have erred through wine, and through strong drink are out of the way; the priest and the prophet have erred through strong drink, they are swallowed up of wine, they are out of the way through strong drink; they err in vision, they stumble *in* judgment.

15. If wine is the symbol of the fierceness of the wrath of God, and if wine is the symbol of the fornications of the great whore (Satan), then how did the same wine become acceptable unto the LORD God Almighty as a symbol of good worship?

16. Do Satan and the LORD God Almighty now share the same doctrines in your estimation, thou filthy ignorant Arch Bishop?

    i. **Jeremiah 25:15 (KJV)** For thus saith the LORD God of Israel unto me; Take the wine cup of this fury at my hand, and cause all the nations, to whom I send thee, to drink it.

    ii. **Revelation 14:10 (KJV)** The same shall drink of the wine of the wrath of God, which is poured out without mixture into the cup of his indignation; and he shall be tormented with fire and brimstone in the presence of the holy angels, and in the presence of the Lamb:

    iii. **Revelation 16:19 (KJV)** And the great city was divided into three parts, and the cities of the nations fell: and great Babylon came in remembrance before God, to give unto her the cup of the wine of the fierceness of his wrath.

    iv. **Revelation 14:8 (KJV)** And there followed another angel, saying, Babylon is fallen, is fallen, that great city, because she made all nations drink of the wine of the wrath of her fornication.

    v. **Revelation 17:1 (KJV)** And there came one of the seven angels which had the seven vials, and talked with me, saying unto me, Come hither; I will shew unto thee the judgment of the great whore that sitteth upon many waters:

    vi. **Revelation 17:2 (KJV)** With whom the kings of the earth have committed fornication, and the inhabitants of the earth have been made drunk with the wine of her fornication.

    vii. **Revelation 18:3 (KJV)** For all nations have drunk of the wine of the wrath of her fornication, and the kings of the earth have committed fornication with her, and the merchants of the earth are waxed rich through the abundance of her delicacies.

17. In conclusion, I ask you all again: Where is the evidence in the entire Holy Scriptures from Genesis to Revelation that the LORD Jesus Christ drank wine and gave wine for Holy Communion sacrifices!

    i. **Luke 24:32 (KJV)** And they said one to another, Did not our heart burn within us, while he talked with us by the way, and while he opened to us the scriptures?

    ii. **Acts 18:28 (KJV)** For he mightily convinced the Jews, *and that* publickly, shewing by the scriptures that Jesus was Christ.

18. If you cannot show me the evidence in the Word of God, and yet you are doing it in all your churches, and have been doing it for several generations already, then from whom did you learn this doctrine?

    i. **Matthew 15:9 (KJV)** But in vain they do worship me, teaching *for* doctrines the commandments of men.

    ii. **Mark 7:7 (KJV)** Howbeit in vain do they worship me, teaching *for* doctrines the commandments of men.

19. Do you now see how Satan is very pleased with you because you have been serving him faithfully all these years?

20. Do you also see how, by this revelation here, you are NOT qualified nor even fit to call yourself a Pastor, an Apostle, an Evangelist, a Bible Teacher, a Prophet, a Bishop, an Arch Bishop, or a General Overseer, because you are a fool, an ignorant bastard, a pervert who has been corrupting the Gospel of the LORD Jesus Christ, teaching false doctrine to help send men and women into Hell?

    i. **2 Corinthians 2:15 (KJV)** For we are unto God a sweet savour of Christ, in them that are saved, and in them that perish:

    ii. **2 Corinthians 2:16 (KJV)** To the one *we are* the savour of death unto death; and to the other the savour of life unto life. And who *is* sufficient for these things?

    iii. **2 Corinthians 2:17 (KJV)** For we are not as many, which corrupt the word of God: but as of sincerity, but as of God, in the sight of God speak we in Christ.

    iv. **2 Peter 2:12 (KJV)** But these, as natural brute beasts, made to be taken and destroyed, speak evil of the things that they understand not; and shall utterly perish in their own corruption;

    v. **2 Peter 2:13 (KJV)** And shall receive the reward of unrighteousness, *as* they that count it pleasure to riot in the day time. Spots *they are* and blemishes, sporting themselves with their own deceivings while they feast with you;

vi. **2 Peter 2:14 (KJV)** Having eyes full of adultery, and that cannot cease from sin; beguiling unstable souls: an heart they have exercised with covetous practices; cursed children:

vii. **2 Peter 2:15 (KJV)** Which have forsaken the right way, and are gone astray, following the way of Balaam *the son* of Bosor, who loved the wages of unrighteousness;

viii. **2 Peter 2:16 (KJV)** But was rebuked for his iniquity: the dumb ass speaking with man's voice forbad the madness of the prophet.

ix. **2 Peter 2:17 (KJV)** These are wells without water, clouds that are carried with a tempest; to whom the mist of darkness is reserved for ever.

x. **2 Peter 2:18 (KJV)** For when they speak great swelling *words* of vanity, they allure through the lusts of the flesh, *through much* wantonness, those that were clean escaped from them who live in error.

xi. **2 Peter 2:19 (KJV)** While they promise them liberty, they themselves are the servants of corruption: for of whom a man is overcome, of the same is he brought in bondage.

xii. **2 Peter 2:20 (KJV)** For if after they have escaped the pollutions of the world through the knowledge of the Lord and Saviour Jesus Christ, they are again entangled therein, and overcome, the latter end is worse with them than the beginning.

xiii. **2 Peter 2:21 (KJV)** For it had been better for them not to have known the way of righteousness, than, after they have known *it*, to turn from the holy commandment delivered unto them.

xiv. **2 Peter 2:22 (KJV)** But it is happened unto them according to the true proverb, The dog *is* turned to his own vomit again; and the sow that was washed to her wallowing in the mire.

21. Now, to all those of you Pastors, Apostles, Evangelists, Teachers, Bishops, Arch Bishops, and General Overseers who claim that the LORD Jesus Christ told you to drink wine and to use wine at your Holy Communion, is this then the description of your Jesus?

i. **Proverbs 23:29 (KJV)** Who hath woe? who hath sorrow? who hath contentions? who hath babbling? who hath wounds without cause? who hath redness of eyes?

    ii.   **Proverbs 23:30 (KJV)** They that tarry long at the wine; they that go to seek mixed wine.

    iii.   **Proverbs 23:31 (KJV)** Look not thou upon the wine when it is red, when it giveth his colour in the cup, *when* it moveth itself aright.

    iv.   **Proverbs 23:32 (KJV)** At the last it biteth like a serpent, and stingeth like an adder.

22. The LORD God Almighty says it plainly in **Proverbs 23:29-35 (KJV)**, that:

    i.   The wine drinker is the one who has woe (meaning curse).

    ii.   The wine drinker is the one who has sorrow.

    iii.   The wine drinker is the one who has contentions/disputations.

    iv.   The wine drinker is the one who is a babbler/speaks nonsense.

    v.   The wine drinker is the one who has wounds without cause.

    vi.   The wine drinker is the one who has redness of eyes.

    vii.   The wine drinker is the one who stays long at the wine place.

    viii.   The wine drinker is the one who mixes different types of wine.

    ix.   The wine drinker is the one whose wine bites him like a serpent.

    x.   The wine drinker is the one whose wine stings him like an adder.

    xi.   The wine drinker is the one who drinks wine and then he beholds strange women and then he begins to lust after her and allows his wicked heart to utter perverse things.

    xii.   The wine drinker is the one who fantasizes himself lying down in the midst of the sea and lying upon the top of a mast.

    xiii.   The wine drinker is the one who has become numb in his senses such that even when he is beaten, he is not aware and even after he awakes and sees the wounds of his beating from the wine, he still says: give me more wine!

23. So, tell me, are all those 13 descriptions that of your Jesus?

24. If your answer is, no, then there are ONLY two choices: either you are a liar or the LORD Jesus Christ who told you to drink wine is a liar!

25. Which one is it? You or Jesus?

26. Do you now see your shame and your curse, Dear Holy Communion fool?

27. The LORD God Almighty will judge you without mercy and it is my fervent prayer that you are never forgiven for this evil doctrine of Holy Communion that you have been peddling for Satan all these years and helping to kill innocent people with all such evil doctrines! Woe unto you!

28. Here are more evidences on the negatives of wine!

    i.   **Proverbs 31:1 (KJV)** The words of king Lemuel, the prophecy that his mother taught him.

ii. **Proverbs 31:2 (KJV)** What, my son? and what, the son of my womb? and what, the son of my vows?

iii. **Proverbs 31:3 (KJV)** Give not thy strength unto women, nor thy ways to that which destroyeth kings.

iv. **Proverbs 31:4 (KJV)** *It is* not for kings, O Lemuel, *it is* not for kings to drink wine; nor for princes strong drink:

v. **Proverbs 31:5 (KJV)** Lest they drink, and forget the law, and pervert the judgment of any of the afflicted.

vi. **Proverbs 31:6 (KJV)** Give strong drink unto him that is ready to perish, and wine unto those that be of heavy hearts.

vii. **Proverbs 31:7 (KJV)** Let him drink, and forget his poverty, and remember his misery no more.

viii. **Proverbs 31:8 (KJV)** Open thy mouth for the dumb in the cause of all such as are appointed to destruction.

29. It is because of all these negative words against wine in the Old Testament:

   i. That is why there is NO mention of wine at all in all the record of the LORD's Supper in the entire Holy Bible!

   ii. And that is also why these very words: "And he took the cup, and gave thanks, and gave *it* to them, saying, Drink ye all of it" CAN NEVER MEAN WINE:

   iii. (1) because there is no record anywhere that refers to wine!

   iv. (2) because the LORD Jesus Christ came to fulfil the Old Testament and therefore, Jesus Christ will never do contrary to the Old Testament!

   v. **Matthew 5:17 (KJV)** Think not that I am come to destroy the law, or the prophets: I am not come to destroy, but to fulfil.

   vi. and (3) because it is not possible for the Scriptures to be broken and it is equally not possible for Jesus Christ to teach contrary to the Word of God whether in the Old Testament or in the New Testament!

   vii. **John 10:35 (KJV)** If he called them gods, unto whom the word of God came, and the scripture cannot be broken;

30. Now, if **Matthew 5:17 (KJV)** is true that the LORD Jesus Christ did NOT come to destroy but to fulfil, and if it is also true in **John 10:35 (KJV)** that the Scriptures cannot be broken, then these very words: "And he took the cup, and gave thanks, and gave *it* to them, saying, Drink ye all of it" CAN NEVER MEAN WINE, because if you translate and interpret those words as referring to wine, then you have

a contradiction and then you have created an opposition between your translation and **Matthew 5:17 (KJV)** and **John 10:35 (KJV)**!

    i. **Matthew 26:26 (KJV)** And as they were eating, Jesus took bread, and blessed *it*, and brake *it*, and gave *it* to the disciples, and said, Take, eat; this is my body.

    ii. **Matthew 26:27 (KJV)** And he took the cup, and gave thanks, and gave *it* to them, saying, Drink ye all of it;

    iii. **Matthew 26:28 (KJV)** For this is my blood of the new testament, which is shed for many for the remission of sins.

    iv. **Matthew 26:29 (KJV)** But I say unto you, I will not drink henceforth of this fruit of the vine, until that day when I drink it new with you in my Father's kingdom.

31. Remember now, that once you have a contradiction and an opposition in your teaching, translation, and interpretation of the Word of God, then you DO NOT HAVE TRUTH BUT YOU HAVE PRODUCED A LIE!

    i. **Isaiah 8:20 (KJV)** To the law and to the testimony: if they speak not according to this word, *it is* because *there is* no light in them.

    ii. **Proverbs 21:30 (KJV)** *There is* no wisdom nor understanding nor counsel against the LORD.

    iii. **Matthew 22:41 (KJV)** While the Pharisees were gathered together, Jesus asked them,

    iv. **Matthew 22:42 (KJV)** Saying, What think ye of Christ? whose son is he? They say unto him, *The Son* of David.

    v. **Matthew 22:43 (KJV)** He saith unto them, How then doth David in spirit call him Lord, saying,

    vi. **Matthew 22:44 (KJV)** The LORD said unto my Lord, Sit thou on my right hand, till I make thine enemies thy footstool?

    vii. **Matthew 22:45 (KJV)** If David then call him Lord, how is he his son?

    viii. **Matthew 22:46 (KJV)** And no man was able to answer him a word, neither durst any *man* from that day forth ask him any more *questions*.

    ix. **Hebrews 7:7 (KJV)** And without all contradiction the less is blessed of the better.

32. The correct methodology of Biblical Hermeneutics prescribes that you CANNOT have any, not even one contradiction or opposition in your Exegesis (Teaching)!

33. If strong drink and wine are for sinners meant for destruction in Hell as **Proverbs 31:6-7 (KJV)** reveals, then surely, the LORD Jesus Christ DID NOT GIVE WINE

TO HIS DISCIPLES TO DRINK, because the lord Jesus Christ DID NOT come to prepare people for Hell but for Heaven!

    i. **Proverbs 31:6 (KJV)** Give strong drink unto him that is ready to perish, and wine unto those that be of heavy hearts.

    ii. **Proverbs 31:7 (KJV)** Let him drink, and forget his poverty, and remember his misery no more.

    iii. **Luke 9:56 (KJV)** For the Son of man is not come to destroy men's lives, but to save *them*. And they went to another village.

34. I have shown you the Truth! You can reject it and continue in your foolishness to drink that wine in your cursed Holy Communion services and the wrath of God is surely waiting for you!

    i. **Proverbs 31:6 (KJV)** Give strong drink unto him that is ready to perish, and wine unto those that be of heavy hearts.

35. All of you who drink wine at your cursed Holy Communion services, the LORD God Almighty says plainly that you are ready to perish, you have heavy heart, you have poverty, and you are miserable!

36. All of you who drink wine at your cursed Holy Communion services, the LORD God Almighty says plainly that "you are appointed to destruction"!

    i. **Proverbs 31:8 (KJV)** Open thy mouth for the dumb in the cause of all such as are appointed to destruction.

37. Therefore, the LORD Jesus Christ DID NOT GIVE WINE TO HIS DISCIPLES TO DRINK, and these very words: "And he took the cup, and gave thanks, and gave *it* to them, saying, Drink ye all of it" CAN NEVER MEAN WINE by any stretch of the Word of God!

38. Instead of all you false Holy Communion Pastors and Bishops drinking that cursed wine in the Pulpit, here is what the LORD God Almighty commands you to do!

    i. **Proverbs 31:8 (KJV)** Open thy mouth for the dumb in the cause of all such as are appointed to destruction.

    ii. **Proverbs 31:9 (KJV)** Open thy mouth, judge righteously, and plead the cause of the poor and needy.

39. Now, what do the words in **Proverbs 31:8-9 (KJV)** mean?

40. Here is the correct meaning:

    i. ONE – Open your mouth, not to put in that filthy wafer, bread, and cursed wine, but open your dumb mouth to produce true Bread of Life (the Word of God) for the dumb and the stupid persons who know not the Word of God and because of their ignorance and foolishness, "they are appointed to destruction in Hell"! **Proverbs 31:8 (KJV)**

ii.   **Psalm 5:5 (KJV)** The foolish shall not stand in thy sight: thou hatest all workers of iniquity.

iii. **Hosea 4:6 (KJV)** My people are destroyed for lack of knowledge: because thou hast rejected knowledge, I will also reject thee, that thou shalt be no priest to me: seeing thou hast forgotten the law of thy God, I will also forget thy children.

iv.   **John 6:32 (KJV)** Then Jesus said unto them, Verily, verily, I say unto you, Moses gave you not that bread from heaven; but my Father giveth you the true bread from heaven.

v.   **John 6:35 (KJV)** And Jesus said unto them, I am the bread of life: he that cometh to me shall never hunger; and he that believeth on me shall never thirst.

vi.   **John 6:51 (KJV)** I am the living bread which came down from heaven: if any man eat of this bread, he shall live for ever: and the bread that I will give is my flesh, which I will give for the life of the world.

vii. TWO – Open your mouth, not to put in that filthy wafer, bread, and cursed wine, but open your dumb mouth to produce true Bread of Life (the Word of God) so that the dumb and the dead in spirit can eat that true Bread of Life and live! Open your dumb mouth and judge righteously, and plead the cause of the poor and needy, so that they can become instructed to enter Heaven! **Proverbs 31:9 (KJV)**

41. When you do those two things in **Proverbs 31:8-9 (KJV)** that I have just shown you, that is when you are doing the true and correct Holy Communion and that is the same correct doctrine of teaching fools the true Word of God that the LORD Jesus Christ was giving to the Disciples in **Matthew 26:26-29 (KJV)**!

i.   **Matthew 26:26 (KJV)** And as they were eating, Jesus took bread, and blessed *it*, and brake *it*, and gave *it* to the disciples, and said, Take, eat; this is my body.

ii.   **Matthew 26:27 (KJV)** And he took the cup, and gave thanks, and gave *it* to them, saying, Drink ye all of it;

iii. **Matthew 26:28 (KJV)** For this is my blood of the new testament, which is shed for many for the remission of sins.

iv.   **Matthew 26:29 (KJV)** But I say unto you, I will not drink henceforth of this fruit of the vine, until that day when I drink it new with you in my Father's kingdom.

42. As the LORD Jesus Christ revealed that He is the true Bread of Life, therefore know now, thou foolish Pastor and Bishop, that the Bread is in the Word and the

Blood/Wine is in the Word, so, give the Word of God to the people and stop those cursed filthy wafers and wine, because that ignorant behavior will surely take you to Hell!

43. Heaven was not made for fools my Dear! Heaven was made for people who use their head to reason the Word of God!

        i. **Isaiah 1:18 (KJV)** Come now, and let us reason together, saith the LORD: though your sins be as scarlet, they shall be as white as snow; though they be red like crimson, they shall be as wool.

The LORD Jesus Christ be with your spirit. The LORD Jesus Christ give you understanding.

Rev. Prof. Peter Pryce, Ph.D.
A Scribe of the Law of the God of Heaven
Prophet of the Word of God
Thursday 30th August 2022 @ 1:10 AM – 3:03 AM
While hearing and meditating on the Word of God
Silver Spring, MD, USA
WWW.THEBIBLEUNIVERSITY.ORG
WWW.BOOKSTORESITE.ORG
WWW.THEBIBLEUNIVERSITYCHURCH.ORG

CHAPTER 3

TO DO JUSTICE AND JUDGMENT IS MORE ACCEPTABLE TO THE LORD THAN HOLY COMMUNION SACRIFICE

AKOFENA

"Sword of war"

Asante philosophical symbol of Courage, Valor

Question 2325

Answer:

1. Unto you Holy Communion and Water Baptism Pastors of today, the LORD God Almighty is speaking! Let us consider the following verses to confirm our doctrine:

      i. **Proverbs 21:3 (KJV)** To do justice and judgment *is* more acceptable to the LORD than sacrifice.

2. Since you claim that you want to worship God, since you claim that you want to please God, since you claim that you want to offer sacrifices unto God, and since there are several sacrifices that a person can offer unto the LORD God Almighty, God is hereby teaching you to compare all the sacrifices, and then choose the one that pleases God most!

3. Now, when you do the comparison, the LORD God Almighty says that God prefers for you to do justice and judgment more than for you to offer Holy Communion and Water Baptism sacrifices and oblations!

4. Please, Mr. Pastor, Apostle, Prophet, Evangelist, Teacher, Bishop, Arch Bishop, General Overseer, is that English too hard for you to comprehend?

i. "To do justice and judgment *is* more acceptable to the LORD than sacrifice." **Proverbs 21:3 (KJV)**

5. If you are too stupid, ignorant, foolish, daft, and unlearned in the Word of Truth and therefore that English is too difficult for you, well, then, is that same **Proverbs 21:3 (KJV)** not written in your own local language, so that you have no excuse at all?

6. Can you tell me why the LORD God Almighty has shown you what is good, and what doth the LORD require of thee, and yet you adamantly insist on and wickedly persist in presenting God Almighty with all these filthy oblations and man-made sacrifices called Holy Communion and Water Baptism when even the term Holy Communion does NOT exist in the entire Holy Bible?

    i. **Micah 6:6 (KJV)** Wherewith shall I come before the LORD, *and* bow myself before the high God? shall I come before him with burnt offerings, with calves of a year old?

    ii. **Micah 6:7 (KJV)** Will the LORD be pleased with thousands of rams, *or* with ten thousands of rivers of oil? shall I give my firstborn *for* my transgression, the fruit of my body *for* the sin of my soul?

    iii. **Micah 6:8 (KJV)** He hath shewed thee, O man, what *is* good; and what doth the LORD require of thee, but to do justly, and to love mercy, and to walk humbly with thy God?

7. How wicked and how dark is your heart that you should do this evil thing against God Sunday after Sunday, year after year, for more than 70 years and in your entire lifetime?

    i. **Ezekiel 16:30 (KJV)** How weak is thine heart, saith the Lord GOD, seeing thou doest all these *things*, the work of an imperious whorish woman;

8. If you Mr. Pastor, Apostle, Prophet, Evangelist, Teacher, Bishop, Arch Bishop, General Overseer, being evil and wicked, know how to present good gifts to your children, then how much more should your Heavenly Father expect you to do much much more unto God who made you!

    i. **Matthew 7:11 (KJV)** If ye then, being evil, know how to give good gifts unto your children, how much more shall your Father which is in heaven give good things to them that ask him?

    ii. **Luke 11:13 (KJV)** If ye then, being evil, know how to give good gifts unto your children: how much more shall *your* heavenly Father give the Holy Spirit to them that ask him?

9. Here is exactly what the LORD God Almighty said:

    i. **Proverbs 21:3 (KJV)** To do justice and judgment *is* more acceptable to the LORD than sacrifice.

10. Now, shall any of you Christian title holders: Mr. Pastor, Apostle, Prophet, Evangelist, Teacher, Bishop, Arch Bishop, General Overseer, being evil and wicked, have children who will tell you:
    i. My father, I like that food better than this one. I don't like this food because it is inferior and hurtful to me.

11. Then you the loving father would respond:
    i. Son, I will continue to give you the food that you do not like.
    ii. I will continue to give you the inferior food.
    iii. I will continue to give you the food that is hurtful to you.
    iv. Because I do what I think is best for my church, not what is "more acceptable to the LORD"!

12. Brother Pastor, is the above scenario not exactly what you are doing unto the LORD God Almighty and still claiming to be a Man of God?

13. Did you ever see a wicked servant entering into the pleasure of his Lord?
    i. **John 8:31 (KJV)** Then said Jesus to those Jews which believed on him, If ye continue in my word, *then* are ye my disciples indeed;
    ii. **John 15:10 (KJV)** If ye keep my commandments, ye shall abide in my love; even as I have kept my Father's commandments, and abide in his love.
    iii. **Colossians 1:23 (KJV)** If ye continue in the faith grounded and settled, and *be* not moved away from the hope of the gospel, which ye have heard, *and* which was preached to every creature which is under heaven; whereof I Paul am made a minister;
    iv. **1 John 2:24 (KJV)** Let that therefore abide in you, which ye have heard from the beginning. If that which ye have heard from the beginning shall remain in you, ye also shall continue in the Son, and in the Father.

14. Now what is Justice and what is Judgment?
    i. **Proverbs 21:3 (KJV)** To do justice and judgment *is* more acceptable to the LORD than sacrifice.

15. Justice is the Word of God and Judgment is the Word of God! The Law of God, the Word of God, the Commandments of God, that you teach your children, family, and congregation in order for them to become Godly and live in Truth and Righteousness, that is Justice and that is Judgment!
    i. **Genesis 18:19 (KJV)** For I know him, that he will command his children and his household after him, and they shall keep the way of the LORD, to do justice and judgment; that the LORD may bring upon Abraham that which he hath spoken of him.

ii. **Deuteronomy 33:21 (KJV)** And he provided the first part for himself, because there, *in* a portion of the lawgiver, *was he* seated; and he came with the heads of the people, he executed the justice of the LORD, and his judgments with Israel.

iii. **2 Samuel 8:15 (KJV)** And David reigned over all Israel; and David executed judgment and justice unto all his people.

iv. **1 Kings 10:9 (KJV)** Blessed be the LORD thy God, which delighted in thee, to set thee on the throne of Israel: because the LORD loved Israel for ever, therefore made he thee king, to do judgment and justice.

v. **1 Chronicles 18:14 (KJV)** So David reigned over all Israel, and executed judgment and justice among all his people.

vi. **2 Chronicles 9:8 (KJV)** Blessed be the LORD thy God, which delighted in thee to set thee on his throne, *to be* king for the LORD thy God: because thy God loved Israel, to establish them for ever, therefore made he thee king over them, to do judgment and justice.

vii. **Job 8:3 (KJV)** Doth God pervert judgment? or doth the Almighty pervert justice?

16. Now, how do I do, or execute, or perform, Justice and Judgment as **Proverbs 21:3 (KJV)** requires?

17. Here is how to do Justice and Judgment!

i. **Psalm 82:3 (KJV)** Defend the poor and fatherless: do justice to the afflicted and needy.

ii. **Psalm 119:121 (KJV)** AIN. I have done judgment and justice: leave me not to mine oppressors.

18. Now, how do I acquire Justice and Judgment as **Proverbs 21:3 (KJV)** requires?

19. Here is how to acquire Justice and Judgment! By means of instruction in the Word of God, you will acquire Justice and Judgment!

i. **Proverbs 1:3 (KJV)** To receive the instruction of wisdom, justice, and judgment, and equity;

20. How do I know when Justice and Judgment are being violated?

21. Anytime that you see the poor and needy person being oppressed, that is Justice and Judgment being violated!

22. Anytime that you see the Word of God being violated and contravened, such as during the filthy Holy Communion and Water Baptism that you impudently offer to God Almighty, something that is contrary to the Word of God, that is Justice and Judgment being violated!

    i. **Ecclesiastes 5:8 (KJV)** If thou seest the oppression of the poor, and violent perverting of judgment and justice in a province, marvel not at the matter: for *he that is* higher than the highest regardeth; and *there be* higher than they.

23. The LORD God Almighty says that, in the Time of Salvation, you should do ONLY is Justice and Judgment and NOT filthy sacrifices such as Holy Communion and Water Baptism!

    i. **Isaiah 56:1 (KJV)** Thus saith the LORD, Keep ye judgment, and do justice: for my salvation *is* near to come, and my righteousness to be revealed.

24. I ask you, therefore, is it the Time of Salvation for you, has the LORD of Salvation Yeshua the Christ already come according to your understanding,?

    i. **Luke 19:9 (KJV)** And Jesus said unto him, This day is salvation come to this house, forsomuch as he also is a son of Abraham.

    ii. **2 Corinthians 6:2 (KJV)** (For he saith, I have heard thee in a time accepted, and in the day of salvation have I succoured thee: behold, now *is* the accepted time; behold, now *is* the day of salvation.)

    iii. **Revelation 12:10 (KJV)** And I heard a loud voice saying in heaven, Now is come salvation, and strength, and the kingdom of our God, and the power of his Christ: for the accuser of our brethren is cast down, which accused them before our God day and night.

25. If your answer is, yes, then why are you still offering filthy sacrifices of Holy Communion and Water Baptism in the Time of Salvation?

26. In other words, in the Time of Salvation, the LORD God Almighty is saying in **Isaiah 56:1 (KJV)** that, in the Days of the Salvation of the LORD Yeshua the Christ, do ONLY Justice and Judgment, and Justice and Judgment are the Word of God!

27. Therefore, when the LORD Jesus Christ commanded to "DO THIS" as often as ye would in remembrance of Me, He was effectively telling you ignorant Bishop Fools to do the Justice and Judgment that He gave with the Cup and Bread as He sat down with His Disciples and spoke to them all evening, which Cup and Bread are useless, material, perishable things that will NOT be acceptable in Heaven!

    i. **Luke 22:19 (KJV)** And he took bread, and gave thanks, and brake *it*, and gave unto them, saying, This is my body which is given for you: this do in remembrance of me.

    ii. **1 Corinthians 11:24 (KJV)** And when he had given thanks, he brake *it*, and said, Take, eat: this is my body, which is broken for you: this do in remembrance of me.

iii. **1 Corinthians 11:25 (KJV)** After the same manner also *he took* the cup, when he had supped, saying, This cup is the new testament in my blood: this do ye, as oft as ye drink *it*, in remembrance of me.

28. In other words, the true Bread that the LORD Jesus Christ gave to the Disciples at the LORD's Supper were the words of Salvation that He gave to them, and NOT the useless, material, perishable Cup and Bread!

   i. **John 6:32 (KJV)** Then Jesus said unto them, Verily, verily, I say unto you, Moses gave you not that bread from heaven; but my Father giveth you the true bread from heaven.

   ii. **John 6:35 (KJV)** And Jesus said unto them, I am the bread of life: he that cometh to me shall never hunger; and he that believeth on me shall never thirst.

   iii. **John 6:51 (KJV)** I am the living bread which came down from heaven: if any man eat of this bread, he shall live for ever: and the bread that I will give is my flesh, which I will give for the life of the world.

   iv. **John 6:63 (KJV)** It is the spirit that quickeneth; the flesh profiteth nothing: the words that I speak unto you, *they* are spirit, and *they* are life.

29. Specifically, therefore, here is the True Bread that the LORD Yeshua the Christ gave them at the LORD's Supper! This is how you calculate the True Bread!

   i. ONE – Jesus Christ revealed that all physical bread in the form and likeness of the bread of Moses is NOT the True bread! **John 6:32 (KJV)**

   ii. TWO – Jesus Christ revealed that "I am the bread of life" **John 6:35 (KJV)**

   iii. THREE – Jesus Christ revealed that "I am the living bread which came down from heaven" **John 6:51 (KJV)**

   iv. FOUR – Jesus Christ revealed that "the flesh profiteth nothing" meaning that anything and everything that you use in church sacrifice such as Holy Communion and Water Baptism sacrifices, since they are "of the flesh", then, as Jesus said: "they profit nothing", meaning that they are useless, material, perishable things that MUST NOT BE USED IN GOD WORSHIP!

   v. FIVE – Since the LORD Jesus Christ gave to the Disciples two sets of things at the LORD's Supper (physical bread, physical cup, AND the Word of God), and now you know by the spiritual calculation that one of them has been eliminated, being the physical bread and physical cup because they are under and part of "the flesh profiteth nothing", that leaves us with only one item left, which item is: the Word of God!

vi. SIX – Therefore, when the LORD Yeshua the Christ said: "this do in remembrance of me", and you know that one of the two items has been eliminated and we have ONLY one left, then, surely, "this do in remembrance of me" refers to the Word of God!

vii. SEVEN – Now, you tell me: Is there anything in Heaven and in the Earth that best reminds you of the LORD Yeshua the Christ more than the Word of God?

30. Do you now see why you are a fool, dear Brother?

31. Do you now understand why there is a place waiting for you and with your name boldly marked on it in Hell?

32. Do you now see and understand how you have been serving Satan all these years, teaching evil doctrines of men on Water Baptism and Holy Communion?

33. I pray that the LORD Jesus Christ never forgive you for all the souls that you have destroyed by teaching them evil doctrines of Satan!

34. Woe unto you ignorant and foolish Pastor, Apostle, Prophet, Evangelist, Teacher, Bishop, Arch Bishop, and General Overseer!

35. Let me take you to another place in the Holy Bible and show you again how very stupid you are, my Dear Brother and Sister!

   i. **Jeremiah 4:22 (KJV)** For my people *is* foolish, they have not known me; they *are* sottish children, and they have none understanding: they *are* wise to do evil, but to do good they have no knowledge.

36. If oil and wine were good items for God-worship, then why would the LORD God put you in the same basket as the one whose only objective is to seek pleasure?

   i. **Proverbs 21:17 (KJV)** He that loveth pleasure *shall be* a poor man: he that loveth wine and oil shall not be rich.

37. Therefore, in **Proverbs 21:17 (KJV)**, you have a joker and a serious person!

38. Then, you have a comedian and a diligent person!

39. Then, you have hedonist and a circumspect person!

40. Now, the LORD God Almighty says that all the three person revealed in **Proverbs 21:17 (KJV)** will become poor!

41. Then, here is the shock in **Proverbs 21:17 (KJV)**!

42. The LORD God Almighty says that "he that loveth wine and oil shall not be rich", but shall surely be poor!

43. Here now is my question to you, ye simple minded and poor wine-loving Holy Communion ignorant and foolish Pastors, Apostle, Prophets, Evangelists, Teachers,

Bishops, Arch Bishops, and General Overseers, why would the LORD God Almighty command you to do a sacrifice that the LORD God has already decreed that it will make you poor?

44. I know that you are a transgressor from the womb and you are already lying to yourself even before you open your lying mouth to explain your filthy Holy Communion and Water Baptism!

> i. **Isaiah 48:8 (KJV)** Yea, thou heardest not; yea, thou knewest not; yea, from that time *that* thine ear was not opened: for I knew that thou wouldest deal very treacherously, and wast called a transgressor from the womb.

45. Here is the Truth, very clear in **Proverbs 21:17 (KJV)**, and you have NOTHING to say or to explain!

46. All of you fools doing Holy Communion in all your churches, the LORD God Almighty says that you are jokers, you are comedians, and you are hedonists!

47. Not only that, because the LORD God Almighty also says in the same **Proverbs 21:17 (KJV)** that, because you love the wine in your dirty Holy Communion (if you did not love it, then you would not be offering it to God), that "he/you that loveth wine and oil shall not be rich", but shall surely be poor!

48. The summary of the revelation in **Proverbs 21:17 (KJV)** is this:

> i. Because you love the wine in your dirty Holy Communion:
> ii. You are jokers
> iii. You are comedians
> iv. You are hedonists, and
> v. You are poor people!

49. Please, I hope that you are not too stupid to open your mouth to dispute and say that: "well, I am not poor but a very rich man and I have properties and millions of money"!

50. O, ye foolish and corrupt idiot of a Bishop, the word "poor" means "destitute of the Truth of the knowledge of God", it does NOT mean what you think, thou filthy fool who is challenging God!

> i. **1 Timothy 6:5 (KJV)** Perverse disputings of men of corrupt minds, and destitute of the truth, supposing that gain is godliness: from such withdraw thyself.

51. So, here you are, that is the Truth of God staring you in the face in **Proverbs 21:17 (KJV)**!

52. So, are you going to humble your proud and foolish self, learn the Truth of God, and stop this filthy wine and bread Holy Communion in all your dwellings and filthy churches?

53. Or, are you going to continue to serve Satan?

54. Choose one!

55. I ask you again, that if oil and wine were good items for God-worship and sacrifices in Holy Communion, then why would the LORD God in **Proverbs 21:17 (KJV)** say that if you use wine because you love to use it, then

    i. You are jokers
    ii. You are comedians
    iii. You are hedonists, and
    iv. You are poor people!

56. Shall the LORD God command you to do something that the same LORD God will use it to condemn you?

57. Did the LORD Jesus Christ ever teach you that obedience to the Word of God brings a reward of sin and condemnation as jokers, comedians, hedonists, and poverty?

58. Is your God such an evil God that after commanding you to love and use wine in Holy Communion, then that same God is counting your sins for using wine, sins as jokers, sins as comedians, sins as hedonists, and sins as poor people?

59. Is that the God that you serve?

60. No wonder that your god is called Satan and lives in Hell!

61. Did the LORD Jesus Christ drink wine? NO! Anyone who drinks wine has forgotten the Law of God!

    i. **Proverbs 23:20 (KJV)** Be not among winebibbers; among riotous eaters of flesh:
    ii. **Matthew 11:19 (KJV)** The Son of man came eating and drinking, and they say, Behold a man gluttonous, and a winebibber, a friend of publicans and sinners. But wisdom is justified of her children.
    iii. **Luke 7:34 (KJV)** The Son of man is come eating and drinking; and ye say, Behold a gluttonous man, and a winebibber, a friend of publicans and sinners!
    iv. **Leviticus 10:9 (KJV)** Do not drink wine nor strong drink, thou, nor thy sons with thee, when ye go into the tabernacle of the congregation, lest ye die: *it shall be* a statute for ever throughout your generations:
    v. **Isaiah 24:9 (KJV)** They shall not drink wine with a song; strong drink shall be bitter to them that drink it.
    vi. **Proverbs 31:3 (KJV)** Give not thy strength unto women, nor thy ways to that which destroyeth kings.

vii. **Proverbs 31:4 (KJV)** *It is* not for kings, O Lemuel, *it is* not for kings to drink wine; nor for princes strong drink:

viii. **Proverbs 31:5 (KJV)** Lest they drink, and forget the law, and pervert the judgment of any of the afflicted.

62. Now, since you claim that it was the LOD Jesus Christ who commanded you to drink wine at Holy Communion, proving that you are a liar destined for Hell because there is no record anywhere that the LORD Jesus Christ drank wine, and since you also know by **Proverbs 31:3-5 (KJV)** that anyone who drinks wine has forgotten the Law of God, then, is your doctrine of Holy Communion testifying that your Jesus Christ is a Perverter of the Law and a Priest of God who did forget the Law of God?

   i. **John 15:10 (KJV)** If ye keep my commandments, ye shall abide in my love; even as I have kept my Father's commandments, and abide in his love.

   ii. **John 17:8 (KJV)** For I have given unto them the words which thou gavest me; and they have received *them*, and have known surely that I came out from thee, and they have believed that thou didst send me.

63. Would the LORD Jesus Christ give you wine to drink when the Word of God clearly forbids it?

   i. **Leviticus 10:9 (KJV)** Do not drink wine nor strong drink, thou, nor thy sons with thee, when ye go into the tabernacle of the congregation, lest ye die: *it shall be* a statute for ever throughout your generations:

   ii. **Mark 15:23 (KJV)** And they gave him to drink wine mingled with myrrh: but he received *it* not.

The LORD Jesus Christ be with your spirit. The LORD Jesus Christ give you understanding.

Rev. Prof. Peter Pryce, Ph.D.
A Scribe of the Law of the God of Heaven
Prophet of the Word of God
Monday 5th September 2022 @ 10:33 AM – 2:01 PM
While hearing and meditating on the Word of God
Silver Spring, MD, USA
WWW.THEBIBLEUNIVERSITY.ORG
WWW.BOOKSTORESITE.ORG
WWW.THEBIBLEUNIVERSITYCHURCH.ORG

CHAPTER 4

THE ORIGIN OF HOLY COMMUNION BREAD

AKOMA

"The heart"

Asante philosophical symbol of Patience, Love, Goodwill, Tolerance, Faithfulness, Fondness, Endurance, Consistency

Question 2385

34. Have you heard these words before: "Take these things hence"?

35. In this Bible Study, we examine once again the subject of Holy Communion and we desire to know whether the origin of the Holy Communion bread has any spiritual significance or impact on the whole exercise of Holy Communion?

36. In other words, is there any reason why the LORD Jesus Christ Himself offers the Holy Communion Bread?

37. Can someone else offer it? Who?

38. Will it have the same spiritual importance and impact if someone else offers the Holy Communion Bread instead of the LORD Jesus Christ?

39. What conditions should be met before a Man of God is qualified to offer Holy Communion?

40. All those are some of the pertinent questions that we seek to examine in this Bible Study in the Light of the Word of God!

41. There is a revelation on Holy Communion in **John 6:1-14 (KJV)** that no other Man of God, Pastor, or Bishop has seen hitherto!

    i. **John 6:1 (KJV)** After these things Jesus went over the sea of Galilee, which is *the sea* of Tiberias.

    ii. **John 6:2 (KJV)** And a great multitude followed him, because they saw his miracles which he did on them that were diseased.

    iii. **John 6:3 (KJV)** And Jesus went up into a mountain, and there he sat with his disciples.

    iv. **John 6:4 (KJV)** And the passover, a feast of the Jews, was nigh.

    v. **John 6:5 (KJV)** When Jesus then lifted up *his* eyes, and saw a great company come unto him, he saith unto Philip, Whence shall we buy bread, that these may eat?

    vi. **John 6:6 (KJV)** And this he said to prove him: for he himself knew what he would do.

    vii. **John 6:7 (KJV)** Philip answered him, Two hundred pennyworth of bread is not sufficient for them, that every one of them may take a little.

    viii. **John 6:8 (KJV)** One of his disciples, Andrew, Simon Peter's brother, saith unto him,

    ix. **John 6:9 (KJV)** There is a lad here, which hath five barley loaves, and two small fishes: but what are they among so many?

    x. **John 6:10 (KJV)** And Jesus said, Make the men sit down. Now there was much grass in the place. So the men sat down, in number about five thousand.

    xi. **John 6:11 (KJV)** And Jesus took the loaves; and when he had given thanks, he distributed to the disciples, and the disciples to them that were set down; and likewise of the fishes as much as they would.

    xii. **John 6:12 (KJV)** When they were filled, he said unto his disciples, Gather up the fragments that remain, that nothing be lost.

    xiii. **John 6:13 (KJV)** Therefore they gathered *them* together, and filled twelve baskets with the fragments of the five barley loaves, which remained over and above unto them that had eaten.

    xiv. **John 6:14 (KJV)** Then those men, when they had seen the miracle that Jesus did, said, This is of a truth that prophet that should come into the world.

42. The reason why the Men of God, the Pastors, the Bishops, and all the Church Leaders have NOT seen any Doctrine of Holy Communion in **John 6:1-14 (KJV)** is that all those verses do NOT have these Holy Communion command words: "this

do in remembrance of me" hence, they have neglected those verses, and yet, the real Holy Communion Doctrine is there!

    i. **Luke 22:19 (KJV)** And he took bread, and gave thanks, and brake *it*, and gave unto them, saying, This is my body which is given for you: this do in remembrance of me.

    ii. **1 Corinthians 11:24 (KJV)** And when he had given thanks, he brake *it*, and said, Take, eat: this is my body, which is broken for you: this do in remembrance of me.

    iii. **1 Corinthians 11:25 (KJV)** After the same manner also *he took* the cup, when he had supped, saying, This cup is the new testament in my blood: this do ye, as oft as ye drink *it*, in remembrance of me.

43. Here is the location of the church!

    i. **John 6:1 (KJV)** After these things Jesus went over the sea of Galilee, which is *the sea* of Tiberias.

44. Here is the church congregation!

    i. **John 6:2 (KJV)** And a great multitude followed him, because they saw his miracles which he did on them that were diseased.

45. Here is the Man of God!

    i. **John 6:3 (KJV)** And Jesus went up into a mountain, and there he sat with his disciples.

46. Here is the church offering called Holy Communion!

    i. **John 6:4 (KJV)** And the passover, a feast of the Jews, was nigh.

47. Here is when the church is looking for bread in order to offer the Holy Communion!

    i. **John 6:5 (KJV)** When Jesus then lifted up *his* eyes, and saw a great company come unto him, he saith unto Philip, Whence shall we buy bread, that these may eat?

48. Here in **John 6:6 (KJV)** is the evidence that you have to engage in Bible Q and A constantly, in order to know which Men of God are far removed from the Kingdom of Heaven and which ones are still connected to Heaven, because "t of the abundance of the heart the mouth speaketh" and also because "Ye shall know them by their fruits"!

    i. **John 6:6 (KJV)** And this he said to prove him: for he himself knew what he would do.

    ii. **Matthew 12:34 (KJV)** O generation of vipers, how can ye, being evil, speak good things? for out of the abundance of the heart the mouth speaketh.

    iii. **Luke 6:45 (KJV)** A good man out of the good treasure of his heart bringeth forth that which is good; and an evil man out of the evil treasure of his heart bringeth forth that which is evil: for of the abundance of the heart his mouth speaketh.

    iv. **Matthew 7:16 (KJV)** Ye shall know them by their fruits. Do men gather grapes of thorns, or figs of thistles?

    v. **Matthew 7:20 (KJV)** Wherefore by their fruits ye shall know them.

49. Here is Man of God Philip giving Christian counsel to go and procure Holy Communion Bread and oblations from the open market, from the superstore, from the supermarket, from the Bible Shop, from the Clergy Store, from the man-made factory, and from the industry-produced store of different varieties and shapes of Holy Communion wafers, bread, and wine!

    i. **John 6:7 (KJV)** Philip answered him, Two hundred pennyworth of bread is not sufficient for them, that every one of them may take a little.

50. Take note very carefully, that Philip is proposing the use of money to buy what we need for the work of God! Now, check the real meaning and implications of Philip's proposal that was contrary to the Word of God in **Leviticus 22:25 (KJV)**! Furthermore, as you can see in **Acts 8:20 (KJV)**, there is a curse when you use money to buy what you think you need for the work of God! Finally, Philip's proposal is also contrary to this Word of God: "freely ye have received" in **Matthew 10:8 (KJV)**!

    i. **Leviticus 22:25 (KJV)** Neither from a stranger's hand shall ye offer the bread of your God of any of these; because their corruption *is* in them, *and* blemishes *be* in them: they shall not be accepted for you.

    ii. **Deuteronomy 23:18 (KJV)** Thou shalt not bring the hire of a whore, or the price of a dog, into the house of the LORD thy God for any vow: for even both these *are* abomination unto the LORD thy God.

    iii. **Deuteronomy 17:1 (KJV)** Thou shalt not sacrifice unto the LORD thy God *any* bullock, or sheep, wherein is blemish, *or* any evilfavouredness: for that *is* an abomination unto the LORD thy God.

    iv. **Matthew 10:8 (KJV)** Heal the sick, cleanse the lepers, raise the dead, cast out devils: freely ye have received, freely give.

    v. **Acts 8:20 (KJV)** But Peter said unto him, Thy money perish with thee, because thou hast thought that the gift of God may be purchased with money.

51. Here is the second Man of God, Andrew, looking for Holy Communion Bread from an impossible source, and he confirms one Truth: It is impossible for the Man of God, humans, to supply the Passover Supper/Holy Communion Bread! This Truth

that Andrew said is the opposite of what all the Holy Communion Pastors and Bishops are doing today in almost all their corrupt churches, because unlike Andrew, they do NOT acknowledge the Truth that they CANNOT and SHOULD NOT attempt to procure, produce, and buy Passover Supper/Holy Communion Bread by themselves!

    i. **John 6:8 (KJV)** One of his disciples, Andrew, Simon Peter's brother, saith unto him,

    ii. **John 6:9 (KJV)** There is a lad here, which hath five barley loaves, and two small fishes: but what are they among so many?

52. Behold, the Truth that Man of God Andrew spoke, it comes from **Zephaniah 1:7 (KJV)** where the LORD God plainly said: "Hold thy peace at the presence of the Lord GOD" because "in the Day of the LORD, the LORD Himself hath prepared HIS Sacrifice/Passover Supper/Holy Communion Bread"!

    i. **Zephaniah 1:7 (KJV)** Hold thy peace at the presence of the Lord GOD: for the day of the LORD *is* at hand: for the LORD hath prepared a sacrifice, he hath bid his guests.

53. Now, after all the other unclean sources were eliminated, see who gives the Sacrifice/Passover Supper/Holy Communion Bread: IT IS THE LORD HIMSELF!

    i. **John 6:10 (KJV)** And Jesus said, Make the men sit down. Now there was much grass in the place. So the men sat down, in number about five thousand.

    ii. **John 6:11 (KJV)** And Jesus took the loaves; and when he had given thanks, he distributed to the disciples, and the disciples to them that were set down; and likewise of the fishes as much as they would.

    iii. **John 6:12 (KJV)** When they were filled, he said unto his disciples, Gather up the fragments that remain, that nothing be lost.

    iv. **John 6:13 (KJV)** Therefore they gathered *them* together, and filled twelve baskets with the fragments of the five barley loaves, which remained over and above unto them that had eaten.

54. Yes, Brother, THE LORD HIMSELF provides/gives the Sacrifice/Passover Supper/Holy Communion Bread, and that is the Truth that all the Holy Communion Pastors and Bishops today have missed, misunderstood, not perceived, and passed over, because they do NOT have the Holy Spirit! Here now is the evidence and the confirmation of what I am showing you!

    i. **Luke 12:37 (KJV)** Blessed *are* those servants, whom the lord when he cometh shall find watching: verily I say unto you, that he shall gird himself, and make them to sit down to meat, and will come forth and serve them.

ii. **Luke 22:27 (KJV)** For whether *is* greater, he that sitteth at meat, or he that serveth? *is* not he that sitteth at meat? but I am among you as he that serveth.

55. So, now how do we get this Sacrifice/Passover Supper/Holy Communion Bread every Sunday? Thou fool! You have it already! It is in your mouth already! It is the Word of God! The Word of God is the true Sacrifice/Passover Supper/Holy Communion Bread!

i. **Deuteronomy 30:11 (KJV)** For this commandment which I command thee this day, it *is* not hidden from thee, neither *is* it far off.

ii. **Deuteronomy 30:12 (KJV)** It *is* not in heaven, that thou shouldest say, Who shall go up for us to heaven, and bring it unto us, that we may hear it, and do it?

iii. **Deuteronomy 30:13 (KJV)** Neither *is* it beyond the sea, that thou shouldest say, Who shall go over the sea for us, and bring it unto us, that we may hear it, and do it?

iv. **Deuteronomy 30:14 (KJV)** But the word *is* very nigh unto thee, in thy mouth, and in thy heart, that thou mayest do it.

v. **Luke 17:20 (KJV)** And when he was demanded of the Pharisees, when the kingdom of God should come, he answered them and said, The kingdom of God cometh not with observation:

vi. **Luke 17:21 (KJV)** Neither shall they say, Lo here! or, lo there! for, behold, the kingdom of God is within you.

56. Here is the evidence that the Word of God is the true Sacrifice/Passover Supper/Holy Communion Bread! All things, including the Sacrifice/Passover Supper/Holy Communion Bread, "were made by him; and without him was not anything made that was made"!

i. **John 1:1 (KJV)** In the beginning was the Word, and the Word was with God, and the Word was God.

ii. **John 1:3 (KJV)** All things were made by him; and without him was not any thing made that was made.

iii. **John 6:32 (KJV)** Then Jesus said unto them, Verily, verily, I say unto you, Moses gave you not that bread from heaven; but my Father giveth you the true bread from heaven.

iv. **John 6:35 (KJV)** And Jesus said unto them, I am the bread of life: he that cometh to me shall never hunger; and he that believeth on me shall never thirst.

v. **John 6:51 (KJV)** I am the living bread which came down from heaven: if any man eat of this bread, he shall live for ever: and the bread that I will give is my flesh, which I will give for the life of the world.

57. Here is another evidence of the LORD Himself giving the Sacrifice/Passover Supper/Holy Communion Bread!

    i. **Luke 9:16 (KJV)** Then he took the five loaves and the two fishes, and looking up to heaven, he blessed them, and brake, and gave to the disciples to set before the multitude.

58. Here is another evidence of the LORD Himself giving the Sacrifice/Passover Supper/Holy Communion Bread!

    i. **Luke 22:19 (KJV)** And he took bread, and gave thanks, and brake *it*, and gave unto them, saying, This is my body which is given for you: this do in remembrance of me.

59. Here is another evidence of the LORD Himself giving the Sacrifice/Passover Supper/Holy Communion Bread!

    i. **Luke 24:30 (KJV)** And it came to pass, as he sat at meat with them, he took bread, and blessed *it*, and brake, and gave to them.

    ii. **Luke 24:31 (KJV)** And their eyes were opened, and they knew him; and he vanished out of their sight.

60. Here is the final evidence of the LORD Himself giving the Sacrifice/Passover Supper/Holy Communion Bread!

    i. **John 21:10 (KJV)** Jesus saith unto them, Bring of the fish which ye have now caught.

    ii. **John 21:11 (KJV)** Simon Peter went up, and drew the net to land full of great fishes, an hundred and fifty and three: and for all there were so many, yet was not the net broken.

    iii. **John 21:12 (KJV)** Jesus saith unto them, Come *and* dine. And none of the disciples durst ask him, Who art thou? knowing that it was the Lord.

    iv. **John 21:13 (KJV)** Jesus then cometh, and taketh bread, and giveth them, and fish likewise.

    v. **John 21:14 (KJV)** This is now the third time that Jesus shewed himself to his disciples, after that he was risen from the dead.

61. Do you know why the final evidence of the LORD Himself giving the Sacrifice/Passover Supper/Holy Communion Bread in **Luke 24:30-31 (KJV)** and in **John 21:10-14 (KJV)** is exclusively different and very important, compared to all the other previous evidences?

62. The spiritual revelation from the Holy Spirit to me is that the LORD Jesus Christ is showing you that, even after HIS Death, HE is still the ONLY ONE to continue giving the Sacrifice/Passover Supper/Holy Communion Bread!

    i. **Hebrews 9:13 (KJV)** For if the blood of bulls and of goats, and the ashes of an heifer sprinkling the unclean, sanctifieth to the purifying of the flesh:

    ii. **Hebrews 9:14 (KJV)** How much more shall the blood of Christ, who through the eternal Spirit offered himself without spot to God, purge your conscience from dead works to serve the living God?

    iii. **Hebrews 9:23 (KJV)** *It was* therefore necessary that the patterns of things in the heavens should be purified with these; but the heavenly things themselves with better sacrifices than these.

63. Thou Holy Communion Pastor and Bishop, does not your hypocrisy and shallow spiritual ignorance and truth-bankruptcy stink continually in your nostrils each time when you pray and you hypocritically say: "Our Father which art in heaven, Give us this day our daily bread", and, then, after you have prayed this prayer, you turn round to go and buy bread from the store to do your filthy Holy Communion!

    i. **Matthew 6:9 (KJV)** After this manner therefore pray ye: Our Father which art in heaven, Hallowed be thy name.

    ii. **Matthew 6:10 (KJV)** Thy kingdom come. Thy will be done in earth, as *it is* in heaven.

    iii. **Matthew 6:11 (KJV)** Give us this day our daily bread.

    iv. **Luke 11:2 (KJV)** And he said unto them, When ye pray, say, Our Father which art in heaven, Hallowed be thy name. Thy kingdom come. Thy will be done, as in heaven, so in earth.

    v. **Luke 11:3 (KJV)** Give us day by day our daily bread.

64. If that is so, then, why don't you just pray to the store in the first place so that all your words and actions would be consistent and not a lie?

65. But you pray to God for bread in your stinking hypocrisy, and then you turn to the store to give you bread to serve God! Thou idiot of a Bishop!

66. How can you be that very stupid, Bishop, having no reasoning at all?

67. How can the same LORD Jesus Christ who trashed and cast out all the food items and money that were used for sacrifices, offerings, and Holy Communion, and that were even brought, approved, sold, and blessed by Priests and Chief Priests, how can this same LORD Jesus Christ, after doing the trashing and destruction and casting all food items out of the church, now turn back and approve for you to go across the road to buy the same food items that HE had just cast out, and that have now been repackaged, and allowed you to bring the same trashed food items unto the altar to

offer them as Sacrifice/Passover Supper/Holy Communion Bread unto God Almighty? Is this your Jesus Christ doing this thing?

    i. **John 2:13 (KJV)** And the Jews' passover was at hand, and Jesus went up to Jerusalem,

    ii. **John 2:14 (KJV)** And found in the temple those that sold oxen and sheep and doves, and the changers of money sitting:

    iii. **John 2:15 (KJV)** And when he had made a scourge of small cords, he drove them all out of the temple, and the sheep, and the oxen; and poured out the changers' money, and overthrew the tables;

    iv. **John 2:16 (KJV)** And said unto them that sold doves, Take these things hence; make not my Father's house an house of merchandise.

    v. **John 2:17 (KJV)** And his disciples remembered that it was written, The zeal of thine house hath eaten me up.

68. See, it is written very plainly in **John 2:13-17 (KJV)**, that the LORD Jesus Christ "found in the temple those that sold oxen and sheep and doves, and the changers of money", all are things that were used for Sacrifice/Passover Supper/Holy Communion!

69. Now, look at what the LORD Jesus Christ did, specifically!

    i. **John 2:15 (KJV)** And when he had made a scourge of small cords, he drove them all out of the temple, and the sheep, and the oxen; and poured out the changers' money, and overthrew the tables;

70. Brother, do you see that what Jesus Christ threw out are Holy Communion things?

71. Now, look at what the LORD Jesus Christ told the Priests and Chief Priests, specifically!

    i. **John 2:16 (KJV)** And said unto them that sold doves, Take these things hence; make not my Father's house an house of merchandise.

72. Brother, do you understand the Word of God at all, that: "Take these things hence" means: "CEASE FROM DOING THIS THING"?

73. So, now if the LORD Jesus Christ commanded you to stop using all these food items in God-worship, how then do you preach that it was the same LORD Jesus Christ who told you to offer the same forbidden food items in your God-worship of Holy Communion?

74. So, is it your Jesus Christ who is a liar, or, is it you yourself who is the liar?

    i. **John 8:43 (KJV)** Why do ye not understand my speech? *even* because ye cannot hear my word.

    ii. **John 8:44 (KJV)** Ye are of *your* father the devil, and the lusts of your father ye will do. He was a murderer from the beginning, and abode not in the truth, because there is no truth in him. When he speaketh a lie, he speaketh of his own: for he is a liar, and the father of it.

    iii. **John 8:45 (KJV)** And because I tell *you* the truth, ye believe me not.

75. When you are educated in the University, when you claim to know how to reason, when you claim to be a Doctor, when you claim to be a Bishop, when you claim to be a Pastor who has headed a congregation in a church for 50 years, and then you go and buy these filthy Holy Communion wafers, bread, and wine, serve them on some filthy altar, wrap them in some filthy white cloth, and offer them to your congregation and lie to them that this is what the LORD Jesus Christ commanded to do, when you do all these things while knowing very well, or, while being very stupidly ignorant of the definition of "meat/food" that the LORD Jesus Christ gave to us, then, how do you deserve any respect, seeing that you are a fool and an idiot?

76. Here is the world and your definition of Holy Communion meat/food!

    i. **John 4:8 (KJV)** (For his disciples were gone away unto the city to buy meat.)

    ii. **John 4:31 (KJV)** In the mean while his disciples prayed him, saying, Master, eat.

77. Then, here is the definition of Holy Communion meat/food given by the LORD Jesus Christ!

    i. **John 4:32 (KJV)** But he said unto them, I have meat to eat that ye know not of.

    ii. **John 4:33 (KJV)** Therefore said the disciples one to another, Hath any man brought him *ought* to eat?

    iii. **John 4:34 (KJV)** Jesus saith unto them, My meat is to do the will of him that sent me, and to finish his work.

    iv. **John 4:35 (KJV)** Say not ye, There are yet four months, and *then* cometh harvest? behold, I say unto you, Lift up your eyes, and look on the fields; for they are white already to harvest.

    v. **John 4:36 (KJV)** And he that reapeth receiveth wages, and gathereth fruit unto life eternal: that both he that soweth and he that reapeth may rejoice together.

    vi. **John 4:37 (KJV)** And herein is that saying true, One soweth, and another reapeth.

    vii. **John 4:38 (KJV)** I sent you to reap that whereon ye bestowed no labour: other men laboured, and ye are entered into their labours.

78. Now, in the New Testament era, the LORD Jesus Christ is showing you that, true food are words, the Word of God, the Gospel of Salvation that you share with

people, but you would rather share filthy Holy Communion wafers, wine, and bread as meat/food!

      i. **John 4:34 (KJV)** Jesus saith unto them, My meat is to do the will of him that sent me, and to finish his work.

79. So, how come that you claim that Jesus Christ called you into the Ministry and yet you have been preaching and acting against the LORD Jesus Christ all these 50 years, teaching lies and doctrines of Devils?

80. That plainly makes you a Man of Satan, NOT a Man of God, and Hell is where you are going to!

81. In conclusion, I show you the answer to our title question: The Origin of Holy Communion Bread, and I show you this revelation to your shame all you Holy Communion Pastors and Bishops!

      i. **ONE** – Here is the evidence that the LORD Jesus Christ was teaching the Doctrine of Sacrifice/Passover Supper/Holy Communion!

          1. **John 6:4 (KJV)** And the passover, a feast of the Jews, was nigh.

      ii. **TWO** – Here is the evidence that they were looking for Sacrifice/Passover Supper/Holy Communion Bread!

          1. **John 6:5 (KJV)** When Jesus then lifted up *his* eyes, and saw a great company come unto him, he saith unto Philip, Whence shall we buy bread, that these may eat?

      iii. **THREE** – Here is the evidence that all the Men of God including the LORD Jesus Christ agreed that it was NOT in the power of men to provide/give the Sacrifice/Passover Supper/Holy Communion Bread!

          1. **John 6:9 (KJV)** There is a lad here, which hath five barley loaves, and two small fishes: but what are they among so many?

      iv. **FOUR** – Here is the evidence that ONLY the LORD Jesus Christ is able to provide/give the Sacrifice/Passover Supper/Holy Communion Bread!

          1. **John 6:11 (KJV)** And Jesus took the loaves; and when he had given thanks, he distributed to the disciples, and the disciples to them that were set down; and likewise of the fishes as much as they would.

      v. **FIVE** – Here is the evidence that simple men and women, common perhaps uneducated folk, men with zero training in Theology, unlearned men, men without spiritual titles of Pastor, Bishop, Archbishop, Prophet, Very Right Reverend, they understood that, truly, ONLY the LORD Jesus Christ is able to provide/give the Sacrifice/Passover Supper/Holy Communion Bread!

1. **John 6:14 (KJV)** Then those men, when they had seen the miracle that Jesus did, said, This is of a truth that prophet that should come into the world.
2. **John 6:24 (KJV)** When the people therefore saw that Jesus was not there, neither his disciples, they also took shipping, and came to Capernaum, seeking for Jesus.
3. **John 6:25 (KJV)** And when they had found him on the other side of the sea, they said unto him, Rabbi, when camest thou hither?

vi. SIX – Here is the evidence of the LORD Jesus Christ saying plainly: DO NOT USE ANY PERISHABLE MEAT/FOOD/BREAD/OBLATIONS AS SACRIFICE/PASSOVER SUPPER/HOLY COMMUNION BREAD!

1. **John 6:26 (KJV)** Jesus answered them and said, Verily, verily, I say unto you, Ye seek me, not because ye saw the miracles, but because ye did eat of the loaves, and were filled.

vii. SEVEN – Here is the evidence of the LORD Jesus Christ identifying Himself as the NLY Person qualified to give/produce Sacrifice/Passover Supper/Holy Communion Bread!

1. **John 6:27 (KJV)** Labour not for the meat which perisheth, but for that meat which endureth unto everlasting life, which the Son of man shall give unto you: for him hath God the Father sealed.

The LORD Jesus Christ be with your spirit. The LORD Jesus Christ give you understanding.

Rev. Prof. PETER PRYCE,
DSEF, BA, MA, B.Soc.Sc Pol Sci, IBA, PhD
A Scribe of the Law of the God of Heaven
Prophet of the Word of God
Professor of French, Silver Spring, MD, USA
Scholar of the Institute of Theologians, USA

WWW.THEBIBLEUNIVERSITY.ORG
WWW.BOOKSTORESITE.ORG
WWW.THEBIBLEUNIVERSITYCHURCH.ORG

Wednesday 13th December 2023 @ 4:00 PM – 11:59 PM
When I had just finished having lunch and washing in the bathroom.

CHAPTER 5

THE CORRECT NAME FOR HOLY COMMUNION IS - BREAKING BREAD

AKOMA NTOASO
"Linked hearts"
Asante philosophical symbol of Understanding, Agreement, Togetherness, Unity

Question 2402

1. Here is the **#26 physical sacrifice and offering of God-worship**.

2. Many have wondered why the LORD Jesus Christ gave a commandment and yet we cannot find it in the New Testament at all, from Matthew to Revelation!

  i.   **Luke 22:14 (KJV)** And when the hour was come, he sat down, and the twelve apostles with him.

  ii. **Luke 22:15 (KJV)** And he said unto them, With desire I have desired to eat this passover with you before I suffer:

  iii. **Luke 22:16 (KJV)** For I say unto you, I will not any more eat thereof, until it be fulfilled in the kingdom of God.

  iv. **Luke 22:17 (KJV)** And he took the cup, and gave thanks, and said, Take this, and divide *it* among yourselves:

  v.   **Luke 22:18 (KJV)** For I say unto you, I will not drink of the fruit of the vine, until the kingdom of God shall come.

  vi. **Luke 22:19 (KJV)** And he took bread, and gave thanks, and brake *it*, and gave unto them, saying, This is my body which is given for you: this do in remembrance of me.

     vii. **Luke 22:20 (KJV)** Likewise also the cup after supper, saying, This cup *is* the new testament in my blood, which is shed for you.

3. The questions is: This eating ritual in **Luke 22:14-20 (KJV)**, where can we find it in the NEW Testament after the Resurrection of the LORD Jesus Christ?

4. Here is where you ca find it!

     i. **Acts 20:7 (KJV)** And upon the first *day* of the week, when the disciples came together to break bread, Paul preached unto them, ready to depart on the morrow; and continued his speech until midnight.

     ii. **Acts 20:8 (KJV)** And there were many lights in the upper chamber, where they were gathered together.

     iii. **Acts 20:9 (KJV)** And there sat in a window a certain young man named Eutychus, being fallen into a deep sleep: and as Paul was long preaching, he sunk down with sleep, and fell down from the third loft, and was taken up dead.

     iv. **Acts 20:10 (KJV)** And Paul went down, and fell on him, and embracing *him* said, Trouble not yourselves; for his life is in him.

     v. **Acts 20:11 (KJV)** When he therefore was come up again, and had broken bread, and eaten, and talked a long while, even till break of day, so he departed.

     vi. **Acts 20:12 (KJV)** And they brought the young man alive, and were not a little comforted.

5. But, why then is the eating ritual in **Luke 22:14-20 (KJV)** not exactly the same as the eating ritual **Acts 20:7-11 (KJV)** is it was the same commandment of the LORD Jesus Christ in **Luke 22:14-20 (KJV)**?

6. Brother, the simple reason is because the Church, the Pastors, the Bishops, the Church Leaders, they have corrupted the eating ritual and the entire commandment of the LORD Jesus Christ, as follows!

     i. ONE – The demonic Church Leaders have corruptly changed the name from "breaking bread" to "Holy Communion", and this strange name "Holy Communion" is NOT even found in the entire Holy Bible from Genesis to Revelation, meaning that it is an evil and satanic addition to the Word of God!

     ii. TWO – As you can see from the evidence in **Luke 22:14-20 (KJV)** and in **Acts 20:7-11 (KJV)**, there are two things that characterized the Passover Supper/Breaking Bread, which are: (1) Breaking of Physical Bread to drive away physical hunger, and (2) Breaking of spiritual

Bread to drive away spiritual hunger where the Spiritual Bread took precedence and greater importance over the Physical Bread!

7. Now, why does the Spiritual Bread take precedence and greater importance over the Physical Bread?

8. Because, the physical Holy Communion is nothing just as the physical Circumcision is nothing, so that, keeping the physical Holy Communion in the churches is one of the useless empty rituals that Church Leaders ever failed to correctly understand!

   i. **1 Corinthians 7:19 (KJV)** Circumcision is nothing, and uncircumcision is nothing, but the keeping of the commandments of God.

9. In fact, the LORD God gave a second emphasis of the nothingness of the physical Holy Communion by saying plainly that "the kingdom of God is not meat and drink", and for this, even a child can see that your physical Holy Communion in all your corrupt churches is nothing but "meat/food and drink"!

   i. **Romans 14:17 (KJV)** For the kingdom of God is not meat and drink; but righteousness, and peace, and joy in the Holy Ghost.

10. Specifically, therefore, the LORD God is showing you plainly in **Romans 14:17 (KJV)** that, the physical "meat/food and drink" Holy Communion that you have been sanctimoniously offering in all your churches have zero connection to Heaven and have zero approval in the Kingdom of God!

11. Truly, not only did the LORD God give a double emphasis of the nothingness of the physical Holy Communion, but the LORD God also gave a triple emphasis of the nothingness of the physical Holy Communion whereby, we see the third condemnation of your physical Holy Communion by the Holy Spirit!

    i. **1 Corinthians 8:8 (KJV)** But meat commendeth us not to God: for neither, if we eat, are we the better; neither, if we eat not, are we the worse.

12. Did you see that plain Word of God in **1 Corinthians 8:8 (KJV)**? Brother, there is absolutely zero connection between your physical Holy Communion and the LORD God Almighty in Heaven, except you want to convince the world that your physical Holy Communion is not "meat/food and drink"?

13. Here is the LORD Jesus Christ doing what I have just shown you: First Jesus Christ gave them physical bread, and then, HE gave them spiritual bread in a greater time in the best part of the night!

14. Here is Part 1: Breaking of Physical Bread to drive away physical hunger!

    i. **John 13:1 (KJV)** Now before the feast of the passover, when Jesus knew that his hour was come that he should depart out of this world unto the Father, having loved his own which were in the world, he loved them unto the end.

ii. **John 13:2 (KJV)** And supper being ended, the devil having now put into the heart of Judas Iscariot, Simon's *son*, to betray him;

15. Here is Part 2: Breaking of spiritual Bread to drive away spiritual hunger!

i. **John 13:25 (KJV)** He then lying on Jesus' breast saith unto him, Lord, who is it?

ii. **John 13:26 (KJV)** Jesus answered, He it is, to whom I shall give a sop, when I have dipped *it*. And when he had dipped the sop, he gave *it* to Judas Iscariot, *the son* of Simon.

iii. **John 13:27 (KJV)** And after the sop Satan entered into him. Then said Jesus unto him, That thou doest, do quickly.

iv. **John 13:28 (KJV)** Now no man at the table knew for what intent he spake this unto him.

v. **John 13:29 (KJV)** For some *of them* thought, because Judas had the bag, that Jesus had said unto him, Buy *those things* that we have need of against the feast; or, that he should give something to the poor.

vi. **John 13:30 (KJV)** He then having received the sop went immediately out: and it was night.

vii. **John 13:31 (KJV)** Therefore, when he was gone out, Jesus said, Now is the Son of man glorified, and God is glorified in him.

viii. **John 13:32 (KJV)** If God be glorified in him, God shall also glorify him in himself, and shall straightway glorify him.

ix. **John 13:33 (KJV)** Little children, yet a little while I am with you. Ye shall seek me: and as I said unto the Jews, Whither I go, ye cannot come; so now I say to you.

x. **John 13:34 (KJV)** A new commandment I give unto you, That ye love one another; as I have loved you, that ye also love one another.

xi. **John 13:35 (KJV)** By this shall all *men* know that ye are my disciples, if ye have love one to another. **John 13:36 (KJV)** Simon Peter said unto him, Lord, whither goest thou? Jesus answered him, Whither I go, thou canst not follow me now; but thou shalt follow me afterwards.

xii. **John 13:36 (KJV)** Simon Peter said unto him, Lord, whither goest thou? Jesus answered him, Whither I go, thou canst not follow me now; but thou shalt follow me afterwards.

xiii. **John 13:37 (KJV)** Peter said unto him, Lord, why cannot I follow thee now? I will lay down my life for thy sake.

xiv. **John 13:38 (KJV)** Jesus answered him, Wilt thou lay down thy life for my sake? Verily, verily, I say unto thee, The cock shall not crow, till thou hast denied me thrice.

16. Here now is Apostle Paul doing what I have just shown you: First Apostle Paul gave them physical bread, and then, Apostle Paul gave them spiritual bread in a greater time in the best part of the night!

17. Here is Part 1: Breaking of Physical Bread to drive away physical hunger!

    i. **Acts 20:7 (KJV)** And upon the first *day* of the week, when the disciples came together to break bread, Paul preached unto them, ready to depart on the morrow; and continued his speech until midnight.

    ii. **Acts 20:11 (KJV)** When he therefore was come up again, and had broken bread, and eaten, and talked a long while, even till break of day, so he departed.

18. Here is Part 2: Breaking of Spiritual Bread to drive away spiritual hunger!

    i. "Paul preached unto them, ready to depart on the morrow; and continued his speech until midnight."

    ii. "and talked a long while, even till break of day"

19. So, I have just demonstrated to you that the eating ritual called "breaking Bread" that the LORD Jesus Christ gave to the Church in **Luke 22:14-20 (KJV)**, the Early Church of Christ followed the commandment exactly and very carefully in **Acts 20:7-11 (KJV)**!

20. Now that you have seen the Truth, I ask you: Is that what you are doing in your church? Have you been obeying the LORD Jesus Christ as the Disciples did in **Acts 20:7-11 (KJV)**?

21. Both you and I know that the answer is, NO, because not only have you Church Leaders of today corrupted the name and diabolically changed it to Holy Communion that is NOT at all in the Holy Bible, but you have even gone further in your depravity and filthy selves by replacing the Spiritual Bread with the useless man-made filthy non-spiritual Satan-directed Physical Bread, wafers, and wine that have zero benefit to the equally dumb and foolish eaters in all your churches!

22. Woe unto you Church leaders!

The LORD Jesus Christ be with your spirit. The LORD Jesus Christ give you understanding.

Rev. Prof. PETER PRYCE,
DSEF, BA, MA, B.Soc.Sc Pol Sci, IBA, PhD

A Scribe of the Law of the God of Heaven
Prophet of the Word of God
Professor of French, Silver Spring, MD, USA
Scholar of the Institute of Theologians, USA
WWW.THEBIBLEUNIVERSITY.ORG
Accreditation Number: 07-QCTO/SDP120723172836
SAQA QUAL ID: Identification # 101997
WWW.BOOKSTORESITE.ORG
WWW.THEBIBLEUNIVERSITYCHURCH.ORG

Wednesday 27th December 2023 @ 12:57 PM – 3:11 PM
While hearing and meditating on the Word of God.

CHAPTER 6

WATER BAPTISM AND HOLY COMMUNION WITHOUT THE RIGHTEOUSNESS OF THE LAW

ANANSE NTENTAN
"Spider's web"
Asante philosophical symbol of Wisdom, Creativity, Craftiness, Shrewdness

Question 2405

1. Here is the **#39 physical sacrifice and offering of God-worship**.

2. If Circumcision and Jewishness are no longer by sight but only according to the unseen spiritual of Faith in the New Testament era, then how are Holy Communion and Water Baptism still based on sight in the New Testament era?

    i. **Romans 2:25 (KJV)** For circumcision verily profiteth, if thou keep the law: but if thou be a breaker of the law, thy circumcision is made uncircumcision.

    ii. **Romans 2:26 (KJV)** Therefore if the uncircumcision keep the righteousness of the law, shall not his uncircumcision be counted for circumcision?

    iii. **Romans 2:27 (KJV)** And shall not uncircumcision which is by nature, if it fulfil the law, judge thee, who by the letter and circumcision dost transgress the law?

    iv. **Romans 2:28 (KJV)** For he is not a Jew, which is one outwardly; neither *is that* circumcision, which is outward in the flesh:

     v. **Romans 2:29 (KJV)** But he *is* a Jew, which is one inwardly; and circumcision *is that* of the heart, in the spirit, *and* not in the letter; whose praise *is* not of men, but of God.

     vi. **1 Corinthians 7:17 (KJV)** But as God hath distributed to every man, as the Lord hath called every one, so let him walk. And so ordain I in all churches.

     vii. **1 Corinthians 7:18 (KJV)** Is any man called being circumcised? let him not become uncircumcised. Is any called in uncircumcision? let him not be circumcised.

     viii. **1 Corinthians 7:19 (KJV)** Circumcision is nothing, and uncircumcision is nothing, but the keeping of the commandments of God.

     ix. **1 Corinthians 7:20 (KJV)** Let every man abide in the same calling wherein he was called.

3. If burnt offerings and Cruxifixion are are no longer by sight but only according to the unseen spiritual of Faith in the New Testament era, then how are Holy Communion and Water Baptism still based on sight in the New Testament era?

     i. **Hebrews 7:27 (KJV)** Who needeth not daily, as those high priests, to offer up sacrifice, first for his own sins, and then for the people's: for this he did once, when he offered up himself.

     ii. **Hebrews 9:7 (KJV)** But into the second *went* the high priest alone once every year, not without blood, which he offered for himself, and *for* the errors of the people:

     iii. **Hebrews 9:28 (KJV)** So Christ was once offered to bear the sins of many; and unto them that look for him shall he appear the second time without sin unto salvation.

     iv. **Hebrews 10:2 (KJV)** For then would they not have ceased to be offered? because that the worshippers once purged should have had no more conscience of sins.

4. If weightier Covenant matters involving blood such as Circumcision and Cruxifixion are no longer effectual by sight in the New Testament era, but now ONLY by the unseen spiritual of Faith in the New Testament era, then, it is wrong for the lesser matters of Holy Communion and Water Baptism to be still based on sight in the New Testament era of Faith?

5. If the strength of Circumcision is in the obedience of the Law, and if the disobedience of the Law changes Circumcision to uncircumcision, and if obedience to the Law converts uncircumcision to Circumcision, then, why can't the same obedience to the Law ensure or convert physical non-Water Baptism to Spiritual

Waterless Baptism by Faith only and not by physical works in a physical performance?

6. Likewise, why can't the same obedience to the Law ensure or convert the physical Holy Communion into a Spiritual Holy Communion by Faith only and not by physical works in a physical performance?

7. It is wrong to have Water Baptism and Holy Communion in the physical, in an era of unseen spiritual Faith of the New Testament when there is not a single law in the entire Holy Bible authorizing that doctrine!

   i. **Romans 2:26 (KJV)** Therefore if the uncircumcision keep the righteousness of the law, shall not his uncircumcision be counted for circumcision?

   ii. **Romans 2:27 (KJV)** And shall not uncircumcision which is by nature, if it fulfil the law, judge thee, who by the letter and circumcision dost transgress the law?

8. If Jewishness and Circumcision are NOT outward and are NOT in the flesh, then why can't my physical Water Baptism and my physical Holy Communion be counted also as NOT outward and NOT in the flesh?

   i. **Romans 2:28 (KJV)** For he is not a Jew, which is one outwardly; neither *is that* circumcision, which is outward in the flesh:

   ii. **Romans 2:29 (KJV)** But he *is* a Jew, which is one inwardly; and circumcision *is that* of the heart, in the spirit, *and* not in the letter; whose praise *is* not of men, but of God.

9. Why can't I keep the righteousness of the Law for my physical Water Baptism and my physical Holy Communion to be counted as already accomplished by Christ Jesus as is the case with my circumcision and uncircumcision?

10. If my circumcision is correct ONLY when it is of the heart, in the spirit, and not in the letter as **Romans 2:29 (KJV)** reveals, then, why can't my Water Baptism and Holy Communion also be correctly located in the heart, in the spirit, and not of the letter?

11. Where is the Law that forbids that?

12. If your Water Baptism and Holy Communion are within the righteousness of the Law as **Romans 2:26 (KJV)** reveals, then should they have been counted fulfilled without the physical works that you have attached to them, but since those physical works remain, and your Water Baptism and Holy Communion are performed in the flesh and by the flesh, therefore, they are NOT in keeping with the righteousness of the Law as **Romans 2:26 (KJV)** requires, and therefore, they are all grievous sins against the LORD!

13. Therefore, your physical flesh Water Baptism and your physical flesh Holy Communion in all the churches are all wrong and contrary to the Word of God, and especially contrary to the Spirit of Faith in Christ Jesus, which Faith is without the works, without the outward, and without the flesh!

14. Bishop, is this not your physical flesh deeds of Water Baptism and your physical flesh deeds of Holy Communion that the LORD God is condemning as evil here in this verse?

    i. **Romans 3:19 (KJV)** Now we know that what things soever the law saith, it saith to them who are under the law: that every mouth may be stopped, and all the world may become guilty before God.

    ii. **Romans 3:20 (KJV)** Therefore by the deeds of the law there shall no flesh be justified in his sight: for by the law *is* the knowledge of sin.

15. Bishop, is this not the Spiritual Waterless Baptism and the Spiritual Holy Communion that the LORD God is approving here as the righteousness of God *which is* by faith of Jesus Christ?

    i. **Romans 3:21 (KJV)** But now the righteousness of God without the law is manifested, being witnessed by the law and the prophets;

    ii. **Romans 3:22 (KJV)** Even the righteousness of God *which is* by faith of Jesus Christ unto all and upon all them that believe: for there is no difference:

16. Bishop, and is this not the physical flesh deeds of Water Baptism and your physical flesh deeds of Holy Communion that the LORD God is saying here plainly that they shall NOT be justified in HIS sight?

    i. **Romans 3:20 (KJV)** Therefore by the deeds of the law there shall no flesh be justified in his sight: for by the law *is* the knowledge of sin.

17. Bishop, how did the LORD God Almighty reckon and count Abraham's righteousness?

18. Was it when Abraham did the physical work of Circumcision or was it when he had NOT yet done it and ONLY believed?

19. Surely, the LORD God Almighty reckoned and counted Abraham's righteousness when Abraham had NOT yet done the physical work of Circumcision! Abraham's righteousness was based ONLY on believing/faith!

    i. **Romans 4:1 (KJV)** What shall we say then that Abraham our father, as pertaining to the flesh, hath found?

    ii. **Romans 4:2 (KJV)** For if Abraham were justified by works, he hath *whereof* to glory; but not before God.

    iii. **Romans 4:3 (KJV)** For what saith the scripture? Abraham believed God, and it was counted unto him for righteousness.

      iv. **Romans 4:10 (KJV)** How was it then reckoned? when he was in circumcision, or in uncircumcision? Not in circumcision, but in uncircumcision.

      v. **Romans 4:11 (KJV)** And he received the sign of circumcision, a seal of the righteousness of the faith which *he had yet* being uncircumcised: that he might be the father of all them that believe, though they be not circumcised; that righteousness might be imputed unto them also:

      vi. **Romans 4:12 (KJV)** And the father of circumcision to them who are not of the circumcision only, but who also walk in the steps of that faith of our father Abraham, which *he had* being *yet* uncircumcised.

      vii. **Romans 4:13 (KJV)** For the promise, that he should be the heir of the world, *was* not to Abraham, or to his seed, through the law, but through the righteousness of faith.

      viii. **Romans 4:14 (KJV)** For if they which are of the law *be* heirs, faith is made void, and the promise made of none effect:

      ix. **Romans 4:15 (KJV)** Because the law worketh wrath: for where no law is, *there is* no transgression.

      x. **Romans 4:16 (KJV)** Therefore *it is* of faith, that *it might be* by grace; to the end the promise might be sure to all the seed; not to that only which is of the law, but to that also which is of the faith of Abraham; who is the father of us all,

20. Bishop, since I suppose that you know this Truth of God in **Romans 4:1-16 (KJV)**, how then do you presume in error that this same God Almighty who reckoned and counted Abraham's righteousness when Abraham had NOT yet done the physical work of Circumcision but ONLY believed, will now turn from HIS own Word and bless you who is approaching God with your physical flesh deeds/works of Water Baptism and your physical flesh deeds/works of Holy Communion?

21. How then are you so brutish and a filthy idiot that you still do not understand that your physical flesh deeds of Water Baptism and your physical flesh deeds of Holy Communion are evil and have zero connection to Heaven?

      i. **Romans 3:28 (KJV)** Therefore we conclude that a man is justified by faith without the deeds of the law.

      ii. **Romans 4:23 (KJV)** Now it was not written for his sake alone, that it was imputed to him;

      iii. **Romans 4:24 (KJV)** But for us also, to whom it shall be imputed, if we believe on him that raised up Jesus our Lord from the dead;

iv. **Romans 4:25 (KJV)** Who was delivered for our offences, and was raised again for our justification.

v. **Romans 8:1 (KJV)** *There is* therefore now no condemnation to them which are in Christ Jesus, who walk not after the flesh, but after the Spirit.

The LORD Jesus Christ be with your spirit. The LORD Jesus Christ give you understanding.

Rev. Prof. PETER PRYCE,
DSEF, BA, MA, B.Soc.Sc Pol Sci, IBA, PhD
A Scribe of the Law of the God of Heaven
Prophet of the Word of God
Professor of French, Silver Spring, MD, USA
Scholar of the Institute of Theologians, USA
WWW.THEBIBLEUNIVERSITY.ORG
Accreditation Number: 07-QCTO/SDP120723172836
SAQA QUAL ID: Identification # 101997
WWW.BOOKSTORESITE.ORG
WWW.THEBIBLEUNIVERSITYCHURCH.ORG

Thursday 28th December 2023 @ 6:37 PM – 8:05 PM
While hearing and meditating on the Word of God.

CHAPTER 7

THE NEW HOLY COMMUNION

ASASE YE DURU

"The Earth is heavy"
Asante philosophical symbol of Divinity of Mother Earth

Question 2460

    1. The word "Holy Communion" is NOT in the entire Holy Bible from Genesis to Revelation, so it is not even recognized in Heaven as a part of God-worship!

    2. When you say "Holy Communion" offering, "Holy Communion" sacrifice, "Holy Communion" worship, or "Holy Communion" service, it has zero resonance in Heaven!

3. "Holy Communion" is NOT recognized in the Spirit realm!

4. The correct name is: Passover, and that was the name that the LORD God gave to that feast in **Exodus 12:11 (KJV)**!

5. Here is the original Old Testament Law of the Passover!

        i. **Exodus 12:1 (KJV)** And the LORD spake unto Moses and Aaron in the land of Egypt, saying,

        ii. **Exodus 12:2 (KJV)** This month *shall be* unto you the beginning of months: it *shall be* the first month of the year to you.

6. The Passover Law stipulated that every male head of household shall offer the lamb sacrifice or offering of Passover for his family to eat it! Passover lamb sacrifice or offering was NOT reserved to the Priests!

   i. **Exodus 12:3 (KJV)** Speak ye unto all the congregation of Israel, saying, In the tenth *day* of this month they shall take to them every man a lamb, according to the house of *their* fathers, a lamb for an house:

   ii. **Exodus 12:4 (KJV)** And if the household be too little for the lamb, let him and his neighbour next unto his house take *it* according to the number of the souls; every man according to his eating shall make your count for the lamb.

7. The Passover lamb sacrifice or offering had to be without blemish, and a male lamb of the first year!

   i. **Exodus 12:5 (KJV)** Your lamb shall be without blemish, a male of the first year: ye shall take *it* out from the sheep, or from the goats:

8. The Passover lamb sacrifice or offering had to be kept alive for 14 days prior to its killing for food!

   i. **Exodus 12:6 (KJV)** And ye shall keep it up until the fourteenth day of the same month: and the whole assembly of the congregation of Israel shall kill it in the evening.

9. The Passover lamb sacrifice or offering was a blood ritual!

   i. **Exodus 12:7 (KJV)** And they shall take of the blood, and strike *it* on the two side posts and on the upper door post of the houses, wherein they shall eat it.

10. The Passover lamb sacrifice or offering had to be eaten at night for the last meal! The Passover lamb sacrifice or offering had to be roasted with fire and eaten with unleavened bread!

   i. **Exodus 12:8 (KJV)** And they shall eat the flesh in that night, roast with fire, and unleavened bread; *and* with bitter *herbs* they shall eat it.

11. The Passover lamb sacrifice or offering could NOT be eaten raw or boiled in water!

   i. **Exodus 12:9 (KJV)** Eat not of it raw, nor sodden at all with water, but roast *with* fire; his head with his legs, and with the purtenance thereof.

12. The Passover lamb sacrifice or offering had to be totally consumed when served, without any leftovers!

   i. **Exodus 12:10 (KJV)** And ye shall let nothing of it remain until the morning; and that which remaineth of it until the morning ye shall burn with fire.

13. The Passover lamb sacrifice or offering had to be eaten while fully dressed, and in a hurry!

i. **Exodus 12:11 (KJV)** And thus shall ye eat it; *with* your loins girded, your shoes on your feet, and your staff in your hand; and ye shall eat it in haste: it *is* the LORD'S passover.

ii. **Exodus 12:12 (KJV)** For I will pass through the land of Egypt this night, and will smite all the firstborn in the land of Egypt, both man and beast; and against all the gods of Egypt I will execute judgment: I *am* the LORD.

iii. **Exodus 12:13 (KJV)** And the blood shall be to you for a token upon the houses where ye *are*: and when I see the blood, I will pass over you, and the plague shall not be upon you to destroy *you*, when I smite the land of Egypt.

iv. **Exodus 12:14 (KJV)** And this day shall be unto you for a memorial; and ye shall keep it a feast to the LORD throughout your generations; ye shall keep it a feast by an ordinance for ever.

14. Here is the LORD Jesus Christ operating in the Old Testament and, therefore, HE is keeping the Passover Feast!

i. **Luke 22:7 (KJV)** Then came the day of unleavened bread, when the passover must be killed.

ii. **Luke 22:8 (KJV)** And he sent Peter and John, saying, Go and prepare us the passover, that we may eat.

iii. **Luke 22:9 (KJV)** And they said unto him, Where wilt thou that we prepare?

iv. **Luke 22:10 (KJV)** And he said unto them, Behold, when ye are entered into the city, there shall a man meet you, bearing a pitcher of water; follow him into the house where he entereth in.

v. **Luke 22:11 (KJV)** And ye shall say unto the goodman of the house, The Master saith unto thee, Where is the guestchamber, where I shall eat the passover with my disciples?

vi. **Luke 22:12 (KJV)** And he shall shew you a large upper room furnished: there make ready.

vii. **Luke 22:13 (KJV)** And they went, and found as he had said unto them: and they made ready the passover.

viii. **Luke 22:14 (KJV)** And when the hour was come, he sat down, and the twelve apostles with him.

ix. **Luke 22:15 (KJV)** And he said unto them, With desire I have desired to eat this passover with you before I suffer:

x. **Luke 22:16 (KJV)** For I say unto you, I will not any more eat thereof, until it be fulfilled in the kingdom of God.

    xi. **Luke 22:17 (KJV)** And he took the cup, and gave thanks, and said, Take this, and divide *it* among yourselves:

    xii. **Luke 22:18 (KJV)** For I say unto you, I will not drink of the fruit of the vine, until the kingdom of God shall come.

    xiii. **Luke 22:19 (KJV)** And he took bread, and gave thanks, and brake *it*, and gave unto them, saying, This is my body which is given for you: this do in remembrance of me.

    xiv. **Luke 22:20 (KJV)** Likewise also the cup after supper, saying, This cup *is* the new testament in my blood, which is shed for you.

15. **Luke 22:7-20 (KJV)** is the record of the Last Passover Feast with the LORD Jesus Christ on Earth because it was HIS last one before HIS Death and Resurrection!

    i. **Luke 22:15 (KJV)** And he said unto them, With desire I have desired to eat this passover with you before I suffer:

16. In this Last Passover Feast, the LORD Jesus Christ also announced that it was the very Last Physical Passover Feast "until [a new Spiritual Passover Feast] be fulfilled in the kingdom of God", and a New Spiritual Passover Feast was going to replace the just ended feast!

    i. **Luke 22:16 (KJV)** For I say unto you, I will not any more eat thereof, until it be fulfilled in the kingdom of God.

17. Furthermore, the LORD Jesus Christ said that the Bread that would be used for the New Spiritual Passover Feast was Himself!

    i. **John 6:33 (KJV)** For the bread of God is he which cometh down from heaven, and giveth life unto the world.

    ii. **John 6:35 (KJV)** And Jesus said unto them, I am the bread of life: he that cometh to me shall never hunger; and he that believeth on me shall never thirst.

    iii. **John 6:51 (KJV)** I am the living bread which came down from heaven: if any man eat of this bread, he shall live for ever: and the bread that I will give is my flesh, which I will give for the life of the world.

18. The record of the Last Passover in **Luke 22:7-20 (KJV)** also shows us that the New Spiritual Passover Feast will be made up of the Body and the Blood of the LORD Jesus Christ!

19. The first New Spiritual Passover Feast that the LORD Jesus Christ said in **Luke 22:16 (KJV)** that it will be done in Heaven, and the same New Spiritual Passover Feast which HE also said in **Luke 22:19-20 (KJV)** that it will be made up of HIS Body and Blood, here is the evidence of it being fulfilled in **Hebrews 9:14 (KJV)** as HE said!

      i. **Luke 22:16 (KJV)** For I say unto you, I will not any more eat thereof, until it be fulfilled in the kingdom of God.

      ii. **Hebrews 9:13 (KJV)** For if the blood of bulls and of goats, and the ashes of an heifer sprinkling the unclean, sanctifieth to the purifying of the flesh:

      iii. **Hebrews 9:14 (KJV)** How much more shall the blood of Christ, who through the eternal Spirit offered himself without spot to God, purge your conscience from dead works to serve the living God?

20. Now, if the Last Physical Passover Feast has changed into the New Spiritual Passover Feast as required by a change in the Law whereby all the Old Testament physical forms and items of God-worship are now in their spiritual state in the New Testament, then:

      i. Continuing with the same Last Physical Passover Feast as is being replicated in all the churches today, is wrong!

      ii. Likewise, the retention of the same physical format of the Old Testament Last Physical Passover Feast with Physical Jesus Christ, is wrong!

      iii. Furthermore, not offering the Physical Passover Feast in its New Spiritual Passover format as the LORD Jesus Christ commanded in **Luke 22:16 (KJV)**, is wrong!

      iv. **Hebrews 7:12 (KJV)** For the priesthood being changed, there is made of necessity a change also of the law.

21. Now, therefore, the next sensible question is this: where can we find the New Spiritual Passover Feast items or oblations so that we can perform it according to the commandment of the LORD Jesus Christ in **Luke 22:16 (KJV)**?

      i. **Luke 22:16 (KJV)** For I say unto you, I will not any more eat thereof, until it be fulfilled in the kingdom of God.

22. The LORD Jesus Christ already told you, so why are you asking again?

      i. **John 6:33 (KJV)** For the bread of God is he which cometh down from heaven, and giveth life unto the world.

      ii. **John 6:35 (KJV)** And Jesus said unto them, I am the bread of life: he that cometh to me shall never hunger; and he that believeth on me shall never thirst.

      iii. **John 6:51 (KJV)** I am the living bread which came down from heaven: if any man eat of this bread, he shall live for ever: and the bread that I will give is my flesh, which I will give for the life of the world.

23. I think that the correct question that you want to pose is: How do we offer the New Spiritual Passover Feast in the correct way that is acceptable in Heaven as the LORD Jesus Christ said in **Luke 22:16 (KJV)**?

24. Here is how to do it!

    i. **1 Corinthians 5:7 (KJV)** Purge out therefore the old leaven, that ye may be a new lump, as ye are unleavened. For even Christ our passover is sacrificed for us:

    ii. **Hebrews 9:13 (KJV)** For if the blood of bulls and of goats, and the ashes of an heifer sprinkling the unclean, sanctifieth to the purifying of the flesh:

    iii. **Hebrews 9:14 (KJV)** How much more shall the blood of Christ, who through the eternal Spirit offered himself without spot to God, purge your conscience from dead works to serve the living God?

25. Did you see how to do it now?

26. Did I hear you say, NO?

27. Well, you want to offer the sacrifice of Passover, which you corruptly call Holy Communion, and the LORD God is saying in **1 Corinthians 5:7 (KJV)** and repeating the same doctrine in **Hebrews 9:13-14 (KJV)** that it has already been offered and sacrificed, so, you have nothing else now to do to add to it, because, truly, no man can add to what the Holy Spirit has already accomplished!

    i. **Deuteronomy 4:2 (KJV)** Ye shall not add unto the word which I command you, neither shall ye diminish *ought* from it, that ye may keep the commandments of the LORD your God which I command you.

    ii. **Deuteronomy 12:32 (KJV)** What thing soever I command you, observe to do it: thou shalt not add thereto, nor diminish from it.

    iii. **Jeremiah 26:2 (KJV)** Thus saith the LORD; Stand in the court of the LORD'S house, and speak unto all the cities of Judah, which come to worship in the LORD'S house, all the words that I command thee to speak unto them; diminish not a word:

28. But, did not the LORD Jesus Christ Himself in **Luke 22:19 (KJV)** command to do the Physical Passover Feast?

    i. **Luke 22:19 (KJV)** And he took bread, and gave thanks, and brake *it*, and gave unto them, saying, This is my body which is given for you: this do in remembrance of me.

29. No, my ignorant Brother Pastor and Bishop, the LORD Jesus Christ never commanded you to do any Physical Passover Feast as you all do in all your churches today!

30. First of all, as you can see, the word "physical" is NOT in **Luke 22:19 (KJV)**!

    i. **John 4:23 (KJV)** But the hour cometh, and now is, when the true worshippers shall worship the Father in spirit and in truth: for the Father seeketh such to worship him.

    ii. **John 4:24 (KJV)** God *is* a Spirit: and they that worship him must worship *him* in spirit and in truth.

31. Second, if it was truly the LORD Jesus Christ who gave this revelation in **John 4:23-24 (KJV)**, then, HE could not be the same Person to tell you to do Physical Passover Feast, therefore, you are a liar, and your father is the Devil!

    i. **John 8:43 (KJV)** Why do ye not understand my speech? *even* because ye cannot hear my word.

    ii. **John 8:44 (KJV)** Ye are of *your* father the devil, and the lusts of your father ye will do. He was a murderer from the beginning, and abode not in the truth, because there is no truth in him. When he speaketh a lie, he speaketh of his own: for he is a liar, and the father of it.

32. So, again, you see that we have come back to the same answer that the LOTD God gave you before, which I showed you here above:

    i. You want to offer the sacrifice of Passover, which you corruptly call Holy Communion, and the LORD God is saying in **1 Corinthians 5:7 (KJV)** and repeating the same doctrine in **Hebrews 9:13-14 (KJV)** that it has already been offered and sacrificed, so, you have nothing else now to do to add to it, because, truly, no man can add to what the Holy Spirit has already accomplished!

33. But, how can we do nothing and still obey or fulfill this command: "this do in remembrance of me"?

    i. **Luke 22:19 (KJV)** And he took bread, and gave thanks, and brake *it*, and gave unto them, saying, This is my body which is given for you: this do in remembrance of me.

34. Did you say that you are saved, born again, and a Christian? And did you say that Abraham is your Father of Faith?

    i. **Luke 1:73 (KJV)** The oath which he sware to our father Abraham,

    ii. **Galatians 3:9 (KJV)** So then they which be of faith are blessed with faithful Abraham.

    iii. **Romans 4:16 (KJV)** Therefore *it is* of faith, that *it might be* by grace; to the end the promise might be sure to all the seed; not to that only which is of the law, but to that also which is of the faith of Abraham; who is the father of us all,

35. Well, then, if you answered, yes, Abraham is your Father of Faith, then, tell me, did Abraham your father do anything physical to obey or to fulfill the commandment of God regarding Circumcision before God Almighty called him righteous?

    i. **Romans 4:1 (KJV)** What shall we say then that Abraham our father, as pertaining to the flesh, hath found?

    ii. **Romans 4:2 (KJV)** For if Abraham were justified by works, he hath *whereof* to glory; but not before God.

    iii. **Romans 4:3 (KJV)** For what saith the scripture? Abraham believed God, and it was counted unto him for righteousness.

    iv. **Romans 4:4 (KJV)** Now to him that worketh is the reward not reckoned of grace, but of debt.

    v. **Romans 4:5 (KJV)** But to him that worketh not, but believeth on him that justifieth the ungodly, his faith is counted for righteousness.

    vi. **Romans 4:6 (KJV)** Even as David also describeth the blessedness of the man, unto whom God imputeth righteousness without works,

    vii. **Romans 4:7 (KJV)** *Saying,* Blessed *are* they whose iniquities are forgiven, and whose sins are covered.

    viii. **Romans 4:8 (KJV)** Blessed *is* the man to whom the Lord will not impute sin.

    ix. **Romans 4:9 (KJV)** *Cometh* this blessedness then upon the circumcision *only,* or upon the uncircumcision also? for we say that faith was reckoned to Abraham for righteousness.

    x. **Romans 4:10 (KJV)** How was it then reckoned? when he was in circumcision, or in uncircumcision? Not in circumcision, but in uncircumcision.

    xi. **Romans 4:11 (KJV)** And he received the sign of circumcision, a seal of the righteousness of the faith which *he had yet* being uncircumcised: that he might be the father of all them that believe, though they be not circumcised; that righteousness might be imputed unto them also:

    xii. **Romans 4:12 (KJV)** And the father of circumcision to them who are not of the circumcision only, but who also walk in the steps of that faith of our father Abraham, which *he had* being *yet* uncircumcised.

    xiii. **Romans 4:13 (KJV)** For the promise, that he should be the heir of the world, *was* not to Abraham, or to his seed, through the law, but through the righteousness of faith.

    xiv. **Romans 4:14 (KJV)** For if they which are of the law *be* heirs, faith is made void, and the promise made of none effect:

xv. **Romans 4:15 (KJV)** Because the law worketh wrath: for where no law is, *there is* no transgression.

xvi. **Romans 4:16 (KJV)** Therefore *it is* of faith, that *it might be* by grace; to the end the promise might be sure to all the seed; not to that only which is of the law, but to that also which is of the faith of Abraham; who is the father of us all,

36. So, as you can see from the evidence in **Romans 4:1-16 (KJV)**, Abraham your father did NOTHING physical to obey or to fulfill the commandment of God regarding Circumcision before God Almighty called him a righteous man!

    i. **Genesis 15:6 (KJV)** And he believed in the LORD; and he counted it to him for righteousness.

    ii. **Romans 4:3 (KJV)** For what saith the scripture? Abraham believed God, and it was counted unto him for righteousness.

    iii. **Galatians 3:6 (KJV)** Even as Abraham believed God, and it was accounted to him for righteousness.

    iv. **James 2:23 (KJV)** And the scripture was fulfilled which saith, Abraham believed God, and it was imputed unto him for righteousness: and he was called the Friend of God.

37. So, now, if Abraham is your Father of Faith, and he ONLY believed, and he did NOTHING, and his believing in the Word of God alone was enough righteousness for him in Heaven, then, why do you call yourself a child of Abraham and you want to do contrary to Abraham by doing physical things for God, in order to attain justification?

38. Brother, Sister, do you see again that, for the second time, I have caught you in guile as a liar and a child of Satan?

    i. **John 8:39 (KJV)** They answered and said unto him, Abraham is our father. Jesus saith unto them, If ye were Abraham's children, ye would do the works of Abraham.

    ii. **John 8:41 (KJV)** Ye do the deeds of your father. Then said they to him, We be not born of fornication; we have one Father, *even* God.

    iii. **John 8:44 (KJV)** Ye are of *your* father the devil, and the lusts of your father ye will do. He was a murderer from the beginning, and abode not in the truth, because there is no truth in him. When he speaketh a lie, he speaketh of his own: for he is a liar, and the father of it.

39. For something as immeasurably gigantic as Salvation, Abraham did NOTHING but only believed God, and God said: That is Righteousness Abraham!

40. However, in your case, for something as little as eating filthy wafers, wine, and bread, you think God will appreciate you more if you deviated from Abraham to obey God in the physical?

41. Thou fool, what do you think this revelation means: "God *is* a Spirit…"?

    i. **John 4:23 (KJV)** But the hour cometh, and now is, when the true worshippers shall worship the Father in spirit and in truth: for the Father seeketh such to worship him.

    ii. **John 4:24 (KJV)** God *is* a Spirit: and they that worship him must worship *him* in spirit and in truth.

42. The same way that Abraham walked in Truth and Righteousness to attain unto the Righteousness of God, in that same way see the LORD God is showing you how to do Holy Communion/New Spiritual Passover Feast without your filthy man-made wafers, bread, and wine!

    i. **1 Corinthians 5:7 (KJV)** Purge out therefore the old leaven, that ye may be a new lump, as ye are unleavened. For even Christ our passover is sacrificed for us:

    ii. **1 Corinthians 5:8 (KJV)** Therefore let us keep the feast, not with old leaven, neither with the leaven of malice and wickedness; but with the unleavened *bread* of sincerity and truth.

43. Do you now see very clearly how the LORD God Almighty is showing you in **1 Corinthians 5:7-8 (KJV)** that "sincerity and truth" are the correct forms of Bread that you should be eating daily?

44. Do you also now see very clearly how these same superior spiritual Bread of "sincerity and truth" will connect you to Heaven and to Jesus Christ in Heaven?

    i. **John 14:6 (KJV)** Jesus saith unto him, I am the way, the truth, and the life: no man cometh unto the Father, but by me.

45. Behold, I have taught you the Truth that the Holy Spirit also taught me!

The LORD Jesus Christ be with your spirit. The LORD Jesus Christ give you understanding.

Rev. Prof. PETER PRYCE,
DSEF, BA, MA, B.Soc.Sc Pol Sci, IBA, PhD
A Scribe of the Law of the God of Heaven
Prophet of the Word of God
Professor of French, Silver Spring, MD, USA
Scholar of the Institute of Theologians, USA
WWW.THEBIBLEUNIVERSITY.ORG

Accreditation Number: 07-QCTO/SDP120723172836
SAQA QUAL ID: Identification # 101997
WWW.BOOKSTORESITE.ORG
WWW.THEBIBLEUNIVERSITYCHURCH.ORG

Friday 5th January 2024 @ 4:10 AM – 5:05 PM
While hearing and meditating on the Word of God in my bed.

CHAPTER 8

THE NEW COMMAND REGARDING HOLY COMMUNION

AYA

"Fern"

Asante philosophical symbol of Endurance, Independence, Defiance against difficulties, Hardiness, Perseverance, and Resourcefulness

Question 2463

1. The same way that the LORD God Almighty sacrificed the LORD Jesus Christ for our sins that HE took upon Himself, same way also you must purge that fornicator away from your midst!

      i. **1 Corinthians 5:7 (KJV)** Purge out therefore the old leaven, that ye may be a new lump, as ye are unleavened. For even Christ our passover is sacrificed for us:

      ii. **1 Corinthians 5:8 (KJV)** Therefore let us keep the feast, not with old leaven, neither with the leaven of malice and wickedness; but with the unleavened *bread* of sincerity and truth.

2. At the same time as the LORD God in **1 Corinthians 5:7-8 (KJV)** is commanding to purge the fornicator out of the church, same time the LORD is also revealing how to perform the spiritual Holy Communion, NOT with physical bread, wine, and wafers as it is corruptly done in all the churches today, but with the spiritual bread, wine, and wafers called: "the unleavened *bread* of sincerity and truth"!

3. So, in **1 Corinthians 5:8 (KJV)**, the new command regarding Holy Communion is this:

i. "Therefore let us keep the feast with the unleavened *bread* of sincerity and truth"!

4. What that means in practise is that, since now "sincerity and truth" are the real Holy Communion bread, wine, and wafers, you as the Christian will set your daily target to accomplish your living in Truth and Righteousness in all things: in your thoughts, in your words, and in your deeds, and as you do that daily, then, it is counted for you as your righteousness in Heaven, just the same way as Abraham's believing in God and obeying God in Truth and Righteousness earned him his own righteousness in Heaven!

   i. **Genesis 15:6 (KJV)** And he believed in the LORD; and he counted it to him for righteousness.

   ii. **Romans 4:3 (KJV)** For what saith the scripture? Abraham believed God, and it was counted unto him for righteousness.

   iii. **Galatians 3:6 (KJV)** Even as Abraham believed God, and it was accounted to him for righteousness.

   iv. **James 2:23 (KJV)** And the scripture was fulfilled which saith, Abraham believed God, and it was imputed unto him for righteousness: and he was called the Friend of God.

5. But, why is the LORD God including this Word on Holy Communion in a chapter on how to judge fornicators and other sinners in the congregation?

6. The reason is that the current Holy Communion as it is practiced in the present form in all the churches, is wrong and a sin, seeing that Pastors, Bishops, and Church Leaders are carnal, corrupt, and practising idolatry by reason of the physical oblations that they use in their filthy Holy Communion whereby, those physical items themselves are contrary to the commandment of the LORD Jesus Christ!

   i. **John 4:23 (KJV)** But the hour cometh, and now is, when the true worshippers shall worship the Father in spirit and in truth: for the Father seeketh such to worship him.

   ii. **John 4:24 (KJV)** God *is* a Spirit: and they that worship him must worship *him* in spirit and in truth.

   iii. **Ephesians 5:9 (KJV)** (For the fruit of the Spirit *is* in all goodness and righteousness and truth;)

7. Furthermore, the LORD God included Holy Communion in the subject of how to judge fornicators because all the Pastors, Bishops, and Church Leaders who have this Holy Communion doctrine that is contrary to **John 4:23-24 (KJV)**, they are also fornicators, harlots, and whores and here is the evidence!

   i. **Hosea 1:2 (KJV)** The beginning of the word of the LORD by Hosea. And the LORD said to Hosea, Go, take unto thee a wife of whoredoms and children of whoredoms: for the land hath committed great whoredom, *departing* from the LORD.

ii. **Hebrews 3:12 (KJV)** Take heed, brethren, lest there be in any of you an evil heart of unbelief, in departing from the living God.

The LORD Jesus Christ be with your spirit. The LORD Jesus Christ give you understanding.

Rev. Prof. PETER PRYCE,
DSEF, BA, MA, B.Soc.Sc Pol Sci, IBA, PhD
A Scribe of the Law of the God of Heaven
Prophet of the Word of God
Professor of French, Silver Spring, MD, USA
Scholar of the Institute of Theologians, USA
WWW.THEBIBLEUNIVERSITY.ORG
Accreditation Number: 07-QCTO/SDP120723172836
SAQA QUAL ID: Identification # 101997
WWW.BOOKSTORESITE.ORG
WWW.THEBIBLEUNIVERSITYCHURCH.ORG

Monday 8th January 2024 @ 10:21 AM – 11:44 AM
While hearing and meditating on the Word of God.

CHAPTER 9

WHERE IS THE COMMAND TO OFFER HOLY COMMUNION WAFERS, WINE, AND BREAD?

BESE SAKA
"Sack of cola nuts"
Asante philosophical symbol of Affluence, Abundance, Unity

Question 2465

1. In other words, when we eat certain foods and meats, does that observance enhance, prolong, advance, or improve our spiritual standing?

2. The short answer is, NO!

3. The potency or the spirituality of any food, meat, or drink that are served unto idols derive their potency and spirituality from the knowledge and belief that the worshippers thereof invest in those same foods, drinks, and meats!

4. In other words, the food, meat, or drink becomes evil when you so think, and the food, meat, or drink is nothing when you so think!

    i. **1 Corinthians 8:1 (KJV)** Now as touching things offered unto idols, we know that we all have knowledge. Knowledge puffeth up, but charity edifieth.

    ii. **1 Corinthians 8:2 (KJV)** And if any man think that he knoweth any thing, he knoweth nothing yet as he ought to know.

    iii. **1 Corinthians 8:4 (KJV)** As concerning therefore the eating of those things that are offered in sacrifice unto idols, we know that an idol *is* nothing in the world, and that *there is* none other God but one.

5. So that concerning foods and meats that are offered unto idols, and asking whether they assume any spiritual potency or importance: they do not, because those foods and meats are as dumb as the lifeless idols themselves that have no power to consume these same foods and drinks that are offered unto them?

6. But, our God is different because our God is the Living God and the Consuming Fire and this attribute of God Almighty, none of the dumb gods and lords is able to do!

    i. **Deuteronomy 5:26 (KJV)** For who *is there of* all flesh, that hath heard the voice of the living God speaking out of the midst of the fire, as we *have*, and lived?

    ii. **Joshua 3:10 (KJV)** And Joshua said, Hereby ye shall know that the living God *is* among you, and *that* he will without fail drive out from before you the Canaanites, and the Hittites, and the Hivites, and the Perizzites, and the Girgashites, and the Amorites, and the Jebusites.

    iii. **Psalm 42:2 (KJV)** My soul thirsteth for God, for the living God: when shall I come and appear before God?

    iv. **Jeremiah 10:10 (KJV)** But the LORD *is* the true God, he *is* the living God, and an everlasting king: at his wrath the earth shall tremble, and the nations shall not be able to abide his indignation.

    v. **Daniel 6:26 (KJV)** I make a decree, That in every dominion of my kingdom men tremble and fear before the God of Daniel: for he *is* the living God, and stedfast for ever, and his kingdom *that* which shall not be destroyed, and his dominion *shall be even* unto the end.

    vi. **Hosea 1:10 (KJV)** Yet the number of the children of Israel shall be as the sand of the sea, which cannot be measured nor numbered; and it shall come to pass, *that* in the place where it was said unto them, Ye *are* not my people, *there* it shall be said unto them, *Ye are* the sons of the living God.

    vii. **Matthew 16:16 (KJV)** And Simon Peter answered and said, Thou art the Christ, the Son of the living God.

7. Here is God Almighty as a Consuming Fire!

    i. **Deuteronomy 4:24 (KJV)** For the LORD thy God *is* a consuming fire, *even* a jealous God.

    ii. **Deuteronomy 9:3 (KJV)** Understand therefore this day, that the LORD thy God *is* he which goeth over before thee; *as* a consuming fire he shall destroy them, and he shall bring them down before thy face: so shalt thou drive them out, and destroy them quickly, as the LORD hath said unto thee.

    iii. **Hebrews 12:29 (KJV)** For our God *is* a consuming fire.

    iv. **Exodus 24:12 (KJV)** And the LORD said unto Moses, Come up to me into the mount, and be there: and I will give thee tables of stone, and a law, and commandments which I have written; that thou mayest teach them.

    v. **Exodus 24:13 (KJV)** And Moses rose up, and his minister Joshua: and Moses went up into the mount of God.

    vi. **Exodus 24:14 (KJV)** And he said unto the elders, Tarry ye here for us, until we come again unto you: and, behold, Aaron and Hur *are* with you: if any man have any matters to do, let him come unto them.

    vii. **Exodus 24:15 (KJV)** And Moses went up into the mount, and a cloud covered the mount.

    viii. **Exodus 24:16 (KJV)** And the glory of the LORD abode upon mount Sinai, and the cloud covered it six days: and the seventh day he called unto Moses out of the midst of the cloud.

    ix. **Exodus 24:17 (KJV)** And the sight of the glory of the LORD *was* like devouring fire on the top of the mount in the eyes of the children of Israel.

8. Now, here is one of the most important differences between the dumb idols and the LORD God Almighty whereby the LORD God can receive meat/food and drink offerings but the dumb idols cannot!

    i. **Leviticus 9:23 (KJV)** And Moses and Aaron went into the tabernacle of the congregation, and came out, and blessed the people: and the glory of the LORD appeared unto all the people.

    ii. **Leviticus 9:24 (KJV)** And there came a fire out from before the LORD, and consumed upon the altar the burnt offering and the fat: *which* when all the people saw, they shouted, and fell on their faces.

    iii. **1 Kings 18:36 (KJV)** And it came to pass at *the time of* the offering of the *evening* sacrifice, that Elijah the prophet came near, and said, LORD God of Abraham, Isaac, and of Israel, let it be known this day that thou *art* God in Israel, and *that* I *am* thy servant, and *that* I have done all these things at thy word.

    iv. **1 Kings 18:37 (KJV)** Hear me, O LORD, hear me, that this people may know that thou *art* the LORD God, and *that* thou hast turned their heart back again.

v. **1 Kings 18:38 (KJV)** Then the fire of the LORD fell, and consumed the burnt sacrifice, and the wood, and the stones, and the dust, and licked up the water that *was* in the trench.

vi. **1 Kings 18:39 (KJV)** And when all the people saw *it*, they fell on their faces: and they said, The LORD, he *is* the God; the LORD, he *is* the God.

9. Therefore, the most important thing is to love God and keep HIS commandments! The dumb idols might call themselves gods and deities and lords, yet they are dumb and have no power over the true child of God who loves God and is known of God as **1 Corinthians 8:3 (KJV)** reveals!

i. **1 Corinthians 8:3 (KJV)** But if any man love God, the same is known of him.

ii. **1 Corinthians 8:5 (KJV)** For though there be that are called gods, whether in heaven or in earth, (as there be gods many, and lords many,)

iii. **1 Corinthians 8:6 (KJV)** But to us *there is but* one God, the Father, of whom *are* all things, and we in him; and one Lord Jesus Christ, by whom *are* all things, and we by him.

10. Agan, it is the knowledge from the worshippers that is invested in the food, drinks, and meats that defiles the man and NOT the food, drinks, and meats themselves! That is why "meat commendeth us not to God", meaning that there is zero spiritual significance in any food, including the useless Holy Communion foods and drinks!

i. **1 Corinthians 8:7 (KJV)** Howbeit *there is* not in every man that knowledge: for some with conscience of the idol unto this hour eat *it* as a thing offered unto an idol; and their conscience being weak is defiled.

ii. **1 Corinthians 8:8 (KJV)** But meat commendeth us not to God: for neither, if we eat, are we the better; neither, if we eat not, are we the worse.

iii. **Mark 7:14 (KJV)** And when he had called all the people *unto him*, he said unto them, Hearken unto me every one *of you*, and understand:

iv. **Mark 7:15 (KJV)** There is nothing from without a man, that entering into him can defile him: but the things which come out of him, those are they that defile the man.

v. **Mark 7:16 (KJV)** If any man have ears to hear, let him hear.

vi. **Matthew 15:15 (KJV)** Then answered Peter and said unto him, Declare unto us this parable.

vii. **Matthew 15:16 (KJV)** And Jesus said, Are ye also yet without understanding?

viii. **Matthew 15:17 (KJV)** Do not ye yet understand, that whatsoever entereth in at the mouth goeth into the belly, and is cast out into the draught?

ix. **Matthew 15:18 (KJV)** But those things which proceed out of the mouth come forth from the heart; and they defile the man.

x. **Matthew 15:19 (KJV)** For out of the heart proceed evil thoughts, murders, adulteries, fornications, thefts, false witness, blasphemies:

xi. **Matthew 15:20 (KJV)** These are *the things* which defile a man: but to eat with unwashen hands defileth not a man.

11. Consequently, the Word of God considers any person who places any spiritual importance into physical food, meat, and drink, as a weak person!

    i. **1 Corinthians 8:9 (KJV)** But take heed lest by any means this liberty of yours become a stumblingblock to them that are weak.

12. All Holy Communion Pastors, Bishops, and Church Leaders are spiritually weak people since they believe that the idolatry of Holy Communion that they perform every Sunday in their churches is able to procure them some spiritual benefit, which it does NOT!

13. If pagans offer foods and drinks to their dumb gods and deities and the dumb gods and deities have no power to eat the food and meat, and then, you who claim to be Christians also offer foods and drinks to your God and your God does not receive nor accept them from your hands hence, you have to eat these same foods and meats by yourselves just as the idol worshippers also consume by themselves the foods and meats that they offer to their idols, then, what is the difference between you two worshippers when both of you do the same thing and both of your gods also do the same thing by NOT accepting the foods and meats at your hands?

    i. **Isaiah 1:10 (KJV)** Hear the word of the LORD, ye rulers of Sodom; give ear unto the law of our God, ye people of Gomorrah.

    ii. **Isaiah 1:11 (KJV)** To what purpose *is* the multitude of your sacrifices unto me? saith the LORD: I am full of the burnt offerings of rams, and the fat of fed beasts; and I delight not in the blood of bullocks, or of lambs, or of he goats.

    iii. **Isaiah 1:12 (KJV)** When ye come to appear before me, who hath required this at your hand, to tread my courts?

    iv. **Isaiah 1:13 (KJV)** Bring no more vain oblations; incense is an abomination unto me; the new moons and sabbaths, the calling of assemblies, I cannot away with; *it is* iniquity, even the solemn meeting.

14. All you Holy Communion Pastors, Bishops, and Church Leaders, is it true that the LORD Jesus Christ said this?

    i. **Matthew 5:17 (KJV)** Think not that I am come to destroy the law, or the prophets: I am not come to destroy, but to fulfil.

    ii. **Matthew 5:18 (KJV)** For verily I say unto you, Till heaven and earth pass, one jot or one tittle shall in no wise pass from the law, till all be fulfilled.

15. All you Holy Communion Pastors, Bishops, and Church Leaders, is it true that the LORD God Almighty said this?

    i. **Psalm 50:7 (KJV)** Hear, O my people, and I will speak; O Israel, and I will testify against thee: I *am* God, *even* thy God.

    ii. **Psalm 50:8 (KJV)** I will not reprove thee for thy sacrifices or thy burnt offerings, *to have been* continually before me.

    iii. **Psalm 50:9 (KJV)** I will take no bullock out of thy house, *nor* he goats out of thy folds.

    iv. **Psalm 50:10 (KJV)** For every beast of the forest *is* mine, *and* the cattle upon a thousand hills.

    v. **Psalm 50:11 (KJV)** I know all the fowls of the mountains: and the wild beasts of the field *are* mine.

    vi. **Psalm 50:12 (KJV)** If I were hungry, I would not tell thee: for the world *is* mine, and the fulness thereof.

    vii. **Psalm 50:13 (KJV)** Will I eat the flesh of bulls, or drink the blood of goats?

16. So, then, why would the LORD Jesus Christ fulfil **Psalm 50:7-13 (KJV)** by telling you to do exactly the opposite of what the LORD God commanded there?

17. When the LORD God removed all your food, meat, and drink offerings in **Psalm 50:7-13 (KJV)**, what did God replace them with? God replaced them with words, just words, the Words of God ONLY!

    i. **Psalm 50:14 (KJV)** Offer unto God thanksgiving; and pay thy vows unto the most High:

    ii. **Psalm 50:15 (KJV)** And call upon me in the day of trouble: I will deliver thee, and thou shalt glorify me.

18. Therefore, when the LORD Jesus Christ fulfilled **Psalm 50:7-13 (KJV)** by telling you to eat bread and drink from the cup, HE never commanded you to make an offering out of them unto God since that would have been a blatant disobedience to **Psalm 50:7-13 (KJV**!

19. Here is exactly what the LORD Jesus Christ commanded!

      i. **Luke 22:14 (KJV)** And when the hour was come, he sat down, and the twelve apostles with him.

      ii. **Luke 22:15 (KJV)** And he said unto them, With desire I have desired to eat this passover with you before I suffer:

      iii. **Luke 22:16 (KJV)** For I say unto you, I will not any more eat thereof, until it be fulfilled in the kingdom of God.

      iv. **Luke 22:17 (KJV)** And he took the cup, and gave thanks, and said, Take this, and divide *it* among yourselves:

      v. **Luke 22:18 (KJV)** For I say unto you, I will not drink of the fruit of the vine, until the kingdom of God shall come.

      vi. **Luke 22:19 (KJV)** And he took bread, and gave thanks, and brake *it*, and gave unto them, saying, This is my body which is given for you: this do in remembrance of me.

      vii. **Luke 22:20 (KJV)** Likewise also the cup after supper, saying, This cup *is* the new testament in my blood, which is shed for you.

20. Now, all you Holy Communion Pastors, Bishops, and Church Leaders, I have reproduced your Holy Communion Law in **Luke 22:14-20 (KJV)**, so, now, show me the exact words that says "OFFERING or SACRIFICE"!

21. **SECOND**, when you have finished showing me the "offering" in the command of the LORD Jesus Christ in **Luke 22:14-20 (KJV)**, then also, show me the worship service that is in **Luke 22:14-20 (KJV)** that empowers you also to do Holy Communion in a church worship service!

22. **THIRD**, when you have finished showing me the "offering" in the command of the LORD Jesus Christ in **Luke 22:14-20 (KJV)**, then also, show me the Altar that the LORD Jesus Christ was using to make HIS "sacrifice and offerings" at the Last Supper!

23. **FOURTH**, when you have finished showing me the "offering" in the command of the LORD Jesus Christ in **Luke 22:14-20 (KJV)**, then also, show me the many wine cups in those verses that empower you to "offer" your Holy Communion in many cups!

24. **FIFTH**, when you have finished showing me the "offering" in the command of the LORD Jesus Christ in **Luke 22:14-20 (KJV)**, then also, show me in those same verses the many different pieces of bread that the LORD Jesus Christ used that empowers you also to use all those many different pieces of bread instead of the only one bread that the LORD Jesus Christ broke and gave to the Apostles!

25. Holy Communion Pastors, Bishops, and Church Leaders, do you now see what despicable filthy fraudsters you have been?

26. Do you now see how very stupid and most ignorant bastards that you are?

27. Do you now see how many millions of innocent equally foolish people like you that you have successfully sent to Hell?

28. Holy Communion Pastors, Bishops, and Church Leaders, do you now see how you are NOT fit to stand in the Pulpit and even to be in the Ministry at all?

29. Shame on you and may the curse of Sodom and Gomorrah be on you forever!

> i. **Jeremiah 23:14 (KJV)** I have seen also in the prophets of Jerusalem an horrible thing: they commit adultery, and walk in lies: they strengthen also the hands of evildoers, that none doth return from his wickedness: they are all of them unto me as Sodom, and the inhabitants thereof as Gomorrah.

30. Again, when the LORD God removed all your food, meat, and drink offerings in **Psalm 50:7-13 (KJV)**, what did God replace them with? God replaced them with words, just words, the Words of God ONLY!

> i. **Psalm 50:14 (KJV)** Offer unto God thanksgiving; and pay thy vows unto the most High:
>
> ii. **Psalm 50:15 (KJV)** And call upon me in the day of trouble: I will deliver thee, and thou shalt glorify me.

31. Therefore, since the LORD Jesus Christ said in **Matthew 5:17-18 (KJV)** that HE came to fulfill the Law and the Prophets, then, the Holy Communion Law of the LORD Jesus Christ in **Luke 22:14-20 (KJV)** can NEVER mean a command for you to disobey **Psalm 50:7-13 (KJV)**, but rather, and specifically, **Luke 22:14-20 (KJV)** is a command to do and obey **Psalm 50:14-15 (KJV)**!

32. How is it that this plain language is in plain sight: "But meat commendeth us not to God", and yet all the Holy Communion Pastors, Bishops, and Church Leaders are so blind that they cannot see it?

> i. **1 Corinthians 8:8 (KJV)** But meat commendeth us not to God: for neither, if we eat, are we the better; neither, if we eat not, are we the worse.

33. The revelation that meat (meaning foods, meats, and drinks) DOES NOT COMMEND US TO GOD means that:

> i. Foods, meats, and drinks, even when offered in sacrifice as Holy Communion, DO NOT commend, approve, entrust, preserve, make us worthy, praise, dedicate, commit, confide, consign, endear, esteem, congratulate, applaud, compliment, endorse, extol, hail, nor justify us before God Almighty!

34. So, then, what is so hard in this sentence: "But meat commendeth us not to God", that educated illiterates and Doctors such as all these Holy Communion Pastors, Bishops, and Church Leaders are NOT able to understand?

    i. **1 Corinthians 8:9 (KJV)** But take heed lest by any means this liberty of yours become a stumblingblock to them that are weak.

35. This particular idolatry and pagan worship in **1 Corinthians 8:10 (KJV)**, is exactly what you have imported into your Holy Communion, and yet it was abolished already in **Psalm 50:7-13 (KJV)**!

    i. **1 Corinthians 8:10 (KJV)** For if any man see thee which hast knowledge sit at meat in the idol's temple, shall not the conscience of him which is weak be emboldened to eat those things which are offered to idols;

36. And this your knowledge and practise of idolatrous Holy Communion has already caused millions of so-called Christians to perish!

    i. **1 Corinthians 8:11 (KJV)** And through thy knowledge shall the weak brother perish, for whom Christ died?

37. You cannot deny that your idolatrous Holy Communion has already caused millions of so-called Christians to perish because the practise of offering and sacrificing food, meat, and drinks before the LORD God Almighty, is NOT even found as a commandment in your own Holy Communion Law of the LORD Jesus Christ in **Luke 22:14-20 (KJV)**!

    i. **1 Corinthians 8:12 (KJV)** But when ye sin so against the brethren, and wound their weak conscience, ye sin against Christ.

    ii. **1 Corinthians 8:13 (KJV)** Wherefore, if meat make my brother to offend, I will eat no flesh while the world standeth, lest I make my brother to offend.

38. Or, if you comprehend the sentence, then what is it that informs your stupidity to continue doing it against the LORD God Almighty?

The LORD Jesus Christ be with your spirit. The LORD Jesus Christ give you understanding.

Rev. Prof. PETER PRYCE,
DSEF, BA, MA, B.Soc.Sc Pol Sci, IBA, PhD
A Scribe of the Law of the God of Heaven
Prophet of the Word of God
Professor of French, Silver Spring, MD, USA
Scholar of the Institute of Theologians, USA

WWW.THEBIBLEUNIVERSITY.ORG
Accreditation Number: 07-QCTO/SDP120723172836
SAQA QUAL ID: Identification # 101997
WWW.BOOKSTORESITE.ORG
WWW.THEBIBLEUNIVERSITYCHURCH.ORG

Wednesday 10th January 2024 @ 9:04 AM – 2:03 PM
While hearing and meditating on the Word of God at home.

CHAPTER 10

CHRISTIAN IDOLATRY IN WATER BAPTISM AND IN HOLY COMMUNION

BI NKA BI

"No one should bite the other"

Asante philosophical symbol of Peace, Harmony, no backbiting, no false witnessing

Question 2468

1. Is it possible for Christianity and idolatry to walk together?
2. Yes, and the consequence for that is Hell!

   i. **1 Samuel 15:23 (KJV)** For rebellion *is as* the sin of witchcraft, and stubbornness *is as* iniquity and idolatry. Because thou hast rejected the word of the LORD, he hath also rejected thee from *being* king.

   ii. **Acts 17:16 (KJV)** Now while Paul waited for them at Athens, his spirit was stirred in him, when he saw the city wholly given to idolatry.

   iii. **Acts 17:21 (KJV)** (For all the Athenians and strangers which were there spent their time in nothing else, but either to tell, or to hear some new thing.)

   iv. **1 Corinthians 10:14 (KJV)** Wherefore, my dearly beloved, flee from idolatry.

   v. **Galatians 5:19 (KJV)** Now the works of the flesh are manifest, which are *these*; Adultery, fornication, uncleanness, lasciviousness,

vi. **Galatians 5:20 (KJV)** Idolatry, witchcraft, hatred, variance, emulations, wrath, strife, seditions, heresies,

vii. **Galatians 5:21 (KJV)** Envyings, murders, drunkenness, revellings, and such like: of the which I tell you before, as I have also told *you* in time past, that they which do such things shall not inherit the kingdom of God.

viii. **Colossians 3:5 (KJV)** Mortify therefore your members which are upon the earth; fornication, uncleanness, inordinate affection, evil concupiscence, and covetousness, which is idolatry:

ix. **Colossians 3:6 (KJV)** For which things' sake the wrath of God cometh on the children of disobedience:

3. So, as you can see from the evidence, the LORD God reveals to us in **1 Samuel 15:23 (KJV)** that rebellion, stubbornness, and rejection/refusal of the Word of God, they are all both witchcraft and idolatry!

4. Then, in **Acts 17:16-21 (KJV)**, you can see that debating politics as a passion and journalism are also idolatry and you know that there are many so-called Christians who love politics more than the Word of God!

5. Then, in **1 Corinthians 10:14 (KJV)**, you can see that Apostle Paul was writing to already saved Brethren and yet he was accusing them of idolatry, and so, yes, Christianity and idolatry can walk together!

6. Then, in **Galatians 5:19-21 (KJV)**, you can see that when people claim to be Christians and they still do the works of the flesh instead of focusing only on the Word of God, such as Water baptism and Holy Communion and Feet Washing, then, they are not only idolaters, but they are also practising witchcraft!

7. Then, in **Colossians 3:5 (KJV)**, you can see that even the very common sin of covetousness/greediness, is also known as idolatry in the spiritual realm!

8. Then, finally in **Colossians 3:6 (KJV)**, you see that anyone who practices idolatry and is therefore a witch and wizard, also has the wrath of God on him, meaning that he/she will go to Hell!

9. Why is 1 Corinthians chapter 10 about idolatry, but already in the second verse, it is talking about Baptism?

i. **1 Corinthians 10:1 (KJV)** Moreover, brethren, I would not that ye should be ignorant, how that all our fathers were under the cloud, and all passed through the sea;

ii. **1 Corinthians 10:2 (KJV)** And were all baptized unto Moses in the cloud and in the sea;

10. Because it is possible to commit idolatry with Water baptism!

11. Look again at **1 Corinthians 10:1-2 (KJV)** and tell me what you see God Almighty revealing to you over there!

12. **ONE** – You see that this expression: "and they all passed through the sea" takes you straight to **Exodus 14:15-22 (KJV)**:

    i. **Exodus 14:15 (KJV)** And the LORD said unto Moses, Wherefore criest thou unto me? speak unto the children of Israel, that they go forward:

    ii. **Exodus 14:16 (KJV)** But lift thou up thy rod, and stretch out thine hand over the sea, and divide it: and the children of Israel shall go on dry *ground* through the midst of the sea.

    iii. **Exodus 14:17 (KJV)** And I, behold, I will harden the hearts of the Egyptians, and they shall follow them: and I will get me honour upon Pharaoh, and upon all his host, upon his chariots, and upon his horsemen.

    iv. **Exodus 14:18 (KJV)** And the Egyptians shall know that I *am* the LORD, when I have gotten me honour upon Pharaoh, upon his chariots, and upon his horsemen.

    v. **Exodus 14:19 (KJV)** And the angel of God, which went before the camp of Israel, removed and went behind them; and the pillar of the cloud went from before their face, and stood behind them:

    vi. **Exodus 14:20 (KJV)** And it came between the camp of the Egyptians and the camp of Israel; and it was a cloud and darkness *to them*, but it gave light by night *to these*: so that the one came not near the other all the night.

    vii. **Exodus 14:21 (KJV)** And Moses stretched out his hand over the sea; and the LORD caused the sea to go *back* by a strong east wind all that night, and made the sea dry *land*, and the waters were divided.

    viii. **Exodus 14:22 (KJV)** And the children of Israel went into the midst of the sea upon the dry *ground*: and the waters *were* a wall unto them on their right hand, and on their left.

13. **TWO** – Then, this Word: "And they were all baptized unto Moses" is evidence that God Almighty is talking about "Baptism"!

14. **THREE** – Then, now look again at **1 Corinthians 10:2 (KJV)**, and then, tell me how the people were baptized, or, with what did Moses baptize the people?

15. **FOUR** – Here is the answer: "And they were all baptized unto Moses in the cloud"!

16. **SIX** – Now, tell me, did you see any water there in **1 Corinthians 10:1-2 (KJV)**?

17. **SEVEN** – The correct answer is, no, and yet, the LORD God says that, even without water, the people still were baptized, meaning that, originally, the very first

time that baptism took place in the entire Holy Bible, it was Waterless Baptism! Can you see that?

18. That revelation of Waterless Baptism that I have just shown you means that the true and correct baptism is NOT with water but waterless, and here is further evidence!

    i. "and the children of Israel shall go on dry *ground* through the midst of the sea" – **Exodus 14:16 (KJV)**

    ii. "and made the sea dry *land*, and the waters were divided" – **Exodus 14:21 (KJV)**

    iii. "And the children of Israel went into the midst of the sea upon the dry *ground*: and the waters *were* a wall unto them on their right hand, and on their left" – **Exodus 14:22 (KJV)**

19. Here is the third evidence that the true and correct baptism is NOT with water but waterless!

    i. **Matthew 3:11 (KJV)** I indeed baptize you with water unto repentance: but he that cometh after me is mightier than I, whose shoes I am not worthy to bear: he shall baptize you with the Holy Ghost, and *with* fire:

    ii. **Mark 1:8 (KJV)** I indeed have baptized you with water: but he shall baptize you with the Holy Ghost.

    iii. **Luke 3:16 (KJV)** John answered, saying unto *them* all, I indeed baptize you with water; but one mightier than I cometh, the latchet of whose shoes I am not worthy to unloose: he shall baptize you with the Holy Ghost and with fire:

20. Here is the fourth evidence that the true and correct baptism is NOT with water but waterless!

    i. **Acts 1:4 (KJV)** And, being assembled together with *them*, commanded them that they should not depart from Jerusalem, but wait for the promise of the Father, which, *saith he*, ye have heard of me.

    ii. **Acts 1:5 (KJV)** For John truly baptized with water; but ye shall be baptized with the Holy Ghost not many days hence.

21. Now, here is the idolatry part that is connected to Water Baptism!

    i. When you move away from the true and correct Waterless Baptism to do the inferior Water Baptism of John the Baptist, then, that water part of your baptism is your idolatry!

    ii. Meaning that you are using a thing as a medium to reach the LORD God Almighty!

22. Now, is it correct Christianity to use things to worship God Almighty? NO!

i. **John 4:23 (KJV)** But the hour cometh, and now is, when the true worshippers shall worship the Father in spirit and in truth: for the Father seeketh such to worship him.

ii. **John 4:24 (KJV)** God *is* a Spirit: and they that worship him must worship *him* in spirit and in truth.

23. Do you remember what the LORD Jesus Christ did to all the people who were using things in God-worship in the Temple?

   i. **John 2:12 (KJV)** After this he went down to Capernaum, he, and his mother, and his brethren, and his disciples: and they continued there not many days.

   ii. **John 2:13 (KJV)** And the Jews' passover was at hand, and Jesus went up to Jerusalem,

   iii. **John 2:14 (KJV)** And found in the temple those that sold oxen and sheep and doves, and the changers of money sitting:

   iv. **John 2:15 (KJV)** And when he had made a scourge of small cords, he drove them all out of the temple, and the sheep, and the oxen; and poured out the changers' money, and overthrew the tables;

   v. **John 2:16 (KJV)** And said unto them that sold doves, Take these things hence; make not my Father's house an house of merchandise.

   vi. **John 2:17 (KJV)** And his disciples remembered that it was written, The zeal of thine house hath eaten me up.

24. In summary so far, we have two baptisms:

   i. The Physical Water Baptism, and

   ii. The Spiritual Waterless Baptism

25. But, the LORD God Almighty is emphasizing the spiritual over the physical, because it is the physical that creates the link to the idolatry!

   i. **Romans 3:27 (KJV)** Where *is* boasting then? It is excluded. By what law? of works? Nay: but by the law of faith.

   ii. **Romans 9:32 (KJV)** Wherefore? Because *they sought it* not by faith, but as it were by the works of the law. For they stumbled at that stumblingstone;

   iii. **Galatians 2:16 (KJV)** Knowing that a man is not justified by the works of the law, but by the faith of Jesus Christ, even we have believed in Jesus Christ, that we might be justified by the faith of Christ, and not by the works of the law: for by the works of the law shall no flesh be justified.

iv. **Galatians 3:5 (KJV)** He therefore that ministereth to you the Spirit, and worketh miracles among you, *doeth he it* by the works of the law, or by the hearing of faith?

v. **Galatians 3:10 (KJV)** For as many as are of the works of the law are under the curse: for it is written, Cursed *is* every one that continueth not in all things which are written in the book of the law to do them.

vi. **Romans 8:13 (KJV)** For if ye live after the flesh, ye shall die: but if ye through the Spirit do mortify the deeds of the body, ye shall live.

26. Idolatry simply means anything that you use to stand in the place of God Almighty! Anything material that represents God is idolatry! Anything or any thought that can draw you away from focusing ONLY on the LORD Jesus Christ is an idol!

27. In other words, when you have any item such as beads, rosary, scarf, mantle, oil, water, cross, graven image, nature, that you claim to need to worship God, then, that thing becomes the idol that replaces God Almighty, why?

28. Because, the Word of God alone is enough to represent God Almighty!

i. **John 1:1 (KJV)** In the beginning was the Word, and the Word was with God, and the Word was God.

ii. **John 1:2 (KJV)** The same was in the beginning with God.

iii. **John 15:7 (KJV)** If ye abide in me, and my words abide in you, ye shall ask what ye will, and it shall be done unto you.

29. So, as you can see from the above two evidences, the ONLY thing that is between you and God Almighty is the Word of God, NOT beads, rosary, scarf, mantle, oil, or water, cross, graven image, nature, etc.!

i. **John 14:6 (KJV)** Jesus saith unto him, I am the way, the truth, and the life: no man cometh unto the Father, but by me.

ii. **1 Timothy 2:5 (KJV)** For *there is* one God, and one mediator between God and men, the man Christ Jesus;

30. It is for the sake of removing idolatry, that is why you no longer need a physical temple or a physical House of God before you can worship God Almighty!

31. That is why you no longer need to repeat the Physical Crucifixion before you can worship God Almighty!

32. That is why you no longer need to repeat the Physical Circumcision before you can worship God Almighty!

33. That is why you no longer need to repeat the Physical Water Baptism before you can worship God Almighty!

34. That is why you no longer need to repeat the Physical Holy Communion/Last Supper before you can worship God Almighty!

35. As you can see, the LORD God is emphasizing the spiritual over the physical, here in these verses! Though it was the LORD God Almighty who gave them the physical water to drink, yet what matters most to God Almighty is the spiritual water and NOT the physical water!

   i. **1 Corinthians 10:3 (KJV)** And did all eat the same spiritual meat;

   ii. **1 Corinthians 10:4 (KJV)** And did all drink the same spiritual drink: for they drank of that spiritual Rock that followed them: and that Rock was Christ.

36. Now, see why the LORD God was angry with them and killed many of them in the wilderness!

   i. **1 Corinthians 10:5 (KJV)** But with many of them God was not well pleased: for they were overthrown in the wilderness.

   ii. **1 Corinthians 10:6 (KJV)** Now these things were our examples, to the intent we should not lust after evil things, as they also lusted.

   iii. **1 Corinthians 10:7 (KJV)** Neither be ye idolaters, as *were* some of them; as it is written, The people sat down to eat and drink, and rose up to play.

37. The LORD God killed those who died because they were idolaters!

38. Now, check again very carefully how they practiced their idolatry!

   i. **Exodus 32:1 (KJV)** And when the people saw that Moses delayed to come down out of the mount, the people gathered themselves together unto Aaron, and said unto him, Up, make us gods, which shall go before us; for *as for* this Moses, the man that brought us up out of the land of Egypt, we wot not what is become of him.

   ii. **Exodus 32:2 (KJV)** And Aaron said unto them, Break off the golden earrings, which *are* in the ears of your wives, of your sons, and of your daughters, and bring *them* unto me.

   iii. **Exodus 32:3 (KJV)** And all the people brake off the golden earrings which *were* in their ears, and brought *them* unto Aaron.

   iv. **Exodus 32:4 (KJV)** And he received *them* at their hand, and fashioned it with a graving tool, after he had made it a molten calf: and they said, These *be* thy gods, O Israel, which brought thee up out of the land of Egypt.

   v. **Exodus 32:5 (KJV)** And when Aaron saw *it*, he built an altar before it; and Aaron made proclamation, and said, To morrow *is* a feast to the LORD.

> vi. **Exodus 32:6 (KJV)** And they rose up early on the morrow, and offered burnt offerings, and brought peace offerings; and the people sat down to eat and to drink, and rose up to play.
>
> vii. **Exodus 32:7 (KJV)** And the LORD said unto Moses, Go, get thee down; for thy people, which thou broughtest out of the land of Egypt, have corrupted *themselves*:
>
> viii. **1 Corinthians 10:7 (KJV)** Neither be ye idolaters, as *were* some of them; as it is written, The people sat down to eat and drink, and rose up to play.

39. Did you see in **Exodus 32:1-7 (KJV)** that the people committed idolatry by introducing a physical tangible object in their worship? That was their idolatry, and that is the same way that when you also introduce a physical thing into your worship, then, for them as well as for you, it also becomes idolatry, no matter what that physical thing is, whether water as in Water Baptism, or wafers, wine, bread as in Holy Communion!

40. Even fornication and adultery, did you know that they are also forms of idolatry? Yes, they are when you love flesh more than the Word of God, or when you love your wife more than the Word of God!

> i. **1 Corinthians 10:8 (KJV)** Neither let us commit fornication, as some of them committed, and fell in one day three and twenty thousand.
>
> ii. **1 Corinthians 10:9 (KJV)** Neither let us tempt Christ, as some of them also tempted, and were destroyed of serpents.
>
> iii. **1 Corinthians 10:10 (KJV)** Neither murmur ye, as some of them also murmured, and were destroyed of the destroyer.

41. Someone will say: But we are in the New Testament and our form of worship is different.

42. Well, they are not dot different rather, the Old Testament is fulfilled in the New Testament!

> i. **Matthew 5:17 (KJV)** Think not that I am come to destroy the law, or the prophets: I am not come to destroy, but to fulfil.
>
> ii. **1 Corinthians 10:11 (KJV)** Now all these things happened unto them for ensamples: and they are written for our admonition, upon whom the ends of the world are come.
>
> iii. **1 Corinthians 10:12 (KJV)** Wherefore let him that thinketh he standeth take heed lest he fall.

43. Here is the connection between the Old and the New Testaments for us, meaning that, the idolatry that the LORD God is showing us in the Old Testament also applies to us in the New Testament!

      i. **1 Corinthians 10:13 (KJV)** There hath no temptation taken you but such as is common to man: but God *is* faithful, who will not suffer you to be tempted above that ye are able; but will with the temptation also make a way to escape, that ye may be able to bear *it*.

     ii. **1 Corinthians 10:14 (KJV)** Wherefore, my dearly beloved, flee from idolatry.

    iii. **1 Corinthians 10:15 (KJV)** I speak as to wise men; judge ye what I say.

44. Thus far, we have finished with the following levels of idolatry:

      i. Christian idolatry in Water Baptism

     ii. Idolatry pertaining to spiritual drink from the Spiritual Rock

    iii. Idolatry pertaining to physical items in worship

    iv. Idolatry pertaining to fornication and adultery

45. Now, we are going to the question of Christian idolatry in Holy Communion!

      i. **1 Corinthians 10:16 (KJV)** The cup of blessing which we bless, is it not the communion of the blood of Christ? The bread which we break, is it not the communion of the body of Christ?

     ii. **1 Corinthians 10:17 (KJV)** For we *being* many are one bread, *and* one body: for we are all partakers of that one bread.

46. Now, when you read **1 Corinthians 10:16-17 (KJV)**, what is the level or the realm that you see the LORD God referring to?

47. There are many, even a majority Christians who will say that **1 Corinthians 10:16-17 (KJV)** is talking about the Physical Water Baptism that we do in our churches, but that will be a false answer!

48. What is physical about "the communion of the blood of Christ" in **1 Corinthians 10:16 (KJV)**?

49. The answer is zero, NONE!

50. Are you able to communicate the Blood of Christ through physical wafers, wine, and bread? NO!

      i. **Hebrews 9:13 (KJV)** For if the blood of bulls and of goats, and the ashes of an heifer sprinkling the unclean, sanctifieth to the purifying of the flesh:

     ii. **Hebrews 9:14 (KJV)** How much more shall the blood of Christ, who through the eternal Spirit offered himself without spot to God, purge your conscience from dead works to serve the living God?

51. Did you see in **Hebrews 9:14 (KJV)** the specific Person who is able to communicate the Blood of Christ? It is the Holy Spirit alone, not you the foolish ignorant filthy Holy Communion Pastor!

52. Are your filthy physical wafers, wine, and bread enough good representations of Christ? NO!

   i. **Luke 1:76 (KJV)** And thou, child, shalt be called the prophet of the Highest: for thou shalt go before the face of the Lord to prepare his ways;

   ii. **Matthew 3:11 (KJV)** I indeed baptize you with water unto repentance: but he that cometh after me is mightier than I, whose shoes I am not worthy to bear: he shall baptize you with the Holy Ghost, and *with* fire:

   iii. **Mark 1:7 (KJV)** And preached, saying, There cometh one mightier than I after me, the latchet of whose shoes I am not worthy to stoop down and unloose.

   iv. **Luke 3:16 (KJV)** John answered, saying unto *them* all, I indeed baptize you with water; but one mightier than I cometh, the latchet of whose shoes I am not worthy to unloose: he shall baptize you with the Holy Ghost and with fire:

   v. **Acts 13:25 (KJV)** And as John fulfilled his course, he said, Whom think ye that I am? I am not *he*. But, behold, there cometh one after me, whose shoes of *his* feet I am not worthy to loose.

53. If John the Baptist who was sent by God from Heaven as the Prophet of the Highest, to introduce the LORD Jesus Christ, said himself that, despite all his holiness, he was still not worthy to even pick up the shoe laces of the LORD Jesus Christ, then how very stupid can you be to think and suppose that your filthy physical wafers, wine, and bread can stand in the place of Christ?

54. We are still on the spirituality of Holy Communion in **1 Corinthians 10:16-17 (KJV)**!

   i. **1 Corinthians 10:16 (KJV)** The cup of blessing which we bless, is it not the communion of the blood of Christ? The bread which we break, is it not the communion of the body of Christ?

   ii. **1 Corinthians 10:17 (KJV)** For we *being* many are one bread, *and* one body: for we are all partakers of that one bread.

55. The LORD God says over there that "The bread which we break, it is the body of Christ"! – **1 Corinthians 10:16 (KJV)**

56. Now, look at the spirituality of the Holy Communion in **1 Corinthians 10:17 (KJV)**!

57. The LORD God says over there, that the same bread which is the body of Christ, that "we *being* many are one bread, *and* one body"!

58. So, the LORD God is saying that both we and the LORD Jesus Christ are eating and drinking this Bread!

59. YES, you got that right: "until that day when I drink it new with you in my Father's kingdom"!

    i. **Matthew 26:26 (KJV)** And as they were eating, Jesus took bread, and blessed *it*, and brake *it*, and gave *it* to the disciples, and said, Take, eat; this is my body.

    ii. **Matthew 26:27 (KJV)** And he took the cup, and gave thanks, and gave *it* to them, saying, Drink ye all of it;

    iii. **Matthew 26:28 (KJV)** For this is my blood of the new testament, which is shed for many for the remission of sins.

    iv. **Matthew 26:29 (KJV)** But I say unto you, I will not drink henceforth of this fruit of the vine, until that day when I drink it new with you in my Father's kingdom.

60. See again what the LORD God said over there: "for we are all partakers of that one bread" – **1 Corinthians 10:17 (KJV)**

61. So, the LORD Jesus Christ is also partaking/eating of this same Bread with us while HE is in Heaven?

62. YES, and the evidence is **Matthew 26:29 (KJV)** and **1 Corinthians 10:17 (KJV)**!

    i. **Matthew 26:29 (KJV)** But I say unto you, I will not drink henceforth of this fruit of the vine, until that day when I drink it new with you in my Father's kingdom.

    ii. **1 Corinthians 10:17 (KJV)** For we *being* many are one bread, *and* one body: for we are all partakers of that one bread.

63. Now, Brethren, that is a very interesting revelation that raises a very seriou question!

64. If, according to **Matthew 26:29 (KJV)** and **1 Corinthians 10:17**, the LORD Jesus Christ is eating the same Bread and drinking the same wine with us as we are doing in our Holy Communion in all the churches, then how did those filthy physical wafers, wine, and bread get to the LORD Jesus Christ in Heaven?

65. Now, Brethren, first of all, is it even possible for those filthy physical wafers, wine, and bread to get to the LORD Jesus Christ in Heaven? Since when did physical items start entering Heaven?

    i. **1 Corinthians 15:50 (KJV)** Now this I say, brethren, that flesh and blood cannot inherit the kingdom of God; neither doth corruption inherit incorruption.

66. Brother, are you now beginning to see the stupidity of you Holy Communion doctrine?

67. Brother, let us consider it again. Here is the condition that the LORD Jesus Christ gave for the Holy Communion that HE commanded us to do: "when I drink it new with you in my Father's kingdom"!

68. But, the truth is that, you know very well that the Holy Communion that you are doing right now in all your churches does NOT meet his spiritual condition, and yet you are still doing it?

69. Or, are you ready to show me what part of those filthy physical wafers, wine, and bread is spiritual and is able to enter Heaven? None of them!

70. If none of them, then, why are you doing it?

71. The simple answer is because you are very stupid! You have no understanding of the Word of God! You do NOT have the Holy Spirit hence you have that carnal Holy Communion doctrine!

72. Or, are you even worse than stupid to tell me that those filthy physical wafers, wine, and bread are not carnal?

73. Are you even aware at all what the word "carnal" means? Here is the meaning of your carnal filthy physical Holy Communion wafers, wine, and bread!

    i. "Carnal" means something related to physical, sexual, sensual, flesh, things that satisfy animal needs, spiritually deficient, uncovered flesh and nakedness like the half-naked choir women in the churches, something that is enmity against God, worldly, lustful, impure, beastly, unchristian, earthly, lewd, wanton, corporal genital, lascivious, lacking Holy Spirit, unbelieving, temporal, something that is not subject to the law of God, selfishness, self-willed, self-focused and self-seeking, legal term for sexual intercourse, crudity, etc.

74. Well, we have come to the point now where, if you had any sense at all, then you would asking:

    i. So, after we have removed this carnal filthy physical Holy Communion wafers, wine, and bread, then what shall we do then?

75. See, the LORD God already gave you the answer in the same **1 Corinthians 10:17 (KJV)** that we have already read several times!

    i. **1 Corinthians 10:17 (KJV)** For we *being* many are one bread, *and* one body: for we are all partakers of that one bread.

76. So, as you read **1 Corinthians 10:17 (KJV)**, where do you think the revelation is, since you claim to be a Pastor, a Bishop, a General Overseer, and you also claim that it was the LORD Jesus Christ who called you into the Ministry, and you also claim that you have the Holy Spirit?

    i. **Jeremiah 3:15 (KJV)** And I will give you pastors according to mine heart, which shall feed you with knowledge and understanding.

    ii. **Malachi 2:7 (KJV)** For the priest's lips should keep knowledge, and they should seek the law at his mouth: for he *is* the messenger of the LORD of hosts.

77. That is the work of the true Man of God, so tell us what the LORD God is saying in **1 Corinthians 10:17 (KJV)** concerning Holy Communion!

78. In answer to your question on what we shall do after we have removed this carnal filthy physical Holy Communion wafers, wine, and bread, here is where the revelation is located: "for we are all partakers of that one bread"!

79. Brother, that is the ONLY ONE BREAD that when you eat it here on the Earth, the LORD Jesus Christ will be eating with you same time in the Kingdom of Heaven as HE promised!

      i. **Matthew 26:29 (KJV)** But I say unto you, I will not drink henceforth of this fruit of the vine, until that day when I drink it new with you in my Father's kingdom.

80. Now, I can hear someone asking: So where is the Bread?

81. Thou fool! Here is the ONLY ONE BREAD!

      i. **John 6:27 (KJV)** Labour not for the meat which perisheth, but for that meat which endureth unto everlasting life, which the Son of man shall give unto you: for him hath God the Father sealed.

      ii. **John 6:32 (KJV)** Then Jesus said unto them, Verily, verily, I say unto you, Moses gave you not that bread from heaven; but my Father giveth you the true bread from heaven.

      iii. **John 6:58 (KJV)** This is that bread which came down from heaven: not as your fathers did eat manna, and are dead: he that eateth of this bread shall live for ever.

82. So, in **John 6:27 (KJV)**, the LORD Jesus Christ said:

      i. Throw away your carnal filthy physical Holy Communion wafers, wine, and bread, because if you refuse and you continue to eat them, you will die!

83. Now, read again **John 6:32 (KJV)**, and tell me: the true Holy Communion Bread, where does it come from?

84. From Heaven, NOT from your filthy sweat-stained polluted bread shop!

85. See here: "my Father giveth you the true bread from heaven"!

      i. **John 6:33 (KJV)** For the bread of God is he which cometh down from heaven, and giveth life unto the world.

86. So, then who will go to Heaven and bring us this Bread?

87. Thou fool again and again! The Bread is already in your mouth according to **Deuteronomy 30:11-14 (KJV)** and confirmed in **Romans 10:8 (KJV)**!

      i. **Deuteronomy 30:11 (KJV)** For this commandment which I command thee this day, it *is* not hidden from thee, neither *is* it far off.

    ii. **Deuteronomy 30:11 (KJV)** For this commandment which I command thee this day, it *is* not hidden from thee, neither *is* it far off.

    iii. **Deuteronomy 30:12 (KJV)** It *is* not in heaven, that thou shouldest say, Who shall go up for us to heaven, and bring it unto us, that we may hear it, and do it?

    iv. **Deuteronomy 30:13 (KJV)** Neither *is* it beyond the sea, that thou shouldest say, Who shall go over the sea for us, and bring it unto us, that we may hear it, and do it?

    v. **Deuteronomy 30:14 (KJV)** But the word *is* very nigh unto thee, in thy mouth, and in thy heart, that thou mayest do it.

    vi. **Romans 10:8 (KJV)** But what saith it? The word is nigh thee, *even* in thy mouth, and in thy heart: that is, the word of faith, which we preach;

88. Here is another evidence that the proper Spiritual Holy Communing Bread is in your mouth and it is the Word of Faith that we preach!

    i. **John 1:1 (KJV)** In the beginning was the Word, and the Word was with God, and the Word was God.

    ii. **John 1:2 (KJV)** The same was in the beginning with God.

89. Here is another evidence that the proper Spiritual Holy Communing Bread is in your mouth and it is the Word of Faith that we preach!

    i. **Revelation 19:11 (KJV)** And I saw heaven opened, and behold a white horse; and he that sat upon him *was* called Faithful and True, and in righteousness he doth judge and make war.

90. Here is another evidence that the proper Spiritual Holy Communing Bread is in your mouth and it is the Word of Faith that we preach!

    i. **Revelation 19:13 (KJV)** And he *was* clothed with a vesture dipped in blood: and his name is called The Word of God.

91. What then is the idolatry in the Holy Communion that we do in the churches?

92. It is the physical oblations, tokens, and elements that we use as representing Christ…they are all works of the flesh and they can never be the point of contact between Heaven and any human being on Earth!

    i. **1 Corinthians 10:18 (KJV)** Behold Israel after the flesh: are not they which eat of the sacrifices partakers of the altar?

    ii. **1 Corinthians 10:19 (KJV)** What say I then? that the idol is any thing, or that which is offered in sacrifice to idols is any thing?

    iii. **1 Corinthians 10:20 (KJV)** But *I say*, that the things which the Gentiles sacrifice, they sacrifice to devils, and not to God: and I would not that ye should have fellowship with devils.

93. As you can from **1 Corinthians 10:18-20 (KJV)**, anything that is after the flesh, or food items that you offer as sacrifice to deities, to devils, and to gods, that is idolatry, except you want to tell me that your carnal filthy physical Holy Communion wafers, wine, and bread, are not of the flesh?

94. Which one is the table of devils and which one is the table of the LORD?

    i. **1 Corinthians 10:21 (KJV)** Ye cannot drink the cup of the Lord, and the cup of devils: ye cannot be partakers of the Lord's table, and of the table of devils.

    ii. **1 Corinthians 10:22 (KJV)** Do we provoke the Lord to jealousy? are we stronger than he?

    iii. **1 Corinthians 10:23 (KJV)** All things are lawful for me, but all things are not expedient: all things are lawful for me, but all things edify not.

95. When the Holy Communion is done with your carnal filthy physical Holy Communion wafers, wine, and bread, then, it is "the table of devils, but when the Holy Communion is done with ONLY the Word of God, then, it is the table of the LORD!

96. Brother, are you able to show me how your carnal filthy physical Holy Communion wafers, wine, and bread are able to edify me spiritually as **1 Corinthians 10:23 (KJV)** requires?

97. The answer is, NO, and you know that very well hence, your Holy Communion is evil and for devils since it cannot edify anyone unto righteousness nor unto the Kingdom of Heaven!

98. There is no record anywhere in the entire Word of God from Genesis to Revelation where food and wine were able to edify and sanctify a people unto righteousness or unto the Kingdom of Heaven! Look at **Micah 6:8 (KJV)** to see what has power to edify worshippers unto Christ!

    i. **Micah 6:6 (KJV)** Wherewith shall I come before the LORD, *and* bow myself before the high God? shall I come before him with burnt offerings, with calves of a year old?

    ii. **Micah 6:7 (KJV)** Will the LORD be pleased with thousands of rams, *or* with ten thousands of rivers of oil? shall I give my firstborn *for* my transgression, the fruit of my body *for* the sin of my soul?

    iii. **Micah 6:8 (KJV)** He hath shewed thee, O man, what *is* good; and what doth the LORD require of thee, but to do justly, and to love mercy, and to walk humbly with thy God?

99. Here is an example of unbelievers who worship using food oblations, so, both you the Christian and the unbelieving Devil worshipper are one, as long as you both use food items that you falsely consider holy oblations!

    i. **1 Corinthians 10:25 (KJV)** Whatsoever is sold in the shambles, *that* eat, asking no question for conscience sake:

    ii. **1 Corinthians 10:26 (KJV)** For the earth *is* the Lord's, and the fulness thereof.

    iii. **1 Corinthians 10:27 (KJV)** If any of them that believe not bid you *to a feast*, and ye be disposed to go; whatsoever is set before you, eat, asking no question for conscience sake.

    iv. **1 Corinthians 10:28 (KJV)** But if any man say unto you, This is offered in sacrifice unto idols, eat not for his sake that shewed it, and for conscience sake: for the earth *is* the Lord's, and the fulness thereof:

    v. **1 Corinthians 10:29 (KJV)** Conscience, I say, not thine own, but of the other: for why is my liberty judged of another *man's* conscience?

    vi. **1 Corinthians 10:30 (KJV)** For if I by grace be a partaker, why am I evil spoken of for that for which I give thanks?

    vii. **1 Corinthians 10:31 (KJV)** Whether therefore ye eat, or drink, or whatsoever ye do, do all to the glory of God.

The LORD Jesus Christ be with your spirit. The LORD Jesus Christ give you understanding.

Rev. Prof. PETER PRYCE,
DSEF, BA, MA, B.Soc.Sc Pol Sci, IBA, PhD
A Scribe of the Law of the God of Heaven
Prophet of the Word of God
Professor of French, Silver Spring, MD, USA
Scholar of the Institute of Theologians, USA
WWW.THEBIBLEUNIVERSITY.ORG
Accreditation Number: 07-QCTO/SDP120723172836
SAQA QUAL ID: Identification # 101997
WWW.BOOKSTORESITE.ORG
WWW.THEBIBLEUNIVERSITYCHURCH.ORG

Thursday 11th January 2024 @ 11:02 PM – Friday 12th January 2024 @ 3:13 AM
While hearing and meditating on the Word of God at home.

CHAPTER 11

THE CHURCH ASSEMBLY IS NOT FOR THE EATING OF HOLY COMMUNION!

BOA ME NA ME MMOA WO
"Help me and let me help you"
Asante philosophical symbol of Cooperation, Interdependence, Co-Existence, Symbiosis

Question 2470

1. We now go to the second main idea or the second theme in 1 Corinthians chapter 11, which is Holy Communion! The first theme is the women's head covering, which we have just finished teaching!

    i. **1 Corinthians 11:20 (KJV)** When ye come together therefore into one place, *this* is not to eat the Lord's supper.

    ii. **1 Corinthians 11:21 (KJV)** For in eating every one taketh before *other* his own supper: and one is hungry, and another is drunken.

    iii. **1 Corinthians 11:22 (KJV)** What? have ye not houses to eat and to drink in? or despise ye the church of God, and shame them that have not? What shall I say to you? shall I praise you in this? I praise *you* not.

2. As you can see in the evidence in **1 Corinthians 11:20 (KJV)**, the church assembly is NOT for the eating of Holy Communion/the Lord's supper!

3. This evidence alone in **1 Corinthians 11:20 (KJV)** is enough to make you stop your Holy Communion eating and drinking in all your churches!

4. The command is as clear as water, saying:

      i. The church assembly is NOT for the eating of Holy Communion/the Lord's supper!

5. Yet, the very opposite of that command is what we see Christians, Pastors, Bishops, and Church Leaders doing Sunday after Sunday after Sunday!

6. If you asked the same Christians, Pastors, Bishops, and Church Leaders to tell you the meaning of: "the body *is* not for fornication", they would tell you correctly, that you cannot be a Christian and still engage in fornication and adultery!

      i. **1 Corinthians 6:13 (KJV)** Meats for the belly, and the belly for meats: but God shall destroy both it and them. Now the body *is* not for fornication, but for the Lord; and the Lord for the body.

7. Do you why they will give you that correct answer?

8. It is because of this negative phrase in the verse:

      i. "the body (**noun**) *is* (**auxiliary verb**) not (**negative**) for fornication (**main verb**)"!

9. Now, read also this verse again!

      i. **1 Corinthians 11:20 (KJV)** When ye come together therefore into one place, *this* is not to eat the Lord's supper.

10. Now, compare the same thing that we have just done above to this:

      i. "when ye (**noun**) come together therefore into one place, *this* is (**auxiliary verb**) not (**negative**) to eat (**main verb**) the Lord's supper"!

11. Now, ask yourself: where is the difference?

12. There is NONE, ZERO!

13. So, then, the question is:

      i. Why would the same Christians, Pastors, Bishops, and Church Leaders answer correctly in **1 Corinthians 6:13 (KJV)**, but lie in **1 Corinthians 11:20 (KJV)** when both verses have the same properties?

      ii. **1 Corinthians 6:13 (KJV)** Meats for the belly, and the belly for meats: but God shall destroy both it and them. Now the body *is* not for fornication, but for the Lord; and the Lord for the body.

      iii. **1 Corinthians 11:20 (KJV)** When ye come together therefore into one place, *this* is not to eat the Lord's supper.

14. The reason why they the same Christians, Pastors, Bishops, and Church Leaders will lie is that they are Devils! They were never born again! They are NOT saved! They are on their way to Hell! They serve Satan and are Ministers of Satan in the Pulpit! They serve the same role as Judas Iscariot who served in the Pulpit but was a Devil!

i. **Matthew 10:4 (KJV)** Simon the Canaanite, and Judas Iscariot, who also betrayed him.

ii. **John 6:70 (KJV)** Jesus answered them, Have not I chosen you twelve, and one of you is a devil?

iii. **John 12:4 (KJV)** Then saith one of his disciples, Judas Iscariot, Simon's *son*, which should betray him,

iv. **John 12:5 (KJV)** Why was not this ointment sold for three hundred pence, and given to the poor?

v. **John 12:6 (KJV)** This he said, not that he cared for the poor; but because he was a thief, and had the bag, and bare what was put therein.

vi. **Matthew 15:9 (KJV)** But in vain they do worship me, teaching *for* doctrines the commandments of men.

vii. **Mark 7:7 (KJV)** Howbeit in vain do they worship me, teaching *for* doctrines the commandments of men.

viii. **1 Timothy 4:1 (KJV)** Now the Spirit speaketh expressly, that in the latter times some shall depart from the faith, giving heed to seducing spirits, and doctrines of devils;

15. If we were still in the physical Old Testament and practiced the carnal ordinances thereof, then we should still be eating and drinking physical Holy Communion food as the Corinthians were doing in **1 Corinthians 11:20 (KJV)**!

i. **1 Corinthians 11:20 (KJV)** When ye come together therefore into one place, *this* is not to eat the Lord's supper.

ii. **1 Corinthians 11:23 (KJV)** For I have received of the Lord that which also I delivered unto you, That the Lord Jesus the *same* night in which he was betrayed took bread:

iii. **1 Corinthians 11:24 (KJV)** And when he had given thanks, he brake *it*, and said, Take, eat: this is my body, which is broken for you: this do in remembrance of me.

iv. **1 Corinthians 11:25 (KJV)** After the same manner also *he took* the cup, when he had supped, saying, This cup is the new testament in my blood: this do ye, as oft as ye drink *it*, in remembrance of me.

v. **1 Corinthians 11:26 (KJV)** For as often as ye eat this bread, and drink this cup, ye do shew the Lord's death till he come.

vi. **Hebrews 9:10 (KJV)** *Which stood* only in meats and drinks, and divers washings, and carnal ordinances, imposed *on them* until the time of reformation.

16. However, because we are NO MORE in the Old Testament of works, but now in the New Testament of Faith, and all the Old Testament physical forms of God-worship have passed away, therefore, to continue to practise the physical works of Holy Communion/the LORD'S Supper that the LORD Jesus Christ accomplished when HE fulfilled HIS Ministry under the Old Testament Laws, it is a sin because of **John 4:23-24 (KJV)** and many other such verses!

    i. **Matthew 5:17 (KJV)** Think not that I am come to destroy the law, or the prophets: I am not come to destroy, but to fulfil.

    ii. **John 4:23 (KJV)** But the hour cometh, and now is, when the true worshippers shall worship the Father in spirit and in truth: for the Father seeketh such to worship him.

    iii. **John 4:24 (KJV)** God *is* a Spirit: and they that worship him must worship *him* in spirit and in truth.

    iv. **Romans 3:20 (KJV)** Therefore by the deeds of the law there shall no flesh be justified in his sight: for by the law *is* the knowledge of sin.

    v. **Galatians 3:23 (KJV)** But before faith came, we were kept under the law, shut up unto the faith which should afterwards be revealed.

    vi. **Galatians 3:24 (KJV)** Wherefore the law was our schoolmaster *to bring us* unto Christ, that we might be justified by faith.

    vii. **Galatians 3:25 (KJV)** But after that faith is come, we are no longer under a schoolmaster.

17. Therefore, because we are now in the New Testament of Faith, we need to, and we should be seeking the Faith/Spiritual meanings of "my body, broken for you, the new testament, my blood, in remembrance of me"!

    i. **1 Corinthians 11:24 (KJV)** And when he had given thanks, he brake *it*, and said, Take, eat: this is my body, which is broken for you: this do in remembrance of me.

    ii. **1 Corinthians 11:25 (KJV)** After the same manner also *he took* the cup, when he had supped, saying, This cup is the new testament in my blood: this do ye, as oft as ye drink *it*, in remembrance of me.

18. And when you search the Scriptures for the correct Faith/Spiritual meanings of "my body, broken for you, the new testament, my blood, in remembrance of me", what you get is this: THE WORD OF GOD!

19. In other words, the Word of God was the real and actual "my body, broken for you, the new testament, my blood, in remembrance of me" that the LORD Jesus Christ was giving to the Apostles!

20. Now, let us test the doctrine that the Word of God is the real and actual "my body, broken for you, the new testament, my blood, in remembrance of me" that the LORD Jesus Christ was giving to the Apostles!

21. The Word of God is the real and actual "my body"!

    i. **John 1:1 (KJV)** In the beginning was the Word, and the Word was with God, and the Word was God.

    ii. **John 1:2 (KJV)** The same was in the beginning with God.

    iii. **John 1:14 (KJV)** And the Word was made flesh, and dwelt among us, (and we beheld his glory, the glory as of the only begotten of the Father,) full of grace and truth.

    iv. **John 6:32 (KJV)** Then Jesus said unto them, Verily, verily, I say unto you, Moses gave you not that bread from heaven; but my Father giveth you the true bread from heaven.

    v. **John 6:33 (KJV)** For the bread of God is he which cometh down from heaven, and giveth life unto the world.

    vi. **John 6:48 (KJV)** I am that bread of life.

    vii. **John 6:51 (KJV)** I am the living bread which came down from heaven: if any man eat of this bread, he shall live for ever: and the bread that I will give is my flesh, which I will give for the life of the world.

22. The Word of God is the real and actual "broken for you", meaning, "rightly dividing the word of truth"!

    i. **Ezekiel 3:1 (KJV)** Moreover he said unto me, Son of man, eat that thou findest; eat this roll, and go speak unto the house of Israel.

    ii. **Ezekiel 3:2 (KJV)** So I opened my mouth, and he caused me to eat that roll.

    iii. **Ezekiel 3:3 (KJV)** And he said unto me, Son of man, cause thy belly to eat, and fill thy bowels with this roll that I give thee. Then did I eat *it*; and it was in my mouth as honey for sweetness.

    iv. **Jeremiah 15:16 (KJV)** Thy words were found, and I did eat them; and thy word was unto me the joy and rejoicing of mine heart: for I am called by thy name, O LORD God of hosts.

    v. **John 5:46 (KJV)** For had ye believed Moses, ye would have believed me: for he wrote of me.

    vi. **2 Timothy 2:15 (KJV)** Study to shew thyself approved unto God, a workman that needeth not to be ashamed, rightly dividing the word of truth.

23. The Word of God is the real and actual "the new testament"!

    i. **Hebrews 9:13 (KJV)** For if the blood of bulls and of goats, and the ashes of an heifer sprinkling the unclean, sanctifieth to the purifying of the flesh:

    ii. **Hebrews 9:14 (KJV)** How much more shall the blood of Christ, who through the eternal Spirit offered himself without spot to God, purge your conscience from dead works to serve the living God?

    iii. **Hebrews 9:15 (KJV)** And for this cause he is the mediator of the new testament, that by means of death, for the redemption of the transgressions *that were* under the first testament, they which are called might receive the promise of eternal inheritance.

    iv. **Hebrews 9:16 (KJV)** For where a testament *is*, there must also of necessity be the death of the testator.

    v. **Hebrews 9:17 (KJV)** For a testament *is* of force after men are dead: otherwise it is of no strength at all while the testator liveth.

24. The Word of God is the real and actual "my blood"!

    i. **Luke 22:20 (KJV)** Likewise also the cup after supper, saying, This cup *is* the new testament in my blood, which is shed for you.

    ii. **Hebrews 9:14 (KJV)** How much more shall the blood of Christ, who through the eternal Spirit offered himself without spot to God, purge your conscience from dead works to serve the living God?

    iii. **Hebrews 9:15 (KJV)** And for this cause he is the mediator of the new testament, that by means of death, for the redemption of the transgressions *that were* under the first testament, they which are called might receive the promise of eternal inheritance.

25. The Word of God is the real and actual "in remembrance of me", meaning that, the Holy Communion wafers, wine, and bread, and all physical food and drinks themselves being dung, excreta, feces, and filthy physical perishable items, they have no power at all to connect into the spiritual, neither do they have any ability at all to cause or to compel the remembrance of the LORD Jesus Christ in any human being by reason of their presence and their eating!

    i. **Mark 7:15 (KJV)** There is nothing from without a man, that entering into him can defile him: but the things which come out of him, those are they that defile the man.

    ii. **Matthew 15:16 (KJV)** And Jesus said, Are ye also yet without understanding?

    iii. **Matthew 15:17 (KJV)** Do not ye yet understand, that whatsoever entereth in at the mouth goeth into the belly, and is cast out into the draught?

      iv. **Mark 7:18 (KJV)** And he saith unto them, Are ye so without understanding also? Do ye not perceive, that whatsoever thing from without entereth into the man, *it* cannot defile him;

      v. **Mark 7:19 (KJV)** Because it entereth not into his heart, but into the belly, and goeth out into the draught, purging all meats?

26. There is no food on Earth that possesses any spiritual properties, therefore, to use physical food to bring the presence of Christ to a physical scene by way of remembrance into the human mind, whether it be in a Holy Communion setting in a church, or whether it be in a voodoo seance as many do in the Akwasidae festival and in the Aboakyer festival of Ghana, both of them are demonic idolatry!!

      i. **John 6:27 (KJV)** Labour not for the meat which perisheth, but for that meat which endureth unto everlasting life, which the Son of man shall give unto you: for him hath God the Father sealed.

      ii. **Micah 6:6 (KJV)** Wherewith shall I come before the LORD, *and* bow myself before the high God? shall I come before him with burnt offerings, with calves of a year old?

      iii. **Micah 6:7 (KJV)** Will the LORD be pleased with thousands of rams, *or* with ten thousands of rivers of oil? shall I give my firstborn *for* my transgression, the fruit of my body *for* the sin of my soul?

      iv. **Micah 6:8 (KJV)** He hath shewed thee, O man, what *is* good; and what doth the LORD require of thee, but to do justly, and to love mercy, and to walk humbly with thy God?

27. Finally, as you can see, we have tested all the five parts and key phrases in the doctrine that the Word of God is the true, the real, and the actual oblation that has power to cause the remembrance of the LORD Jesus Christ in Christians, and we found out from the testing that the doctrine is perfect and there is not even one single part lacking! I have demonstrated the doctrine to you fully!

28. Therefore, you should continue to use your physical filthy Holy Communion wafers, wine and bread at your own peril in Hell!

29. How is it that the LORD Jesus Christ is God, and HE said that HE came to fulfill the Law, and the Law says that what God gives HIS Servants to eat are words, NOT physical food, and yet you are able to conclude that the same Jesus Christ gave food to HIS Servants and not words! How does that reasoning match up to you if you are not a fool?

      i. **Isaiah 9:6 (KJV)** For unto us a child is born, unto us a son is given: and the government shall be upon his shoulder: and his name shall be called Wonderful, Counseller, The mighty God, The everlasting Father, The Prince of Peace.

    ii. **Jeremiah 32:18 (KJV)** Thou shewest lovingkindness unto thousands, and recompensest the iniquity of the fathers into the bosom of their children after them: the Great, the Mighty God, the LORD of hosts, *is* his name,

    iii. **Matthew 5:17 (KJV)** Think not that I am come to destroy the law, or the prophets: I am not come to destroy, but to fulfil.

    iv. **Jeremiah 15:16 (KJV)** Thy words were found, and I did eat them; and thy word was unto me the joy and rejoicing of mine heart: for I am called by thy name, O LORD God of hosts.

    v. **Ezekiel 3:1 (KJV)** Moreover he said unto me, Son of man, eat that thou findest; eat this roll, and go speak unto the house of Israel.

    vi. **Ezekiel 3:2 (KJV)** So I opened my mouth, and he caused me to eat that roll.

    vii. **John 17:8 (KJV)** For I have given unto them the words which thou gavest me; and they have received *them*, and have known surely that I came out from thee, and they have believed that thou didst send me.

30. Since the world began, is it recorded anywhere that a man became guilty before God because of some food that he did not eat and drink, or, is it rather recorded that a man became guilty before God because of the words of the Covenant of God that he did not obey?

    i. **1 Corinthians 11:27 (KJV)** Wherefore whosoever shall eat this bread, and drink *this* cup of the Lord, unworthily, shall be guilty of the body and blood of the Lord.

    ii. **1 Corinthians 11:28 (KJV)** But let a man examine himself, and so let him eat of *that* bread, and drink of *that* cup.

    iii. **1 Corinthians 11:29 (KJV)** For he that eateth and drinketh unworthily, eateth and drinketh damnation to himself, not discerning the Lord's body.

    iv. **1 Corinthians 10:31 (KJV)** Whether therefore ye eat, or drink, or whatsoever ye do, do all to the glory of God.

31. You know certainly that a man's spirituality, holiness or guilt is never derived from some food that he ate or failed to eat and drink, but instead, a man became guilty before God because of the words of the Covenant of God that he did not obey!

    i. **Matthew 15:10 (KJV)** And he called the multitude, and said unto them, Hear, and understand:

    ii. **Matthew 15:11 (KJV)** Not that which goeth into the mouth defileth a man; but that which cometh out of the mouth, this defileth a man.

     iii. **Mark 7:15 (KJV)** There is nothing from without a man, that entering into him can defile him: but the things which come out of him, those are they that defile the man.

32. How could you know all this and still be that very stupid not to know that you have the wrong doctrine of Holy Communion which derives holiness from perishable food and drink and NOT from the Covenant of God?

     i. **Luke 22:20 (KJV)** Likewise also the cup after supper, saying, This cup *is* the new testament in my blood, which is shed for you.

     ii. **1 Corinthians 11:25 (KJV)** After the same manner also *he took* the cup, when he had supped, saying, This cup is the new testament in my blood: this do ye, as oft as ye drink *it*, in remembrance of me.

33. If the cup is inside the New Testament, and you being the Pastor and Bishop of the church, you are always going outside the New Testament in order to procure holiness, spirituality, worship, remembrance of Christ, and blessings from outside the New Testament, then where are your senses Brother?

34. Can you be that incorrigibly stupid and perpetually cursed unto Satan, that the LORD Jesus Christ has told you plainly that the bread and the cup are inside the New Testament, but yet still you decided to seek the same bread and the cup from OUTSIDE the New Testament?

35. Here is another evidence of your incorrigible stupidity and your perpetual curse unto Satan!

     i. **1 Corinthians 11:30 (KJV)** For this cause many *are* weak and sickly among you, and many sleep.

36. Now, after you have read **1 Corinthians 11:30 (KJV)**, can you show me any evidence from Genesis to Revelation where a man or many people became weak, sickly, and died because they failed to eat some physical food?

37. Do not weakness, sickness, and death actually and truly come from NOT eating the spiritual food of the Word of God, the same as Jesus Christ told you in **Luke 22:20 (KJV)** and **1 Corinthians 11:25 (KJV)**?

38. How very stupid can you be Brother, Sister?

     i. **1 Corinthians 11:31 (KJV)** For if we would judge ourselves, we should not be judged.

     ii. **1 Corinthians 11:32 (KJV)** But when we are judged, we are chastened of the Lord, that we should not be condemned with the world.

39. Brother, Sister, are you under any illusion at all that there are two types of eating in 1 Corinthians chapter 11, and that one of then is the physical useless eating of physical

foods whereas the other is the preferred spiritual eating as I have showed you many times in the very chapter?

    i. **1 Corinthians 11:33 (KJV)** Wherefore, my brethren, when ye come together to eat, tarry one for another.

    ii. **1 Corinthians 11:34 (KJV)** And if any man hunger, let him eat at home; that ye come not together unto condemnation. And the rest will I set in order when I come.

The LORD Jesus Christ be with your spirit. The LORD Jesus Christ give you understanding.

Rev. Prof. PETER PRYCE,
DSEF, BA, MA, B.Soc.Sc Pol Sci, IBA, PhD
A Scribe of the Law of the God of Heaven
Prophet of the Word of God
Professor of French, Silver Spring, MD, USA
Scholar of the Institute of Theologians, USA
WWW.THEBIBLEUNIVERSITY.ORG
Accreditation Number: 07-QCTO/SDP120723172836
SAQA QUAL ID: Identification # 101997
WWW.BOOKSTORESITE.ORG
WWW.THEBIBLEUNIVERSITYCHURCH.ORG

Friday 12th January 2024 @ 4:55 PM – 7:27 PM
While hearing and meditating on the Word of God at home.

CHAPTER 12

THE CORRUPTION IN THE OFFERING OF HOLY COMMUNION AND WATER BAPTISM!

DAME-DAME

"Name of a board game"

Asante philosophical symbol of Intelligence, Ingenuity, Foresightedness, Preemption

Question 2479

1. Now, here in **1 Corinthians 15:50 (KJV)** is a revelation that has a very profound meaning for many things that we do in the churches!

   i. **1 Corinthians 15:50 (KJV)** Now this I say, brethren, that flesh and blood cannot inherit the kingdom of God; neither doth corruption inherit incorruption.

2. The revelation in **1 Corinthians 15:50 (KJV)** is a confirmation of the Truth of Christ that God Almighty is Spirit, therefore, God-worship must always be conducted at the spirit level and NOT at the physical level to which many Christians are often accustomed, howbeit in error!

   i. **John 4:23 (KJV)** But the hour cometh, and now is, when the true worshippers shall worship the Father in spirit and in truth: for the Father seeketh such to worship him.

   ii. **John 4:24 (KJV)** God *is* a Spirit: and they that worship him must worship *him* in spirit and in truth.

   iii. **1 Corinthians 2:12 (KJV)** Now we have received, not the spirit of the world, but the spirit which is of God; that we might know the things that are freely given to us of God.

     iv. **1 Corinthians 2:13 (KJV)** Which things also we speak, not in the words which man's wisdom teacheth, but which the Holy Ghost teacheth; comparing spiritual things with spiritual.

     v. **Deuteronomy 30:14 (KJV)** But the word *is* very nigh unto thee, in thy mouth, and in thy heart, that thou mayest do it.

     vi. **Romans 10:8 (KJV)** But what saith it? The word is nigh thee, *even* in thy mouth, and in thy heart: that is, the word of faith, which we preach;

3. If "flesh and blood cannot inherit the kingdom of God", and the Kingdom of God is in your mouth, and the Kingdom of God is the Word of Faith which we preach, then how do you not understand that the fleshly-produced wafers, wine, and bread of your Holy Communion cannot inherit the kingdom of God since you agree that your wafers, wine, and bread are flesh, your wafers, wine, and bread are blood, and your wafers, wine, and bread are corruption, as condemned in **1 Corinthians 15:50 (KJV)**?

4. How also do you not understand that your flesh-based Water Baptism cannot inherit the kingdom of God since you agree that your Water Baptism is flesh, your Water Baptism is blood, and your Water Baptism is corruption, as condemned in **1 Corinthians 15:50 (KJV)**?

5. How also do you not understand that any part of your God-worship that is accomplished through the works of flesh, blood, and corruption are all disqualified by the same **1 Corinthians 15:50 (KJV)** which says that "flesh and blood cannot inherit the kingdom of God; neither doth corruption inherit incorruption"?

6. Or, are you able to contradict the Word of God in **John 4:23-24 (KJV)** and in **1 Corinthians 15:50 (KJV)** to show me that your Holy Communion wafers, wine, and bread, and your Water Baptism, and all your physical worship man-made items, do not come from corruption and are not done with corrupt filthy human hands?

     i. **Leviticus 22:25 (KJV)** Neither from a stranger's hand shall ye offer the bread of your God of any of these; because their corruption *is* in them, *and* blemishes *be* in them: they shall not be accepted for you.

     ii. **Romans 8:21 (KJV)** Because the creature itself also shall be delivered from the bondage of corruption into the glorious liberty of the children of God.

     iii. **1 Corinthians 15:42 (KJV)** So also *is* the resurrection of the dead. It is sown in corruption; it is raised in incorruption:

     iv. **Galatians 6:8 (KJV)** For he that soweth to his flesh shall of the flesh reap corruption; but he that soweth to the Spirit shall of the Spirit reap life everlasting.

    v. **Haggai 2:10 (KJV)** In the four and twentieth *day* of the ninth *month*, in the second year of Darius, came the word of the LORD by Haggai the prophet, saying,

    vi. **Haggai 2:11 (KJV)** Thus saith the LORD of hosts; Ask now the priests *concerning* the law, saying,

    vii. **Haggai 2:12 (KJV)** If one bear holy flesh in the skirt of his garment, and with his skirt do touch bread, or pottage, or wine, or oil, or any meat, shall it be holy? And the priests answered and said, No.

    viii. **Haggai 2:13 (KJV)** Then said Haggai, If *one that is* unclean by a dead body touch any of these, shall it be unclean? And the priests answered and said, It shall be unclean.

    ix. **Haggai 2:14 (KJV)** Then answered Haggai, and said, So *is* this people, and so *is* this nation before me, saith the LORD; and so *is* every work of their hands; and that which they offer there *is* unclean.

7. If you agree that there is no good thing dwelling in your flesh, then how do you presume that God Almighty will be pleased to take Holy Communion offering and Water Baptism offering from your dirty hands?

    i. **Romans 7:18 (KJV)** For I know that in me (that is, in my flesh,) dwelleth no good thing: for to will is present with me; but *how* to perform that which is good I find not.

8. Brother Bishop, in both the Old and New Testaments of Christ, the LORD God has identified for you, clearly and very plainly, the specific part and spot of your human flesh that all God-worship should come from, should proceed, and should be accomplished, and that place is YOUR MOUTH!

    i. **Deuteronomy 30:14 (KJV)** But the word *is* very nigh unto thee, in thy mouth, and in thy heart, that thou mayest do it.

    ii. **Romans 10:8 (KJV)** But what saith it? The word is nigh thee, *even* in thy mouth, and in thy heart: that is, the word of faith, which we preach;

    iii. **Micah 6:8 (KJV)** He hath shewed thee, O man, what *is* good; and what doth the LORD require of thee, but to do justly, and to love mercy, and to walk humbly with thy God?

    iv. **Joshua 1:7 (KJV)** Only be thou strong and very courageous, that thou mayest observe to do according to all the law, which Moses my servant commanded thee: turn not from it *to* the right hand or *to* the left, that thou mayest prosper whithersoever thou goest.

    v. **Joshua 1:8 (KJV)** This book of the law shall not depart out of thy mouth; but thou shalt meditate therein day and night, that thou mayest observe to do according to all that is written therein: for then thou shalt make thy way prosperous, and then thou shalt have good success.

vi. **1 Corinthians 5:8 (KJV)** Therefore let us keep the feast, not with old leaven, neither with the leaven of malice and wickedness; but with the unleavened *bread* of sincerity and truth.

vii. **Hebrews 13:15 (KJV)** By him therefore let us offer the sacrifice of praise to God continually, that is, the fruit of *our* lips giving thanks to his name.

9. So, I have shown you only seven evidences (there are many) why your worship to Godward should proceed from your mouth and NOT from corruptible things such as Holy Communion wafers, wine, bread, and filthy Water Baptism river waters!

The LORD Jesus Christ be with your spirit. The LORD Jesus Christ give you understanding.

Rev. Prof. PETER PRYCE,
DSEF, BA, MA, B.Soc.Sc Pol Sci, IBA, PhD
A Scribe of the Law of the God of Heaven
Prophet of the Word of God
Professor of French, Silver Spring, MD, USA
Scholar of the Institute of Theologians, USA
WWW.THEBIBLEUNIVERSITY.ORG
Accreditation Number: 07-QCTO/SDP120723172836
SAQA QUAL ID: Identification # 101997
WWW.BOOKSTORESITE.ORG
WWW.THEBIBLEUNIVERSITYCHURCH.ORG

Thursday 18th January 2024 @ 11:00 AM – 12:46 PM
While hearing and meditating on the Word of God at home.

CHAPTER 13

OFFER UNTO GOD – WORDS, LIVING WORDS!

DWENNIMMEN

"Ram's horns"
Asante philosophical symbol of Humility and Strength in Mind, Body, and Soul

Question 2487

1.   As the LORD Jesus Christ showed us that the flesh profiteth nothing, and again as the LORD showed us that the flesh is weak but the spirit is willing, and again as the LORD showed us that HE was cricified in the flesh but quickened in the Spirit, so also we have this treasure in an earthern temporary vessel of flesh that is also weak and base but carrying the excellency of the eternal knowledge of Christ!

   i.   **2 Corinthians 10:1 (KJV)** Now I Paul myself beseech you by the meekness and gentleness of Christ, who in presence *am* base among you, but being absent am bold toward you:

   ii. **2 Corinthians 10:2 (KJV)** But I beseech *you*, that I may not be bold when I am present with that confidence, wherewith I think to be bold against some, which think of us as if we walked according to the flesh.

2.   It is for this very reason of the weakness, unrpifitableness, and baseness of the flesh that everything that we do with the flesh, such as Holy Communion offerings and Water Baptism sacrifices, are already filthy and condemned and unacceptable in Heaven!

   i.   **Matthew 26:41 (KJV)** Watch and pray, that ye enter not into temptation: the spirit indeed *is* willing, but the flesh *is* weak.

    ii. **Mark 14:38 (KJV)** Watch ye and pray, lest ye enter into temptation. The spirit truly *is* ready, but the flesh *is* weak.

    iii. **John 6:63 (KJV)** It is the spirit that quickeneth; the flesh profiteth nothing: the words that I speak unto you, *they* are spirit, and *they* are life.

    iv. **Romans 7:18 (KJV)** For I know that in me (that is, in my flesh,) dwelleth no good thing: for to will is present with me; but *how* to perform that which is good I find not.

3. Moreover, and most imprtantly, the LORD God Almighty DOES NOT accept dead lifeless things as sacrifice, and if God did NOT accept them from Cain, then, how deep is your stupidity to think that the same God will accept from your filthy hands what God already rejected?

    i. **Genesis 4:3 (KJV)** And in process of time it came to pass, that Cain brought of the fruit of the ground an offering unto the LORD.

    ii. **Genesis 4:4 (KJV)** And Abel, he also brought of the firstlings of his flock and of the fat thereof. And the LORD had respect unto Abel and to his offering:

    iii. **Genesis 4:5 (KJV)** But unto Cain and to his offering he had not respect. And Cain was very wroth, and his countenance fell.

    iv. **Genesis 4:6 (KJV)** And the LORD said unto Cain, Why art thou wroth? and why is thy countenance fallen?

    v. **Genesis 4:7 (KJV)** If thou doest well, shalt thou not be accepted? and if thou doest not well, sin lieth at the door. And unto thee *shall be* his desire, and thou shalt rule over him.

    vi. **Micah 6:6 (KJV)** Wherewith shall I come before the LORD, *and* bow myself before the high God? shall I come before him with burnt offerings, with calves of a year old?

    vii. **Micah 6:7 (KJV)** Will the LORD be pleased with thousands of rams, *or* with ten thousands of rivers of oil? shall I give my firstborn *for* my transgression, the fruit of my body *for* the sin of my soul?

    viii. **Micah 6:8 (KJV)** He hath shewed thee, O man, what *is* good; and what doth the LORD require of thee, but to do justly, and to love mercy, and to walk humbly with thy God?

4. The above reasons are also why the Old Testament was condemned unto removal and abogation by reason of its weakness and unprofitableness seeing that it leadeth to the works of the Law and of the flesh, which works cannot save anyone, but the New Testament was deemed excellent and better Covenant because it tendeth and leadeth to the spirit and NOT to the flesh/letter!

- i. **Galatians 2:16 (KJV)** Knowing that a man is not justified by the works of the law, but by the faith of Jesus Christ, even we have believed in Jesus Christ, that we might be justified by the faith of Christ, and not by the works of the law: for by the works of the law shall no flesh be justified.

- ii. **Hebrews 7:18 (KJV)** For there is verily a disannulling of the commandment going before for the weakness and unprofitableness thereof.

- iii. **Hebrews 7:19 (KJV)** For the law made nothing perfect, but the bringing in of a better hope *did*; by the which we draw nigh unto God.

- iv. **Hebrews 7:20 (KJV)** And inasmuch as not without an oath *he was made priest*:

- v. **Hebrews 8:6 (KJV)** But now hath he obtained a more excellent ministry, by how much also he is the mediator of a better covenant, which was established upon better promises.

- vi. **Hebrews 12:24 (KJV)** And to Jesus the mediator of the new covenant, and to the blood of sprinkling, that speaketh better things than *that of* Abel.

5. By reason of the perpetual condition of the flesh as weak, unprfitable, and base, everything that we do with the flesh, such as Holy Communion offerings and Water Baptism sacrifices, are already filthy and condemned and unacceptable in Heaven!

  - i. **Haggai 2:10 (KJV)** In the four and twentieth *day* of the ninth *month*, in the second year of Darius, came the word of the LORD by Haggai the prophet, saying,

  - ii. **Haggai 2:11 (KJV)** Thus saith the LORD of hosts; Ask now the priests *concerning* the law, saying,

  - iii. **Haggai 2:12 (KJV)** If one bear holy flesh in the skirt of his garment, and with his skirt do touch bread, or pottage, or wine, or oil, or any meat, shall it be holy? And the priests answered and said, No.

  - iv. **Haggai 2:13 (KJV)** Then said Haggai, If *one that is* unclean by a dead body touch any of these, shall it be unclean? And the priests answered and said, It shall be unclean.

  - v. **Haggai 2:14 (KJV)** Then answered Haggai, and said, So *is* this people, and so *is* this nation before me, saith the LORD; and so *is* every work of their hands; and that which they offer there *is* unclean.

vi. **Romans 7:18 (KJV)** For I know that in me (that is, in my flesh,) dwelleth no good thing: for to will is present with me; but *how* to perform that which is good I find not.

vii. **Philippians 3:21 (KJV)** Who shall change our vile body, that it may be fashioned like unto his glorious body, according to the working whereby he is able even to subdue all things unto himself.

6. There is no Man of God living who has yet attained unto the spiritual level of Apostle Paul! Therefore, if Apostle Paul can say in **Romans 7:18 (KJV)** that I know that in me (that is, in my flesh,) dwelleth no good thing, then, you the Holy Communion and Water Baptism Pastors of today, there is far more filth in your flesh than there was in Apostle Paul who went to Paradise in Heaven and returned, whereas you did not!

i. **2 Corinthians 12:1 (KJV)** It is not expedient for me doubtless to glory. I will come to visions and revelations of the Lord.

ii. **2 Corinthians 12:2 (KJV)** I knew a man in Christ above fourteen years ago, (whether in the body, I cannot tell; or whether out of the body, I cannot tell: God knoweth;) such an one caught up to the third heaven.

iii. **2 Corinthians 12:3 (KJV)** And I knew such a man, (whether in the body, or out of the body, I cannot tell: God knoweth;)

iv. **2 Corinthians 12:4 (KJV)** How that he was caught up into paradise, and heard unspeakable words, which it is not lawful for a man to utter.

v. **2 Corinthians 12:5 (KJV)** Of such an one will I glory: yet of myself I will not glory, but in mine infirmities.

vi. **2 Corinthians 12:6 (KJV)** For though I would desire to glory, I shall not be a fool; for I will say the truth: but *now* I forbear, lest any man should think of me above that which he seeth me *to be*, or *that* he heareth of me.

vii. **2 Corinthians 12:7 (KJV)** And lest I should be exalted above measure through the abundance of the revelations, there was given to me a thorn in the flesh, the messenger of Satan to buffet me, lest I should be exalted above measure.

viii. **2 Corinthians 12:8 (KJV)** For this thing I besought the Lord thrice, that it might depart from me.

ix. **2 Corinthians 12:9 (KJV)** And he said unto me, My grace is sufficient for thee: for my strength is made perfect in weakness. Most gladly therefore will I rather glory in my infirmities, that the power of Christ may rest upon me.

    x. **2 Corinthians 12:10 (KJV)** Therefore I take pleasure in infirmities, in reproaches, in necessities, in persecutions, in distresses for Christ's sake: for when I am weak, then am I strong.

   xi. **Philippians 3:21 (KJV)** Who shall change our vile body, that it may be fashioned like unto his glorious body, according to the working whereby he is able even to subdue all things unto himself.

7. And so, if by way of comparison, you are worse and filthier than Apostle Paul, and Apostle Paul did NOT water baptize people, then, where is your scriptural justification to do Water Baptism and Holy Communion?

    i. **1 Corinthians 1:17 (KJV)** For Christ sent me not to baptize, but to preach the gospel: not with wisdom of words, lest the cross of Christ should be made of none effect.

   ii. **1 Corinthians 6:20 (KJV)** For ye are bought with a price: therefore glorify God in your body, and in your spirit, which are God's.

  iii. **1 Corinthians 11:20 (KJV)** When ye come together therefore into one place, *this* is not to eat the Lord's supper.

  iv. **1 Corinthians 15:50 (KJV)** Now this I say, brethren, that flesh and blood cannot inherit the kingdom of God; neither doth corruption inherit incorruption.

8. The sum of what I have said so far is this:

    i. You have flesh and you have a spirit. **1 Corinthians 6:20 (KJV)**

   ii. Your flesh is weak, unrpifitable, and base. **John 6:63 (KJV), Romans 7:18 (KJV)**

  iii. Everything that your flesh offers to God Almighty is filthy and unacceptable in Heaven! **Micah 6:6-8 (KJV), Haggai 2:10-14 (KJV)**

  iv. Therefore, the flesh is forever disqualified from offering anytging unto God Almighty!

   v. What you now have left is only your spirit!

  vi. The spirit eats and produces only one thing: words!

 vii. Therefore, offer unto God words, living words, living words that come from a living human spirit, living words that are produced from the spirit in which dwells the Holy Spirit, living words that are produced from the spirit that is washed with the water of the Word, living words that are produced from the spirit that is a well of rivers of living waters, living words that are produced from the spirit that has been and is being renewed everyday in the Gospel of Christ, living words that God Almighty Himself has given you!

viii. **Micah 6:8 (KJV)** He hath shewed thee, O man, what *is* good; and what doth the LORD require of thee, but to do justly, and to love mercy, and to walk humbly with thy God?

ix. **Hosea 14:2 (KJV)** Take with you words, and turn to the LORD: say unto him, Take away all iniquity, and receive *us* graciously: so will we render the calves of our lips.

x. **John 3:34 (KJV)** For he whom God hath sent speaketh the words of God: for God giveth not the Spirit by measure *unto him*.

xi. **1 Corinthians 6:17 (KJV)** But he that is joined unto the Lord is one spirit.

xii. **John 14:17 (KJV)** *Even* the Spirit of truth; whom the world cannot receive, because it seeth him not, neither knoweth him: but ye know him; for he dwelleth with you, and shall be in you.

xiii. **Romans 8:11 (KJV)** But if the Spirit of him that raised up Jesus from the dead dwell in you, he that raised up Christ from the dead shall also quicken your mortal bodies by his Spirit that dwelleth in you.

xiv. **Ephesians 5:26 (KJV)** That he might sanctify and cleanse it with the washing of water by the word,

xv. **John 4:10 (KJV)** Jesus answered and said unto her, If thou knewest the gift of God, and who it is that saith to thee, Give me to drink; thou wouldest have asked of him, and he would have given thee living water.

xvi. **John 4:14 (KJV)** But whosoever drinketh of the water that I shall give him shall never thirst; but the water that I shall give him shall be in him a well of water springing up into everlasting life.

xvii. **John 7:38 (KJV)** He that believeth on me, as the scripture hath said, out of his belly shall flow rivers of living water.

xviii. **John 15:3 (KJV)** Now ye are clean through the word which I have spoken unto you.

xix. **Ephesians 4:23 (KJV)** And be renewed in the spirit of your mind;

xx. **John 17:8 (KJV)** For I have given unto them the words which thou gavest me; and they have received *them*, and have known surely that I came out from thee, and they have believed that thou didst send me.

9. All the above are the reasons why "we do not war after the flesh"! All the above are the reasons why "the weapons of our warfare *are* not carnal"!

      i. **2 Corinthians 10:3 (KJV)** For though we walk in the flesh, we do not war after the flesh:

      ii. **2 Corinthians 10:4 (KJV)** (For the weapons of our warfare *are* not carnal, but mighty through God to the pulling down of strong holds;)

10. Now, pause a while and ask yourself:

11. The filthy Water Baptism river and pool waters, and the Holy Comunion wafers, wine, and bread that we offer in all the churches, are they "in the flesh"? YES!

      i. Then, they are disqualified because they stand against and are contrary to **2 Corinthians 10:3-4 (KJV)**!

12. The filthy Water Baptism river and pool waters, and the Holy Comunion wafers, wine, and bread that we offer in all the churches, are they "after the flesh"? YES!

      i. Then, they are disqualified because they stand against and are contrary to **2 Corinthians 10:3-4 (KJV)**!

13. The filthy Water Baptism river and pool waters, and the Holy Comunion wafers, wine, and bread that we offer in all the churches, are they part of the Christian life of war? NO!

      i. Then, they are disqualified because they stand against and are contrary to **2 Corinthians 10:3-4 (KJV)**!

14. The filthy Water Baptism river and pool waters, and the Holy Comunion wafers, wine, and bread that we offer in all the churches, are they "weapons of our warfare"? NO!

      i. Then, they are disqualified because they stand against and are contrary to **2 Corinthians 10:3-4 (KJV)**!

15. The filthy Water Baptism river and pool waters, and the Holy Comunion wafers, wine, and bread that we offer in all the churches, are they mighty warfare items in God? NO!

      i. Then, they are disqualified because they stand against and are contrary to **2 Corinthians 10:3-4 (KJV)**!

16. The filthy Water Baptism river and pool waters, and the Holy Comunion wafers, wine, and bread that we offer in all the churches, are you able to use them to pull down of strong holds? NO!

      i. Then, they are disqualified because they stand against and are contrary to **2 Corinthians 10:3-4 (KJV)**!

17. Will demons of the strong holds recognize, fear, respond to, and obey your filthy Water Baptism river and pool waters, and your Holy Comunion wafers, wine, and bread that we offer in all the churches? NO!

      i. Then, they are disqualified because they stand against and are contrary to **2 Corinthians 10:3-4 (KJV)**!

18. Let us conside some more evidences:
    i. **2 Corinthians 10:5 (KJV)** Casting down imaginations, and every high thing that exalteth itself against the knowledge of God, and bringing into captivity every thought to the obedience of Christ;
    ii. **2 Corinthians 10:6 (KJV)** And having in a readiness to revenge all disobedience, when your obedience is fulfilled.

19. Furthermore, are you able to use your filthy Water Baptism river and pool waters, and your Holy Comunion wafers, wine, and bread to "cast down imaginations, and every high thing that exalteth itself against the knowledge of God"? NO!
    i. Then, they are disqualified because they stand against and are contrary to **2 Corinthians 10:5-6 (KJV)**!

20. Then, are you able to use your filthy Water Baptism river and pool waters, and your Holy Comunion wafers, wine, and bread to "bring into captivity every thought to the obedience of Christ"? NO!
    i. Then, they are disqualified because they stand against and are contrary to **2 Corinthians 10:5-6 (KJV)**!

21. Brother Pastor and Bishop, do you now see how nakedly shameful you look because you do NOT know the Holy Scriptures and yet you claim to have been called into the Ministry?

22. Did you ever read anywhere in the entire Holy Bible Bible from Genesis to Revelation, that the LORD God Almighty sends fools and ignorant bastards like you into the Ministry?
    i. **Exodus 28:3 (KJV)** And thou shalt speak unto all *that are* wise hearted, whom I have filled with the spirit of wisdom, that they may make Aaron's garments to consecrate him, that he may minister unto me in the priest's office.
    ii. **Exodus 31:3 (KJV)** And I have filled him with the spirit of God, in wisdom, and in understanding, and in knowledge, and in all manner of workmanship,
    iii. **Exodus 35:31 (KJV)** And he hath filled him with the spirit of God, in wisdom, in understanding, and in knowledge, and in all manner of workmanship;
    iv. **Luke 2:40 (KJV)** And the child grew, and waxed strong in spirit, filled with wisdom: and the grace of God was upon him.

23. Do you now see that it was NOT the LORD Jesus Christ who called you into the Ministry and that you called yourself?

24. Do you now see that if you were not a liar and you truly had the Holy Spirit, then HE would have taught you all these mysteries in the Gospel of Christ?

25. Brother, Sister, do you now see and admit that it is ONLY words, living words, the words of God, that are able to do all the above things that your filthy Water Baptism river and pool waters, and your Holy Comunion wafers, wine, and bread are NOT able to do?

26. So, therefore, USE ONLY WORDS, THE WORD OF GOD, TO ACCOMPLISH ALL WORSHIP AND ALL SACRIFICES, INCLUDING WATER BAPTISM AND HOLY COMMUNION!

27. As a true man of God, should you operate by what you see and feel? NO!

    i. **2 Corinthians 10:7 (KJV)** Do ye look on things after the outward appearance? If any man trust to himself that he is Christ's, let him of himself think this again, that, as he *is* Christ's, even so *are* we Christ's.

    ii. **2 Corinthians 4:18 (KJV)** While we look not at the things which are seen, but at the things which are not seen: for the things which are seen *are* temporal; but the things which are not seen *are* eternal.

28. If, therefore, the LORD God commanded you to NOT operate in Ministry by what you see and feel because all those things are temporal, carnal, worldly, defiled, corrupt, and NOT of God, but instead God commanded you to operate by "the things which are not seen" because they share the same eternal attributes with God Almighty, and now, you on your part, you have defied God Almighty and you are operating and serving God in Ministry with "the things which are seen" such as your filthy Water Baptism river and pool waters, and your Holy Comunion wafers, wine, and bread, then, is it not plainly obvious that it was NOT the LORD Jesus Christ who called you into the Ministry?

29. Is it not plainly obvious that it was NOT the LORD Holy Spirit who called you into the Ministry?

30. Is it not plainly obvious that it was Satan who called you into the Ministry and that is why you are defying God Almighty and obeying Satan?

31. If the LORD God Almighty gave you four commands in **2 Corinthians 10:5-8 (KJV)**, and you failed all of them, you are not obeying any of them, then, how is it that you do not have shame to continue to call yourself a Pastor or a bishop? Can a Man oif God defy God and still be a Man of God?

    i. **Amos 3:3 (KJV)** Can two walk together, except they be agreed?

    ii. **2 Corinthians 6:15 (KJV)** And what concord hath Christ with Belial? or what part hath he that believeth with an infidel?

    iii. **2 Corinthians 6:16 (KJV)** And what agreement hath the temple of God with idols? for ye are the temple of the living God; as God hath said, I will dwell in them, and walk in *them*; and I will be their God, and they shall be my people.

32. Now, when that which is perfect is already come, it is only the preaching and teaching of the Word of God that is now needful and NOT the offering of useless physical oblations in useless church sacrifices that have zero ability to save anyone!

    i. **2 Corinthians 10:16 (KJV)** To preach the gospel in the *regions* beyond you, *and* not to boast in another man's line of things made ready to our hand.

    ii. **2 Corinthians 10:17 (KJV)** But he that glorieth, let him glory in the Lord.

    iii. **2 Corinthians 10:18 (KJV)** For not he that commendeth himself is approved, but whom the Lord commendeth.

    iv. **1 Corinthians 13:10 (KJV)** But when that which is perfect is come, then that which is in part shall be done away.

    v. **Luke 10:41 (KJV)** And Jesus answered and said unto her, Martha, Martha, thou art careful and troubled about many things:

    vi. **Luke 10:42 (KJV)** But one thing is needful: and Mary hath chosen that good part, which shall not be taken away from her.

    vii. **Revelation 1:11 (KJV)** Saying, I am Alpha and Omega, the first and the last: and, What thou seest, write in a book, and send *it* unto the seven churches which are in Asia; unto Ephesus, and unto Smyrna, and unto Pergamos, and unto Thyatira, and unto Sardis, and unto Philadelphia, and unto Laodicea.

33. The LORD God Almighty, the LORD Jesus Christ, never commended anyone for excellent in sacrificing sheep and goats, neither did the LORD Jesus Christ commend anyone for excellence in sacrificing Holy Communion wafers, wine, and bread, but the LORD Jesus Christ surely commended HIS Disciples for excellence in Teaching the Word of God unto Salvation! So, then, choose which function you want to receive commendation in: whether in the carnal filthy Holy Communion physical things, and Water Baptism, or, in the teaching of the Word of God ONLY!

    i. **2 Corinthians 10:18 (KJV)** For not he that commendeth himself is approved, but whom the Lord commendeth.

    ii. **Acts 18:9 (KJV)** Then spake the Lord to Paul in the night by a vision, Be not afraid, but speak, and hold not thy peace:

    iii. **Acts 18:10 (KJV)** For I am with thee, and no man shall set on thee to hurt thee: for I have much people in this city.

    iv. **Acts 18:11 (KJV)** And he continued *there* a year and six months, teaching the word of God among them.

v. **Acts 23:11 (KJV)** And the night following the Lord stood by him, and said, Be of good cheer, Paul: for as thou hast testified of me in Jerusalem, so must thou bear witness also at Rome.

vi. **Amos 5:21 (KJV)** I hate, I despise your feast days, and I will not smell in your solemn assemblies.

vii. **Amos 5:22 (KJV)** Though ye offer me burnt offerings and your meat offerings, I will not accept *them*: neither will I regard the peace offerings of your fat beasts.

viii. **Amos 5:23 (KJV)** Take thou away from me the noise of thy songs; for I will not hear the melody of thy viols.

ix. **Amos 5:24 (KJV)** But let judgment run down as waters, and righteousness as a mighty stream.

x. **Amos 5:25 (KJV)** Have ye offered unto me sacrifices and offerings in the wilderness forty years, O house of Israel?

xi. **Amos 5:26 (KJV)** But ye have borne the tabernacle of your Moloch and Chiun your images, the star of your god, which ye made to yourselves.

xii. **Amos 5:27 (KJV)** Therefore will I cause you to go into captivity beyond Damascus, saith the LORD, whose name *is* The God of hosts.

xiii. **Acts 7:42 (KJV)** Then God turned, and gave them up to worship the host of heaven; as it is written in the book of the prophets, O ye house of Israel, have ye offered to me slain beasts and sacrifices *by the space of* forty years in the wilderness?

The LORD Jesus Christ be with your spirit. The LORD Jesus Christ give you understanding.

Rev. Prof. PETER PRYCE,
DSEF, BA, MA, B.Soc.Sc Pol Sci, IBA, PhD
A Scribe of the Law of the God of Heaven
Prophet of the Word of God
Professor of French, Silver Spring, MD, USA
Scholar of the Institute of Theologians, USA
WWW.THEBIBLEUNIVERSITY.ORG
Accreditation Number: 07-QCTO/SDP120723172836
SAQA QUAL ID: Identification # 101997
WWW.BOOKSTORESITE.ORG

Wednesday 24th January 2024 @ 11:01 AM – 3:27 PM
While hearing and meditating on the Word of God at home.

CHAPTER 14

THE CORRECT BREAD IS THE WORD OF GOD

EBAN
"Fence"
Asante philosophical symbol of Love, Safety, Security

Question 2498

1. The LORD God reveals that Water Baptism and Holy Communion are NOT done with physical items such as physical filthy wine, physical filthy river, physical filthy pool water, physical filthy man-made wafers, physical filthy bread but, or any such things, BUT with the water of the Word and with the wine of the Spirit!

   i. **Ephesians 5:18 (KJV)** And be not drunk with wine, wherein is excess; but be filled with the Spirit;

   ii. **Ephesians 5:26 (KJV)** That he might sanctify and cleanse it with the washing of water by the word,

   iii. **Ephesians 5:27 (KJV)** That he might present it to himself a glorious church, not having spot, or wrinkle, or any such thing; but that it should be holy and without blemish.

   iv. **John 6:35 (KJV)** And Jesus said unto them, I am the bread of life: he that cometh to me shall never hunger; and he that believeth on me shall never thirst.

   v. **John 6:41 (KJV)** The Jews then murmured at him, because he said, I am the bread which came down from heaven.

   vi. **John 6:51 (KJV)** I am the living bread which came down from heaven: if any man eat of this bread, he shall live for ever: and the bread that I will give is my flesh, which I will give for the life of the world.

vii. **John 1:1 (KJV)** In the beginning was the Word, and the Word was with God, and the Word was God.

viii. **Deuteronomy 8:3 (KJV)** And he humbled thee, and suffered thee to hunger, and fed thee with manna, which thou knewest not, neither did thy fathers know; that he might make thee know that man doth not live by bread only, but by every *word* that proceedeth out of the mouth of the LORD doth man live.

ix. **Matthew 4:4 (KJV)** But he answered and said, It is written, Man shall not live by bread alone, but by every word that proceedeth out of the mouth of God.

x. **Luke 4:4 (KJV)** And Jesus answered him, saying, It is written, That man shall not live by bread alone, but by every word of God.

2. So, as you can see from the evidences above, the correct bread is the Word of God and the correct wine is the wine of the Spirit and the correct water is the water of the Word! So, why do you claim that it was the LORD Jesus Christ who called you into the Ministry and yet, every Sunday, you have been insulting God Almighty and Jesus Christ by offering unto them physical filthy man-made water and wine and bread!

3. There is no man-made wine in the entire world that is not filthy and polluted! There is no river or pool water in the entire world that is not filthy, polluted, and corrupted, and so, you ask yourself as a Pastor, shall we offer filthy and polluted river and pool water to the Almighty God? Did not the LORD God command to offer ONLY that which has NO BLEMISH AT ALL?

i. **Exodus 12:5 (KJV)** Your lamb shall be without blemish, a male of the first year: ye shall take *it* out from the sheep, or from the goats:

ii. **Leviticus 1:3 (KJV)** If his offering *be* a burnt sacrifice of the herd, let him offer a male without blemish: he shall offer it of his own voluntary will at the door of the tabernacle of the congregation before the LORD.

iii. **Leviticus 3:1 (KJV)** And if his oblation *be* a sacrifice of peace offering, if he offer *it* of the herd; whether *it be* a male or female, he shall offer it without blemish before the LORD.

iv. **Leviticus 22:25 (KJV)** Neither from a stranger's hand shall ye offer the bread of your God of any of these; because their corruption *is* in them, *and* blemishes *be* in them: they shall not be accepted for you.

v. **Malachi 1:6 (KJV)** A son honoureth *his* father, and a servant his master: if then I *be* a father, where *is* mine honour? and if I *be* a master, where *is* my fear? saith the LORD of hosts unto you, O priests, that despise my name. And ye say, Wherein have we despised thy name?

vi. **Malachi 1:7 (KJV)** Ye offer polluted bread upon mine altar; and ye say, Wherein have we polluted thee? In that ye say, The table of the LORD *is* contemptible.

vii. **Malachi 1:8 (KJV)** And if ye offer the blind for sacrifice, *is it* not evil? and if ye offer the lame and sick, *is it* not evil? offer it now unto thy governor; will he be pleased with thee, or accept thy person? saith the LORD of hosts.

viii. **Malachi 1:9 (KJV)** And now, I pray you, beseech God that he will be gracious unto us: this hath been by your means: will he regard your persons? saith the LORD of hosts.

4. Pastor and Bishop, can you guarantee with your life that the water in your Water Baptism, and the wafers, wine, and bread in your Holy Communion have no single blemish at all and that they are all 100% pure?

    i. **Ephesians 5:27 (KJV)** That he might present it to himself a glorious church, not having spot, or wrinkle, or any such thing; but that it should be holy and without blemish.

5. Since you know that you cannot give such a guarantee, then, you acquiesce that you are guilty of offering into God Almighty: evil polluted corrupted filthy cursed Water Baptism and Holy Communion, and should you not be equally cursed and sent to Hell for this your evil?

6. Since you know that the Holy Communion and the Water Baptism that you have been offering unto God ARE NOT "holy and without blemish" as God commanded, then, why are you still doing them if it is not Satan that you actually serve?

7. As **Ephesians 5:27 (KJV)** reveals, it is ONLY when you use the correct holy and without blemish Bread of the Word of God, and the correct holy and without blemish Wine of the Spirit in the Word of God, that your Holy Communion and your Water Baptism shall be accepted in Heaven!

The LORD Jesus Christ be with your spirit. The LORD Jesus Christ give you understanding.

Rev. Prof. PETER PRYCE,
DSEF, BA, MA, B.Soc.Sc Pol Sci, IBA, PhD
A Scribe of the Law of the God of Heaven

Prophet of the Word of God
Professor of French, Silver Spring, MD, USA
Scholar of the Institute of Theologians, USA
WWW.THEBIBLEUNIVERSITY.ORG
Accreditation Number: 07-QCTO/SDP120723172836
SAQA QUAL ID: Identification # 101997
WWW.BOOKSTORESITE.ORG
WWW.THEBIBLEUNIVERSITYCHURCH.ORG

Wednesday 7th February 2024 @ 12:31 PM – 12:53 PM
While hearing and meditating on the Word of God in the office.

CHAPTER 15

YOU DO NOT GAIN ACCESS TO GOD OR TO HEAVEN THROUGH FOOD, MEAT, AND WINE!

EBAN

"Fence"

Asante philosophical symbol of Love, Safety, Security

Question 2500

1. Now, concerning Holy Communion, I counsel you by the Holy Ghost, that you do NOT gain access to the LORD or to Heaven through food, meat, and wine!

> i. **1 Corinthians 8:8 (KJV)** But meat commendeth us not to God: for neither, if we eat, are we the better; neither, if we eat not, are we the worse.
>
> ii. **Hosea 4:11 (KJV)** Whoredom and wine and new wine take away the heart.

2. Food/meat is NOT a medium by which you reach or connect the Kingdom of God in Heaven!

3. The LORD God Almighty does NOT operate through food/meat, but ONLY through the Word of God!

> i. **Psalm 50:7 (KJV)** Hear, O my people, and I will speak; O Israel, and I will testify against thee: I *am* God, *even* thy God.
>
> ii. **Psalm 50:8 (KJV)** I will not reprove thee for thy sacrifices or thy burnt offerings, *to have been* continually before me.
>
> iii. **Psalm 50:9 (KJV)** I will take no bullock out of thy house, *nor* he goats out of thy folds.

    iv.   **Psalm 50:10 (KJV)** For every beast of the forest *is* mine, *and* the cattle upon a thousand hills.

    v.   **Psalm 50:11 (KJV)** I know all the fowls of the mountains: and the wild beasts of the field *are* mine.

    vi.   **Psalm 50:12 (KJV)** If I were hungry, I would not tell thee: for the world *is* mine, and the fulness thereof.

    vii.   **Psalm 50:13 (KJV)** Will I eat the flesh of bulls, or drink the blood of goats?

    viii.   **Psalm 50:14 (KJV)** Offer unto God thanksgiving; and pay thy vows unto the most High:

    ix.   **Psalm 50:15 (KJV)** And call upon me in the day of trouble: I will deliver thee, and thou shalt glorify me.

4. Food/meat are products fit for the dunghill and for the toilet, but the Words of God are the Keys to open Heaven!

    i.   **Matthew 15:10 (KJV)** And he called the multitude, and said unto them, Hear, and understand:

    ii.   **Matthew 15:11 (KJV)** Not that which goeth into the mouth defileth a man; but that which cometh out of the mouth, this defileth a man.

    iii.   **Matthew 15:12 (KJV)** Then came his disciples, and said unto him, Knowest thou that the Pharisees were offended, after they heard this saying?

    iv.   **Matthew 15:13 (KJV)** But he answered and said, Every plant, which my heavenly Father hath not planted, shall be rooted up.

    v.   **Matthew 15:14 (KJV)** Let them alone: they be blind leaders of the blind. And if the blind lead the blind, both shall fall into the ditch.

    vi.   **Matthew 15:15 (KJV)** Then answered Peter and said unto him, Declare unto us this parable.

    vii.   **Matthew 15:16 (KJV)** And Jesus said, Are ye also yet without understanding?

    viii.   **Matthew 15:17 (KJV)** Do not ye yet understand, that whatsoever entereth in at the mouth goeth into the belly, and is cast out into the draught?

5. Food/meat are oblations for sacrifice unto Devils but the Word of God is the correct sacrifice and offering unto God!

    i.   **Exodus 32:1 (KJV)** And when the people saw that Moses delayed to come down out of the mount, the people gathered themselves together unto Aaron, and said unto him, Up, make us gods, which shall go before us; for *as for* this Moses, the man that brought us up out of the land of Egypt, we wot not what is become of him.

ii. **Exodus 32:2 (KJV)** And Aaron said unto them, Break off the golden earrings, which *are* in the ears of your wives, of your sons, and of your daughters, and bring *them* unto me.

iii. **Exodus 32:3 (KJV)** And all the people brake off the golden earrings which *were* in their ears, and brought *them* unto Aaron.

iv. **Exodus 32:4 (KJV)** And he received *them* at their hand, and fashioned it with a graving tool, after he had made it a molten calf: and they said, These *be* thy gods, O Israel, which brought thee up out of the land of Egypt.

v. **Exodus 32:5 (KJV)** And when Aaron saw *it*, he built an altar before it; and Aaron made proclamation, and said, To morrow *is* a feast to the LORD.

vi. **Exodus 32:6 (KJV)** And they rose up early on the morrow, and offered burnt offerings, and brought peace offerings; and the people sat down to eat and to drink, and rose up to play.

vii. **Exodus 32:7 (KJV)** And the LORD said unto Moses, Go, get thee down; for thy people, which thou broughtest out of the land of Egypt, have corrupted *themselves*:

viii. **Exodus 32:8 (KJV)** They have turned aside quickly out of the way which I commanded them: they have made them a molten calf, and have worshipped it, and have sacrificed thereunto, and said, These *be* thy gods, O Israel, which have brought thee up out of the land of Egypt.

6. The Word of God is the correct sacrifice and offering unto God!

   i. **Psalm 50:14 (KJV)** Offer unto God thanksgiving; and pay thy vows unto the most High:

   ii. **Psalm 50:15 (KJV)** And call upon me in the day of trouble: I will deliver thee, and thou shalt glorify me.

   iii. **Hebrews 9:13 (KJV)** For if the blood of bulls and of goats, and the ashes of an heifer sprinkling the unclean, sanctifieth to the purifying of the flesh:

7. You approach the LORD God Almighty with words, the Words of God, NOT with food/meat/drinks!

   i. **Hosea 14:2 (KJV)** Take with you words, and turn to the LORD: say unto him, Take away all iniquity, and receive *us* graciously: so will we render the calves of our lips.

8. Holy Communion food and drink are the evil and wrong oblations and sacrifices unto God!

  i. **Isaiah 1:13 (KJV)** Bring no more vain oblations; incense is an abomination unto me; the new moons and sabbaths, the calling of assemblies, I cannot away with; *it is* iniquity, even the solemn meeting.

  ii. **Psalm 40:6 (KJV)** Sacrifice and offering thou didst not desire; mine ears hast thou opened: burnt offering and sin offering hast thou not required.

  iii. **Psalm 40:7 (KJV)** Then said I, Lo, I come: in the volume of the book *it is* written of me,

  iv. **Psalm 40:8 (KJV)** I delight to do thy will, O my God: yea, thy law *is* within my heart.

  v. **Hebrews 9:14 (KJV)** How much more shall the blood of Christ, who through the eternal Spirit offered himself without spot to God, purge your conscience from dead works to serve the living God?

  vi. **Hebrews 10:5 (KJV)** Wherefore when he cometh into the world, he saith, Sacrifice and offering thou wouldest not, but a body hast thou prepared me:

  vii. **Hebrews 10:8 (KJV)** Above when he said, Sacrifice and offering and burnt offerings and *offering* for sin thou wouldest not, neither hadst pleasure *therein*; which are offered by the law;

The LORD Jesus Christ be with your spirit. The LORD Jesus Christ give you understanding.

Rev. Prof. PETER PRYCE,
DSEF, BA, MA, B.Soc.Sc Pol Sci, IBA, PhD
A Scribe of the Law of the God of Heaven
Prophet of the Word of God
Professor of French, Silver Spring, MD, USA
Scholar of the Institute of Theologians, USA
WWW.THEBIBLEUNIVERSITY.ORG
Accreditation Number: 07-QCTO/SDP120723172836
SAQA QUAL ID: Identification # 101997
WWW.BOOKSTORESITE.ORG
WWW.THEBIBLEUNIVERSITYCHURCH.ORG

Friday 9th February 2024 @ 9:00 AM – 9:40 AM
While hearing and meditating on the Word of God at home.

CHAPTER 16

DO NOT EAT PHYSICAL FOOD OF HOLY COMMUNION AT THE ALTAR!

EPA

"Handcuffs"

Asante philosophical symbol of Law, Justice, Slavery, Captivity, and the Crime of white people's Colonization of Black People, including both Physical Colonization on the Continent of Africa and Spiritual and Mental Colonization of all Black People in the Diaspora through the economic shackles of Racism and false historical narratives about the Black People

Question 2531

53. This last chapter of the Book of Hebrews is dedicated to an in-depth study of Holy Communion, where the word "communion" simply means "speaking with, interacting with, communicating with"!

54. In other words how do I as a Christian interact with the Brethren, and how do I demonstrate that the Holy Ghost is interacting with me?

55. Another way to understand the main idea of this chapter is to ask:

    i. What signs show that I have good interaction with the Brethren?

    ii. What signs show that I have good interaction with the Holy Spirit?

56. **How to eat the true and proper Holy Communion: #1**:

57. The first sign that you are eating the true and proper Holy Communion is your obedience to the commandment of brotherly love and your communication and demonstration of the same to the true Children of God:

    i. **Hebrews 13:1 (KJV)** Let brotherly love continue.

ii. **John 13:34 (KJV)** A new commandment I give unto you, That ye love one another; as I have loved you, that ye also love one another.

iii. **John 13:35 (KJV)** By this shall all *men* know that ye are my disciples, if ye have love one to another.

iv. **John 15:12 (KJV)** This is my commandment, That ye love one another, as I have loved you.

v. **John 15:17 (KJV)** These things I command you, that ye love one another.

vi. **Romans 12:10 (KJV)** *Be* kindly affectioned one to another with brotherly love; in honour preferring one another;

vii. **Romans 13:8 (KJV)** Owe no man any thing, but to love one another: for he that loveth another hath fulfilled the law.

viii. **Galatians 5:13 (KJV)** For, brethren, ye have been called unto liberty; only *use* not liberty for an occasion to the flesh, but by love serve one another.

ix. **Ephesians 4:2 (KJV)** With all lowliness and meekness, with longsuffering, forbearing one another in love;

x. **1 Thessalonians 3:12 (KJV)** And the Lord make you to increase and abound in love one toward another, and toward all *men*, even as we *do* toward you:

xi. **1 Thessalonians 4:9 (KJV)** But as touching brotherly love ye need not that I write unto you: for ye yourselves are taught of God to love one another.

xii. **Hebrews 10:24 (KJV)** And let us consider one another to provoke unto love and to good works:

xiii. **1 Peter 1:22 (KJV)** Seeing ye have purified your souls in obeying the truth through the Spirit unto unfeigned love of the brethren, *see that ye* love one another with a pure heart fervently:

xiv. **1 Peter 3:8 (KJV)** Finally, *be ye* all of one mind, having compassion one of another, love as brethren, *be* pitiful, *be* courteous:

xv. **1 John 3:11 (KJV)** For this is the message that ye heard from the beginning, that we should love one another.

xvi. **1 John 3:23 (KJV)** And this is his commandment, That we should believe on the name of his Son Jesus Christ, and love one another, as he gave us commandment.

xvii. **1 John 4:7 (KJV)** Beloved, let us love one another: for love is of God; and every one that loveth is born of God, and knoweth God.

xviii. **1 John 4:11 (KJV)** Beloved, if God so loved us, we ought also to love one another.

xix. **1 John 4:12 (KJV)** No man hath seen God at any time. If we love one another, God dwelleth in us, and his love is perfected in us.

xx. **2 John 5 (KJV)** And now I beseech thee, lady, not as though I wrote a new commandment unto thee, but that which we had from the beginning, that we love one another.

58. **How to eat the true and proper Holy Communion: #2**:

59. The second sign that you are eating the true and proper Holy Communion is when you are helping the poor, the needy, the widow, the stranger, the fatherless, and the destitute, communicating with them according to their needs, and helping them as unto the LORD Jesus Christ:

i. **Hebrews 13:2 (KJV)** Be not forgetful to entertain strangers: for thereby some have entertained angels unawares.

ii. **Ezekiel 22:29 (KJV)** The people of the land have used oppression, and exercised robbery, and have vexed the poor and needy: yea, they have oppressed the stranger wrongfully.

iii. **Ezekiel 22:30 (KJV)** And I sought for a man among them, that should make up the hedge, and stand in the gap before me for the land, that I should not destroy it: but I found none.

iv. **Deuteronomy 15:11 (KJV)** For the poor shall never cease out of the land: therefore I command thee, saying, Thou shalt open thine hand wide unto thy brother, to thy poor, and to thy needy, in thy land.

v. **Psalm 9:18 (KJV)** For the needy shall not alway be forgotten: the expectation of the poor shall *not* perish for ever.

60. **How to eat the true and proper Holy Communion: #3**:

61. The third sign that you are eating the true and proper Holy Communion is to obey the commandment to empathize with those who suffer in adversity and are in need of comfort and care!

62. When you do all these things and help all such persons, that is when you do show that you have good interaction/communion with the Brethren and with the Holy Ghost!

i. **Hebrews 13:3 (KJV)** Remember them that are in bonds, as bound with them; *and* them which suffer adversity, as being yourselves also in the body.

ii. **Matthew 25:40 (KJV)** And the King shall answer and say unto them, Verily I say unto you, Inasmuch as ye have done *it* unto one of the least of these my brethren, ye have done *it* unto me.

      iii. **Matthew 25:45 (KJV)** Then shall he answer them, saying, Verily I say unto you, Inasmuch as ye did *it* not to one of the least of these, ye did *it* not to me.

63. **How to eat the true and proper Holy Communion: #4**:

64. The fourth sign that you are eating the true and proper Holy Communion and having good interaction/communion with the Brethren and with the Holy Ghost is that you are obeying the commandment of God to NOT defraud your wife and the wife also seeing that she defraud NOT her husband in anything!

      i. **Hebrews 13:4 (KJV)** Marriage *is* honourable in all, and the bed undefiled: but whoremongers and adulterers God will judge.

65. The title of a man or a woman who is obeying this commandment is: "Honorable Man and Honorable Woman", NOT those evil, wicked, demonic, lying, corrupt, stealing, robbing, ignorant, inordinate, reprobate, ungodly, bribe-taking Politicians who falsely call themselves "Honorable Member of Parliament" …THEY ARE NOT!

66. **How to eat the true and proper Holy Communion: #5**:

67. The fifth sign that you are eating the true and proper Holy Communion and having good interaction/communion with the Brethren and with the Holy Ghost is that your obedience to the Word of God are both evident in your speech and utterances!

      i. **Hebrews 13:5 (KJV)** *Let your* conversation *be* without covetousness; *and be* content with such things as ye have: for he hath said, I will never leave thee, nor forsake thee.

      ii. **Hebrews 13:6 (KJV)** So that we may boldly say, The Lord *is* my helper, and I will not fear what man shall do unto me.

68. Let it not be understood from your utterances that you are a greedy person more interested in acquiring, amassing, and hoarding money, riches, and wealth to yourself and to your family while neglecting the Brethren as if you have not seen their plight or you have not known of their suffering and their adversity!

69. You have pursued money and chased after money, rising up early at dawn to get out into the streets and into the offices to chase after money, and yet, after all the many thousands of money and after all the many millions of money that you have acquired, yet you are NOT satisfied, and you continue to chase after money all your life to the very moment when you take you last breath, and right before death you are still talking about money, bank accounts, properties, inheritance, and NOT Christ! Woe unto you!

      i. **Luke 6:24 (KJV)** But woe unto you that are rich! for ye have received your consolation.

    ii. **James 5:1 (KJV)** Go to now, *ye* rich men, weep and howl for your miseries that shall come upon *you*.

    iii. **James 5:2 (KJV)** Your riches are corrupted, and your garments are motheaten.

    iv. **James 5:3 (KJV)** Your gold and silver is cankered; and the rust of them shall be a witness against you, and shall eat your flesh as it were fire. Ye have heaped treasure together for the last days.

    v. **James 5:4 (KJV)** Behold, the hire of the labourers who have reaped down your fields, which is of you kept back by fraud, crieth: and the cries of them which have reaped are entered into the ears of the Lord of sabaoth.

    vi. **James 5:5 (KJV)** Ye have lived in pleasure on the earth, and been wanton; ye have nourished your hearts, as in a day of slaughter.

    vii. **James 5:6 (KJV)** Ye have condemned *and* killed the just; *and* he doth not resist you.

    viii. **James 5:7 (KJV)** Be patient therefore, brethren, unto the coming of the Lord. Behold, the husbandman waiteth for the precious fruit of the earth, and hath long patience for it, until he receive the early and latter rain.

    ix. **James 5:8 (KJV)** Be ye also patient; stablish your hearts: for the coming of the Lord draweth nigh.

70. Woe unto you false Christians who claim to have Christ and yet you harden your hearts to NOT help the poor, the needy, the widow, the stranger, the fatherless, and the destitute!

71. You go to your home to eat excess and over abundant thanksgiving meals right after church while you look at other poor brethren and sisters in the face and tell them: the Lord be with you and help you!

72. Behold, I tell you, that you shall give account in Hell of this your wickedness of NOT helping the poor!

73. How to eat the true and proper Holy Communion: #6:

74. The sixth sign that you are eating the true and proper Holy Communion and having good interaction/communion with the Brethren and with the Holy Ghost is that you acknowledge the Truth of God that anyone "who have spoken unto you the word of God", who is teaching you the Word of God, who is giving you deep understanding in the Word of God, who is helping you to understand things in the Word of God that you never understood before or knew before, that person is your Elder who has rule over you and the LORD God commands you to give reverence that Man of

God! The LORD God commands you to verify what he teaches you by the Word of God!

    i. **Hebrews 13:7 (KJV)** Remember them which have the rule over you, who have spoken unto you the word of God: whose faith follow, considering the end of *their* conversation.

    ii. **Jeremiah 3:15 (KJV)** And I will give you pastors according to mine heart, which shall feed you with knowledge and understanding.

    iii. **Malachi 2:7 (KJV)** For the priest's lips should keep knowledge, and they should seek the law at his mouth: for he *is* the messenger of the LORD of hosts.

    iv. **Acts 17:10 (KJV)** And the brethren immediately sent away Paul and Silas by night unto Berea: who coming *thither* went into the synagogue of the Jews.

    v. **Acts 17:11 (KJV)** These were more noble than those in Thessalonica, in that they received the word with all readiness of mind, and searched the scriptures daily, whether those things were so.

    vi. **Acts 17:12 (KJV)** Therefore many of them believed; also of honourable women which were Greeks, and of men, not a few.

    vii. **1 Thessalonians 5:21 (KJV)** Prove all things; hold fast that which is good.

    viii. **1 John 4:1 (KJV)** Beloved, believe not every spirit, but try the spirits whether they are of God: because many false prophets are gone out into the world.

75. **How to eat the true and proper Holy Communion: #7**:

76. The seventh sign that you are eating the true and proper Holy Communion and having good interaction/communion with the Brethren and with the Holy Ghost is that you know and you recognize the end/aim/object/target of the conversation/interaction/communion of every true Man of God, and this target of conversation is the LORD Jesus Christ!

    i. **Hebrews 13:8 (KJV)** Jesus Christ the same yesterday, and to day, and for ever.

    ii. **Hebrews 13:9 (KJV)** Be not carried about with divers and strange doctrines. For *it is* a good thing that the heart be established with grace; not with meats, which have not profited them that have been occupied therein.

77. This word: "considering the end of *their* conversation", in **Hebrews 13:7 (KJV)**, continues in **Hebrews 13:8 (KJV)** by naming the end/aim/object/target of your conversation, interaction, and communion, which end is the LORD Jesus Christ!

78. Therefore, what **Hebrews 13:7-8 (KJV)** is showing you is that when you meet a Man of God whose speech, utterances, conversation, preaching, teaching, and explanations do NOT conform 100% to the Word of God, then you must condemn him as a liar and a servant of Satan!

    i. **1 Thessalonians 5:21 (KJV)** Prove all things; hold fast that which is good.
    ii. **1 John 4:1 (KJV)** Beloved, believe not every spirit, but try the spirits whether they are of God: because many false prophets are gone out into the world.

79. Now, the specifics of the conversation that you should expect from a true Man of God are these:

    i. Christ came into the world.
    ii. Christ took all our sins and died for our forgiveness and Salvation by the shedding of HIS own Blood.
    iii. Christ arose from the dead on the third according to the Scriptures.
    iv. Christ ascended back into Heaven.
    v. Christ sent down HIS Holy Ghost into the heart of everyone who believes in HIS Name and Work of Salvation from sin!
    vi. Christ sent Apostles to testify of all the above in preaching, in teaching, and in writing Books!

80. So, then, when you meet a Man of God and his conversation, preaching, teaching, interaction is about money, prosperity gospel, marriage, wives, husbands, visa to travel abroad, properties, branches of churches, stories to laugh, people, celebrities, his family, and material things, then know immediately, that he is NOT a Man of God but a Man of Satan!

81. The ONLY ONE Gospel that all the Apostles taught was what I have shown you here above, and so, any Man of God who deviates from those words and teachings is a fool, an ignorant bastard, a demon-possessed idiot, and a candidate for Hell, and in this very teaching, the Word of God also bears me witness in **Hebrews 13:9 (KJV)**!

    i. **Galatians 1:8 (KJV)** But though we, or an angel from heaven, preach any other gospel unto you than that which we have preached unto you, let him be accursed.
    ii. **Galatians 1:9 (KJV)** As we said before, so say I now again, If any *man* preach any other gospel unto you than that ye have received, let him be accursed.
    iii. **2 John 9 (KJV)** Whosoever transgresseth, and abideth not in the doctrine of Christ, hath not God. He that abideth in the doctrine of Christ, he hath both the Father and the Son.

iv. **2 John 10 (KJV)** If there come any unto you, and bring not this doctrine, receive him not into *your* house, neither bid him God speed:

v. **2 John 11 (KJV)** For he that biddeth him God speed is partaker of his evil deeds.

vi. **Ephesians 4:4 (KJV)** *There is* one body, and one Spirit, even as ye are called in one hope of your calling;

vii. **Ephesians 4:5 (KJV)** One Lord, one faith, one baptism,

viii. **Ephesians 4:6 (KJV)** One God and Father of all, who *is* above all, and through all, and in you all.

82. **How to eat the true and proper Holy Communion: #8**:

83. The eighth sign that you are eating the true and proper Holy Communion and having good interaction/communion with the Brethren and with the Holy Ghost is that you learn, recognize, understand, and teach that there is nothing called: "Holy Communion" in the entire Holy Bible from Genesis to Revelation!

   i. **Hebrews 13:9 (KJV)** Be not carried about with divers and strange doctrines. For *it is* a good thing that the heart be established with grace; not with meats, which have not profited them that have been occupied therein.

84. What is falsely called "Holy Communion" in the churches by ignorant men and women is actually called: "The Lord's Last Passover Supper"!

   i. **Exodus 12:43 (KJV)** And the LORD said unto Moses and Aaron, This *is* the ordinance of the passover: There shall no stranger eat thereof:

   ii. **Matthew 26:17 (KJV)** Now the first *day* of the *feast of* unleavened bread the disciples came to Jesus, saying unto him, Where wilt thou that we prepare for thee to eat the passover?

   iii. **Matthew 26:18 (KJV)** And he said, Go into the city to such a man, and say unto him, The Master saith, My time is at hand; I will keep the passover at thy house with my disciples.

   iv. **Matthew 26:19 (KJV)** And the disciples did as Jesus had appointed them; and they made ready the passover.

   v. **Matthew 26:20 (KJV)** Now when the even was come, he sat down with the twelve.

85. Now, here is what transpired at "The Lord's Last Passover Supper"!

   i. **Luke 22:14 (KJV)** And when the hour was come, he sat down, and the twelve apostles with him.

   ii. **Luke 22:15 (KJV)** And he said unto them, With desire I have desired to eat this passover with you before I suffer:

iii. **Luke 22:16 (KJV)** For I say unto you, I will not any more eat thereof, until it be fulfilled in the kingdom of God.

iv. **Luke 22:17 (KJV)** And he took the cup, and gave thanks, and said, Take this, and divide *it* among yourselves:

v. **Luke 22:18 (KJV)** For I say unto you, I will not drink of the fruit of the vine, until the kingdom of God shall come.

vi. **Luke 22:19 (KJV)** And he took bread, and gave thanks, and brake *it*, and gave unto them, saying, This is my body which is given for you: this do in remembrance of me.

vii. **Luke 22:20 (KJV)** Likewise also the cup after supper, saying, This cup *is* the new testament in my blood, which is shed for you.

viii. **1 Corinthians 11:23 (KJV)** For I have received of the Lord that which also I delivered unto you, That the Lord Jesus the *same* night in which he was betrayed took bread:

ix. **1 Corinthians 11:24 (KJV)** And when he had given thanks, he brake *it*, and said, Take, eat: this is my body, which is broken for you: this do in remembrance of me.

x. **1 Corinthians 11:25 (KJV)** After the same manner also *he took* the cup, when he had supped, saying, This cup is the new testament in my blood: this do ye, as oft as ye drink *it*, in remembrance of me.

xi. **1 Corinthians 11:26 (KJV)** For as often as ye eat this bread, and drink this cup, ye do shew the Lord's death till he come.

86. We know that this was the last Passover Dinner because the LORD Jesus Christ said this: "I will not any more eat thereof"!

    i. **Luke 22:16 (KJV)** For I say unto you, I will not any more eat thereof, until it be fulfilled in the kingdom of God.

87. We also know that the LORD Jesus Christ said this: "this do in remembrance of me"!

88. We also ask this question:

    i. How do many churches and Pastors continue the physical practise of The Lord's Last Passover Supper" when the LORD Jesus Christ said: "I will not any more eat thereof"!

    ii. Was it therefore that the LORD Jesus Christ ended the practise and then immediately also told the Apostles to continue doing it?

    iii. Where then is the sense in that?

89. We also ask whether, aside from that one time during the meal, there is another evidence where the LORD Jesus Christ again commanded that "The Lord's Last Passover Supper" was over?

90. Here is the reason why we seek a second confirmation that "The Lord's Last Passover Supper" is over?

      i. **Deuteronomy 17:6 (KJV)** At the mouth of two witnesses, or three witnesses, shall he that is worthy of death be put to death; *but* at the mouth of one witness he shall not be put to death.

      ii. **Deuteronomy 19:15 (KJV)** One witness shall not rise up against a man for any iniquity, or for any sin, in any sin that he sinneth: at the mouth of two witnesses, or at the mouth of three witnesses, shall the matter be established.

      iii. **Matthew 18:20 (KJV)** For where two or three are gathered together in my name, there am I in the midst of them.

      iv. **John 8:17 (KJV)** It is also written in your law, that the testimony of two men is true.

91. Here then is the second confirmation, as plain as water!

      i. **1 Corinthians 11:20 (KJV)** When ye come together therefore into one place, *this* is not to eat the Lord's supper.

92. So, therefore, when you add this: "I will not any more eat thereof" [**Luke 22:16 (KJV)**] to this "When ye come together therefore into one place, *this* is not to eat the Lord's supper" [**1 Corinthians 11:20 (KJV)**], you get those two witnesses that the LORD Jesus Christ said in **John 8:17 (KJV)** that you need in order to establish that the record is True!

93. So, now that we have established by the Scriptures that the record of the end of "The Lord's Last Passover Supper" is true, we now need to search and find out what then did the LORD Jesus Christ mean by "this do in remembrance of me"!

      i. **Luke 22:19 (KJV)** And he took bread, and gave thanks, and brake *it*, and gave unto them, saying, This is my body which is given for you: this do in remembrance of me.

94. We shall prove that by five evidences, as follows!

95. **Evidence #1** of what the LORD Jesus Christ meant by "this do in remembrance of me"!

      i. **Luke 22:14 (KJV)** And when the hour was come, he sat down, and the twelve apostles with him.

      ii. **Luke 22:15 (KJV)** And he said unto them, With desire I have desired to eat this passover with you before I suffer:

      iii. **Luke 22:16 (KJV)** For I say unto you, I will not any more eat thereof, until it be fulfilled in the kingdom of God.

      iv. **Luke 22:17 (KJV)** And he took the cup, and gave thanks, and said, Take this, and divide *it* among yourselves:

96. Now, take note very carefully, that in **Luke 22:14-17 (KJV)**, the LORD Jesus Christ is comparing and juxtaposing two things, namely: "HIS Words" and "the physical bread", and HE is emphasizing to choose "HIS Words" over "the physical bread"!

97. Evidence #2 of what the LORD Jesus Christ meant by "this do in remembrance of me"!

> i. **John 6:52 (KJV)** The Jews therefore strove among themselves, saying, How can this man give us *his* flesh to eat?
>
> ii. **John 6:53 (KJV)** Then Jesus said unto them, Verily, verily, I say unto you, Except ye eat the flesh of the Son of man, and drink his blood, ye have no life in you.
>
> iii. **John 6:54 (KJV)** Whoso eateth my flesh, and drinketh my blood, hath eternal life; and I will raise him up at the last day.
>
> iv. **John 6:55 (KJV)** For my flesh is meat indeed, and my blood is drink indeed.
>
> v. **John 6:56 (KJV)** He that eateth my flesh, and drinketh my blood, dwelleth in me, and I in him.
>
> vi. **John 6:57 (KJV)** As the living Father hath sent me, and I live by the Father: so he that eateth me, even he shall live by me.
>
> vii. **John 6:58 (KJV)** This is that bread which came down from heaven: not as your fathers did eat manna, and are dead: he that eateth of this bread shall live for ever.
>
> viii. **John 6:59 (KJV)** These things said he in the synagogue, as he taught in Capernaum.
>
> ix. **John 6:60 (KJV)** Many therefore of his disciples, when they had heard *this*, said, This is an hard saying; who can hear it?
>
> x. **John 6:61 (KJV)** When Jesus knew in himself that his disciples murmured at it, he said unto them, Doth this offend you?
>
> xi. **John 6:62 (KJV)** *What* and if ye shall see the Son of man ascend up where he was before?
>
> xii. **John 6:63 (KJV)** It is the spirit that quickeneth; the flesh profiteth nothing: the words that I speak unto you, *they* are spirit, and *they* are life.

98. Again, now, take note very carefully, that in **John 6:52-63 (KJV)**, the LORD Jesus Christ is comparing and juxtaposing two things, namely: "HIS Words" and "the physical bread", and HE is emphasizing to choose "HIS Words" over "the physical bread"!

99. Evidence #3 of what the LORD Jesus Christ meant by "this do in remembrance of me"!

     i.   **Luke 24:25 (KJV)** Then he said unto them, O fools, and slow of heart to believe all that the prophets have spoken:

    ii.   **Luke 24:26 (KJV)** Ought not Christ to have suffered these things, and to enter into his glory?

   iii.   **Luke 24:27 (KJV)** And beginning at Moses and all the prophets, he expounded unto them in all the scriptures the things concerning himself.

   iv.   **Luke 24:28 (KJV)** And they drew nigh unto the village, whither they went: and he made as though he would have gone further.

    v.   **Luke 24:29 (KJV)** But they constrained him, saying, Abide with us: for it is toward evening, and the day is far spent. And he went in to tarry with them.

   vi.   **Luke 24:30 (KJV)** And it came to pass, as he sat at meat with them, he took bread, and blessed *it*, and brake, and gave to them.

  vii.   **Luke 24:31 (KJV)** And their eyes were opened, and they knew him; and he vanished out of their sight.

100.   Again, now, take note very carefully, that in **Luke 24:25-31 (KJV)**, the LORD Jesus Christ is comparing and juxtaposing two things, namely: "HIS Words" and "the physical bread", and HE is emphasizing to choose "HIS Words" over "the physical bread"!

101.   How do we know that the LORD Jesus Christ emphasized to choose "HIS Words" over "the physical bread"?

102.   We know because the LORD Jesus Christ took time and great effort with the two men, and "beginning at Moses and all the prophets, he expounded unto them in all the scriptures the things concerning himself", BUT when it came to "the physical bread" the LORD Jesus Christ abandoned it and all of them left "the physical bread" UNEATEN!

103.   So, by that act alone, both the LORD Jesus Christ and the two men demonstrated with great clarity and indisputable precision that they did not care for "the physical bread" at all!

104.   Secondly, by that very act alone of abandoning the physical bread, the LORD Jesus Christ demonstrated to the Church that, when HE took physical bread during "The Lord's Last Passover Supper" and told them: "this do in remembrance of me", that HE DID NOT mean for the Church to focus on perishable useless toilet-destined physical bread, BUT RATHER on the everlasting Bread from Heaven which Bread is Himself as the Word of God, because, surely, The Word of God is the true Bread which came down from Heaven!

105.   **Evidence #4** of what the LORD Jesus Christ meant by "this do in remembrance of me"!

      i. **John 6:26 (KJV)** Jesus answered them and said, Verily, verily, I say unto you, Ye seek me, not because ye saw the miracles, but because ye did eat of the loaves, and were filled.

      ii. **John 6:32 (KJV)** Then Jesus said unto them, Verily, verily, I say unto you, Moses gave you not that bread from heaven; but my Father giveth you the true bread from heaven.

      iii. **John 6:33 (KJV)** For the bread of God is he which cometh down from heaven, and giveth life unto the world.

      iv. **John 6:35 (KJV)** And Jesus said unto them, I am the bread of life: he that cometh to me shall never hunger; and he that believeth on me shall never thirst.

      v. **Matthew 15:17 (KJV)** Do not ye yet understand, that whatsoever entereth in at the mouth goeth into the belly, and is cast out into the draught?

      vi. **Mark 7:18 (KJV)** And he saith unto them, Are ye so without understanding also? Do ye not perceive, that whatsoever thing from without entereth into the man, *it* cannot defile him;

      vii. **Mark 7:19 (KJV)** Because it entereth not into his heart, but into the belly, and goeth out into the draught, purging all meats?

106.   Again, now, take note very carefully, that in **John 6:26-35 (KJV)**, in **Matthew 15:17 (KJV)**, and in **Mark 7:18-19 (KJV)**, the LORD Jesus Christ is comparing and juxtaposing two things, namely: "HIS Words" and "the physical bread", and HE is emphasizing to choose "HIS Words" over "the physical bread"!

107.   How do we know that the LORD Jesus Christ emphasized to choose "HIS Words" over "the physical bread"?

108.   We know because in **John 6:26 (KJV)**, the LORD Jesus Christ condemned all food and all physical bread that is used as part of God-worship!

109.   We know because in **John 6:32-35 (KJV)**, the LORD Jesus Christ gives us to understand that even the better manna/bread and Angels' food under Moses does NOT qualify as bread that has any connection to Heaven and CANNOT at all be used as part of God-worship!

110.   We know because in **Matthew 15:17 (KJV** and in **Mark 7:18-19 (KJV)**, the LORD Jesus Christ revealed to us that all physical food has zero spiritual significance because all food is toilet/draught, and therefore, you CANNOT IN YOUR RIGHT MIND use toilet materials to offer them as holy sacrifices unto the LORD God Almighty!

111.   **Evidence #5** of what the LORD Jesus Christ meant by "this do in remembrance of me"!

> i. **John 21:9 (KJV)** As soon then as they were come to land, they saw a fire of coals there, and fish laid thereon, and bread.
>
> ii. **John 21:10 (KJV)** Jesus saith unto them, Bring of the fish which ye have now caught.
>
> iii. **John 21:11 (KJV)** Simon Peter went up, and drew the net to land full of great fishes, an hundred and fifty and three: and for all there were so many, yet was not the net broken.
>
> iv. **John 21:12 (KJV)** Jesus saith unto them, Come *and* dine. And none of the disciples durst ask him, Who art thou? knowing that it was the Lord.
>
> v. **John 21:13 (KJV)** Jesus then cometh, and taketh bread, and giveth them, and fish likewise.
>
> vi. **John 21:14 (KJV)** This is now the third time that Jesus shewed himself to his disciples, after that he was risen from the dead.
>
> vii. **John 21:15 (KJV)** So when they had dined, Jesus saith to Simon Peter, Simon, *son* of Jonas, lovest thou me more than these? He saith unto him, Yea, Lord; thou knowest that I love thee. He saith unto him, Feed my lambs.
>
> viii. **John 21:16 (KJV)** He saith to him again the second time, Simon, *son* of Jonas, lovest thou me? He saith unto him, Yea, Lord; thou knowest that I love thee. He saith unto him, Feed my sheep.
>
> ix. **John 21:17 (KJV)** He saith unto him the third time, Simon, *son* of Jonas, lovest thou me? Peter was grieved because he said unto him the third time, Lovest thou me? And he said unto him, Lord, thou knowest all things; thou knowest that I love thee. Jesus saith unto him, Feed my sheep.
>
> x. **John 21:18 (KJV)** Verily, verily, I say unto thee, When thou wast young, thou girdedst thyself, and walkedst whither thou wouldest: but when thou shalt be old, thou shalt stretch forth thy hands, and another shall gird thee, and carry *thee* whither thou wouldest not.

112.   Again, now, take note very carefully, that in **John 21:9-18 (KJV)**, the LORD Jesus Christ is comparing and juxtaposing two things, namely: "HIS Words" and "the physical bread", and HE is emphasizing to choose "HIS Words" over "the physical bread"!

113.   How do we know that the LORD Jesus Christ emphasized to choose "HIS Words" over "the physical bread"?

114. We know because the LORD Jesus Christ is asking Peter in **John 21:15 (KJV)** whether he loves all these food, bread, and fish more than Jesus the Word?

　　　　i. **John 1:1 (KJV)** In the beginning was the Word, and the Word was with God, and the Word was God.

　　　　ii. **Revelation 19:13 (KJV)** And he *was* clothed with a vesture dipped in blood: and his name is called The Word of God.

115. We know because, three times in **John 21:15-17 (KJV)**, the LORD Jesus Christ told Peter to focus on "Feeding my sheep" with the true Bread that came down from Heaven, which Bread is the Word of God!

116. So, now, I have proved to you, in five solid evidences, using ONLY the Holy Scriptures, that when the LORD Jesus Christ, during "The Lord's Last Passover Supper", told them these words: "this do in remembrance of me", HE NEVER meant for them and the Church to start meeting together to eat filthy perishable useless toilet-destined physical bread!

117. It is because of all the above five reasons/evidences, and specifically because the churches, the Pastors, the Bishops, and the Church Leaders, have completely misunderstood "The Lord's Last Passover Supper", first by getting the name even wrong and falsely calling it "Holy Communion", a name which is NOT found in the entire Holy Bible, showing clearly that "Holy Communion" is completely a human invention and human tradition, and, second, by these same ignorant Church Leaders focusing on filthy perishable useless toilet-destined physical bread to connect Heaven instead of focusing on the true Bread which is the Word of God!

118. Because of that grave foolishness of Pastors and Bishops, the LORD God commanded that "church gathering is NOT to eat the Lord's supper"!

　　　　i. **1 Corinthians 11:20 (KJV)** When ye come together therefore into one place, *this* is not to eat the Lord's supper. why the LORD Jesus Christ would

119. And as if that command in **1 Corinthians 11:20 (KJV)** was not enough, again, showing the utter depravity, ignorance, foolishness, and idiocy of Church leaders, the LORD God Almighty again came back in **Hebrews 13:9 (KJV)** to issue the same warning that YOU CANNOT IN YOUR RIGHT MIND use toilet materials (food items) to offer them as holy sacrifices unto the LORD God Almighty!

　　　　i. **Hebrews 13:9 (KJV)** Be not carried about with divers and strange doctrines. For *it is* a good thing that the heart be established with grace; not with meats, which have not profited them that have been occupied therein.

120.   See it very clearly in **Hebrews 13:9 (KJV)** the LORD God saying plainly that:

        i. "The good thing is that the heart/mind/spirit be established with Grace/Word of God; NOT WITH MEATS"!

121.   And as if that command was not enough again, showing the utter depravity, ignorance, foolishness, and idiocy of Church leaders, the LORD God Almighty again came back in **1 Corinthians 8:8 (KJV)** to issue the same warning that YOU CANNOT IN YOUR RIGHT MIND use toilet materials (food items) to offer them as holy sacrifices unto the LORD God Almighty!

        i. **1 Corinthians 8:8 (KJV)** But meat commendeth us not to God: for neither, if we eat, are we the better; neither, if we eat not, are we the worse.

122.   See it very clearly in **1 Corinthians 8:8 (KJV)** the LORD God saying plainly that:

        i. "meat commendeth us not to God", meaning that FOOD DOES NOT CONNECT ANYONE TO HEAVEN!

123.   So, as you can see, I have shown you altogether eight (8) different times, those earlier five evidences plus these last three making eight warnings, that the LORD God Almighty is issuing the same warning to you bastard Pastor and stupid dumb dog Bishop, that YOU CANNOT IN YOUR RIGHT MIND use toilet materials (food items) to offer them as holy sacrifices unto the LORD God Almighty!

124.   Will you listen, or will you choose to go to Hell instead?

125.   Again, Brother, the LORD God is saying: DO NOT EAT PHYSICAL FOOD AT THE ALTAR, but rather, go to the LORD Jesus Christ "bearing his reproach"!

        i. **Hebrews 13:10 (KJV)** We have an altar, whereof they have no right to eat which serve the tabernacle.

        ii. **Hebrews 13:11 (KJV)** For the bodies of those beasts, whose blood is brought into the sanctuary by the high priest for sin, are burned without the camp.

        iii. **Hebrews 13:12 (KJV)** Wherefore Jesus also, that he might sanctify the people with his own blood, suffered without the gate.

        iv. **Hebrews 13:13 (KJV)** Let us go forth therefore unto him without the camp, bearing his reproach.

126.   What is the meaning of "bearing his reproach"?

127.   It simply means "the Word of God", because the Word of God is our reproach that we bear in order to turn away from sin and iniquity unto Truth and Righteousness unto Salvation!

    i.   **Psalm 69:7 (KJV)** Because for thy sake I have borne reproach; shame hath covered my face.

    ii.   **Psalm 109:25 (KJV)** I became also a reproach unto them: *when* they looked upon me they shaked their heads.

    iii.   **Jeremiah 6:10 (KJV)** To whom shall I speak, and give warning, that they may hear? behold, their ear *is* uncircumcised, and they cannot hearken: behold, the word of the LORD is unto them a reproach; they have no delight in it.

    iv.   **Jeremiah 20:8 (KJV)** For since I spake, I cried out, I cried violence and spoil; because the word of the LORD was made a reproach unto me, and a derision, daily.

    v.   **Galatians 5:11 (KJV)** And I, brethren, if I yet preach circumcision, why do I yet suffer persecution? then is the offence of the cross ceased.

    vi.   **Hebrews 11:26 (KJV)** Esteeming the reproach of Christ greater riches than the treasures in Egypt: for he had respect unto the recompence of the reward.

128.   Therefore, in essence, the LORD God Almighty is showing you in **Hebrews 13:10-13 (KJV)** that when you go to the LORD Jesus Christ, when you go to the LORD God Almighty, you MUST be carrying/bearing the Gospel of Christ, NOT physical food, and here is another evidence that I am showing you as the Holy Spirit has revealed it to me on this very subject of Holy Communion!

    i.   **Hosea 14:1 (KJV)** O Israel, return unto the LORD thy God; for thou hast fallen by thine iniquity.

    ii.   **Hosea 14:2 (KJV)** Take with you words, and turn to the LORD: say unto him, Take away all iniquity, and receive *us* graciously: so will we render the calves of our lips.

    iii.   **Hosea 14:3 (KJV)** Asshur shall not save us; we will not ride upon horses: neither will we say any more to the work of our hands, *Ye are* our gods: for in thee the fatherless findeth mercy.

129.   Brother, did you see it plainly and very clearly in **Hosea 14:1-3 (KJV)** the following revelations?

    i.   ONE – When you go to the LORD Jesus Christ, when you go to the LORD God Almighty, do you see it plainly in **Hosea 14:2 (KJV)** that you MUST be carrying/bearing words, the Gospel of Christ, NOT physical food?

ii. **TWO** – The food, the calves, the wafers, the wine, the bread that you offer at your filthy Holy Communion, do you see it plainly in **Hosea 14:2 (KJV)** that they HAVE TO BE "rendered as the calves of our lips"?

iii. **THREE** – Do you also know surely, and in very deed, that "the calves of our lips" ARE PLAIN WORDS AND NOT FILTHY FOOD?

130. This will be evidence #10 that I am showing you that YOU CANNOT IN YOUR RIGHT MIND use toilet materials (food items) to offer them as holy sacrifices unto the LORD God Almighty!

i. **Hebrews 13:14 (KJV)** For here have we no continuing city, but we seek one to come.

ii. **Hebrews 13:15 (KJV)** By him therefore let us offer the sacrifice of praise to God continually, that is, the fruit of *our* lips giving thanks to his name.

131. Again, can any words be plainer than these words from God Almighty?

132. Do you see it plainly in **Hebrews 13:14-15 (KJV)** that the ONLY sacrifice that the LORD God will accept from your filthy hands is "the sacrifice of praise to God continually, that is, the fruit of *our* lips"?

133. So, then, why has Satan filled your heart to despise the Word of God and to be offering unto God Almighty all these years filthy perishable useless toilet-destined physical bread and wine as Holy Communion?

134. Let me show you evidence #11!

i. **Hebrews 13:16 (KJV)** But to do good and to communicate forget not: for with such sacrifices God is well pleased.

135. Brother, did you see the key word "communicate" in **Hebrews 13:16 (KJV)**?

136. What do you think that word means?

137. It means "communion" and "communion" means "to commune/to speak with/to interact/to communicate"!

138. Then, now, read again the same **Hebrews 13:16 (KJV)** and see what God Almighty calls "communication, communion/to commune/to speak with/to interact/to communicate"!

139. The LORD God says that "communication/communion/to commune/to speak with/to interact/to communicate" are: "SUCH SACRIFICES THAT GOD IS WELL PLEASED WITH"!

140. So, then, without any shadow of doubt:

          i. THE CORRECT SACRIFICE OF HOLY COMMUNION IS TO USE WORDS, NOT FOOD!

141.   So, then, COMMUNICATION IS SACRIFICE!

142.   Now, some fool will ask: What kind of communication is God talking about here?

143.   Here is your answer!

          i. **Philippians 1:27 (KJV)** Only let your conversation be as it becometh the gospel of Christ: that whether I come and see you, or else be absent, I may hear of your affairs, that ye stand fast in one spirit, with one mind striving together for the faith of the gospel;

144.   So, then, without any shadow of doubt, according to **Philippians 1:27 (KJV)**:

          i. THE SPECIFIC AND EXACT SACRIFICE OF COMMUNICATION THAT YOU NEED TO BE OFFERING UNTO GOD ALMIGHTY AT THE ALTAR IS THE GOSPEL OF CHRIST!

145.   Brother, Sster, what more can I say to you regarding this vexing question of fraudulent Holy Communion? Behold, I have told you all that the Holy Spirit has taught me on this matter!

146.   Receive it if you will, and forebear if you will not, but this remember, that someday, sometime, the LORD God Almighty will surely bring you into judgment for this my teaching that I give unto you this day!

147.   Fare well!

The LORD Jesus Christ be with your spirit. The LORD Jesus Christ give you understanding.

Rev. Prof. PETER PRYCE,
DSEF, BA, MA, B.Soc.Sc Pol Sci, IBA, PhD
A Scribe of the Law of the God of Heaven
Prophet of the Word of God
Professor of French, Silver Spring, MD, USA
Scholar of the Institute of Theologians, USA
WWW.THEBIBLEUNIVERSITY.ORG
Accreditation Number: 07-QCTO/SDP120723172836
SAQA QUAL ID: Identification # 101997
WWW.BOOKSTORESITE.ORG

WWW.THEBIBLEUNIVERSITYCHURCH.ORG

Wednesday 20th March 2024 @ 5:17 AM – 12:37 PM

While hearing and meditating on the Word of God in the office.

CHAPTER 17

HOLY COMMUNION WINE IS MEANT FOR THEM THAT PERISH IN HELL!

ESE NE TEKREMA

"The teeth and the tongue"

Asante philosophical symbol of Friendship, Interdependence, Co-Existence, Tolerance

Question 2537

1. There was a Church in the wilderness!
    i. **Acts 7:38 (KJV)** This is he, that was in the church in the wilderness with the angel which spake to him in the mount Sina, and *with* our fathers: who received the lively oracles to give unto us:
2. Though there was a Church in the wilderness, yet, there was NO Holy Communion!
    i. **Deuteronomy 29:5 (KJV)** And I have led you forty years in the wilderness: your clothes are not waxen old upon you, and thy shoe is not waxen old upon thy foot.
    ii. **Deuteronomy 29:6 (KJV)** Ye have not eaten bread, neither have ye drunk wine or strong drink: that ye might know that I *am* the LORD your God.
3. Someone will say that, well, they did not drink Holy Communion wine in the church in the wilderness because they were in the wilderness and because they were not yet in the Promised Land!
4. Alright, then, let us see what was the Law of Wine even in the Promised Land throughout your generations!
    i. **Leviticus 10:8 (KJV)** And the LORD spake unto Aaron, saying,

ii. **Leviticus 10:9 (KJV)** Do not drink wine nor strong drink, thou, nor thy sons with thee, when ye go into the tabernacle of the congregation, lest ye die: *it shall be* a statute for ever throughout your generations:

5. Furthermore, if your reasoning is that they did not drink Holy Communion wine in the church in the wilderness because they were in the wilderness and because they were not yet in the Promised Land, and so that is your excuse for your present New Testament Holy Communion wine, then, aside from **Leviticus 10:8-9 (KJV)**, let us see another Truth of God when they dwelt in the Promised Land many generations!

     i. **Proverbs 31:1 (KJV)** The words of king Lemuel, the prophecy that his mother taught him.

     ii. **Proverbs 31:2 (KJV)** What, my son? and what, the son of my womb? and what, the son of my vows?

     iii. **Proverbs 31:3 (KJV)** Give not thy strength unto women, nor thy ways to that which destroyeth kings.

     iv. **Proverbs 31:4 (KJV)** *It is* not for kings, O Lemuel, *it is* not for kings to drink wine; nor for princes strong drink:

     v. **Proverbs 31:5 (KJV)** Lest they drink, and forget the law, and pervert the judgment of any of the afflicted.

     vi. **Proverbs 31:6 (KJV)** Give strong drink unto him that is ready to perish, and wine unto those that be of heavy hearts.

     vii. **Proverbs 31:7 (KJV)** Let him drink, and forget his poverty, and remember his misery no more.

6. So, now, have you seen the Truth in **Leviticus 10:8-9 (KJV)** and in **Proverbs 31:1-7 (KJV)**?

7. Have you seen the Truth that there are only two things in this world that destroy men and kings, which things are women and wine?

8. When you read these words: "*It is* not for kings, O Lemuel, *it is* not for kings to drink wine", do you just read them and then mock God Almighty in your Pulpits and at your so-called Holy Communion service?

9. When you read those words, do you close your ears and eyes and pretend that you did not hear or see them?

10. When you read those words, do you tell yourself that God is NOT speaking to you but to someone else?

11. When you read those words, do you begin to think that the words appeared there by mistake in the Holy Scriptures?

12. When you read those words, do you feel any conviction in your conscience, heart, and mind that you are doing something very evil, very dirty, and do you understand

at all that by giving wine to people in the Pulpit, under the false label of Holy Communion,, that you are actually helping to kill people just as **Proverbs 31:1-7 (KJV)** says?

13. Now, when I warn you of the evil of your Holy Communion rituals, you tell me that:

    i.   Oh, but it was the LORD Jesus Christ Himself who commanded us to do Holy Communion and to serve the wine!

14. Well, is your LORD Jesus Christ a sinner?

    i.   **Galatians 2:17 (KJV)** But if, while we seek to be justified by Christ, we ourselves also are found sinners, *is* therefore Christ the minister of sin? God forbid.

15. Is your LORD Jesus Christ a Minister of sin?

16. Did your LORD Jesus Christ come to violate, contradict, and destroy the Scriptures?

    i.   **Matthew 5:17 (KJV)** Think not that I am come to destroy the law, or the prophets: I am not come to destroy, but to fulfil.

    ii. **Luke 9:56 (KJV)** For the Son of man is not come to destroy men's lives, but to save *them.* And they went to another village.

    iii. **John 10:10 (KJV)** The thief cometh not, but for to steal, and to kill, and to destroy: I am come that they might have life, and that they might have *it* more abundantly.

17. If the Word of God clearly said that: "*It is* not for kings, O Lemuel, *it is* not for kings to drink wine", and, again, if the Word of God said that "the scripture cannot be broken", then, why would you be that very stupid to claim that it was the LORD Jesus Christ who gave you wine to drink and also commanded you to drink wine?

    i.   **John 10:35 (KJV)** If he called them gods, unto whom the word of God came, and the scripture cannot be broken;

18. So, you mean that your Jesus Christ commanded you to drink Holy Communion wine so that He can destroy you, as **Proverbs 31:3 (KJV)** says?

    i.   **Proverbs 31:3 (KJV)** Give not thy strength unto women, nor thy ways to that which destroyeth kings.

19. So, you mean that your Jesus Christ commanded you to drink Holy Communion wine so that He can demonstrate it to you that you are NOT Kings and Princes?

    i.   **Proverbs 31:4 (KJV)** *It is* not for kings, O Lemuel, *it is* not for kings to drink wine; nor for princes strong drink:

    ii. **Exodus 19:6 (KJV)** And ye shall be unto me a kingdom of priests, and an holy nation. These *are* the words which thou shalt speak unto the children of Israel.

    iii. **1 Peter 2:9 (KJV)** But ye *are* a chosen generation, a royal priesthood, an holy nation, a peculiar people; that ye should shew forth the praises of him who hath called you out of darkness into his marvellous light:

    iv. **Revelation 1:6 (KJV)** And hath made us kings and priests unto God and his Father; to him *be* glory and dominion for ever and ever. Amen.

20. So, you mean that your Jesus Christ commanded you to drink Holy Communion wine so that He can lead you to forget the Law of God, as **Proverbs 31:5 (KJV)** says?

    i. **Proverbs 31:5 (KJV)** Lest they drink, and forget the law, and pervert the judgment of any of the afflicted.

21. So, you mean that your Jesus Christ commanded you to drink Holy Communion wine so that He can lead you to pervert the judgment of God against the afflicted, as **Proverbs 31:5 (KJV)** says?

22. So, you mean that your Jesus Christ commanded you to drink Holy Communion wine so that He can destroy and kill you, just as **Proverbs 31:6 (KJV)** says?

    i. **Proverbs 31:6 (KJV)** Give strong drink unto him that is ready to perish, and wine unto those that be of heavy hearts.

    ii. **Matthew 5:17 (KJV)** Think not that I am come to destroy the law, or the prophets: I am not come to destroy, but to fulfil.

    iii. **Luke 9:56 (KJV)** For the Son of man is not come to destroy men's lives, but to save *them.* And they went to another village.

23. Aside the wine and women that you can use to destroy men in this world, there is one other thing that you can use to deceive men and women, and that is wine!

24. Here is another evidence why the LORD Jesus Christ DID NOT give any unclean wine to the Apostles! Except you want to read **Proverbs 20:1 (KJV)** and teach that Jesus Christ was mocking HIS Apostles and wanted to deceive them hence HE gave them wine to drink?

    i. **Proverbs 20:1 (KJV)** Wine *is* a mocker, strong drink *is* raging: and whosoever is deceived thereby is not wise.

    ii. **Proverbs 23:31 (KJV)** Look not thou upon the wine when it is red, when it giveth his colour in the cup, *when* it moveth itself aright.

    iii. **Proverbs 23:32 (KJV)** At the last it biteth like a serpent, and stingeth like an adder.

25. There are three key words in **Proverbs 20:1 (KJV)**: namely, a mocker, a deceiver, and a fool! Which of those three key words is you since you use wine in church?

26. In fact, all the three key words are you, because what the LORD God Almighty is showing you over there in **Proverbs 20:1 (KJV)** is that, anyone who uses wine is a mocker, is a deceiver, and is a fool!

27. Brother, since the many evidences above show that your Jesus Christ is doing all these evil deeds, then surely, your Holy Communion Jesus Christ is the Devil and Satan, and NOT the real Christ!

     i. **John 10:10 (KJV)** The thief cometh not, but for to steal, and to kill, and to destroy: I am come that they might have life, and that they might have *it* more abundantly.

28. Now, concerning the claim and the accusation that it was the LORD Jesus Christ who gave you Holy Communion wine to drink and also commanded you to drink wine, let us put your claim, argument, and accusation to the test, by the Scriptures!

     i. **1 Thessalonians 5:21 (KJV)** Prove all things; hold fast that which is good.

     ii. **1 John 4:1 (KJV)** Beloved, believe not every spirit, but try the spirits whether they are of God: because many false prophets are gone out into the world.

29. Here is the evidence to examine in order to correctly conclude the test!

     i. **Luke 22:7 (KJV)** Then came the day of unleavened bread, when the passover must be killed.

     ii. **Luke 22:8 (KJV)** And he sent Peter and John, saying, Go and prepare us the passover, that we may eat.

     iii. **Luke 22:14 (KJV)** And when the hour was come, he sat down, and the twelve apostles with him.

     iv. **Luke 22:15 (KJV)** And he said unto them, With desire I have desired to eat this passover with you before I suffer:

     v. **Luke 22:16 (KJV)** For I say unto you, I will not any more eat thereof, until it be fulfilled in the kingdom of God.

     vi. **Luke 22:17 (KJV)** And he took the cup, and gave thanks, and said, Take this, and divide *it* among yourselves:

     vii. **Luke 22:18 (KJV)** For I say unto you, I will not drink of the fruit of the vine, until the kingdom of God shall come.

     viii. **Luke 22:19 (KJV)** And he took bread, and gave thanks, and brake *it*, and gave unto them, saying, This is my body which is given for you: this do in remembrance of me.

     ix. **Luke 22:20 (KJV)** Likewise also the cup after supper, saying, This cup *is* the new testament in my blood, which is shed for you.

30. In **Luke 22:17 (KJV)**, the Word of God says that "And he took the cup":

     i. There is no mention of any wine!

31. In **Luke 22:18 (KJV)**, the Word of God says that "I will not drink of the fruit of the vine", and this declaration is consistent with:

      i. **Leviticus 10:8 (KJV)** And the LORD spake unto Aaron, saying,

      ii. **Leviticus 10:9 (KJV)** Do not drink wine nor strong drink, thou, nor thy sons with thee, when ye go into the tabernacle of the congregation, lest ye die: *it shall be* a statute for ever throughout your generations:

      iii. **Leviticus 10:10 (KJV)** And that ye may put difference between holy and unholy, and between unclean and clean;

      iv. **Leviticus 10:11 (KJV)** And that ye may teach the children of Israel all the statutes which the LORD hath spoken unto them by the hand of Moses.

32. The same declaration, to wit: "I will not drink of the fruit of the vine", is also consistent with **Proverbs 31:1-7 (KJV)**!

33. The same declaration, to wit: "I will not drink of the fruit of the vine", is also consistent with **Matthew 5:17 (KJV)**!

      i. **Matthew 5:17 (KJV)** Think not that I am come to destroy the law, or the prophets: I am not come to destroy, but to fulfil.

34. The same declaration, to wit: "I will not drink of the fruit of the vine", is also consistent with **Jeremiah 35:5-19 (KJV)**, where we see that the Salvation of God is with those who drink NO WINE!

      i. **Jeremiah 35:5 (KJV)** And I set before the sons of the house of the Rechabites pots full of wine, and cups, and I said unto them, Drink ye wine.

      ii. **Jeremiah 35:6 (KJV)** But they said, We will drink no wine: for Jonadab the son of Rechab our father commanded us, saying, Ye shall drink no wine, *neither* ye, nor your sons for ever:

      iii. **Jeremiah 35:7 (KJV)** Neither shall ye build house, nor sow seed, nor plant vineyard, nor have *any*: but all your days ye shall dwell in tents; that ye may live many days in the land where ye *be* strangers.

      iv. **Jeremiah 35:8 (KJV)** Thus have we obeyed the voice of Jonadab the son of Rechab our father in all that he hath charged us, to drink no wine all our days, we, our wives, our sons, nor our daughters;

      v. **Jeremiah 35:9 (KJV)** Nor to build houses for us to dwell in: neither have we vineyard, nor field, nor seed:

      vi. **Jeremiah 35:10 (KJV)** But we have dwelt in tents, and have obeyed, and done according to all that Jonadab our father commanded us.

      vii. **Jeremiah 35:11 (KJV)** But it came to pass, when Nebuchadrezzar king of Babylon came up into the land, that we said, Come, and let us go to Jerusalem for fear of the army of the Chaldeans, and for fear of the army of the Syrians: so we dwell at Jerusalem.

viii. **Jeremiah 35:12 (KJV)** Then came the word of the LORD unto Jeremiah, saying,

ix. **Jeremiah 35:13 (KJV)** Thus saith the LORD of hosts, the God of Israel; Go and tell the men of Judah and the inhabitants of Jerusalem, Will ye not receive instruction to hearken to my words? saith the LORD.

x. **Jeremiah 35:14 (KJV)** The words of Jonadab the son of Rechab, that he commanded his sons not to drink wine, are performed; for unto this day they drink none, but obey their father's commandment: notwithstanding I have spoken unto you, rising early and speaking; but ye hearkened not unto me.

xi. **Jeremiah 35:15 (KJV)** I have sent also unto you all my servants the prophets, rising up early and sending *them*, saying, Return ye now every man from his evil way, and amend your doings, and go not after other gods to serve them, and ye shall dwell in the land which I have given to you and to your fathers: but ye have not inclined your ear, nor hearkened unto me.

xii. **Jeremiah 35:16 (KJV)** Because the sons of Jonadab the son of Rechab have performed the commandment of their father, which he commanded them; but this people hath not hearkened unto me:

xiii. **Jeremiah 35:17 (KJV)** Therefore thus saith the LORD God of hosts, the God of Israel; Behold, I will bring upon Judah and upon all the inhabitants of Jerusalem all the evil that I have pronounced against them: because I have spoken unto them, but they have not heard; and I have called unto them, but they have not answered.

xiv. **Jeremiah 35:18 (KJV)** And Jeremiah said unto the house of the Rechabites, Thus saith the LORD of hosts, the God of Israel; Because ye have obeyed the commandment of Jonadab your father, and kept all his precepts, and done according unto all that he hath commanded you:

xv. **Jeremiah 35:19 (KJV)** Therefore thus saith the LORD of hosts, the God of Israel; Jonadab the son of Rechab shall not want a man to stand before me for ever.

35. So, now we have examined the evidence of the Law of Holy Communion in **Luke 22:7-20 (KJV)**, and we have found out that there is nothing, zero word in it, that allows you to drink wine as Holy Communion in the Churches!

36. So, what do you say now, Brother?

37. Do you still claim that it was the LORD Jesus Christ who gave you Holy Communion wine to drink and also commanded you to drink wine, a commandment that is clearly contradicting the Word of God and is in violation of the entire Law of wine in the Word of God?

38. Therefore, again, Holy Communion wine is for them that perish, and as you the ignorant foolish Pastor and Bishop, you are helping your equally dumb congregation to perish in Hell by giving them wine to drink, prepare for yourself also, your own place in Hell!

39. Moreover, I tell you that wine and anything that comes from the vine tree is NOT for true Men of God and the Word of God confirms that!

    i. **Judges 13:1 (KJV)** And the children of Israel did evil again in the sight of the LORD; and the LORD delivered them into the hand of the Philistines forty years.

    ii. **Judges 13:2 (KJV)** And there was a certain man of Zorah, of the family of the Danites, whose name *was* Manoah; and his wife *was* barren, and bare not.

    iii. **Judges 13:3 (KJV)** And the angel of the LORD appeared unto the woman, and said unto her, Behold now, thou *art* barren, and bearest not: but thou shalt conceive, and bear a son.

    iv. **Judges 13:4 (KJV)** Now therefore beware, I pray thee, and drink not wine nor strong drink, and eat not any unclean *thing*:

    v. **Judges 13:8 (KJV)** Then Manoah intreated the LORD, and said, O my Lord, let the man of God which thou didst send come again unto us, and teach us what we shall do unto the child that shall be born.

    vi. **Judges 13:9 (KJV)** And God hearkened to the voice of Manoah; and the angel of God came again unto the woman as she sat in the field: but Manoah her husband *was* not with her.

    vii. **Judges 13:10 (KJV)** And the woman made haste, and ran, and shewed her husband, and said unto him, Behold, the man hath appeared unto me, that came unto me the *other* day.

    viii. **Judges 13:11 (KJV)** And Manoah arose, and went after his wife, and came to the man, and said unto him, *Art* thou the man that spakest unto the woman? And he said, I *am*.

    ix. **Judges 13:12 (KJV)** And Manoah said, Now let thy words come to pass. How shall we order the child, and *how* shall we do unto him?

    x. **Judges 13:13 (KJV)** And the angel of the LORD said unto Manoah, Of all that I said unto the woman let her beware.

       xi. **Judges 13:14 (KJV)** She may not eat of any *thing* that cometh of the vine, neither let her drink wine or strong drink, nor eat any unclean *thing*: all that I commanded her let her observe.

40. Bother, did you hear these words very loudly and clearly from the mouth of God, or, you did not hear them?

       i. "She may not eat of any *thing* that cometh of the vine, neither let her drink wine or strong drink, nor eat any unclean thing" **Judges 13:14 (KJV)**

       ii. Please, did you see how the LORD God commanded to NOT eat or drink ANYTHING that comes from the vine tree if you are Man of God or a Child of God?

       iii. Please, did you see how the LORD God said that ANYTHING that comes from the vine tree is an unclean thing?

41. So, now, tell me: Did the LORD Jesus Christ know of **Judges 13:1-14 (KJV)** before HE commanded you to drink Holy Communion wine per your claim?

42. If the LORD Jesus Christ knew of **Judges 13:1-14 (KJV)** and HE still went ahead and commanded you to drink wine in the church, then, is your Jesus Christ a Minister of sin? Or, is your Jesus Christ the High Priest of unclean things?

43. If your answer is, no, then, why are you drinking the unclean thing of the vine and also claiming that it was Jesus Christ who told you to do so when HE never told you to do so?

44. The LORD Jesus Christ gave you a Cup! HE never gave you wine to drink!

       i. **Luke 22:17 (KJV)** And he took the cup, and gave thanks, and said, Take this, and divide *it* among yourselves:

       ii. **Luke 22:18 (KJV)** For I say unto you, I will not drink of the fruit of the vine, until the kingdom of God shall come.

45. So, then what was in the Cup?

46. It was the Covenant just as **Luke 22:20 (KJV)** reveals, it was the New Testament, it was Words, it was the Word of God that was in the Cup, NOT WINE!

47. That was what was in the Cup, NOT WINE, because wine destroys men and causes men to forget the Law of God as God revealed in **Proverbs 31:3-6 (KJV)**, so Jesus Christ could NEVER have thought to give you something that HE already knew would destroy you and cause you to forget HIM the Word of God, thou fool!

       i. **Luke 22:20 (KJV)** Likewise also the cup after supper, saying, This cup *is* the new testament in my blood, which is shed for you.

       ii. **John 10:10 (KJV)** The thief cometh not, but for to steal, and to kill, and to destroy: I am come that they might have life, and that they might have *it* more abundantly.

  iii. **Proverbs 31:3 (KJV)** Give not thy strength unto women, nor thy ways to that which destroyeth kings.

  iv. **Proverbs 31:4 (KJV)** *It is* not for kings, O Lemuel, *it is* not for kings to drink wine; nor for princes strong drink:

  v. **Proverbs 31:5 (KJV)** Lest they drink, and forget the law, and pervert the judgment of any of the afflicted.

  vi. **Proverbs 31:6 (KJV)** Give strong drink unto him that is ready to perish, and wine unto those that be of heavy hearts.

48. Now, as for the dog-Pastors and swine-Bishops who continue to wallow in the mire of the vomit of their filthy thoughts, they will say to me that in the Cup that the LORD Jesus Christ gave to the Apostles was wine that represented HIS Blood, and they cite the following verses to support their false claim even when, truly, there is not a single verse in the entire Holy Bible where the LORD Jesus Christ drank wine and also gave wine to Men of God to drink!

  i. **John 6:53 (KJV)** Then Jesus said unto them, Verily, verily, I say unto you, Except ye eat the flesh of the Son of man, and drink his blood, ye have no life in you.

  ii. **John 6:54 (KJV)** Whoso eateth my flesh, and drinketh my blood, hath eternal life; and I will raise him up at the last day.

  iii. **John 6:55 (KJV)** For my flesh is meat indeed, and my blood is drink indeed.

  iv. **John 6:56 (KJV)** He that eateth my flesh, and drinketh my blood, dwelleth in me, and I in him.

  v. **John 6:57 (KJV)** As the living Father hath sent me, and I live by the Father: so he that eateth me, even he shall live by me.

  vi. **John 6:58 (KJV)** This is that bread which came down from heaven: not as your fathers did eat manna, and are dead: he that eateth of this bread shall live for ever.

49. Now, to all the dog-Pastors and swine-Bishops who serve wine in the churches as Holy Communion and use **John 6:53-58 (KJV)** as your justification, has your LORD Jesus Christ then become altogether as sinful and corrupt as you are? How would Jesus Christ know of the following verses and still give you wine and Blood to drink?

  i. **1 Samuel 1:9 (KJV)** So Hannah rose up after they had eaten in Shiloh, and after they had drunk. Now Eli the priest sat upon a seat by a post of the temple of the LORD.

  ii. **1 Samuel 1:10 (KJV)** And she *was* in bitterness of soul, and prayed unto the LORD, and wept sore.

     iii. **1 Samuel 1:11 (KJV)** And she vowed a vow, and said, O LORD of hosts, if thou wilt indeed look on the affliction of thine handmaid, and remember me, and not forget thine handmaid, but wilt give unto thine handmaid a man child, then I will give him unto the LORD all the days of his life, and there shall no rasor come upon his head.

     iv. **1 Samuel 1:12 (KJV)** And it came to pass, as she continued praying before the LORD, that Eli marked her mouth.

     v. **1 Samuel 1:13 (KJV)** Now Hannah, she spake in her heart; only her lips moved, but her voice was not heard: therefore Eli thought she had been drunken.

     vi. **1 Samuel 1:14 (KJV)** And Eli said unto her, How long wilt thou be drunken? put away thy wine from thee.

     vii. **1 Samuel 1:15 (KJV)** And Hannah answered and said, No, my lord, I *am* a woman of a sorrowful spirit: I have drunk neither wine nor strong drink, but have poured out my soul before the LORD.

     viii. **1 Samuel 1:16 (KJV)** Count not thine handmaid for a daughter of Belial: for out of the abundance of my complaint and grief have I spoken hitherto.

50. If wine was a good thing to be given to congregations in the churches, then why would Eli the High Priest be commanding a congregant to: "put away thy wine from thee"?

51. If wine was a good thing to be given to congregations in the churches, then why would Hannah be denying ever drinking wine?

52. If wine was a good thing to be given to congregations in the churches, then why would wine-drinking be counted as an activity of the children of Belial/Satan?

53. Finally, to all those who say that the Cup that the LORD Jesus Christ gave to the Apostles was HIS Blood, then, my question to them is this: What about these verses here that specifically forbid the eating and drinking of blood?

     i. **Genesis 9:4 (KJV)** But flesh with the life thereof, *which is* the blood thereof, shall ye not eat.

     ii. **Leviticus 19:26 (KJV)** Ye shall not eat *any thing* with the blood: neither shall ye use enchantment, nor observe times.

     iii. **Deuteronomy 12:16 (KJV)** Only ye shall not eat the blood; ye shall pour it upon the earth as water.

     iv. **Deuteronomy 12:23 (KJV)** Only be sure that thou eat not the blood: for the blood *is* the life; and thou mayest not eat the life with the flesh.

    v. **Deuteronomy 15:23 (KJV)** Only thou shalt not eat the blood thereof; thou shalt pour it upon the ground as water.

    vi. **1 Samuel 14:34 (KJV)** And Saul said, Disperse yourselves among the people, and say unto them, Bring me hither every man his ox, and every man his sheep, and slay *them* here, and eat; and sin not against the LORD in eating with the blood. And all the people brought every man his ox with him that night, and slew *them* there.

54. Did the LORD Jesus Christ know about all the above verses, and HE still gave you Blood and wine to drink?

55. Did your Jesus Christ know about **Ezekiel 44:21 (KJV)** when HE gave the Cup to the Apostles?

    i. **Ezekiel 44:21 (KJV)** Neither shall any priest drink wine, when they enter into the inner court.

    ii. **Psalm 110:4 (KJV)** The LORD hath sworn, and will not repent, Thou *art* a priest for ever after the order of Melchizedek.

    iii. **Hebrews 5:6 (KJV)** As he saith also in another *place*, Thou *art* a priest for ever after the order of Melchisedec.

    iv. **Hebrews 5:10 (KJV)** Called of God an high priest after the order of Melchisedec.

    v. **Hebrews 6:20 (KJV)** Whither the forerunner is for us entered, *even* Jesus, made an high priest for ever after the order of Melchisedec.

    vi. **Hebrews 7:17 (KJV)** For he testifieth, Thou *art* a priest for ever after the order of Melchisedec.

    vii. **Hebrews 7:21 (KJV)** (For those priests were made without an oath; but this with an oath by him that said unto him, The Lord sware and will not repent, Thou *art* a priest for ever after the order of Melchisedec:)

56. Is your Jesus Christ a Priest forever after the order of Melchizedek?

57. Is the Priesthood of your Jesus Christ a perpetual Priesthood both on Earth and in Heaven?

58. Then how can you be that very stupid to say that your LORD Jesus Christ knew about **Ezekiel 44:21 (KJV)** and yet still HE violated the Word of God and give you wine to drink?

59. Is your LORD Jesus Christ therefore become the Apostle and High Priest of sin and a violator of the Word of God?

60. O, Holy Communion Pastors and Bishops, is this Word of God in the Bok of Hosea written in your Holy Bible?

     i. **Hosea 4:11 (KJV)** Whoredom and wine and new wine take away the heart.

     ii. **Hosea 7:5 (KJV)** In the day of our king the princes have made *him* sick with bottles of wine; he stretched out his hand with scorners.

61. According to **Hosea 4:11 (KJV)**, and because of the fact that you serve and drink wine, sweet wine, and new wine in your churches, would it be all right for me to call you a whore?

62. Would it be all right for me to prophesy to you that your heart is already taken away into Hell??

63. Would it be all right for me to prophesy to you that you Holy Communion Pastors and Bishops are all sick in the head and in the flesh because of the bottles of wine that you have already consumed in your filthy Holy Communion at the altar every Sunday?

64. Would it be all right for me to prophesy to you that you Holy Communion Pastors and Bishops are all scorners who daily mock and scorn the LORD God Almighty with your filthy Holy Communion at the altar every Sunday?

65. Therefore, will the sin of your Holy Communion wine find you out and send you all to Hell!

The LORD Jesus Christ be with your spirit. The LORD Jesus Christ give you understanding.

Rev. Prof. PETER PRYCE,
DSEF, BA, MA, B.Soc.Sc Pol Sci, IBA, PhD
A Scribe of the Law of the God of Heaven
Prophet of the Word of God
Professor of French, Silver Spring, MD, USA
Scholar of the Institute of Theologians, USA
WWW.THEBIBLEUNIVERSITY.ORG
Accreditation Number: 07-QCTO/SDP120723172836
SAQA QUAL ID: Identification # 101997
WWW.BOOKSTORESITE.ORG
WWW.THEBIBLEUNIVERSITYCHURCH.ORG

Friday 5th April 2024 @ 8:45 AM – 10:31 AM

While hearing and meditating on the Word of God at home.

CHAPTER 18

THIS CUP IS THE NEW TESTAMENT!

FAWOHODIE
"Independence"
Asante philosophical symbol of Independence, Freedom, Emancipation, Self-Governance

Question 2542

1.   On Wednesday 10th April 2024, between 2:44 AM and 3:24 AM, I was praying in my room and the prayer took a different turn where the Holy Spirit began to teach me something new about the LORD's Last Supper and the Holy Communion that churches have made out of it! Here is what the Holy Spirit taught me:

2.   It is time for the Passover Meal!

   i.   **Luke 22:7 (KJV)** Then came the day of unleavened bread, when the passover must be killed.

   ii. **Luke 22:8 (KJV)** And he sent Peter and John, saying, Go and prepare us the passover, that we may eat.

   iii. **Luke 22:14 (KJV)** And when the hour was come, he sat down, and the twelve apostles with him.

3.   The Passover Meal is a token, a sign, an emblem, a pointer, a reminder, and NOT the actual main thing!

   i.   **Luke 22:15 (KJV)** And he said unto them, With desire I have desired to eat this passover with you before I suffer:

4. The actual main thing behind the Passover Meal are words, the Word of God, a commandment of God, a revelation of God, a prophecy of God, and this is the full text!

    i. **Exodus 12:1 (KJV)** And the LORD spake unto Moses and Aaron in the land of Egypt, saying,

    ii. **Exodus 12:2 (KJV)** This month *shall be* unto you the beginning of months: it *shall be* the first month of the year to you.

    iii. **Exodus 12:3 (KJV)** Speak ye unto all the congregation of Israel, saying, In the tenth *day* of this month they shall take to them every man a lamb, according to the house of *their* fathers, a lamb for an house:

    iv. **Exodus 12:4 (KJV)** And if the household be too little for the lamb, let him and his neighbour next unto his house take *it* according to the number of the souls; every man according to his eating shall make your count for the lamb.

    v. **Exodus 12:5 (KJV)** Your lamb shall be without blemish, a male of the first year: ye shall take *it* out from the sheep, or from the goats:

    vi. **Exodus 12:6 (KJV)** And ye shall keep it up until the fourteenth day of the same month: and the whole assembly of the congregation of Israel shall kill it in the evening.

    vii. **Exodus 12:7 (KJV)** And they shall take of the blood, and strike *it* on the two side posts and on the upper door post of the houses, wherein they shall eat it.

    viii. **Exodus 12:8 (KJV)** And they shall eat the flesh in that night, roast with fire, and unleavened bread; *and* with bitter *herbs* they shall eat it.

    ix. **Exodus 12:9 (KJV)** Eat not of it raw, nor sodden at all with water, but roast *with* fire; his head with his legs, and with the purtenance thereof.

    x. **Exodus 12:10 (KJV)** And ye shall let nothing of it remain until the morning; and that which remaineth of it until the morning ye shall burn with fire.

    xi. **Exodus 12:11 (KJV)** And thus shall ye eat it; *with* your loins girded, your shoes on your feet, and your staff in your hand; and ye shall eat it in haste: it *is* the LORD'S passover.

    xii. **Exodus 12:12 (KJV)** For I will pass through the land of Egypt this night, and will smite all the firstborn in the land of Egypt, both man and beast; and against all the gods of Egypt I will execute judgment: I *am* the LORD.

xiii. **Exodus 12:13 (KJV)** And the blood shall be to you for a token upon the houses where ye *are*: and when I see the blood, I will pass over you, and the plague shall not be upon you to destroy *you*, when I smite the land of Egypt.

xiv. **Exodus 12:14 (KJV)** And this day shall be unto you for a memorial; and ye shall keep it a feast to the LORD throughout your generations; ye shall keep it a feast by an ordinance for ever. **Exodus 12:15 (KJV)** Seven days shall ye eat unleavened bread; even the first day ye shall put away leaven out of your houses: for whosoever eateth leavened bread from the first day until the seventh day, that soul shall be cut off from Israel.

xv. **Exodus 12:16 (KJV)** And in the first day *there shall be* an holy convocation, and in the seventh day there shall be an holy convocation to you; no manner of work shall be done in them, save *that* which every man must eat, that only may be done of you.

xvi. **Exodus 12:17 (KJV)** And ye shall observe *the feast of* unleavened bread; for in this selfsame day have I brought your armies out of the land of Egypt: therefore shall ye observe this day in your generations by an ordinance for ever.

xvii. **Exodus 12:18 (KJV)** In the first *month*, on the fourteenth day of the month at even, ye shall eat unleavened bread, until the one and twentieth day of the month at even.

xviii. **Exodus 12:19 (KJV)** Seven days shall there be no leaven found in your houses: for whosoever eateth that which is leavened, even that soul shall be cut off from the congregation of Israel, whether he be a stranger, or born in the land.

xix. **Exodus 12:20 (KJV)** Ye shall eat nothing leavened; in all your habitations shall ye eat unleavened bread.

5. Then, this is the specific text/Word of God that the Passover Meal is invoking whenever you do it, which the Holy Spirit taught me!

6. ONE – A Lamb – **Exodus 12:3 (KJV)**

7. TWO – The Lamb is for eating and the eating is for the preservation of the soul! – **Exodus 12:4 (KJV)**

8. THREE – The Lamb shall be without blemish, without sin, without guile, a male, and a firstborn Lamb! – **Exodus 12:5 (KJV)**

9. FOUR – The Lamb has to die/be killed at the same time as the evening sacrifice! – **Exodus 12:6 (KJV)**

10. **FIVE** – The Blood of the Lamb shall flow on wooden side and top posts, like a Cross! – **Exodus 12:7 (KJV)**

11. **SIX** – The eating of the Lamb to sustain the soul or for the preservation of the soul or for the saving of the soul, shall happen in the night, and "night" means that you do not know when and you do not know how! – **Exodus 12:8 (KJV)**

   i. **John 3:8 (KJV)** The wind bloweth where it listeth, and thou hearest the sound thereof, but canst not tell whence it cometh, and whither it goeth: so is every one that is born of the Spirit.

12. **EIGHT** – The Lamb shall be tempered with the same entity of fire that the real Lamb of God (Jesus Christ) is also made of! – **Exodus 12:10 (KJV)**

   i. **Matthew 3:11 (KJV)** I indeed baptize you with water unto repentance: but he that cometh after me is mightier than I, whose shoes I am not worthy to bear: he shall baptize you with the Holy Ghost, and *with* fire:

   ii. **Luke 3:16 (KJV)** John answered, saying unto *them* all, I indeed baptize you with water; but one mightier than I cometh, the latchet of whose shoes I am not worthy to unloose: he shall baptize you with the Holy Ghost and with fire:

13. **NINE** – The entire Passover Meal celebration is a token, a sign, an emblem, a pointer, a reminder of the destruction of the plague of Judgment Day and Hell from which plague and destruction you have ONLY ONE escape route: the Blood of Christ! – **Exodus 12:12-13 (KJV)**

14. **TEN** – The day of your escape from the wrath, destruction, and plague of Judgment and Hell is your Day of Salvation! – **Exodus 12:14 (KJV)**

15. **ELEVEN** – Leaven means sin, and so your separation from leaven is your separation from sin! – **Exodus 12:15 (KJV)**

16. **TWELVE** – In addition, because leaven is sin and the Lamb is without blemish and without sin, hence, you are commanded to NOT bring leaven into contact with the Lamb!

   i. **Leviticus 6:17 (KJV)** It shall not be baken with leaven. I have given it *unto them for* their portion of my offerings made by fire; it *is* most holy, as *is* the sin offering, and as the trespass offering.

   ii. **Matthew 16:6 (KJV)** Then Jesus said unto them, Take heed and beware of the leaven of the Pharisees and of the Sadducees.

   iii. **Matthew 16:11 (KJV)** How is it that ye do not understand that I spake *it* not to you concerning bread, that ye should beware of the leaven of the Pharisees and of the Sadducees?

    iv. **Matthew 16:12 (KJV)** Then understood they how that he bade *them* not beware of the leaven of bread, but of the doctrine of the Pharisees and of the Sadducees.

    v. **Mark 8:15 (KJV)** And he charged them, saying, Take heed, beware of the leaven of the Pharisees, and *of* the leaven of Herod.

    vi. **Luke 12:1 (KJV)** In the mean time, when there were gathered together an innumerable multitude of people, insomuch that they trode one upon another, he began to say unto his disciples first of all, Beware ye of the leaven of the Pharisees, which is hypocrisy.

17. **THIRTEEN** – No manner of work shall be done for your Salvation save only to believe on HIM who gave you the Salvation free of charge! – **Exodus 12:16 (KJV)**

18. **FOURTEEN** – You shall never forget how you were once a sinner in the past, and now, the LORD God Almighty has had mercy on you to make you free form Hell by HIS SON Jesus Christ! – **Exodus 12:17 (KJV)**

19. **FIFTEEN** – The correct food that you shall eat in order to sustain your Salvation is Bread, unleavened Bread, unblemished Bread, Bread that came down from Heaven, Bread without sin and that Bread is Jesus Christ! – **Exodus 12:18 (KJV)**

    i. **John 6:35 (KJV)** And Jesus said unto them, I am the bread of life: he that cometh to me shall never hunger; and he that believeth on me shall never thirst.

    ii. **John 6:51 (KJV)** I am the living bread which came down from heaven: if any man eat of this bread, he shall live for ever: and the bread that I will give is my flesh, which I will give for the life of the world.

20. **SIXTEEN** – The number seven is the number of completion and perpetuity hence, if you are commanded to NOT eat leaven for seven days, and leaven means sin, then, it means that you are commanded to NOT return to sin at all forever after you become saved! – **Exodus 12:19 (KJV)**

21. **SEVENTEEN** – The words: "in all your habitations ye shall eat nothing leavened" means in your entire life, for the rest of your life after you have become born again, you shall NOT return to sin, and sin shall not be once named among you! – **Exodus 12:20 (KJV)**

    i. **Luke 9:62 (KJV)** And Jesus said unto him, No man, having put his hand to the plough, and looking back, is fit for the kingdom of God.

    ii. **Ephesians 5:3 (KJV)** But fornication, and all uncleanness, or covetousness, let it not be once named among you, as becometh saints;

      iii. **Ezekiel 33:12 (KJV)** Therefore, thou son of man, say unto the children of thy people, The righteousness of the righteous shall not deliver him in the day of his transgression: as for the wickedness of the wicked, he shall not fall thereby in the day that he turneth from his wickedness; neither shall the righteous be able to live for his *righteousness* in the day that he sinneth.

22. So, anytime that you do the LORD's Passover (Holy Communion) in the churches, those are the seventeen points/text/Word of God that you are spiritually invoking!

23. In other words, the LORD's Passover (Holy Communion) itself means nothing since it is a token, a sign, an emblem, a pointer, a reminder, a shadow, because its real meaning is the text that it represents, is the Word of God that it invokes, and because the LORD's Passover (Holy Communion) was in all those years pointing to the coming of the LORD Jesus Christ, and now this same LORD Jesus Christ has come, therefore, the LORD Jesus Christ ended it since it has already served its purpose and intent: "I will not any more eat thereof"!

      i. **Luke 22:15 (KJV)** And he said unto them, With desire I have desired to eat this passover with you before I suffer:

      ii. **Luke 22:16 (KJV)** For I say unto you, I will not any more eat thereof, until it be fulfilled in the kingdom of God.

      iii. **Luke 22:17 (KJV)** And he took the cup, and gave thanks, and said, Take this, and divide *it* among yourselves:

      iv. **Luke 22:18 (KJV)** For I say unto you, I will not drink of the fruit of the vine, until the kingdom of God shall come.

24. Now, take note again very carefully of **Luke 22:15-18 (KJV)**, and see the revelation in those words, as follows:

25. **ONE** – The LORD Jesus Christ ended the physical LORD's Passover (Holy Communion)! **Luke 22:15 (KJV)**

26. **TWO** – Immediately the LORD Jesus Christ ended the physical LORD's Passover (Holy Communion), HE replaced it with a spiritual LORD's Passover (Holy Communion) that should "be fulfilled in the kingdom of God"! **Luke 22:16 (KJV)**

27. **THREE** – Now, what is the Kingdom of God or where is the Kingdom of God? Here is the answer!

      i. **Deuteronomy 30:11 (KJV)** For this commandment which I command thee this day, it *is* not hidden from thee, neither *is* it far off.

      ii. **Deuteronomy 30:12 (KJV)** It *is* not in heaven, that thou shouldest say, Who shall go up for us to heaven, and bring it unto us, that we may hear it, and do it?

    iii. **Deuteronomy 30:13 (KJV)** Neither *is* it beyond the sea, that thou shouldest say, Who shall go over the sea for us, and bring it unto us, that we may hear it, and do it?

    iv. **Deuteronomy 30:14 (KJV)** But the word *is* very nigh unto thee, in thy mouth, and in thy heart, that thou mayest do it.

    v. **Luke 17:20 (KJV)** And when he was demanded of the Pharisees, when the kingdom of God should come, he answered them and said, The kingdom of God cometh not with observation:

    vi. **Luke 17:21 (KJV)** Neither shall they say, Lo here! or, lo there! for, behold, the kingdom of God is within you.

28. **FOUR** – So, you see from the evidence above that, the Kingdom of God the Word of God that is in your mouth, in your heart, and in your mind!

29. **FIVE** – In other words, if the Kingdom of God is the Word of God in your heart/mind/mouth, then, the new spiritual LORD's Passover (Holy Communion) that the LORD Jesus Christ is bringing and is promising to drink and to eat, also has to be inside the Word of God! how do we know that?

30. Here is the answer!

    i. **Luke 22:19 (KJV)** And he took bread, and gave thanks, and brake *it*, and gave unto them, saying, This is my body which is given for you: this do in remembrance of me.

31. So, you see that the new Passover Bread is "unleavened bread"!

32. Well, what is the difference between this unleavened bread of the New Testament in **Luke 22:19 (KJV)** and the same unleavened bread of the Old Testament in **Exodus 12:1-20 (KJV)**?

33. The most important difference is that the unleavened bread of the Old Testament is a physical bread that leads to death and with zero spiritual significance, but the unleavened bread of the New Testament is the Flesh of the Lord Jesus Christ Himself and gives life!

    i. **John 6:48 (KJV)** I am that bread of life.

    ii. **John 6:49 (KJV)** Your fathers did eat manna in the wilderness, and are dead.

    iii. **John 6:50 (KJV)** This is the bread which cometh down from heaven, that a man may eat thereof, and not die.

    iv. **John 6:51 (KJV)** I am the living bread which came down from heaven: if any man eat of this bread, he shall live for ever: and the bread that I will give is my flesh, which I will give for the life of the world.

     v. **John 6:53 (KJV)** Then Jesus said unto them, Verily, verily, I say unto you, Except ye eat the flesh of the Son of man, and drink his blood, ye have no life in you.

     vi. **John 6:54 (KJV)** Whoso eateth my flesh, and drinketh my blood, hath eternal life; and I will raise him up at the last day.

     vii. **John 6:55 (KJV)** For my flesh is meat indeed, and my blood is drink indeed.

     viii. **John 6:56 (KJV)** He that eateth my flesh, and drinketh my blood, dwelleth in me, and I in him.

     ix. **John 6:57 (KJV)** As the living Father hath sent me, and I live by the Father: so he that eateth me, even he shall live by me.

     x. **John 6:58 (KJV)** This is that bread which came down from heaven: not as your fathers did eat manna, and are dead: he that eateth of this bread shall live for ever.

34. So, then, should we serve physical bread just as we were doing in the Old Testament?

35. No, thou fool!

36. The LORD Jesus Christ revealed that the physical bread that HE was talking about in **John 6:48-58 (KJV)** is actually the Spiritual Bread!

     i. **John 6:61 (KJV)** When Jesus knew in himself that his disciples murmured at it, he said unto them, Doth this offend you?

     ii. **John 6:62 (KJV)** *What* and if ye shall see the Son of man ascend up where he was before?

     iii. **John 6:63 (KJV)** It is the spirit that quickeneth; the flesh profiteth nothing: the words that I speak unto you, *they* are spirit, and *they* are life.

37. So, then, where is this Spiritual Bread of Christ?

38. Again, thou fool! Here is it!

     i. **John 1:1 (KJV)** In the beginning was the Word, and the Word was with God, and the Word was God.

39. So, the Spiritual Bread of Christ that you must eat is the Word of God, NOT corrupt physical bread that cannot take you to Heaven!

40. So, the Word of God is food to eat?

41. Yes, thou fool!

     i. **Jeremiah 15:16 (KJV)** Thy words were found, and I did eat them; and thy word was unto me the joy and rejoicing of mine heart: for I am called by thy name, O LORD God of hosts.

ii. **Ezekiel 3:1 (KJV)** Moreover he said unto me, Son of man, eat that thou findest; eat this roll, and go speak unto the house of Israel.

iii. **Ezekiel 3:2 (KJV)** So I opened my mouth, and he caused me to eat that roll.

iv. **Ezekiel 3:3 (KJV)** And he said unto me, Son of man, cause thy belly to eat, and fill thy bowels with this roll that I give thee. Then did I eat *it*; and it was in my mouth as honey for sweetness.

v. **Ezekiel 3:4 (KJV)** And he said unto me, Son of man, go, get thee unto the house of Israel, and speak with my words unto them.

vi. **Revelation 10:8 (KJV)** And the voice which I heard from heaven spake unto me again, and said, Go *and* take the little book which is open in the hand of the angel which standeth upon the sea and upon the earth.

vii. **Revelation 10:9 (KJV)** And I went unto the angel, and said unto him, Give me the little book. And he said unto me, Take *it*, and eat it up; and it shall make thy belly bitter, but it shall be in thy mouth sweet as honey.

viii. **Revelation 10:10 (KJV)** And I took the little book out of the angel's hand, and ate it up; and it was in my mouth sweet as honey: and as soon as I had eaten it, my belly was bitter.

ix. **Revelation 10:11 (KJV)** And he said unto me, Thou must prophesy again before many peoples, and nations, and tongues, and kings.

42. The final revelation that the Holy Spirit taught me on the LORD's Last Supper (Holy Communion) is this!

i. **Luke 22:20 (KJV)** Likewise also the cup after supper, saying, This cup *is* the new testament in my blood, which is shed for you.

43. Now, what do you think was in the Cup?

44. Please, do be one of those very stupid Pastors, Ministers, and Bishops who say that there was wine in the Cup that Jesus gave to the Apostles!

45. Here is the reason why the LORD Jesus Christ DID NOT give wine to the Apostles!

i. **Proverbs 31:1 (KJV)** The words of king Lemuel, the prophecy that his mother taught him.

ii. **Proverbs 31:2 (KJV)** What, my son? and what, the son of my womb? and what, the son of my vows?

iii. **Proverbs 31:3 (KJV)** Give not thy strength unto women, nor thy ways to that which destroyeth kings.

iv. **Proverbs 31:4 (KJV)** *It is* not for kings, O Lemuel, *it is* not for kings to drink wine; nor for princes strong drink:

     v. **Proverbs 31:5 (KJV)** Lest they drink, and forget the law, and pervert the judgment of any of the afflicted.

     vi. **Proverbs 31:6 (KJV)** Give strong drink unto him that is ready to perish, and wine unto those that be of heavy hearts.

     vii. **Proverbs 31:7 (KJV)** Let him drink, and forget his poverty, and remember his misery no more.

46. Here is another evidence why the LORD Jesus Christ DID NOT give wine to the Apostles!

     i. **Matthew 5:17 (KJV)** Think not that I am come to destroy the law, or the prophets: I am not come to destroy, but to fulfil.

     ii. **Luke 9:56 (KJV)** For the Son of man is not come to destroy men's lives, but to save *them*. And they went to another village.

     iii. **John 10:10 (KJV)** The thief cometh not, but for to steal, and to kill, and to destroy: I am come that they might have life, and that they might have *it* more abundantly.

47. Here is another evidence why the LORD Jesus Christ DID NOT give wine to the Apostles!

     i. **John 10:35 (KJV)** If he called them gods, unto whom the word of God came, and the scripture cannot be broken;

48. Here is another evidence why the LORD Jesus Christ DID NOT give wine to the Apostles!

     i. **Leviticus 10:8 (KJV)** And the LORD spake unto Aaron, saying,

     ii. **Leviticus 10:9 (KJV)** Do not drink wine nor strong drink, thou, nor thy sons with thee, when ye go into the tabernacle of the congregation, lest ye die: *it shall be* a statute for ever throughout your generations:

49. Here is another evidence why the LORD Jesus Christ DID NOT give any unclean wine to the Apostles!

     i. **Judges 13:12 (KJV)** And Manoah said, Now let thy words come to pass. How shall we order the child, and *how* shall we do unto him?

     ii. **Judges 13:13 (KJV)** And the angel of the LORD said unto Manoah, Of all that I said unto the woman let her beware.

     iii. **Judges 13:14 (KJV)** She may not eat of any *thing* that cometh of the vine, neither let her drink wine or strong drink, nor eat any unclean *thing*: all that I commanded her let her observe.

50. Here is another evidence why the LORD Jesus Christ DID NOT give any unclean wine to the Apostles! Except you want to read **Proverbs 20:1 (KJV)** and teach that

Jesus Christ was mocking HIS Apostles and wanted to deceive them hence HE gave them wine to drink?

      i. **Proverbs 20:1 (KJV)** Wine *is* a mocker, strong drink *is* raging: and whosoever is deceived thereby is not wise.

      ii. **Proverbs 23:31 (KJV)** Look not thou upon the wine when it is red, when it giveth his colour in the cup, *when* it moveth itself aright.

      iii. **Proverbs 23:32 (KJV)** At the last it biteth like a serpent, and stingeth like an adder.

51. There are three key words in **Proverbs 20:1 (KJV)**: namely, a mocker, a deceiver, and a fool! Which of those three key words is you since you use wine in church?

52. In fact, all the three key words are you, because what the LORD God Almighty is showing you over there in **Proverbs 20:1 (KJV)** is that, anyone who uses wine is a mocker, is a deceiver, and is a fool!

53. So, again what do you think was in the Cup that Jesus Christ gave to the Apostles?

      i. **Luke 22:20 (KJV)** Likewise also the cup after supper, saying, This cup *is* the new testament in my blood, which is shed for you.

54. Brother, the answer is right there in your face, but because you do NOT have the Holy Spirit, you are very ignorant of what you asay?

55. The LORD Jesus Christ said: "This cup *is* the new testament", clearly meaning that: "in this Cup is the New Testament"!

56. Therefore, in the LORD's Last Supper (Holy Communion) Cup, there were words, there was the New Covenant, there was the Commandments of God, there was the New Testament, just as Christ Himself specified!

57. Another confirmation that in the LORD's Last Supper (Holy Communion) Cup were the words of the New Testament are the words: "in my blood, which is shed for you"! how so?

58. Because you need the shedding of Blood BEFORE a Testament can come into force!

59. In other words, even though the Blood points to the Will/Testament of the Dead Man Christ, the Blood itself alone has none effect except it is revealing what is behind the Blood, and it is the Covenant of the New Testament hence, the LORD Jesus Christ was NOT commanding you to be drinking and eating physical blood and bread, neither was the LORD Jesus Christ telling you to go to the market and shops to buy filthy Holy Communion wafers, wine, and bread, BUT Jesus was communing with you in parables to turn rather to the words behind the Blood, to the words in the Cup, and to the true Bread which is the Word of God, which true Bread the Word of God is the ONLY superior medium "which is given in Heaven and in Earth in remembrance of me"!

    i. **Luke 22:19 (KJV)** And he took bread, and gave thanks, and brake *it*, and gave unto them, saying, This is my body which is given for you: this do in remembrance of me.

    ii. **Hebrews 9:13 (KJV)** For if the blood of bulls and of goats, and the ashes of an heifer sprinkling the unclean, sanctifieth to the purifying of the flesh:

    iii. **Hebrews 9:14 (KJV)** How much more shall the blood of Christ, who through the eternal Spirit offered himself without spot to God, purge your conscience from dead works to serve the living God?

    iv. **Hebrews 9:15 (KJV)** And for this cause he is the mediator of the new testament, that by means of death, for the redemption of the transgressions *that were* under the first testament, they which are called might receive the promise of eternal inheritance.

    v. **Hebrews 9:16 (KJV)** For where a testament *is*, there must also of necessity be the death of the testator.

    vi. **Hebrews 9:17 (KJV)** For a testament *is* of force after men are dead: otherwise it is of no strength at all while the testator liveth.

60. Brethren, I guarantee you, I testify to you by the Holy Spirit, and I vouch to you 100%, that if you show up in Heaven with your physical Holy Communion wafers, wine, and bread in your hands and in your mouth, you will immediately be booted and flung in to Hell for insulting Heaven with physical filthy man-made things!

61. BUT, again I guarantee you, I testify to you by the Holy Spirit, and I vouch to you 100%, that if you show up in Heaven with the Bread of Heaven, with the Word of God, which is the true Bread of Life, all the Spirits in Heaven will smile at you, they will welcome you for bringing with you the Word of God the ONLY begotten Son of God the Father, and they will worship that true Bread the Word of God that you are holding in your hands, and by extension they will also worship you alongside the Son of God in whom you are actually planted in Heavenly Places far above all principality, and power, and might, and dominion, and every name that is named, not only in this world, but also in that which is to come!

    i. **Psalm 97:9 (KJV)** For thou, LORD, *art* high above all the earth: thou art exalted far above all gods.

    ii. **Ephesians 1:17 (KJV)** That the God of our Lord Jesus Christ, the Father of glory, may give unto you the spirit of wisdom and revelation in the knowledge of him:

    iii. **Ephesians 1:18 (KJV)** The eyes of your understanding being enlightened; that ye may know what is the hope of his calling, and what the riches of the glory of his inheritance in the saints,

iv. **Ephesians 1:19 (KJV)** And what *is* the exceeding greatness of his power to us-ward who believe, according to the working of his mighty power,

v. **Ephesians 1:20 (KJV)** Which he wrought in Christ, when he raised him from the dead, and set *him* at his own right hand in the heavenly *places*,

vi. **Ephesians 1:21 (KJV)** Far above all principality, and power, and might, and dominion, and every name that is named, not only in this world, but also in that which is to come:

vii. **Ephesians 1:22 (KJV)** And hath put all *things* under his feet, and gave him *to be* the head over all *things* to the church,

viii. **Ephesians 1:23 (KJV)** Which is his body, the fulness of him that filleth all in all.

62. Brethren, the above was what the Holy Spirit taught me on the LORD's Supper (Holy Communion) on Wednesday 10th April 2024, between 2:44 AM and 3:24 AM, as I was praying in my room!

The LORD Jesus Christ be with your spirit. The LORD Jesus Christ give you understanding.

Rev. Prof. PETER PRYCE,
DSEF, BA, MA, B.Soc.Sc Pol Sci, IBA, PhD
A Scribe of the Law of the God of Heaven
Prophet of the Word of God
Professor of French, Silver Spring, MD, USA
Scholar of the Institute of Theologians, USA
WWW.THEBIBLEUNIVERSITY.ORG
Accreditation Number: 07-QCTO/SDP120723172836
SAQA QUAL ID: Identification # 101997
WWW.BOOKSTORESITE.ORG
WWW.THEBIBLEUNIVERSITYCHURCH.ORG

Wednesday 10th April 2024 @ 7:30 AM – 1:00 PM

While praying at home.

CHAPTER 19
GENERAL CONCLUSION

FIHANKRA
"Compound house"

Asante philosophical symbol of Security, Safety

We have come to the end of this Book – *Holy Communion, Vol. 1 – Research Study from Genesis to Revelation* – in which we have taught all and everything that the LORD God Almighty has embedded and revealed to me concerning *Holy Communion* and how to verify the doctrines of Pastors who preach and practise *Holy Communion* in the Churches, in order to know whether they were called of God or whether they work for Satan!

This is a most valuable study and reference material for the Spiritual Bible Training of Ministers so that the Man of God should be well equipped and adequately furnished to respond to all spiritual questions regarding the Doctrine of *Holy Communion* in the Holy Bible.

> **Jeremiah 3:15 (KJV)** And I will give you pastors according to mine heart, which shall feed you with knowledge and understanding.

> **Malachi 2:7 (KJV)** For the priest's lips should keep knowledge, and they should seek the law at his mouth: for he *is* the messenger of the LORD of hosts.

> **2 Timothy 3:16 (KJV)** All Scripture *is* given by inspiration of God, and *is* profitable for doctrine, for reproof, for correction, for instruction in righteousness:

2 Timothy 3:17 (KJV) That the Man of God may be perfect, throughly furnished unto all good works.

We used the Scriptures from Genesis to Revelation as our main and only research material according to the methodology of Bible research and doctrine that God Almighty revealed in the Holy Scriptures:

Isaiah 8:20 (KJV) To the law and to the testimony: if they speak not according to this word, *it is* because *there is* no light in them.

Jeremiah 23:28 (KJV) The prophet that hath a dream, let him tell a dream; and he that hath my word, let him speak my word faithfully. What *is* the chaff to the wheat? saith the LORD.

Galatians 1:8 (KJV) But though we, or an angel from heaven, preach any other gospel unto you than that which we have preached unto you, let him be accursed.

Galatians 1:9 (KJV) As we said before, so say I now again, If any *man* preach any other gospel unto you than that ye have received, let him be accursed.

Throughout our research, we have solidified our belief that while all other things shall pass away, only the Word of God will remain. That observation further reveals that, given the capital importance of the Word of God and its power of Salvation to them that believe, in other words, its ability to become your Ticket to Heaven, God Almighty also did not leave carnal humans to decide how to teach it, nor even to determine the foolishness or otherwise of the Scriptures, seeing that God Almighty uses the foolish things of the world to confound the wise:

1 Corinthians 1:26 (KJV) For ye see your calling, brethren, how that not many wise men after the flesh, not many mighty, not many noble, *are called*:

1 Corinthians 1:27 (KJV) But God hath chosen the foolish things of the world to confound the wise; and God hath chosen the weak things of the world to confound the things which are mighty;

1 Corinthians 1:28 (KJV) And base things of the world, and things which are despised, hath God chosen, *yea*, and things which are not, to bring to nought things that are:

1 Corinthians 1:29 (KJV) That no flesh should glory in his presence.

The following groups of people will find excellent use for this Christian Theological Research Textbook:

1. Already established Ministers who are still teaching the Word of God.
2. Newly ordained Ministers in churches who are seeking Pastoral Training on how to approach and understanding spiritual proverbs and parables as a foundation to understanding the entire Holy Bible.
3. Theological Scholars who are researching theological questions in the Holy Scriptures.
4. Bible Students at the following levels of academic and spiritual pursuit:
5. **SUMMARY OF BIBLICAL STUDIES DEGREE PROGRAMS IN THE BIBLE UNIVERSITY**: The Bible University offers the following Online Biblical Studies Degree Programs:
   i. Occupational Certificate: **Religious Associate Professional (Christian Religious Practitioner): South African Qualifications Authority (SAQA)ID 101997**.
   ii. Certificate in Theology (C. Th.) (for just one topic or two) – 1 month
   iii. Diploma in Theology (Dip. Th.) is a self-paced one-year diploma program of purely Bible Study, Bible Translation, and Bible Interpretation
   iv. Bachelor of Theology (B.Th.) – 2-year degree program to complete 22 self-selected Books of the Holy Bible
   v. Master of Theology (M.Th.) – 2-year degree program to complete 44 self-selected Books of the Holy Bible
   i. Doctor of Theology (Th.D.) – 4-year degree program to complete all 66 Books of the Holy Bible
   ii. Diploma in Chaplaincy Training Program for Pastors
   iii. Diploma in Church Financial Management Training Program for Pastors
   iv. Diploma in General Counseling Training Program for Pastors
   v. Diploma in Marriage Counseling Training Program for Pastors
   vi. Diploma in Sermon Preparation for Ministers of the Gospel
   vii. Preparation of Bible Topics for Christian Conference and award of Conference Certificates to Participants

The Scriptures the Word of God are in two parts, and possessing one part but lacking the other invalidates what you have! The two parts are:

     i.   The written Scriptures, and

    ii.   The Holy Spirit

When those two do not combine, you do not have the Word of God! Just as you do not have a ship and you will die if you purchase one from the market and you lack the professionally approved Pilot to captain the ship and navigate the treacherous waters for you, so also, you do not have Scriptures the Word of God, and you will die, if you purchase one Holy Bible from the open market but you lack the Driver called Holy Spirit to help you navigate the treacherous spiritual realm within it! Here is the evidence:

Luke 24:48 (KJV) And ye are witnesses of these things.

Luke 24:49 (KJV) And, behold, I send the promise of my Father upon you: but tarry ye in the city of Jerusalem, until ye be endued with power from on high.

John 14:15 (KJV) If ye love me, keep my commandments.

John 14:16 (KJV) And I will pray the Father, and he shall give you another Comforter, that he may abide with you for ever;

John 14:17 (KJV) *Even* the Spirit of truth; whom the world cannot receive, because it seeth him not, neither knoweth him: but ye know him; for he dwelleth with you, and shall be in you.

John 16:12 (KJV) I have yet many things to say unto you, but ye cannot bear them now.

John 16:13 (KJV) Howbeit when he, the Spirit of truth, is come, he will guide you into all truth: for he shall not speak of himself; but whatsoever he shall hear, *that* shall he speak: and he will shew you things to come.

John 16:14 (KJV) He shall glorify me: for he shall receive of mine, and shall shew *it* unto you.

Romans 8:9 (KJV) But ye are not in the flesh, but in the Spirit, if so be that the Spirit of God dwell in you. Now if any man have not the Spirit of Christ, he is none of his.

Romans 8:14 (KJV) For as many as are led by the Spirit of God, they are the sons of God.

THE DOCTRINE OF THE BIBLE UNIVERSITY

In this section, I identify thirteen foundational pillars of The Bible University Doctrine! This is our doctrine and this is where we stand in the Holy Scriptures. Let us consider the following verses to confirm our doctrine:

1. In The Bible University, we teach ONLY the Holy Bible the Word of God, from Genesis to Revelation, without any denominational influence!

    i. **Matthew 28:18 (KJV)** And Jesus came and spake unto them, saying, All power is given unto me in heaven and in earth.

    ii. **Matthew 28:19 (KJV)** Go ye therefore, and teach all nations, baptizing them in the name of the Father, and of the Son, and of the Holy Ghost:

    iii. **Matthew 28:20 (KJV)** Teaching them to observe all things whatsoever I have commanded you: and, lo, I am with you alway, *even* unto the end of the world. Amen.

2. In The Bible University, we question everything by the Scriptures, we question every church practise, we question every church doctrine, we judge everything, and we judge every Man of God... by the Scriptures!

    i. **John 7:24 (KJV)** Judge not according to the appearance, but judge righteous judgment.

    ii. **Acts 17:11 (KJV)** These were more noble than those in Thessalonica, in that they received the word with all readiness of mind, and searched the scriptures daily, whether those things were so.

    iii. **1 Corinthians 14:29 (KJV)** Let the prophets speak two or three, and let the other judge.

    iv. **1 Thessalonians 5:21 (KJV)** Prove all things; hold fast that which is good.

    v. **1 John 4:1 (KJV)** Beloved, believe not every spirit, but try the spirits whether they are of God: because many false prophets are gone out into the world.

3. In The Bible University, our foundational doctrine is that there is ONLY ONE WAY to teach, to translate, and to interpret the Word of God, which is: YOU

MUST TEACH THE WORD OF GOD TO AGREE WITH THE WORD OF GOD!

     i. **Proverbs 21:30 (KJV)** *There is* no wisdom nor understanding nor counsel against the LORD.

    ii. **Isaiah 8:20 (KJV)** To the law and to the testimony: if they speak not according to this word, *it is* because *there is* no light in them.

   iii. **Jeremiah 23:28 (KJV)** The prophet that hath a dream, let him tell a dream; and he that hath my word, let him speak my word faithfully. What *is* the chaff to the wheat? saith the LORD.

   iv. **John 10:35 (KJV)** If he called them gods, unto whom the word of God came, and the scripture cannot be broken;

    v. **Galatians 1:8 (KJV)** But though we, or an angel from heaven, preach any other gospel unto you than that which we have preached unto you, let him be accursed.

   vi. **Galatians 1:9 (KJV)** As we said before, so say I now again, If any *man* preach any other gospel unto you than that ye have received, let him be accursed.

4. In The Bible University, our foundational doctrine is that: TO QUALIFY AS A MAN OF GOD, YOU MUST THINK, SPEAK, AND OBEY THE WORD OF GOD COMPLETELY TO REFLECT THAT HOLY SPIRIT LIVES IN YOU!

     i. **Joshua 1:8 (KJV)** This book of the law shall not depart out of thy mouth; but thou shalt meditate therein day and night, that thou mayest observe to do according to all that is written therein: for then thou shalt make thy way prosperous, and then thou shalt have good success.

    ii. **John 6:63 (KJV)** It is the spirit that quickeneth; the flesh profiteth nothing: the words that I speak unto you, *they* are spirit, and *they* are life.

   iii. **John 14:17 (KJV)** *Even* the Spirit of truth; whom the world cannot receive, because it seeth him not, neither knoweth him: but ye know him; for he dwelleth with you, and shall be in you.

   iv. **John 15:7 (KJV)** If ye abide in me, and my words abide in you, ye shall ask what ye will, and it shall be done unto you.

    v. **Colossians 1:9 (KJV)** For this cause we also, since the day we heard *it*, do not cease to pray for you, and to desire that ye might be filled with the knowledge of his will in all wisdom and spiritual understanding;

5. In The Bible University, by means of the Word of God, we identify, analyze, dissect, point out, prove, show, expose, and overthrow evil church doctrines and practices that have no basis in the Holy Bible, that violate the Holy Scriptures, and that are contrary to the Gospel of Jesus Christ! We rebuke sharply, sparing no man or woman, to the intent "that they may be sound in the faith"!

   i. **2 Corinthians 13:10 (KJV)** Therefore I write these things being absent, lest being present I should use sharpness, according to the power which the Lord hath given me to edification, and not to destruction.

   ii. **1 Timothy 5:20 (KJV)** Them that sin rebuke before all, that others also may fear.

   iii. **Titus 1:13 (KJV)** This witness is true. Wherefore rebuke them sharply, that they may be sound in the faith;

6. In The Bible University, we judge the spiritual controversies of Jesus Christ and Apostle Paul with the Word of God Almighty!

   i. **Deuteronomy 17:8 (KJV)** If there arise a matter too hard for thee in judgment, between blood and blood, between plea and plea, and between stroke and stroke, *being* matters of controversy within thy gates: then shalt thou arise, and get thee up into the place which the LORD thy God shall choose;

   ii. **Deuteronomy 19:17 (KJV)** Then both the men, between whom the controversy *is*, shall stand before the LORD, before the priests and the judges, which shall be in those days;

   iii. **Deuteronomy 21:5 (KJV)** And the priests the sons of Levi shall come near; for them the LORD thy God hath chosen to minister unto him, and to bless in the name of the LORD; and by their word shall every controversy and every stroke be *tried*:

   iv. **Deuteronomy 25:1 (KJV)** If there be a controversy between men, and they come unto judgment, that *the judges* may judge them; then they shall justify the righteous, and condemn the wicked.

   v. **Jeremiah 25:31 (KJV)** A noise shall come *even* to the ends of the earth; for the LORD hath a controversy with the nations, he will plead with all flesh; he will give them *that are* wicked to the sword, saith the LORD.

   vi. **Ezekiel 44:24 (KJV)** And in controversy they shall stand in judgment; *and* they shall judge it according to my judgments: and they shall keep my laws and my statutes in all mine assemblies; and they shall hallow my sabbaths.

    vii. **1 Timothy 3:16 (KJV)** And without controversy great is the mystery of godliness: God was manifest in the flesh, justified in the Spirit, seen of angels, preached unto the Gentiles, believed on in the world, received up into glory.

    viii. **2 Chronicles 19:8 (KJV)** Moreover in Jerusalem did Jehoshaphat set of the Levites, and *of* the priests, and of the chief of the fathers of Israel, for the judgment of the LORD, and for controversies, when they returned to Jerusalem.

7. In The Bible University, we maintain The Offence of the Cross!

    i. **John 6:61 (KJV)** When Jesus knew in himself that his disciples murmured at it, he said unto them, Doth this offend you?

    ii. **Galatians 5:11 (KJV)** And I, brethren, if I yet preach circumcision, why do I yet suffer persecution? then is the offence of the cross ceased.

    iii. **James 3:2 (KJV)** For in many things we offend all. If any man offend not in word, the same *is* a perfect man, *and* able also to bridle the whole body.

8. In The Bible University, we do not shy away from Bible errors and contradictions, because we have Bible theories to explain the errors, omissions, corruptions, contradictions, inconsistences and foolishness in the Holy Bible as God-ordained spiritual seals and sieves for good purpose, and for the weeding out and cleansing of the corrupt!

    i. **Isaiah 30:28 (KJV)** And his breath, as an overflowing stream, shall reach to the midst of the neck, to sift the nations with the sieve of vanity: and *there shall be* a bridle in the jaws of the people, causing *them* to err.

    ii. **Amos 9:9 (KJV)** For, lo, I will command, and I will sift the house of Israel among all nations, like as *corn* is sifted in a sieve, yet shall not the least grain fall upon the earth.

    iii. **2 Corinthians 2:17 (KJV)** For we are not as many, which corrupt the word of God: but as of sincerity, but as of God, in the sight of God speak we in Christ.

9. In The Bible University, we are only virtual and worldwide!

    i. **Matthew 28:18 (KJV)** And Jesus came and spake unto them, saying, All power is given unto me in heaven and in earth.

    ii. **Matthew 28:19 (KJV)** Go ye therefore, and teach all nations, baptizing them in the name of the Father, and of the Son, and of the Holy Ghost:

iii. **Matthew 28:20 (KJV)** Teaching them to observe all things whatsoever I have commanded you: and, lo, I am with you alway, *even* unto the end of the world. Amen.

10. In The Bible University, our aim is Salvation by The Bible <u>only</u>!

    i. **1 Timothy 4:13 (KJV)** Till I come, give attendance to reading, to exhortation, to doctrine.

    ii. **1 Timothy 4:16 (KJV)** Take heed unto thyself, and unto the doctrine; continue in them: for in doing this thou shalt both save thyself, and them that hear thee.

    iii. **James 1:21 (KJV)** Wherefore lay apart all filthiness and superfluity of naughtiness, and receive with meekness the engrafted word, which is able to save your souls.

11. In The Bible University, we teach that Christianity is a School whose only pursuit is to seek the knowledge of God Almighty and Jesus Christ, from Genesis to Revelation!

    i. **Hosea 6:6 (KJV)** For I desired mercy, and not sacrifice; and the knowledge of God more than burnt offerings.

    ii. **Psalm 2:10 (KJV)** Be wise now therefore, O ye kings: be instructed, ye judges of the earth.

    iii. **Proverbs 9:10 (KJV)** The fear of the LORD *is* the beginning of wisdom: and the knowledge of the holy *is* understanding.

    iv. **Proverbs 15:28 (KJV)** The heart of the righteous studieth to answer: but the mouth of the wicked poureth out evil things.

    v. **Jeremiah 3:15 (KJV)** And I will give you pastors according to mine heart, which shall feed you with knowledge and understanding.

    vi. **Jeremiah 6:8 (KJV)** Be thou instructed, O Jerusalem, lest my soul depart from thee; lest I make thee desolate, a land not inhabited.

    vii. **Matthew 13:52 (KJV)** Then said he unto them, Therefore every scribe *which is* instructed unto the kingdom of heaven is like unto a man *that is* an householder, which bringeth forth out of his treasure *things* new and old.

    viii. **Matthew 28:18 (KJV)** And Jesus came and spake unto them, saying, All power is given unto me in heaven and in earth.

    ix. **Matthew 28:19 (KJV)** Go ye therefore, and teach all nations, baptizing them in the name of the Father, and of the Son, and of the Holy Ghost:

    x. **Matthew 28:20 (KJV)** Teaching them to observe all things whatsoever I have commanded you: and, lo, I am with you alway, *even* unto the end of the world. Amen.

    xi. **1 Timothy 4:13 (KJV)** Till I come, give attendance to reading, to exhortation, to doctrine.

    xii. **2 Timothy 2:15 (KJV)** Study to shew thyself approved unto God, a workman that needeth not to be ashamed, rightly dividing the word of truth.

12. In The Bible University, we teach that the best way to know God is to obey the commandments of Jesus Christ!

    i. **Exodus 19:5 (KJV)** Now therefore, if ye will obey my voice indeed, and keep my covenant, then ye shall be a peculiar treasure unto me above all people: for all the earth *is* mine:

    ii. **Jeremiah 7:23 (KJV)** But this thing commanded I them, saying, Obey my voice, and I will be your God, and ye shall be my people: and walk ye in all the ways that I have commanded you, that it may be well unto you.

    iii. **Jeremiah 9:23 (KJV)** Thus saith the LORD, Let not the wise *man* glory in his wisdom, neither let the mighty *man* glory in his might, let not the rich *man* glory in his riches:

    iv. **Jeremiah 9:24 (KJV)** But let him that glorieth glory in this, that he understandeth and knoweth me, that I *am* the LORD which exercise lovingkindness, judgment, and righteousness, in the earth: for in these *things* I delight, saith the LORD.

    v. **Jeremiah 22:15 (KJV)** Shalt thou reign, because thou closest *thyself* in cedar? did not thy father eat and drink, and do judgment and justice, *and* then *it was* well with him?

    vi. **Jeremiah 22:16 (KJV)** He judged the cause of the poor and needy; then *it was* well *with him: was* not this to know me? saith the LORD.

    vii. **John 14:23 (KJV)** Jesus answered and said unto him, If a man love me, he will keep my words: and my Father will love him, and we will come unto him, and make our abode with him.

    viii. **John 14:24 (KJV)** He that loveth me not keepeth not my sayings: and the word which ye hear is not mine, but the Father's which sent me.

13. In The Bible University, we teach that the best way to obey the commandments of Jesus Christ is to correctly understand them!

    i. **Nehemiah 8:3 (KJV)** And he read therein before the street that *was* before the water gate from the morning until midday, before the men and the women, and those that could understand; and the ears of all the people *were attentive* unto the book of the law.

ii. **Nehemiah 8:7 (KJV)** Also Jeshua, and Bani, and Sherebiah, Jamin, Akkub, Shabbethai, Hodijah, Maaseiah, Kelita, Azariah, Jozabad, Hanan, Pelaiah, and the Levites, caused the people to understand the law: and the people *stood* in their place.

iii. **Nehemiah 8:8 (KJV)** So they read in the book in the law of God distinctly, and gave the sense, and caused *them* to understand the reading.

iv. **Nehemiah 8:13 (KJV)** And on the second day were gathered together the chief of the fathers of all the people, the priests, and the Levites, unto Ezra the scribe, even to understand the words of the law.

v. **Psalm 14:2 (KJV)** The LORD looked down from heaven upon the children of men, to see if there were any that did understand, *and* seek God.

vi. **Psalm 53:2 (KJV)** God looked down from heaven upon the children of men, to see if there were *any* that did understand, that did seek God.

vii. **Isaiah 28:9 (KJV)** Whom shall he teach knowledge? and whom shall he make to understand doctrine? *them that are* weaned from the milk, *and* drawn from the breasts.

viii. **Daniel 8:16 (KJV)** And I heard a man's voice between *the banks of* Ulai, which called, and said, Gabriel, make this *man* to understand the vision.

ix. **Matthew 15:10 (KJV)** And he called the multitude, and said unto them, Hear, and understand:

x. **Mark 13:14 (KJV)** But when ye shall see the abomination of desolation, spoken of by Daniel the prophet, standing where it ought not, (let him that readeth understand,) then let them that be in Judaea flee to the mountains:

xi. **Luke 24:45 (KJV)** Then opened he their understanding, that they might understand the scriptures,

The best way to correctly understand the Word of God and the commandments of Jesus Christ is why The Bible University textbooks were written for you: *Complete Bible Curriculum!* There are two channels of training as follows. Everything is virtual:

1. Pastoral Training for Ministry
2. Personal Training for Spiritual Growth

Group 1 Members will register at

WWW.THEBIBLEUNIVERSITY.ORG for Pastoral training and a Degree Certificate at completion.

Group 2 Members will register at

WWW.THEBIBLEUNIVERSITYCHURCH.ORG for proper Christian education and spiritual growth.

The LORD Jesus Christ be with your spirit. The LORD Jesus Christ give you understanding.

Rev. Prof. PETER PRYCE,
DSEF, BA, MA, B.Soc.Sc Pol Sci, IBA, PhD
A Scribe of the Law of the God of Heaven
Prophet of the Word of God
Professor of French, Silver Spring, MD, USA
Scholar of the Institute of Theologians, USA
WWW.THEBIBLEUNIVERSITY.ORG
Accreditation Number: 07-QCTO/SDP120723172836
SAQA QUAL ID: Identification # 101997
WWW.BOOKSTORESITE.ORG
WWW.THEBIBLEUNIVERSITYCHURCH.ORG

Tuesday 15th March 2022 @ 3:37 PM – 5:07 PM
While hearing and meditating on the Word of God

RESEARCH METHODOLOGY

We used the Christian Holy Scriptures the Bible as the main and only source of research data, beginning from ***Genesis to Revelation***. In this discovery research specifically focused on the ***Holy Communion*** in the Holy Bible, we began from the broad to the specific. We searched the Scriptures from Genesis to Revelation in order to find out everything that God Almighty has embedded in the Holy Scriptures, for the purpose of strengthening the Body of Christ by these teachings, so that Ministers and Christians alike would be fully equipped for Ministry Service.

The type of Bible Interpretation exemplified in this book is ***intralingual translation*** and we used the English Bible, the King James Version, throughout. It is well understood that in translation, you render ***meaning of thought*** by means of entities called *words* or *identifiers* or *signs* or *symbols* that constitute into a main idea text or speech. Therefore, *words, identifiers, signs,* and *symbols* are ***linguistic vehicles*** that carry meanings.

Just as meaning does not derive independent of the pre-text, the text, the context, the post-text, as well as the unseen spirit behind the text, so also Bible Translation, whether interlingual or intralingual, must respect the correct Biblical Hermeneutics of the ***perfect harmony of the Scriptures.***

The ***Perfect Harmony Theory for Bible Translation and Interpreting (Pryce, 2011)*** simply means that Bible teaching or interpreting must not in any way contradict any part of the Bible from Genesis to Revelation, and, therefore, the meaning of the text must come from the text itself, not from outside the text!

The exposition of the ***Perfect Harmony Theory for Bible Translation and Interpreting (Pryce, 2011)*** prescribes that there is ONLY ONE methodology to teach, to translate, to explain, to interpret, to write, and to expound the Holy Scriptures the Word of God, which methodology is this: YOU MUST TEACH THE WORD OF GOD TO AGREE WITH THE WORD OF GOD, and here are the evidences!

      i. **Proverbs 21:30 (KJV)** *There is* no wisdom nor understanding nor counsel against the LORD.

ii. **Isaiah 8:20 (KJV)** To the law and to the testimony: if they speak not according to this word, *it is* because *there is* no light in them.

iii. **Jeremiah 23:28 (KJV)** The prophet that hath a dream, let him tell a dream; and he that hath my word, let him speak my word faithfully. What *is* the chaff to the wheat? saith the LORD.

iv. **John 10:35 (KJV)** If he called them gods, unto whom the word of God came, and the Scripture cannot be broken;

v. **Galatians 1:8 (KJV)** But though we, or an angel from heaven, preach any other gospel unto you than that which we have preached unto you, let him be accursed.

vi. **Galatians 1:9 (KJV)** As we said before, so say I now again, If any *man* preach any other gospel unto you than that ye have received, let him be accursed.

To master the Hermeneutics of the ***Perfect Harmony Theory for Bible Translation and Interpreting (Pryce, 2011)*** is to successfully blend the communicative objective of translation and interpreting with thorough Bible scholarship enriched by research and the study of the Word of God from Genesis to Revelation, without losing the scientific edge of Bible Interpretation where ***scientific*** means that the interpretation that is finally presented is independently verifiable and replicable through research in much the same intellectual way as you can subject a text to translation analysis using proper ***translation assessment strategies***.

The hallmark of this method is a total agreement between what is presented as the meaning of the verse and what the rest of the Bible, from Genesis to Revelation, says. There must be no variation or contradiction between what is presented as meaning of the verses and what the Bible says in order to fulfil the commandment of God that we must be of one mind and in one accord with the Scriptures:

> **2 Corinthians 13:11 (KJV)** Finally, brethren, farewell. Be perfect, be of good comfort, be of one mind, live in peace; and the God of love and peace shall be with you.

> **Philippians 1:27 (KJV)** Only let your conversation be as it becometh the gospel of Christ: that whether I come and see you, or else be absent, I may hear of your affairs, that ye stand fast in one spirit, with one mind striving together for the faith of the gospel;

Philippians 2:2 (KJV) Fulfil ye my joy, that ye be likeminded, having the same love, *being* of one accord, of one mind.

1 Peter 3:8 (KJV) Finally, *be ye* all of one mind, having compassion one of another, love as brethren, *be* pitiful, *be* courteous:

In other words, one interpretation at one part of the Bible should not contradict another interpretation at another part of the Bible thus, creating perfect harmony. Due to the verse comparison and verification that is required, the ***Perfect Harmony Theory (Pryce, 2011)*** is also a tool to test ***faithfulness*** in Bible Translation and Interpreting.

RESEARCH APPROACH

This has been a qualitative research in as much as it aligns with a Biblical Exegesis and constructivist paradigm of re-interpreting Scripture in a way that impacts spiritual and redemptive thought to the saving of the soul:

> **Exodus 20:20 (KJV)** And Moses said unto the people, Fear not: for God is come to prove you, and that his fear may be before your faces, that ye sin not.

> **1 John 2:1 (KJV)** My little children, these things write I unto you, that ye sin not. And if any man sin, we have an advocate with the Father, Jesus Christ the righteous:

We approached this research with methodical data collection from Genesis to Revelation. In fact, we did a verse-by-verse reading and analysis of each verse. We followed the Bible reference selections with an in-depth critical analysis of Scripture and hypotheses, using both inductive and deductive reasoning as part of the methodical approach:

> **1 Samuel 12:7 (KJV)** Now therefore stand still, that I may reason with you before the LORD of all the righteous acts of the LORD, which he did to you and to your fathers.

> **Job 13:3 (KJV)** Surely I would speak to the Almighty, and I desire to reason with God.

> **Job 37:19 (KJV)** Teach us what we shall say unto him; *for* we cannot order *our speech* by reason of darkness.

> **Isaiah 1:18 (KJV)** Come now, and let us reason together, saith the LORD: though your sins be as scarlet, they shall be as white as snow; though they be red like crimson, they shall be as wool.

> **Isaiah 41:21 (KJV)** Produce your cause, saith the LORD; bring forth your strong *reasons*, saith the King of Jacob.

Ecclesiastes 8:5 (KJV) Whoso keepeth the commandment shall feel no evil thing: and a wise man's heart discerneth both time and judgment.

Hebrews 5:14 (KJV) But strong meat belongeth to them that are of full age, *even* those who by reason of use have their senses exercised to discern both good and evil.

1 Peter 3:15 (KJV) But sanctify the Lord God in your hearts: and *be* ready always to *give* an answer to every man that asketh you a reason of the hope that is in you with meekness and fear:

The research in this textbook also draws from two research methods: (1) Constructive Research methods, using the ***Perfect Harmony Theory for Translation and Interpreting (Pryce, 2011)***, by which we have thus far developed solutions and answers to some **2551** Scripture questions on multiple platforms, producing some 64 Christian Theological Research Textbooks of Holy Scriptures and Bible Commentaries in the process. Just a few of the full list of all my 127 books are listed at the end of this book.

The second research method used in this book is the Empirical Research by which we tested the feasibility and applicability of the ***Perfect Harmony Theory for Translation and Interpreting (Pryce, 2011)*** in order to discover scriptural solutions to relevant spiritual questions. The multiple testing platforms were:

- Face-to-face Bible Lecture Series
- Campus Students' Bible Lecture Series
- Writing Christian Theological Research Textbooks and Bible Commentary
- Bible Lecture Series in churches
- Radio Bible Lecture Series on Channel-R Radio on 92.7 FM in Accra, Ghana
- Radio Bible Lecture Series on Radio Spring 102.7 FM in Accra, Ghana
- Radio Bible Lecture Series on Radio Peace 88.9 FM in Winneba
- TV Bible Lecture Series on 1st Digital TV in Accra, Ghana
- Bible and Qur'an Lecture Series on Qibla FM Radio in New York, USA
- Bible Lecture Series on ELWA and ELBC FM Radio stations in Liberia
- Bible Lecture Series via WhatsApp
- Pastors' Bible Lecture Series
- YouTube Bible Lecture Series – type Rev. Prof. Peter Pryce and scroll down for all his 100 works

- Radio Bible Lecture Series on 90.3 FM WDIH Radio in Salisbury, Maryland, USA
- **Bible Lecture Series of the Christian Sunday Live Zoom Podcast, USA – Sunday, October 23, 2022**

Quite specifically, there is ONLY ONE spiritual law that governs how to translate, interpret, explain, teach, and understand the Word of God! That law is stated twice: one in the Old Testament and the other in the New Testament, as follows: "turn not from it *to* the right hand or *to* the left"! That was the spiritual approach that we adopted throughout our Bible research:

> **Proverbs 21:30 (KJV)** *There is* no wisdom nor understanding nor counsel against the LORD.

> **Isaiah 8:20 (KJV)** To the law and to the testimony: if they speak not according to this word, *it is* because *there is* no light in them.

> **Deuteronomy 28:14 (KJV)** And thou shalt not go aside from any of the words which I command thee this day, *to* the right hand, or *to* the left, to go after other gods to serve them.

> **Joshua 1:7 (KJV)** Only be thou strong and very courageous, that thou mayest observe to do according to all the law, which Moses my servant commanded thee: turn not from it *to* the right hand or *to* the left, that thou mayest prosper whithersoever thou goest.

> **Galatians 1:8 (KJV)** But though we, or an Angel from heaven, preach any other gospel unto you than that which we have preached unto you, let him be accursed.

> **Galatians 1:9 (KJV)** As we said before, so say I now again, If any *man* preach any other gospel unto you than that ye have received, let him be accursed.

In other words, the only approach to Bible Teaching that is acceptable in Heaven is the one that will "turn not from it *to* the right hand or *to* the left"!

EXPRESSION OF PERSONAL OPINION

We hope that Ministers and Christians will verify the contents of this textbook by the Holy Scriptures, and yield to the teachings contained herein in as much as they conform 100% to the Holy Bible. Then, their spiritual life would greatly advance to the acknowledgment of the Truth of the Gospel of Jesus Christ and, most importantly, to the obedience of the Word of God unto Salvation.

It is our hope that you will trust the Word of God the Scriptures as the final authority in all matters spiritual while using this textbook as supplementary reading material in your Spiritual School of Heaven on Earth. In whatever way this book is useful to you, believe only the Word of God, believe the LORD Jesus Christ as the final authority in all matters spiritual:

> **Ephesians 6:19 (KJV)** And for me, that utterance may be given unto me, that I may open my mouth boldly, to make known the mystery of the gospel,

> **Ephesians 6:20 (KJV)** For which I am an ambassador in bonds: that therein I may speak boldly, as I ought to speak.

> **Ephesians 6:21 (KJV)** But that ye also may know my affairs, *and* how I do, Tychicus, a beloved brother and faithful minister in the Lord, shall make known to you all things:

The following groups of people will find an excellent use for the **Complete Bible Curriculum** series:

1. Already established Ministers who are still teaching the Word of God.
2. Newly ordained Ministers in churches who are seeking Pastoral Training in sermon preparation.
3. Theological Scholars who are researching theological questions in the Holy Scriptures.
4. **The Bible University** students who are in the following levels of academic and spiritual education:

6. **SUMMARY OF BIBLICAL STUDIES DEGREE PROGRAMS IN THE BIBLE UNIVERSITY**: The Bible University offers the following Online Biblical Studies Degree Programs:

    vi. Occupational Certificate: **Religious Associate Professional (Christian Religious Practitioner): South African Qualifications Authority (SAQA)ID 101997**.

    vii. Certificate in Theology (C. Th.) (for just one topic or two) – 1 month

    viii. Diploma in Theology (Dip. Th.) is a self-paced one-year diploma program of purely Bible Study, Bible Translation, and Bible Interpretation

    ix. Bachelor of Theology (B. Th.) – 2-year degree program to complete 22 self-selected Books of the Holy Bible

    x. Master of Theology (M. Th.) – 2-year degree program to complete 44 self-selected Books of the Holy Bible

    xii. Doctor of Theology (Th. D.) – 4-year degree program to complete all 66 Books of the Holy Bible

    xiii. Diploma in Chaplaincy Training Program for Pastors

    xiv. Diploma in Church Financial Management Training Program for Pastors

    xv. Diploma in General Counseling Training Program for Pastors

    xvi. Diploma in Marriage Counseling Training Program for Pastors

    xvii. Diploma in Sermon Preparation for Ministers of the Gospel

    xviii. Preparation of Bible Topics for Christian Conference and award of Conference Certificates to Participants

Jeremiah 23:15 (KJV) Therefore thus saith the LORD of hosts concerning the prophets; Behold, I will feed them with wormwood, and make them drink the water of gall: for from the prophets of Jerusalem is profaneness gone forth into all the land.

2 Corinthians 2:17 (KJV) For we are not as many, which corrupt the word of God: but as of sincerity, but as of God, in the sight of God speak we in Christ.

1 Timothy 4:13 (KJV) Till I come, give attendance to reading, to exhortation, to doctrine.

1 Timothy 6:5 (KJV) Perverse disputings of men of corrupt minds, and destitute of the truth, supposing that gain is godliness: from such withdraw thyself.

2 Timothy 2:15 (KJV) Study to shew thyself approved unto God, a workman that needeth not to be ashamed, rightly dividing the word of truth.

I pray that by the power of the knowledge and wisdom of the Holy Spirit, I shall continue to be able to make known the mystery of the Gospel of Jesus Christ according to the will of the LORD God Almighty:

> **Romans 16:25 (KJV)** Now to him that is of power to stablish you according to my gospel, and the preaching of Jesus Christ, according to the revelation of the mystery, which was kept secret since the world began,
>
> **Ephesians 6:18 (KJV)** Praying always with all prayer and supplication in the Spirit, and watching thereunto with all perseverance and supplication for all saints;
>
> **Ephesians 6:19 (KJV)** And for me, that utterance may be given unto me, that I may open my mouth boldly, to make known the mystery of the gospel,
>
> **Ephesians 6:20 (KJV)** For which I am an ambassador in bonds: that therein I may speak boldly, as I ought to speak.

Please, do not just quietly steal the ideas and teachings in this intellectual project/work and use them without any form of reward to me, so that you do not reveal yourself as a thief bound for Hell rather than as a true Minister of Jesus Christ. Instead of stealing my work, contact me, work with me, collaborate with me, and partner with me, so that I can also receive the due reward for my many hours, days, months, and years of labour in the Wisdom of God Almighty, for the edification of the Body of Christ:

> **Jeremiah 22:13 (KJV)** Woe unto him that buildeth his house by unrighteousness, and his chambers by wrong; *that* useth his neighbour's service without wages, and giveth him not for his work;
>
> **1 Thessalonians 4:6 (KJV)** That no *man* go beyond and defraud his brother in *any* matter: because that the Lord *is* the avenger of all such, as we also have forewarned you and testified.
>
> **1 Thessalonians 4:7 (KJV)** For God hath not called us unto uncleanness, but unto holiness.

FUTURE EXPECTATIONS

For the future, as we are able to secure funding for research, interior formatting, graphic designing, printing, and publishing, we pray to be able to continue writing Scriptures, and to keep writing on relevant topics that the Holy Spirit would teach us so that we can produce Christian Theological Research Textbooks to the world, especially to edify the Body of Christ in knowledge and in Truth.

These are intellectual, academic, and spiritual resources to all people around the world, who desire study materials for Spiritual Pastoral Training, for the edification of the Christian, and for the edification of the Church.

> **2 Timothy 2:15 (KJV)** Study to shew thyself approved unto God, a workman that needeth not to be ashamed, rightly dividing the word of truth.

As we conducted the research to produce this textbook, take note very carefully that we used only the Word of God the Scriptures and allowed the Holy Bible to speak for itself, not turning to the right or to the left to use any other book according to the requirement for research in Bible Translation and Interpretation that is laid down in **Deuteronomy 28:14 (KJV)** and in the following Scriptures:

> **Deuteronomy 17:18 (KJV)** And it shall be, when he sitteth upon the throne of his kingdom, that he shall write him a copy of this law in a book out of *that which is* before the priests the Levites:

> **Deuteronomy 17:19 (KJV)** And it shall be with him, and he shall read therein all the days of his life: that he may learn to fear the LORD his God, to keep all the words of this law and these statutes, to do them:

> **Deuteronomy 28:14 (KJV)** And thou shalt not go aside from any of the words which I command thee this day, *to* the right hand, or *to* the left, to go after other gods to serve them.

> **Joshua 1:8 (KJV)** This book of the law shall not depart out of thy mouth; but thou shalt meditate therein day and night, that thou mayest observe to do

according to all that is written therein: for then thou shalt make thy way prosperous, and then thou shalt have good success.

Luke 10:26 (KJV) He said unto him, What is written in the law? how readest thou?

John 5:39 (KJV) Search the Scriptures; for in them ye think ye have eternal life: and they are they which testify of me.

2 Peter 1:19 (KJV) We have also a more sure word of prophecy; whereunto ye do well that ye take heed, as unto a light that shineth in a dark place, until the day dawn, and the day star arise in your hearts:

2 Peter 1:20 (KJV) Knowing this first, that no prophecy of the Scripture is of any private interpretation.

The LORD God Almighty let His face shine upon you. The LORD Jesus Christ give you understanding. The Holy Spirit be with your spirit…Amen.

THE END!
Wednesday 24th April 2024 @ 4:37 PM
While hearing and meditating on the Word of God.

+ + + + + + +
Rev. Prof. PETER PRYCE,
DSEF, BA, MA, B.Soc.Sc Pol Sci, IBA, PhD
A Scribe of the Law of the God of Heaven
Prophet of the Word of God
Professor of French, Silver Spring, MD, USA
Scholar of the Institute of Theologians, USA
WWW.THEBIBLEUNIVERSITY.ORG
Accreditation Number: 07-QCTO/SDP120723172836
SAQA QUAL ID: Identification # 101997
WWW.BOOKSTORESITE.ORG
WWW.THEBIBLEUNIVERSITYCHURCH.ORG

Contact Info:
Phone: +1-301-793-7190
E-mail: Dr.Pryce@gmail.com

PRINCIPAL REFERENCE

The Holy Scriptures - King James Version

OTHER PRINCIPAL REFERENCES

Abdullah, Yusuf Ali. "The Meanings of the Holy Qur'an."
http://www.islam101.com/quran/YusufAli/index.htm:
9 October 2013.

http://www.islam101.com/quran/yusufAli/
14th September 2016.

https://www.google.com/?gfe_rd=cr&ei=g9EPVrb6Euyr8wf0m44CA#safe=active&q=abdullah+yusuf+ali
(Friday 16th September, 2016).

For a detailed study of the Holy Qur'an: English Translation and Commentary by Abdullah Yusuf Ali, both his original and modified versions, see these three works:
https://www.al-islam.org/tahrif/yusufali/
(Friday 16th September, 2016).

Original
The Glorious Kur'an - Translation and Commentary
 (Dar al-Fikr, Beirut) (n.d.)

Amana
The Meaning of The Holy Qur'an
New Edition with Revised Translation, Commentary and Newly Compiled Comprehensive Index. Amana Publications, First edition, 1408 AH/1989 AC by Amana Corporation

IFTA
The Holy Qur'an - English Translation of the Meanings and Commentary Revised and Edited by The Presidency of Islamic Researches, IFTA, Call and Guidance, King Fahd Holy Qur'an Printing Complex

Abdullah, Yusuf Ali. *The Meaning of the Holy Qur'an: [English] Translation and Commentary*. 10th Edition. Maryland: Amana Corporation, 1935, 1989, 1993.

Ally, Dr. Shabir. "What Are Some Examples of Parables in the Quran?"
http://www.onislam.net/english/ask-about-islam/faith-and-worship/quran-andScriptures/462015-what-are-some-examples-of-parables-in-thequran.html?Scriptures:
30th October 2014.

Khali, Ibrahim. "The Sons of God in Bible and Quran."
http://www.streetdirectory.com/travel_guide/105306/religion/the_sons_of_god_in_bibl_and_quran.html:
1 August 2014.

King Fahd Holy Qur'an. The Holy Qur'an: English Translation of the Meanings and Commentary, King Fahd Holy Qur'an Printing Complex, P O Box 3561, Al-Madinah, Al-Munawarah:
http://qurancomplex.gov.sa/Quran/Targama/Targama.asp?TabID=4&SubItemID=1&l=eng&t=eng&SecOrder=4&SubSecOrder=1)

King Fahd Complex for the Printing of the Holy Qur'an,
http://qurancomplex.gov.sa/Quran/Targama/Targama.asp?TabID=4&SubItemID=1&l=eng&t=eng&SecOrder=4&SubSecOrder=1

Memsuah, Mansoor "The Son of God in the Bible and the Qur'an."
http://www.answeringislam.org/Authors/Memsuah/son_of_god_bq.htm:
1 August 2014.

"Father and Son Definitions".
http://www.answering-christianity.com,
http://www.answeringchristianity.com/definition_son_of_god.htm:
1 August 2014.

GENERAL BIBLIOGRAPHY

Allen, Jeff. "The Bible as Resource for Translation Software". http://www.multilingual.com/articleDetaillosthisislam.php?id=614: December 21, 2012.

Bearth T. « Exégèse et herméneutique biblique du point de vue d'un linguiste ». *Cahiers de traduction biblique 15*, 1991.

Beekman, John and **Callow, John**. *Translating "the Word of God"*. Grand Rapids Michigan: Zondervan Publishing House, 1997, pp. 23, 24, 33-39.

Berman, A. "Translation and the Trials of the Foreign", in Lawrence Venuti (ed.), *The Translation Studies Reader*. London: Routledge, 2000, p. 297.

Bernard, H. Russell. *Research Methods in Anthropology: Qualitative and Quantitative Approaches, 6th Edition*. Lanham: Rowman and Littlefield, 2002, pp. 437-490.

Blum-Kulka, Shoshana. "Shifts of Cohesion and Coherence in Translation", in J. House and S. Blum-Kulka (eds), *Interlingual and Intercultural Communication*. Tübingen: Gunter Narr, 1986, pp. 17-35.

Bodine J. E. « Discourse Analysis of Biblical Literature: What it is and what it offers ». *Discourse Analysis of Biblical Literature*. Atlanta: Scholars Press, 1995, pp. 1-20.

Catford, John C. *A Linguistic Theory of Translation*. Oxford: Oxford University Press. 1965.

Chesterman, Andrew. *Memes of Translation*. Amsterdam: Benjamins, 1997.

Delisle, Jean et al. *Terminologie de la traduction*. Amsterdam: Benjamins. 1999.

Dye, Thurlow Wayne. *Bible Translation Strategy, an Analysis of Its Spiritual Impact*. Rev. ed. Dallas, TX: Wycliffe Bible Translators, 1985.

Escande J. « Pour une réflexion sémiotique sur la traduction des textes bibliques », *ETR 53,3*, 1978.

Even-Zohar, Itamar. "The Position of Translated Literature within the Literary Polysystem", in *Poetics Today 11/1*, 1990 pp. 45-51.

Even-Zohar, Itamar. "Polysystem Theory" in *Poetics Today 11*: 1 Spring, 1990, pp. 9-26.

Fairclough, Norman. *Analysing Discourse, Textual Analysis for Social Research*, London, Routledge. 2001, pp. 19-39.

Garnet, Paul. « The Concept of a Sacred Language: Help or Hindrance in New Testament Translation? » *TTR, 3, 2, 2e semestre*, 1990, pp. 71-79.

Gentzler, Edwin. "Translation without Borders". http://translation.fusp.it/. October 4, 2014.

Gentzler, Edwin. *Contemporary Translation Theories*. Clevedon: Cromwell Press Ltd. 2001.

Greimas A. J. « La traduction et La Bible ». *Sémiotique et Bible 32*, 1983.

Greenstein E. L. *Essays on biblical method and translation*. Atlanta: Scholars Press, 1989.

Gutt, Ernst-August. Translation and Relevance, Oxford: Basil Blackwell, 1991.

Gutt, Ernst-August. "Translation as Interlingual Interpretive Use." in *The Translation Studies Reader*. Lawrence Venuti (ed.), London: Routledge, 1991, 2000, 2001 pp. 376-96.

Hatim, Basil, and **Ian Mason**. The Translator as Communicator, London & New York: Routledge, vii, 1997, pp. 14, 193.

Hervey, Sándor and **Higgins, Ian**. *Thinking Translation: A Course in Translation Method: French to English*. London: Routledge, 1992.

Irving, Thomas Ballantine, Ahmad, Khurshid, and **Ahsan, Mohammad Manazir**. The Qur'an. Basic Teachings. Leicester, UK. The Islamic Foundation, 1992, pp. 109-112.

Jakobson, Roman. "On Linguistic Aspects of Translation." in R. Jakobson (ed.), *Selected Writings, II*, The Hague: Mouton, 1971 [1959], pp. 260-266.

Jakobson, Roman O. "On Linguistic Aspects of Translation" in L. Venuti (ed), *The Translation Studies Reader*. London, New York and Canada: Routledge, 2004, pp. 113-118.

Lategan, B.C. "Target Audience and Bible Translation", *JNSL 19*, 1993.

Lefevere, André. (ed.) Translation, History and Culture, London: Pinter Publishing Ltd. 1990.

Lockyer, Sharon. In Lisa M. Given (ed.), *The Sage Encyclopaedia of Qualitative Research Methods Vols. 1 & 2*, Thousand Oaks, California, SAGE Publications, Inc., 2008. pp. 706-711.

Margot, Jean-Claude. « Langues sacrées et méthode de traduction ». *TTR, 3, 2, 2e semestre*, 1990, pp. 15-31.

Mossop, Brian. *"Translating as Reporting: A Theoretical Characterization of the Translator"*. Paper read at EST Congress "Translating / Interpreting as Intercultural Communication", Prague 28-30 September, 1995.

Mossop, Brian. "Objective Translational Error and the Cultural Norm of Translation" in R. Larose (ed.), *L'Erreur en Traduction, TTR 2/2*, 1989, pp. 55-70.

Mullins P. « Sacred Text in Electronic Age », *BTB 20/3002E*, 1990.

Newmark, Peter. *Approaches to Translation*. New York and London: Prentice Hall, 1988a.

Nida, Eugene A. *Toward a Science of Translating*, Leiden: E. J. Brill, 1964.

Nida, Eugene A, and William D. Reyburn. *Meaning across Cultures*. Maryknoll, New York: Orbis Press, 1981.

O'Donnell M. B. « Translation and the Exegetical Process, Using Mark 5:1-10, "The Binding of the Strong Man" as a Test Case ». *Translating the Bible*, Sheffield: Academic Press, 1999.

Patte D. « Speech Act Theory and Biblical Exegesis. » *Semeia 41*, 1988, pp. 85-102.

Popovic, Anton. "Aspects of metatext". *Canadian Review of Comparative Literature* 3, 1976, pp. 225-235.

Pryce, Peter. *Measuring Attitudes in Translation: A Study of Nokia Business Reports*, Helsinki: Helsinki University Printing House, 2006, p. 150.

Reiss, Katharina and **Vermeer, Hans J**. *Grundlegung einer allgemeinen Translationstheorie*. Tübingen: Niemeyer, 1984.

Rivers, W. M. and **Temperley, M. S**. A Practical Guide to the Teaching of English as a Second or Foreign Language, Oxford: Oxford University Press, 1978, p. 329.

Robyns, Clem. *Translation and Discursive Identity*, in Robyns, C. (ed.), 1994, pp. 57-81.

Seleskovitch, Danica. « Take care of the sense and the sounds will take care of themselves or Why interpreting is not tantamount to Translating Languages. » *The Incorporated Linguist*, *16*, 1977, pp. 27-33.

Seleskovitch, Danica. & Lederer, Marianne. *Traduire pour interpréter*. Publication de la Sorbonne: Didier Erudition, Coll. « Traductologie 1 », 1993.

Seleskovitch, Danica, et Marianne Lederer. *Interpréter pour traduire*, *Quatrième édition*. Paris: Didier Erudition, 2001.

Simon, Sherry. « La traduction biblique : Modèle des Modèles? ». *TTR*, *3, 2, 2e semestre*, 1990, pp. 111-120.

Simms, Karl, (ed.) *Translating Sensitive Texts: Linguistic Aspects*. Amsterdam: Rodopi, 1997.

Toury, Gideon. *Descriptive Translation Studies and Beyond*. Amsterdam: Benjamins, 1995.

Turner, Charles. V. *Biblical Bible Translating*. Lafayette: Sovereign Grace Publishers Inc., Lighting Source Inc., 2001.

Vatican Insider Newspaper, La Stampa, of Tuesday 8th March 2011.
http://vaticaninsider.lastampa.it/en/documents/detail/articolo/bibbia-bible-biblia-6531/
Friday April 12, 2013.

Venuti, Lawrence. *The Translation Studies Reader London: Routledge*. 2000.

Vinay, Jean-Paul, and **Jean Darbelnet**. *Comparative Stylistics of French and English: a Methodology for Translation*. Juan C. Sager and M.-J. Hamel, (ed. and translators), Amsterdam: John Benjamin, 1995 [1958].

Wilhelm, J. E. « Herméneutique et traduction: La question de l'appropriation ou le rapport du propre à l'étranger ». *Meta*, *49, 4*, 2004, pp. 768-776.

BIBLIOGRAPHY FOR BIBLE TRANSLATION METHODS

Barnwell, Katharine G. L. *Bible Translation an Introductory Course in Translation Principles*. 3d ed. Dallas, TX: Institute of Linguistics, 1992.

Barnwell, Katharine G. L., and Summer Institute of Linguistics. *Introduction to Semantics and Translation with Special Reference to Bible Translation*. 2d ed. Introduction to Practical Linguistics. High Wycombe: Summer Institute of Linguistics, 1980.

Bible. *The Psalms in English*. Penguin Classics. London New York: Penguin Books, 1996.

Bible., and **Norman Messenger**. *The Creation Story*. New York: DK Pub., 2001.

Budick, Sanford, and **Wolfgang. Iser**. *The Translatability of Cultures Figurations of the Space Between*. Stanford, Calif.: Stanford University Press, 1996.

Cavanaugh, Jack. *Beyond the Sacred Page a Novel : The Tyndale Translation*. Grand Rapids, Mich.: Zondervan, 2003.

Clendenen, E. Ray. *Inclusive Language in Bible Translation a Reply to Mark Strauss*, 1998.

De Groot, Martien. *Assessment of Bible Translation and Literacy Needs of the Samburu Language Group*. Nairobi: Bible Translation and Literacy (EA), 1987.

Dye, Thurlow Wayne. *Bible Translation Strategy an Analysis of Its Spiritual Impact*. Rev. (ed.) Dallas, TX: Wycliffe Bible Translators, 1985.

Fritz, Paul J. *Sermons for the Nigerian Pastor*. Jos, Nigeria: Nigeria Bible Translation Trust, 1989.

General Conference of Seventh-Day Adventists. *Problems in Bible Translation*. Washington: Review and Herald, 1954.

Griffiths, Richard. *The Bible in the Renaissance Essays on Biblical Commentary and Translation in the Fifteenth and the Sixteenth Centuries*. St. Andrews Studies in Reformation History. Aldershot, Hants, UK Burlington, USA: Ashgate, 2001.

Hammer, Reuven. *The Classic Midrash Tannaitic Commentaries on the Bible*. Classics of Western Spirituality. New York: Paulist Press, 1995.

Hampton, Roberta S. *A Guide to Reading is Easy, Understand with Your Eyes!* Tamale, Ghana: Ghana Institute of Linguistics, Literacy and Bible Translation, 1994.

Lewins, Frank. (1992). *Social Science Methodology: A Brief but Critical Introduction*, South Melbourne, Australia: Macmillan Education Australia, Pty Ltd. P. 11.

Louw, J. P. *Lexicography and Translation with Special Reference to Bible Translation*. Cape Town: Bible Society of South Africa, 1985.

McGrath, Alister E. *In the Beginning the Story of the King James Bible and How It Changed a Nation, a Language and a Culture*. London: Hodder & Stoughton, 2002.

Pryce, Peter. "Méthode de traduction intralinguale de thèmes bibliques." Paper presented at the 8th Inter-University Conference on the Co-Existence of Languages in West Africa, Department of French Education, University of Education, Winneba, Ghana, Monday, 13th June 2011 – Saturday 18th June, 2011.

Strauss, Mark L. *Distorting Scripture? The Challenge of Bible Translation & Gender Accuracy*. Downers Grove, Ill: Inter Varsity Press, 1998.

Turner, Charles V. *Biblical Bible Translating the Biblical Basis for Bible Translating: With an Introduction to Semantics and Applications Made to Bible Translation Principles*. Bowie, Tex. (Box 1450, Bowie 76230): Baptist Bible Translators, Institute of Missiology International, 1988.

OTHER BOOKS BY THE SAME AUTHOR

These Christian Research Theological Textbooks are recommended as **Supplementary Course Literature** for training in The Bible University (WWW.THEBIBLEUNIVERSITY.ORG), and for a better understanding of the Holy Scriptures. They are methodically reasoned and are perfectly harmonized expositions of the Scriptures – written by Rev. Prof. Peter Pryce for the *Bible Lecture Series*.

1. Studies and Teachings on The Prophetic
2. Translation of Dreams
3. The Law of Writing Scriptures
4. Key to the Bible - Complete Bible Curriculum Vol. 1
5. Key to the Bible - Complete Bible Curriculum Vol. 2
6. Studies and Teachings on Abraham
7. Studies and Teachings on Water Baptism – From Genesis to Revelation
8. BOOK # 5 – Studies and Teachings on The Gentile
9. Studies and Teachings on Fasting
10. BOOK # 9 – Studies and Teachings on The Child of God
11. Studies and Teachings on Sin
12. BOOK # 15 – Studies and Teachings on Perfect
13. Studies and Teachings on The Spiritual
14. Studies and Teachings on Freely ye have received, Freely Give
15. Studies and Teachings on Prayer
16. Studies and Teachings on The Dog
17. Studies and Teachings on The Church
18. Studies and Teachings on Kingdom of Heaven, Kingdom of God
19. Studies and Teachings on Miracle
20. Studies and Teachings on Healing
21. Studies and Teachings on The Holy Communion
22. Studies and Teachings on The Poor
23. Studies and Teachings on The Servant of God
24. Studies and Teachings on Understanding Parables
25. Studies and Teachings on Death
26. Studies and Teachings on Faith

27. Studies and Teachings on Angels
28. Studies and Teachings on Christian Conflict Resolution
29. Studies and Teachings on Bible Translation and Interpreting
30. Studies and Teachings on Suffering
31. Studies and Teachings on Sabbath
32. Studies and Teachings on Definition of Jews
33. Studies and Teachings on Birthday
34. Studies and Teachings on The Multi-Dimensional Personalities of Jesus Christ
35. Studies and Teachings on Reincarnation
36. Studies and Teachings on The Scribe
37. Studies and Teachings on Tongues
38. Studies and Teachings on The Bereaved
39. Studies and Teachings on The Place of Worship
40. Studies and Teachings on Customs, Culture, and Traditions
41. Studies and Teachings on Discernment
42. Studies and Teachings on Deliverance
43. Topics in Translation Review – Testing the Perfect Harmony Theory of Translation and Interpreting
44. Qibla Files
45. Bible Translation of the Qur'an
46. Spirituals of Money
47. Hope for Christian-Muslim Fellowship
48. Perfect Harmony Theory for Translators and Interpreters – Méthode de traduction intralinguale de thèmes bibliques.

SCHOLAR OF THE INSTITUTE OF THEOLOGIANS

Institute Of Theologians

hereby elect

Dr. Peter Pryce, *S.Inst.T.*

Scholar of the Institute Of Theologians

Together with all the rights, privileges, and honor appertaining thereunto in consideration of satisfactory completion of the prescribed requirements.

In testimony wherefore, the seal of the Institute and Signatures as authorized by the Board of Trustees are hereunto affixed in the State of North Carolina. Given at Dallas, North Carolina, in the year of our Lord, Two Thousand Eighteen, The Month of December.

Dr. Moses Nueman Sr., Th.D., D.Miss., President

Dr. Robert Eng III Ph.D. Th.D., Vice President

INDEX

C

D

E

F

G

H

I

U

V

W

Y